Young People and the Politics of Outrage and Hope

Youth in a Globalizing World

Series Editor

Vincenzo Cicchelli (*GEMASS, Université Paris-Sorbonne/
CNRS* and *University Paris Descartes*)

Editorial Board

Valentina Cuzzocrea (*Universität Erfurt, Germany*)
Ratiba Hadj-Moussa (*York University, Canada*)
Claudia Jacinto (*PREJET-Instituto de Desarrollo
Económico y Social, Argentina*)
Jeylan Mortimer (*University of Minnesota, United States of America*)
Sylvie Octobre (*GEMASS, Université Paris-Sorbonne/
CNRS* and *la DEPS au Ministère de la Culture, France*)
Andrea Pirni (*Università di Genova, Italy*)
Dan Woodman (*University of Melbourne, Australia*)
Chin-Chun Yi (*Academia Sinica, Taiwan*)

VOLUME 7

The titles published in this series are listed at *brill.com/ygw*

Young People and the Politics of Outrage and Hope

Edited by

Peter Kelly
Perri Campbell
Lyn Harrison
Chris Hickey

BRILL

LEIDEN | BOSTON

Cover illustration: Retro style clenched fist held high in protest against grunge concrete wall background indicating revolution or aggression. Image by Kunal Mehta.

Library of Congress Cataloging-in-Publication Data

Names: Kelly, Peter, 1957- editor.
Title: Young people and the politics of outrage and hope / edited by Peter Kelly [and three others].
Description: Leiden ; Boston : Brill, [2019] | Series: Youth in a globalizing world ; 7 | Includes bibliographical references.
Identifiers: LCCN 2018047362 (print) | LCCN 2018049042 (ebook) | ISBN 9789004387492 (E-book) | ISBN 9789004337077 (hardback : alk. paper)
Subjects: LCSH: Youth--Political activity. | Youth--Social conditions--21st century. | Youth--Economic conditions--21st century.
Classification: LCC HQ799.2.P6 (ebook) | LCC HQ799.2.P6 Y646 2019 (print) | DDC 320.0835--dc23
LC record available at http://lccn.loc.gov/2018047362

Typeface for the Latin, Greek, and Cyrillic scripts: "Brill". See and download: brill.com/brill-typeface.

ISSN 2212-9383
ISBN 978-90-04-33707-7 (hardback)
ISBN 978-90-04-38749-2 (e-book)

Copyright 2019 by Koninklijke Brill NV, Leiden, The Netherlands.
Koninklijke Brill NV incorporates the imprints Brill, Brill Hes & De Graaf, Brill Nijhoff, Brill Rodopi, Brill Sense, Hotei Publishing, mentis Verlag, Verlag Ferdinand Schöningh and Wilhelm Fink Verlag.
All rights reserved. No part of this publication may be reproduced, translated, stored in a retrieval system, or transmitted in any form or by any means, electronic, mechanical, photocopying, recording or otherwise, without prior written permission from the publisher.
Authorization to photocopy items for internal or personal use is granted by Koninklijke Brill NV provided that the appropriate fees are paid directly to The Copyright Clearance Center, 222 Rosewood Drive, Suite 910, Danvers, MA 01923, USA. Fees are subject to change.

This book is printed on acid-free paper and produced in a sustainable manner.

Contents

Acknowledgements IX
List of Illustrations X
Notes on Contributors XI

Young People and the Politics of Outrage and Hope: An Introduction   1
  Peter Kelly, Perri Campbell, Lyn Harrison and Chris Hickey

PART 1
Neo-Liberal Capitalism and the Politics of Outrage

1 Neoliberal Violence against Youth in the Age of Orwellian Nightmares   27
  Henry A. Giroux

2 Channelling Hope through Peer to Peer Technology: Education and Participatory Practice   44
  Judith Bessant

3 Performing Dispossession: Young People and the Politics of the Guerrilla Self   60
  Perri Campbell and Luke Howie

4 New Politics: The Anonymous Politics of 4chan, Outrage and the New Public Sphere   73
  Rob Watts

5 Hacking the Future: Youth, Digital Disruption and the Promise of the New   90
  Shane B. Duggan

6 Neo-Liberal Capitalism and the War on Young People: Growing Up with the Illusion of Choice and the Ambivalence of Freedom   105
  Peter Kelly

PART 2
Education, Work and the Promise of Hope

7 Making the Hopeful Citizen in Precarious Times   123
   Rosalyn Black

8 Indigenous Young Australians and Pathways to Hope in the Struggle to 'get real'   140
   Chris Hickey and Lyn Harrison

9 Dreams of Ordinariness: The "missing middle" of Youth Aspirations in Sardinia   155
   Giuliana Mandich

10 Beyond Hope and Outrage: Conceptualizing and Harnessing Adversity Capital in Young People   169
   Lucas Walsh

11 The Youth Bulge: Remaking Precarity in Times of Illegitimacy   186
   Emma E. Rowe

PART 3
Cultures of Democracy and the Politics of Belonging

12 The Moral Emotions of Youthful Politics and Anti-Politics   209
   Kerry Montero and Judith Bessant

13 Young Muslims and Everyday Political Practice: A DIY Citizenship Approach   226
   Anita Harris and Joshua Roose

14 Young Indonesians and WikiDPR: Between Apathy and Engagement   241
   Michael Hatherell

15 Strategic Space for Progressive Alternatives: Syriza and Democracy in Greece   256
   John Bourdouvalis

16 The Socio-Demographic and Political Contexts and Legacies of the Arab Spring   272
    Ken Roberts

17 Outrageous Disparities: Young Peoples' Perspectives on Wealth Inequality, Collectivity, and Hope in New York City   289
    Madeline Fox and Brett Stoudt

18 2011 and World Revolutionary Moments: Mapping New Strategies and Alliances in Australian Youth Activism   307
    Freg J Stokes

    Index   327

Acknowledgements

This collection was compiled in the years following the global unrest and uprisings of 2011, during which people around the world contested the conditions in which they lived. These uprisings – the so-called Arab Spring, Occupy, 15-M – inspired the title of this collection alongside Manuel Castells 2012 book *Networks of Outrage and Hope*. Written in the years immediately following these uprisings, Castells considers the possibilities of digital technology for building new ways of knowing each other and our capacity for change. In recent years more skeptical and necessarily critical engagements with digital technology have emerged. In this context Castells reminds us of the role that hope, digital tools and relationship building can and have to play in reimagining the future.

We acknowledge those who seek better futures in complex and dangerous times, to our contributors who have engaged with the ambiguity of hope and outrage to contribute to the unfolding conversation about young people's futures. The many different ways our contributions engage with the possibilities and limitations of the present speaks to the passion and concern that persists among teachers and researchers today.

This collection is also inspired by our research with the Australian social enterprise Charcoal Lane and Mission Australia. The stories of the Charcoal Lane trainees and staff continue to educate us about the outrageous inequality that structures our everyday lives in Australia.

We would also like to acknowledge the support of the School of Education at Deakin University; the Alfred Deakin Research Fellowship Scheme; the School of Education, and the Centre for Education and Training in the Asian Century at RMIT University; and the Centre for Research in Higher Education and Training at La Trobe University.

To our friends and family who have supported us along the way we say thank you:
Peter – Georgia and Julie
Perri – Craig, Margaret, Chantelle and Hamish Campbell, Luke Howie.
Lyn – Archie, Kate and Campbell McLaren
Chris – Sue, Alex, James & Polly
Finally we extend a special thanks to Kate for her fine editorial work.

Illustrations

Figures

- 11.1 The Youth Bulge and the Arab Revolution   191
- 17.1 PFJ Survey question asking for explanation of wealth disparity   293
- 17.2 PFJ Survey explanations for inequality thematic tree   295
- 17.3 Themes that emerged from the question: Is there anything you have done about some groups being poorer or wealthier than others?   301
- 17.4 Themes that emerged from the question: Is there anything you have done about some groups being poorer or wealthier than others?   301
- 17.5 A selection of PFJ responses to: What three questions do you think we should be asking NYC teens?   304

Tables

- 16.1 Fertility rates by country (in percentages)   274
- 16.2 Unemployment rates (in percentages)   275
- 16.3 Youth unemployment rates (in percentages)   275
- 16.4 Labour force participation rates (in percentages)   276
- 16.5 Female labour force participation rates (in percentages)   276
- 16.6 Types of employment: 15–29 year olds in Egypt, 2009   277
- 18.1 World Revolutions, 1789–1917   310
- 18.2 World Revolutions, 1968–2011   311

Notes on Contributors

Judith Bessant
is Professor of Youth Studies and Sociology at RMIT University, Melbourne, Australia. She publishes in the areas policy, sociology, politics, youth studies, media and history. She is currently working on a book *The Great Transformation, Politics, Labour and Learning in the Digital Age*, Routledge and 2017. Her most recent books are *The Precarious Generation: A Political Economy of Young People*, 2017 (Routledge) with Rys Farthing and Rob Watts, and edited an collection, *Young People and the Regeneration of Politics Times of Crises* 2017, with Sarah Pickard. Judith has also worked for many years with government and Non Government Organizations in a policy advisory capacity.

Rosalyn Black
is Senior Lecturer in Education at Deakin University. Her research interests meet at the intersection of the sociologies of education and youth: she has published widely on young people's experience of citizenship in precarious contexts and the role of education policy and practice in relation to diverse social inequalities. Her coming co-authored books include *Rethinking Youth Citizenship after the Age of Entitlement* (Bloomsbury) and *Young People in Digital Society: Control Shift* (Palgrave Macmillan).

John A. Bourdouvalis
is a PhD candidate in the School of Humanities and Social Sciences at Deakin University. His dissertation involves examining the future of social democracy and progressive social mobilisations since the 2008 Global Financial Crisis. John's research focuses on critiques of neoliberalism, post-Marxism, social democracy and political economy. He is particularly interested in the effects of neoliberal austerity on democracy in Southern Europe after the Global Financial Crisis, and the progressive movements that have emerged in response.

Perri Campbell
is a Postdoctoral Research Fellow at Swinburne University. She is the author of *Digital Selves* (Common Ground, 2015) and has published widely in critical youth studies on young women and the Iraq War, and young people's use of digital media in the Occupy and Black Lives Matter movements. She has been an Alfred Deakin Postdoctoral Research Fellow at Deakin University, and Visiting Scholar at the University of California, Berkeley. Perri's forthcoming book *Crisis and Terror in the Age of Anxiety* (Palgrave, 2017) explores the challenges facing young people as they carve out a life and future.

Shane B. Duggan
is a Vice Chancellor's Postdoctoral Fellow in the School of Education, RMIT University. His work explores how young people understand and engage in higher education and work in the context of shifting social, cultural and economic conditions. His recent research has contributed to reforms to higher education admissions policy in Australia and he maintains an active voice in advocating for change in Senior Secondary Certification and the Australian Tertiary Admissions Ranking (ATAR) through scholarly and media channels. Shane is currently working on his first book, *Impossible Machines,* which traces shifting notions of value and aspirations in higher education.

Madeline Fox
is an Assistant Professor of Children & Youth Studies and Sociology at Brooklyn College, City University of New York. She engages in participatory action research with young people to investigate every day experiences of public policy and the overlap between art and participatory knowledge production all towards making social justice claims. Her writing can be found in journals such as *Children & Society, Social and Personality Psychology Compass,* and in *Qualitative Psychology.* Maddy co-edited the volume *Telling Stories to Change the World: Global Voices on the Power of Narrative to Build Community and Make Social Justice Claims* with Rickie Solinger and Kayhan Irani.

Henry A. Giroux
currently holds the McMaster University Chair for Scholarship in the Public Interest in the English and Cultural Studies Department. He is also the Paulo Freire distinguished Scholar in Critical Pedagogy. His most recent books include *Dangerous Thinking in the Age of the New Authoritarianism* (Routledge 2015); coauthored with Brad Evans, *Disposable Futures: The Seduction of Violence in the Age of Spectacle; (City Lights, 2015), America's Addiction to Terrorism* (Monthly Review Press, 2016) and *America at War with Itself* (City Lights 2017). Giroux is also a member of Truthout's Board of Directors and a contributing editor at Tikkun magazine. His web site is www.henryagiroux.com.

Anita Harris
is a Research Professor in the Institute for Citizenship and Globalisation at Deakin University, Australia. Her research areas include youth citizenship, youth cultures, and participatory practice in changing times, with a focus on gender and cultural diversity. She is working on an Australian Research Council Future Fellowship 'Young People and Social Inclusion in the Multicultural City', a major project on the civic life of young Muslim Australians, and a new

study on transnational mobility and youth transitions (with Loretta Baldassar & Shanthi Robertson). She is the author of several books in youth studies, most recently *Young People and Everyday Multiculturalism* (2013, Routledge New York).

Lyn Harrison

is an Honorary Associate Professor in the School of Education at Deakin University, Victoria, Australia. She is the co-author of two books: *Working in Jamie's Kitchen: Salvation, Passion and Young Workers* and *Smashed! The many meanings of intoxication and* drunkenness. She has also co-authored a major monograph *Sexuality Education Matters: Preparing pre-service teachers to teach sexuality education*. Lyn's core interests are in Critical Youth Studies, Health and Wellbeing and Sexuality Education. She is in the latter stages of an Australian Research Council (ARC) Linkage project *Engaging Young People in Sexuality Education* focusing on student voice.

Michael Hatherell

is a lecturer in Strategic Studies at Deakin University, and is currently seconded to the Centre for Defence and Strategic Studies in Canberra, Australia. His research interests include political representation, political leadership and democratic theory, with a particular focus on interpretive approaches. Michael previously completed his PhD at Deakin University, with a thesis focused on Indonesia's political party system and different understandings of political representation. His recent publications and projects focus on charismatic leadership and populism in Indonesia and the role of local leaders as representatives.

Chris Hickey

is a Professor of Health and Physical Education and Chair of Academic Board at Deakin University, Australia. His research is broadly focused on the ways in which gendered identities are theorised, researched and regulated and the links between identity and issues of social cohesion and exclusion. He has recently been involved in major research projects focusing on educational pathways for marginalized youth, and youth resilience in overcoming social disadvantage. He is the founder and Chief Editor of the *Asia-Pacific Journal of Health, Sport and Physical Education*.

Luke Howie

is in the Politics and International Relations department at the School of Social Sciences, Monash University and Deputy Director of the Global Terrorism Research Centre (GTReC). Luke's research sits across terrorism studies, youth studies and digital media. Luke is a Visiting Scholar at the University of California, Berkeley where he carries out research in politics, popular culture, and youth transitions. Luke's recent book, *Terror on the Screen*, examines how terrorism has reverberated through our pop-culture artefacts by engaging with TV shows such as South Park, The Simpsons, Family Guy, and films which integrate terrorism into their canon.

Peter Kelly
is a Professor of Education, and Head of UNESCO UNEVOC in the School of Education, RMIT University. He has published extensively on young people, the practice of youth studies, social theory and globalisation. His books include, *Working in Jamie's Kitchen: Salvation, Passion and Young Workers* (2009), *The Self as Enterprise: Foucault and the "Spirit" of 21st Century Capitalism* (2013), *The Moral Geographies of Children, Young People and Food* (2014), *A Critical Youth Studies for the 21st Century* (2015), *Young People and the Aesthetics of Health Promotion* (2016), *and Neo-Liberalism and Austerity: The Moral Economies of Young People's Health and Well-being* (2017).

Giuliana Mandich
is Professor of Sociology at Cagliari University. She is a social theorist who has published extensively on space and time as constitutive dimensions of everyday life and young people. Her recent interest is on the future, both as a specific focus of analysis of youth in contemporary society, and as an essential topic in rethinking social theory today. Her articles are published in journals such as *Space and Culture, City and Society, Journal of Youth Studies*.

Kerry Montero
is Senior Lecturer and Program Manager in the Bachelor of Social Science (Youth Work) program at RMIT University. Kerry has been teaching in youth work education for over two decades and has an extensive background in youth work, health promotion and health service delivery to young people. A focus of Kerry's research and practice over the past twenty years has been in the area of young people and road safety education and policy. She is co-author of *Young People and the Aesthetics of Health Promotion: Beyond Reason, Rationality and Risk* (with Peter Kelly).

Ken Roberts
is Emeritus Professor of Sociology and Honorary Research Fellow at the University of Liverpool. He has a long track record in youth research. From 1989 until 2010 he coordinated a series of projects among youth in transforming post-communist countries. His most recent research has been as member of a

European Union Consortium investigating the roles of youth during and since the Arab Spring of 2011. His books include *Surviving Post-Communism: Young People in the Former Soviet Union* (2000), *Youth in Transition: Eastern Europe and in the West* (2009), *Class in Contemporary Britain* (2011), *Sociology: An Introduction* (2012), *The Business of Leisure* (2016), and *Social Theory, Sport, Leisure* (2016).

Joshua Roose
is the Director of the Institute for Religion, Politics and Society at the Australian Catholic University and a visiting Scholar at the East Asian Legal Studies Program at Harvard Law School (2014-). He is a political sociologist with research interests in political Islam, populism, masculinity, legal pluralism and legal theory. His latest book is *Political Islam and Masculinity: Muslim Men in the West* (2016).

Emma E. Rowe
is an early-career researcher and lecturer in the School of Education, Deakin University. Emma's work is published in *Journal of Education Policy*, *Critical Studies in Education* and *International Studies in Sociology of Education*. Emma contributed to the UNESCO Global Education Monitoring Report (Australia), and the International Handbook on Urban Education. Her monograph is published by Routledge and is entitled, *Middle-class school choice in urban spaces: the economics of public schooling and globalized education reform* (2017). Emma's PhD was the recipient of the 'Outstanding Dissertation Award' from the American Association of Research in Education, Qualitative Research SIG (2015).

Freg J Stokes
is a PhD candidate at the University of Melbourne, with his research focusing on Guarani Mbyá responses to deforestation in Brazil, Paraguay and Argentina. For his honours thesis investigation (Political Science, University of Melbourne, 2011), he collaborated with Happy Valley, a youth theatre co-operative in Bhutan. He has written for *The Journal of Postcolonial Studies*, *The Lifted Brow*, *Overland*, *Arena*, *Voiceworks* and *Crikey*. His alter ego Twiggy Palmcock, CEO of Excretum mining, is a close friend and confidante of former prime minister Tony Abbott.

Brett C. Stoudt
PhD is an Associate Professor in the Psychology Department with a joint appointment in the Gender Studies Program at John Jay College of Criminal justice as well as the Psychology and Social Welfare Doctoral Programs at

the Graduate Center. His interests include the social psychology of privilege and oppression as well as aggressive and discriminatory policing practices. Dr. Stoudt's work has been published in volumes such as *Geographies of Privilege* as well as journals such as *The Journal of Social Issues*. He is the recipient of *The Michele Alexander Early Career Award for Scholarship and Service* from The Society for the Psychology Study of Social Issues.

Lucas Walsh
is Deputy Dean of the Faculty of Education at Monash University, where he is Professor of Education Policy and Practice, Youth Studies. Lucas has worked in corporate, government and not-for-profit sectors and held four research fellowships. His recent books include "Educating Generation Next: Young People, Teachers and Schooling in Transition" (Palgrave Macmillan) and "Rethinking Youth Citizenship After the Age of Entitlement" with Rosalyn Black (Bloomsbury Academic).

Rob Watts
is Professor of Social Policy in the justice and legal studies program at RMIT University. He has wide-ranging interests including social policy, history, social and political theory and criminology. Books include *The Foundations of the National Welfare State, Arguing About the Australian Welfare State, Sociology Australia* and *International Criminology: A Critical Introduction, Talking Policy: Australian Social Policy.* More recent books *include, States of Violence and the Civilising Process: on criminology and state crime* (2016) and *Public Universities, Managerialism and the value of the university* published in January 2017.

Young People and the Politics of Outrage and Hope: An Introduction

Peter Kelly, Perri Campbell, Lyn Harrison and Chris Hickey

Nearing the end of the second decade of the 21st century millions of young people around the globe are marginalised in educational, cultural, social, economic and political contexts that are local and global; that are characterised by increasing wealth and poverty, and a widening gap between them; by the remaking of the markers of marginalisation in which some forms appear to wane while new forms seem to emerge; by global ruptures that are marked by austerity, recession and the remaking of the welfare state in the aftermath of the GFC; and which have been characterised, variously, and not unproblematically, as signalling a 'clash of civilisations' (Huntington 1993) and the 'end times' (Žižek 2010).

During the so-called Year of the Protester (Time 2011) we witnessed many young people around the world – the Spanish *Indignados*, the global Occupy movement, the young people of the various and different revolutions in the so-called 'Arab Spring', and those participating in, and caught up by, the riots in many cities in the UK during August 2011 – voice their anxiety, uncertainty and anger about their experience of these diverse and emerging circumstances. In the years that have followed, these and other movements, for example, the Black Lives Matter movement and the March for our Lives anti-gun violence movements in the US, have seen young people continue to be involved in diverse ways in different forms of political action in relation to issues that matter – to them.

High levels of youth unemployment and precarious employment, student debt accompanying increased costs for higher education, housing costs that lock many out of home ownership, and the challenges for young people's physical and mental health and well-being are re-shaping young people's sense of self and of their chances for meaningful participation in relationships and settings that have, in the past, identified someone as an adult, as a citizen (Kelly 2017). As we will suggest later, we see in these movements, these protests, these interventions, on-going experiments – some more 'successful' than others – in new 'cultures of democracy' (Taylor 2007).

This collection has emerged from a number of projects that we have been involved in over a number of years. Including, most recently, an Australian Research Council (ARC) Linkage project examining a social enterprise based, transitional labour market program providing training and, *hopefully*, pathways into employment for marginalised Aboriginal young people,[1] and an Alfred Deakin Postdoctoral Research Fellowship[2] that focused on young people's participation in post-2011 global uprisings and the Occupy movement.

In our call for contributions to this collection, and to a two day conference that we hosted in December 2015, our 'hope' was that contributors would draw on a range of theoretical, methodological and empirical work to identify, explore, map and debate some of the challenges and opportunities of the politics of outrage and hope that should accompany academic, community and political discussions about the futures that young people will inherit and make. In doing this work we have found the ways in which Manuel Castells (2012) engaged with the possibilities of 2011, building on his earlier work on identity and network logics, to be particularly useful. Indeed, Castell's (2012: 224, emphasis in original) suggestion that the *'transition from outrage to hope is accomplished by deliberation in the space of autonomy'* was generative of the title for this collection. In addition, the related problematics of young people, 'outrage', 'hope', the 'future', among others, are given a provocative shape by the ways in which Castell's (2012: 228) addresses the positive potentialities of futures that are rendered knowable in a particular way by the idea of 'utopias':

> Utopias are not mere fantasy. Most modern political ideologies at the roots of political systems (liberalism, socialism, communism) originated from utopias. Because utopias become material force by incarnating in people's minds, by inspiring their dreams, by guiding their actions and inducing their reactions. What these networked social movements are proposing in their practice is a new utopia at the heart of the culture of the network society: the utopia of the autonomy of the subject vis-à-vis the institutions of society. Indeed, when societies fail in managing their structural crises by the existing institutions, change can only take place out of the system by a transformation of power relations that starts in people's minds and develops in the form of networks built by the projects of new actors constituting themselves as the subjects of the new history in the making.

---

1 Australian Research Council Linkage Project (LP100200153): 'Capacity Building and Social Enterprise: Individual and organisational transformation in transitional labour market programs', Deakin University.
2 Alfred Deakin Postdoctoral Fellowship: 'The Young Men and Women of the Global Uprisings: Generations, Gender, Social Media and Cultures of Democracy', Deakin University.

Before we explore the *hopes* and aspirations that shape this collection in more detail we want to switch gear a little and think about how popular culture, and commentary on popular culture, is touching on some of the themes we identified for the collection. Our point of reference here is the hugely successful *Hunger Games* franchise, which was initially a series of 3 novels by Suzanne Collins, adapted to film and starring, among others, Jennifer Lawrence as the hero Katniss Everdeen. We won't provide too much detail on the plot and themes of the franchise at this time, but as two contributors to this collection, Perri Campbell and Luke Howie, have argued elsewhere (Howie and Campbell 2017a), in a post-GFC world pop-culture has played a significant role in questioning neo-Liberal common sense. For Howie and Campbell (2017a) *The Hunger Games* novels and films can be read as moments that imagine the future in 'other terms' and are, in this sense, possible catalysts for change, for hope.

So, what does the *Hunger Games* book series and movie franchise offer us at the start of this collection? Sarah Hughes (2015) has made the case that the popularity of the *Hunger Games* novels and films indicates that many young people around the globe identify with the anxieties, fears and distrust of 'elites' that shape the storylines we have sketched for this collection. Citing the economist and academic Noreena Hertz, who coined the term *Generation K* – after Jennifer Lawrence's character Katniss Everdeen – for those born between 1995 and 2002, Hughes (2015) claims 'that this is a generation riddled with anxiety, distrustful of traditional institutions from government to marriage', and, 'like their heroine Katniss Everdeen, [are energised by] a strong sense of what is right and fair'. Hughes also references Louise O'Neill, whose bestselling novel *Only Ever Yours* has struck a 'chord with the millennial generation'. O'Neill thinks that the popularity of dystopian tales such as the Hunger Games is an echo of the times:

> Millennials are the first generation unlikely to achieve a higher standard of living than their parents enjoyed. They've been priced out of the housing market, unemployment is almost a given and they've been saddled with economic debt which they did nothing to accumulate.
> HUGHES 2015

What is more: 'The anger they have about this, coupled with their genuine concern about social, political, and ecological crises, has created an atmosphere of fear and anxiety'. That, suggests O'Neill, is 'why so many of this generation are drawn to dystopian fiction' (Hughes 2015).

From another perspective, Hughes (2015) makes reference to novelist Daniel José Older, whose recent book for young adults, *Shadowshaper*, is, apparently, 'an addictive story of magic, music, art and death on the streets of Brooklyn'. For Older, what draws a young audience to these tales, is the way that stories like *The Hunger Games* deal with the tendency of the mass media to make a spectacle of brutality (Hughes 2015). Older goes on to suggest that:

> The idea that today's teenagers respond so strongly because of what's happening in the world is a simplification, but what's interesting about the books is the way in which they take violence seriously and tackle the lasting effects of war and trauma. That's what gives the work its power and makes it so unsettling.
>
> HUGHES 2015

There is much that could be discussed here – if this was a chapter about the *Hunger Games* – including, how in the end – spoiler alert!! – the revolutionary hope that was invested in a reluctant Mockingjay is transferred to a very traditional heterosexual relationship and Katniss as the mother of two children. Is the promise of the privatised, domesticated family all that young people can hope for?

Though we possibly did not have a direct eye to the figure of Katniss and generation K when we started our discussions and planning, the themes of injustice, violence, outrage, hope and the possibility of change that are embedded in much of the dystopian fiction that is popular with young people, connects so well to our own interests in the politics of outrage and hope for the futures that young people will inherit and make. In the following sections, we provide a brief sketch of some of the key ideas that shaped the framing of this project, and this collection.

1   'Networks of Outrage and Hope'[3]

Over the past seven or more years a number of protest movements, 'uprisings', and 'revolutions' in countries around the world have demonstrated the different ways in which young people are able to mobilise and organise against unfair and unjust social conditions. Much has been written about the use of social media in these movements with a particular emphasis on the ways in which young people's online networks transform their understanding of society, politics and each other (see for instance, Castells 2012; Wellington 2015;

---

[3] This is the title of Manuel Castells 2012 book: *Networks of Outrage and Hope: Social Movements in the Internet Age*.

Wulf et al. 2013; Collin 2015). From catch cries such as the 'Twitter Revolution' (see Hounshell 2011), to 'Revolution 2.0' (Ghonim 2012: 294), the use of social media has been understood as 'one of the unequivocal generational virtues of these movements' (Stengel 2011: 29). The everyday use of Facebook, Twitter, Tumblr and other social networking sites, keeps young people's outrage and hope 'suspended' in the public imaginary. These conversations are preserved online for us to engage with, to take notice of and to find hope in (Braidotti 2014).

Digital communication technologies enable a different kind of protest practice and self-awareness for young people (Campbell 2018, 2015). Manuel Castells (2013) argues that the speed at which internet-facilitated networks were able to grow, increased the likelihood of international, collective action around particular issues. Digital support for many of these uprisings grew quickly. For instance, between 2008 and 2009 Tunisia's Facebook presence grew from 30,000 to 800,000. Facebook became the 'GPS', the guiding tool for the Tunisian revolution (Rosen 2011; Anderson 2011). Created by people working in New York, the 'We are the 99 Percent' Tumblr became a platform for an, at first glance, 'leaderless movement'. The Tumblr captured the stories of young people struggling to survive with university debt and unemployment leading to financial hardship, stress and, for some, poor physical and mental health (Howie and Campbell 2017b). Uprisings and movements across the globe were united by a 'new sociological type' argues Paul Manson (2013): 'the graduate with no future':

> To survive, the young have become a generation of drifters [who] ... in the west, will never accumulate pay, conditions or savings at the level their parents did. What they are accumulating is resentment.

In Tunisia in late 2010, in a 'moment' that came to be seen as important in the emergence of the so-called 'Arab Spring' during early-mid 2011, a 26 year-old street vendor by the name of Mohamed Bouazizi set himself on fire outside a government building in Sidi Bouzid after local police prevented him, yet again, from working. A video of the protest was recorded and distributed over the Internet. Bouazizi inspired large numbers of people in a youthful population to try to 'reclaim' their dignity and honour (Castells 2012: 13; see also: Pollock 2011). Following events in Tunisia, uprisings unfolded in Egypt, Spain, and Greece. In September 2011, young men and women gathered in lower Manhattan to protest against the role that Wall Street based banks, financial institutions and multinational businesses played in the GFC (Gould-Wartofsky 2015:8). They protested against wealth and income inequalities, and the social structures that helped sustain a life of privilege for the few, and a life of poverty for the many. The Spanish *Indignados* movement staged protests in the capital Madrid against the effects of the Euro-crisis, such as high rates of youth unemployment. In Spain, young people protesting carried signs that read: 'worried for our future, because this is the place we will spend the rest of our lives' (*Indignados* protest banner in Castells 2012: 116).

While these protest groups' each have their own demands that were/are shaped by location, culture and context, the groups did refer to each other and engage in acts of solidarity. New Yorkers, occupying public spaces around Wall St, named their first encampment Tahrir Square, and so did the occupiers in Barcelona.[4] In Spain, protesters shouted 'Iceland is the solution', and for those occupying Tahrir square: 'Tunisia was the solution' (Castells 2012: 20). The Occupy Wall Street movement spread throughout the US, and when authorities attempted to shut the encampment down, rallies were held in Hong Kong, Athens, Rome, Nairobi, and Johannesburg (Occupytogether.org, 2015).[5] Internet based communication supported public awareness of these groups, and also enabled inter-group (and 'inter-Occupy') connections to be forged that facilitated the sharing of legal and philosophical knowledge, resistance and protest techniques, and information about democratic processes.

Throughout this collection we do not argue for or against the idea of a *digital revolution*. What we and our contributors hope to convey about young people's networks, protests, and use of digital communication technologies, is how young people's everyday struggles in shaping a self, a life and a future are intimately connected to their political concerns, digital networks, educational and employment experiences, and participation in protests online and in the streets. Many of the chapters we present engage with the idea of outrage, struggle and the ethical self-shaping practices/politics young people are adopting. In this sense, it is how the uprisings are embodied that is significant – the process whereby we come to understand ourselves and each other differently (Butler & Athanasiou, 2013: xi). For Castells (2012: 144):

> This is the true revolutionary transformation: the material production of social change not from programmatic goals but from the networked experiences of the actors of the movement ... the movement is the most

---

4 Occupiers renamed Zucotti Park 'Liberty Square as an homage to the Egyptian uprising that began in Tahrir Square in January' (Occupytogether.org, 2015).
5 Occupy participants registered with the Occupy.org website are located particularly along the East and West coast of the US (see: Occupy.org Interactive Map of Occupy Attendees, http://occupywallst.org/attendees/).

important mental transformation, they accept the slowness of the process, and they place themselves in the long haul, because slowness is a virtue: it allows for self-reflection.

From the perspective of post-human philosophy, Rosi Braidotti's (2013) idea of 'relational becoming' offers another means to productively frame those processes in which self-making, digital networks, politics, neo-liberalism, community, organisms and animals, biological environments and friendships forged in encampments, collide. Such relational becoming is one reason why Braidotti (2013) argues that we need to look beyond established modes of thought regarding our understandings of *self* in order to catch up with our unfolding posthuman reality. Some of the possibilities opened here are taken up by a number of our colleagues in the chapters that follow.

2   Education, Work, Transitions and Hope

As we go past the midway point of the second decade of the twenty-first century, the place of schooling in the life course of young people is increasingly precarious (Kelly 2017). Amid an expanding gap in social inequality, that sees the upward redistribution of wealth and power coupled with public disinvestment in social welfare programs for the most vulnerable and needy, the distribution of opportunity through education and schooling becomes increasingly polarised. In an age of austerity, many young people are becoming dispossessed of any hope for a secure future.

Alongside local shifts, is an increasingly globalised context, in which multi-national conglomerates exploit dissolved boundaries to find the best business and financial settings and cheapest labour. Here, multi-national and trans-national engagements interact to blur the boundaries that sustain established life patterns and pathways. The flow of refugees and other forms of unskilled labour complexify shared notions of normal life courses. However, for all the instability and uncertainty, the unequal distribution of resources and opportunities continues to undermine neo-liberal assertions of 'biographies of choice' (Beck 1992). Ulrich Beck's (1992; 2016) characterisation of a 'risk society' provides a useful framework through which to question the utility of structure and social status as unifying frameworks for knowing the underpinning assumptions, practices and dispositions of someone's life course. Among the core conditions of a risk society, Beck (1992, 2016) argues, are a range of identity questions, contradictions and challenges. Here, class, culture, gender and geography become much less stable categories with which to make assumptions about life courses, and how we measure success. There exists a significant body of research on the nature of educational underachievement, which is most often linked with familial characteristics, such as one's socio economic background. In a risk society, however, the increasingly complex and unstable nature of the human enterprise unsettles such couplings. As one example, the coupling between a 'university degree' and a 'known future' is increasingly problematic. However, those who do not invest in this increasingly normalised pathway, and opt rather to enter the labour market directly, are understood to be placing themselves in a much higher category of uncertainty and risk. These concerns are energised through wider public discourse around *failed pathways* and *youth at risk* (Kelly 2006).

Against this backdrop, educational policy has a tendency to be normative and promote a particular vocabulary in which disadvantage is framed in terms of individual 'lacks' and 'deficit'. Here, the construction of a 'drop out' attributes failure to the young person rather than the system. Failure is defined and measured in terms of attrition rates that do not account for the complexity of individual pathways. The discourses that support notions of social disadvantage draw on pathological or essentialist views of young people to develop common-sense understandings of 'educational failure'. In this framework, educational failure is framed via a meritocratic structure in which the victims are charged with the responsibility for their 'failure'.

In this collection many of our contributors look to open up new possibilities for understanding and theorising notions of inequality and the place of education, and its role in facilitating transitions to work and the hope of a prosperous and meaningful life.

3   Cultures of Democracy and Belonging

Part of the work of this collection is to explore some of the new ways in which young people are imagining themselves, their relationships with Others, who the Other is, what 'difference' means, and what it means to 'belong'. In this sense the ideas of 'cultures of democracy' and 'belonging' are important in thinking through a politics of outrage and hope. Our purposes at this time are well served by a detailed engagement with an article by Charles Taylor (2007) from a special of *Public Culture* titled, 'Cultures of Democracy and Citizen Efficacy'. This article, and others in the special issue, is particularly instructive and helpful in mapping what it is that we want to describe as *cultures of democracy*. A key concept in Taylor's discussion is what he calls *social imaginary*:

> What I am trying to get at with this term is something much broader and deeper than the intellectual schemes people may entertain when they think about social reality in a disengaged mode. I am thinking rather of the ways in which they imagine their social existence – how they fit together with others and how things go on between them and their fellows, the expectations that are normally met and the deeper normative notions and images that underlie these expectations.
> TAYLOR 2007: 119

The way in which Taylor (2007: 118–119) conceives of this *social imaginary* is useful because it points to the shared, the normalised, the enduring, the changing and the complex aspects of people's sense of themselves and their possible relations with others:

> Our social imaginary at any given time is complex. It incorporates a sense of the normal expectations that we have of each other, the kind of common understanding that enables us to carry out the collective practices that make up our social life. It also incorporates some sense of how we all fit together in carrying out the common practice. This understanding is both factual and normative; that is, we have a sense of how things usually go, but this is interwoven with an idea of how they ought to go, of what missteps would invalidate the practice.

The plural (*cultures*) is important in our framing of such things as Iran's 'Green Revolution', the 'Arab Spring', the European protests of 2011, the Occupy movement. Iran in 2008–09, is not Egypt in 2011, is not Tunisia in 2011, is not Yemen or Syria or Libya or Greece or Spain. Nor is it Wall St, or London, or Melbourne, or Sydney. Dilip Parameshwar Gaonkar (2007: 21–22), in an introduction to the special issue on *Cultures of Democracy*, touches on some of the issues that shape our interests in young people's construction of, and participation in, cultures of democracy:

> After nearly a century of incessant experimentation, democracy remains on trial in a variety of national/cultural sites. It has good days, and it has bad days. Through its many travails and failings, democracy has endured. For us, the moderns, it is the inescapable horizon of our political lives and imaginings. Its presence, as well as its absence, can no longer be measured narrowly in terms of how we elect those who would govern us. It is more than a method. It is a way of being in the world politically as a

people. Democracy is one among many ways of being a people, perhaps the most vexing way due to the sheer plurality of its constituents and their claims to difference.

Taylor (2007: 118) also suggests, in this light, that:

> It may well be that the attempt to answer totally general questions—such as, what are the conditions of democracy?—is misguided. General questions assume that there is some recognizable political culture of democracy and a set of economic and social conditions that enable this. In fact, it would seem more sensible to start from another basic assumption: that there are cultures of democracy, in the plural.

The problem for analysis and interpretation then, is to seek to grasp, to hold on to, to examine aspects of these cultures in order to explore what is happening, in general and in particular. For Taylor (2007: 119):

> Comparison here does not aim at general truths, but rather is the search for enlightening contrasts, where the particular features of each system stand out in their differences. Of course, contrasts require likenesses as their essential background; therefore the point is not to catalogue the similarities, but to grasp what is particular to each.

Gaonkar (2007: 22) also suggests that this concept of cultures of democracy requires that analysis and interpretation broadens the scope of what might be identified and understood as democratic practices, particularly as we shift our attention to different spaces, places, movements and cultures, which enable or provoke the emergence of these practices:

> That difference, now globally mobile, cannot be mastered, nor recognized by electoral politics alone. Hence, the future of democracy and its flourishing, will depend decisively on our capacity to imagine a more capacious rather than a constricted view of its possibilities and also of its fragilities.

In the last few years the concept of 'belonging' has been taken up in youth studies to examine diverse ways of 'linking' individual young people, and groups of young people, to an array of transformations at the levels of neighbourhoods, communities, cities, nations, the globe. This idea of belonging has useful linkages to the concept of cultures of democracy – if we are being capacious in our thinking. Vanessa May (2011: 374), for example, has argued that the concept of 'belonging', situated as it is in 'the everyday realities of people', allows an examination of 'the mutual interaction between social change and the self'. She argues that this interaction is mutually constitutive. For May (2011), 'belonging' links the person with the social and our sense of belonging is bound up in our sense of place. John Crowley (1999) has referred to the politics of belonging as 'the dirty work of boundary maintenance'. While Nisa Yuval-Davis (2011: 12), in her book *The Politics of Belonging: Intersectional Contestations*, makes a distinction between belonging as 'naturalized' in everyday life, and the 'politics of belonging' which comprises 'specific political projects aimed at constructing belonging to particular collectivity/ies which are themselves being constructed in these projects in very specific ways'. Yuval-Davis also points out that the boundaries produced in these processes are often spatial and location specific. Yuval-Davis (2011: 18) uses what she terms:

> three major analytical facets; social locations, people's identifications and emotional attachments, and their ethical and political value systems' which she employs to interrogate how people make judgements about who belongs/does not belong. In this way the politics of belonging not only constructs boundaries but includes/excludes particular people, social categories and groupings.

It is against this briefly sketched theoretical and analytical background that some of our contributors have positioned their engagement with our interest in young people and the politics of outrage and hope. As should be expected in a collection of this type, these contributions engage with diverse aspects of these concerns from a variety of perspectives, and via a number of general, and more specific, aspects of young people's lives in different parts of the world at the start of the 21st century. These contributions have been 'curated' here in relation to our themes: *Neo-Liberal Capitalism and the Politics of Outrage*; *Education, Work and the Promise of Hope*; and *Cultures of Democracy and the Politics of Belonging*.

4   Part One: Neo-Liberal Capitalism and the Politics of Outrage

In Part One of this collection our contributors examine young people's experiences growing up in a time that could be described as post-GFC, and shaped by neo-liberal social modalities, relationships and digital communication technologies. In many respects our contributors ask: what hope can young people have for *their* future? How can young people push back against the limitations imposed by neo-liberal modes of governmentality to shape a self and build fulfilling relationships with others? Many of our contributors frame their critique by referring to global unrest, uprisings and the downstream effects of the GFC, such as: high-unemployment rates, high levels of student debt, major disruptions to the transition to adulthood or the permanence of 'waithood' (Honwana, 2014). At a time when young people face an increasing range of challenges related to transitions into precarious labour markets in any meaningful way to set up a life and future that is less precarious, our contributors consider how next generations can be best prepared, and the role education has to play. From entrepreneurial to Guerrilla ethics, our contributors explore how young people are reimagining the ways in which they are encouraged to develop relationships and a sense of self at a time when individualised, competitive ethics are so dominant. Community connections and social intuitions have a significant role to play here for those struggling with neo-liberal modes of dispossession.

Henry Giroux begins this edited collection with a provocative description of Canada and the United States in which George Orwell's nightmarish vision of a totalitarian society casts a large shadow. He describes a landscape where institutions designed to protect the public from market excesses have been weakened or abolished and the erosion of 'the social contract' and the concomitant rise of free market policies and deregulation shape every major political and economic institution in both countries. Under these circumstances progressive ideas and critical dialogue in public spheres are increasingly commercialized or else these spheres are transferred to corporate settings where profit margins are king. Henry argues that as a result it 'becomes more difficult to reclaim a history in which the culture of business is not the culture of education'. He presents compelling evidence of the erosion of the social contract and its devastating effect on marginalised people in both countries. Without resiling from his portrayal of this bleak dystopian landscape, Henry demonstrates that he has not lost all hope when he argues, after Hannah Arendt, that 'history is open and the space of the possible is always larger than the one currently on display'. He concludes by urging us to take seriously Jacques Derrida's provocation to think and do the impossible if we do not want a future where we are doomed to endlessly repeat the present.

In Chapter 2 Judith Bessant engages the dominance of neo-Liberal capitalism and its effects by focusing on two problems, one relatively new and one old. In the first instance, Judith discusses the transformation of the Western industrial social and economic order through recent developments such as the Internet and biotechnology. She argues that these developments call into question what it is to be human and how we should live our lives. The second problem she identifies is the appeal of a state-sponsored educational system based on the transmission and reproduction of knowledge focused on the three R's. Her argument is that this focus is primarily about socialising young people and preparing them for 'work and life'. The question for educators is, given the rapid changes in technology and their effects on humanity, what exactly is it that we should be teaching? Judith focuses on the challenge the intersection of these two problems pose for institutions such as schools and universities who are struggling to meet the demands of the world their students will enter. She ponders how these institutions will enable young people to make informed choices about what they value, who they wish to be and how they will live. Here, the old idea of democratic education perhaps holds some promise and contemporary relevance as it enables us to understand the use of 'peer-to-peer' technology as a way of fostering more cooperative practices among diverse groups, enabling students to become user-creators rather than passive consumers of new knowledges.

In the next chapter Perri Campbell and Luke Howie draw on an ethnographic study of young people in a west coast college town in the US. They argue that these students, although severely affected by the Global Financial Crisis, demonstrated resilience and hope for the future. Drawing on Haraway's notion of figures as 'material-semiotic nodes or knots' (2008: 4) that 'map universes of knowledge, practice and power', Perri and Luke develop a figure they call the *guerrilla self*. This figure gathers up stories about young people's transitions and pathways into the future told by the young people interviewed and those stories found in the youth studies cannon. They employ this figure as a marker for the combination of complex social, cultural and political forces which have had particularly adverse effects on young people globally. They share a concern, also expressed by Henry Giroux, that this is a world characterised by economic disaster, the rise of ISIS, the dominance of the 'authoritarian right', and widespread distrust of traditional authority figures and the media, and an ever-increasing divide between the haves and the have nots. These global events form the backdrop for understanding the experiences of young people in these times of 'dangerous dreaming'. Perri and Luke argue that by adopting entrepreneurial or guerrilla tactics for carving out a life and a self, young people are practicing an ethos of survival and responsibilisation which affords a critical engagement with available avenues for living *life as we know it*. Young people are aware that they are being dispossessed of social connectedness in its many forms and secure socio-economic futures. The guerrilla self offers a politics of hope inspired by movements such as Black Lives Matter, Occupy and the search for a sense of community.

The ways in which young people are calling for different modes of relationality and communication and the social structures that support these, is explored further by Rob Watts in Chapter 4. Rob examines the relationship between democracy and digital media by engaging with the users of an internet site called 4chan set up by 15 year-old New Yorker Christopher Poole in 2003, and which, by 2008, had become famous for its Manga-style porn and for its politics. Users of this site started a campaign against Islamic State in 2015, and, following the Paris attacks of 13 November 2015, Anonymous used 4chan to mount a digital attack on thousands of ISIS Twitter accounts. This online campaign was typical of both 4chan and Anonymous (a name adopted by a decentralised network of young people) whose trademark qualities include 'humour, vulgarity, offensive trolling, and distributed denial of service activity'. Since 2007–8 'Anonymous' has targeted governments, corporations and high-profile individuals. The group relies on Poole's design features that all users are to be anonymous and that anything posted on 4chan is not permanent. Poole defends both design features on the grounds that they promote increased rationality and freedom of expression. For Rob, the reliance on anonymity and planned amnesia raise a number of important intellectual and practical problems about *what the political is* and how we should think about it today. Sharing the sentiment expressed by Judith Bessant and Kerry Montero in Chapter 11, Rob says: 'The point of 4chan is that it points to new conceptions of the political. This is not grounded in an austere conception of deliberative rationality. Rather it invokes the imaginary, the poetic, the capacity to ridicule, the ethical and the emotional in striking new ways'.

In Chapter Five Shane Duggan suggests that community, media and policy debates about young people's education and training over the last decade have come to be concerned with the changing notions of the 'future' and the 'new' within the digital information economy, and the implications of these formulations for how young people make a life. The chapter examines the variety of ways in which different notions of the 'future' and the 'new' have been mobilised as a response to the conditions which have accompanied the emergence of the networked digital information economy. Shane references, and makes an innovative contribution to, debates in youth studies about the experience and orientation of temporal processes, and their intersections with emerging understandings of new commodity forms and digital informational flows. In his examination of the ways in which these ideas orient discussions about young people Shane argues that the 'abstraction' of traditional forms of information and labour has emerged as a key driver of popular and policy understandings of young people's lives. Shane frames much of his discussion via a reference to McKenzie Wark's concept of the 'hacker class' to explore how traditional notions of labour market participation are being abstracted in ways that expose young people to new forms of governance and intervention. This abstraction creates the possibility of 'the new'—and the benefits it brings for the most advantaged—yet displaces the vast majority of young people in material and symbolic ways.

Peter Kelly's contribution in Chapter 6 builds on a large body of work that examines and critiques 21st century neo-liberal capitalism: a form of capitalism that is characterised by privatisation, commodification and individualisation in the pursuit of profit. He argues that this version of capitalism 'individualises and atomises' the person over the life span. As a result, individuals are made to feel responsible for their choices and the consequences of these. Peter suggests that these processes can be thought about in terms of 'the *mythic dimensions of choice*', mythic in the sense that they dominate our stories of what it is to be human, and the accompanying ambivalence that comes with the practice of freedom under these conditions. Peter draws on the recent political philosophy of John Gray, the sociological work of Zygmunt Bauman on ambivalence, and the ethics of Michel Foucault to argue that 'choice and freedom are not, as Nikolas Rose would say, *shams*. But they may well be, as Freud would argue, *illusions*'. He draws on these theorists to examine the plight of many young people who now live in a world where education is becoming increasingly privatised and commodified, where work is precarious, where they are subject to increased State surveillance and are denied refuge, and where the 'Internet of Things' has changed what it means to be human, and which brings into question how we all should practice our humanity. Peter's aim in this chapter is to unsettle the moral project of responsibilisation that is integral to the workings of neo-Liberal capitalism.

5   Part Two: Education, Work and the Promise of Hope

Part Two of this collection brings together work that addresses common themes including: youth transitions and unemployment, precarity, false hopes, imagined futures, educational interventions, and 2011 as the so-called year of the protestor. Our contributors variously engage with the idea of 'cruel optimism' (Berlant, 2011) to provide a warning to those who attempt to imagine a hopeful future from within the bounds of neo-liberal capitalist social structures. As Berlant (2011: 1) herself says:

> A relation of cruel optimism exists when something you desire is actually an obstacle to your flourishing. It might involve food, or a kind of love; it

might be a fantasy of the good life, or a political project ... They become cruel only when the object that draws your attachment actively impedes the aim that bought you to it initially.

The fundamental problem of freedom, agency and structure underlies the contributions in this section, as authors grapple with what it means to try and give shape to a future from the embrace of neo-liberalism. Our contributors ask: *How can young people adopt new skills to navigate precarious times? What skills are required? Can youthful visions of the future breathe new life into education? What role can educational institutions play in articulating new moral economies?*

In the first chapter in Part Two Ros Black examines the projects, practices and policies in educational settings that aim to produce resilient and hopeful young citizens who can ensure their own participation in all facets of society in the increasingly precarious contexts of contemporary life. She argues that these projects, practices and policies create deeply ambiguous experiences for young people who are already bearing the brunt of precarity, both globally and locally. In the process of encouraging them to be or become 'hopeful young citizens', these processes also seek to make them docile, 'channelling or containing other responses that they may have to precarity, such as outrage, protest or democratic disengagement'. These processes, as Peter Kelly suggests in the previous chapter, are deeply ambiguous. Ros draws on data from a small scale qualitative study in two Australian schools to examine the ways in which hope is employed as a neo-liberal strategy for making or remaking active young citizens in these precarious times. She employs Appadurai's ideas about the politics of hope to explore these young people's experiences. She also deploys work that is concerned with the making of citizens by 'governmental projects, practices and policies', as she questions whether educational technologies designed to produce active citizenship are enabling for young people or are a form of cruel optimism generating false hope.

In their contribution, Chris Hickey and Lyn Harrison discuss a particular dimension of a three-year project undertaken to explore the potential for a social enterprise Transitional Labour Market Program (TLMP) to re-engage disadvantaged Indigenous young people. Through its alignments with a number of key stakeholders, including a national community service organisation, a registered training organisation, and an employment transition agency, the program offers an accredited training pathway in hospitality alongside sustained work experience in a social enterprise restaurant. It was envisaged that participants would develop transferable labour market skills and knowledge that had currency across the hospitality industry in a learning environment that was culturally respectful and enabling. Chris and Lyn suggest that the 'wicked problem' associated with mediating the competing tensions between the social and financial goals of social enterprise endeavours had consequences for participant recruitment, and for gaining the support of the local Indigenous community. They suggest that it soon became clear that the intention to create a place of cultural inclusivity was not supported by accompanying values and practices that genuinely embraced and celebrated Aboriginal culture. Many trainees found the program reproduced the mainstream educational ideologies and methodologies that had previously caused them to drop out of school. Chris and Lyn use two case studies, drawn from interviews and observations, to examine how the trainees negotiated this training environment and what the consequences were for them and the TLMP itself.

Giuliana Mandich takes us to Sardinia in Chapter 9 to report on a research project about young people's imagined futures. The project's aim was to encourage young Sardinian's *capacity to aspire* in a regional environment that offers a very limited range of opportunities in the labour market, and in the educational system. Giuliana uses Appadurai's work on aspiration to analyse young people's writing about their imagined futures. She identifies a broad set of cultural resources used by young people to project themselves into the future. Drawing inspiration from a UK based research project 'Living and Working in Sheppey', the Sardinian students were asked to write an essay imagining what life they were living at the age of 90, and from this vantage point to tell how their lives had unfolded. Giuliana argues that the 'capacity to aspire' is a demand for recognition of a space in society – not necessarily creative or innovative – where 're-enchantment of the ordinary' is possible. For many of these young people the imagined future constitutes a 'politics of hope'.

Lucas Walsh seeks to develop an argument for how to equip young people and educational institutions with the skills and competencies to navigate fluidity and uncertainty in contemporary society. He builds on previous work to develop the concept of 'adversity capital' as both a way of understanding, and as a basis to respond to, certain challenges confronting young people today. He documents growing international interest in developing certain 'soft skills', for example problem solving and communication skills, in order to enable young people to become more adaptive and resilient as they navigate uncertain times. In this chapter, Lucas explores how adversity capital can be embedded in institutions, and be useful in youth political participation, work and culture. His discussion of adversity capital and resilience critically engages with the incentive to give shape to an entrepreneurial self which Lucas argues offers a neo-liberal form of subjectivity. This chapter raises a number of questions about how moral economies can push back against neoliberal responsibilisation.

In Chapter 11, Emma Rowe builds on the focus on youth precarity and its consequences in relation to cultural and social movements for education. Emma explores collaborative methods of democratic participation and how these may speak to the reimagining of education within the 'technocapitalist' global landscape. She argues that expressions of hope are central to precarity, and that doom and gloom predictions, are not necessarily shared by young people. Challenges to education, democracy and government can be seen as expressions of a reinvention of hope. For Emma, this is a valuable process, which sees both young and old exchanging ideas and negotiating and articulating values, hopes and ambitions. She argues that during these exchanges young people are articulating their expression of the future and reimagining the status quo. Emma sees these spaces as offering innovative and new visions of how to imagine educational spaces as 'critical, cooperative and democratic'.

6   Part Three: Cultures of Democracy and the Politics of Belonging

In this section our contributors turn their attention to the ways in which young people have been involved in forging new political spaces of belonging, in some cases from the ground up. For many young people this involves agitating for change and engaging everyday civic and political practices across digital and non-digital spaces. Many of our authors argue that there are limited forms of formal political participation on offer for young people, and that formalised categories of civic and political participation do not account for the ways in which young people *are* being political. Rob Watts frames this as a 'crisis of democracy and youth participation'. This crisis has been understood and experienced in a range of different ways in different geographical locations around the world. For instance, it can be understood in relation to young people's experiences of marginalisation from the labour market. As Judith Bessant and Kerry Montero note, young people are angry about searching tirelessly for a job after graduating from university, only to find unpaid internships or employment which does not pay enough to support a family. Within these precarious conditions young people are giving shape to different forms of civic and political participation, through, for instance, 'DIY citizenship' and DIY careers (Threadgold 2015), activist organisations such as Anonymous, Occupy Melbourne and Sydney, WikiDPR, and the rise of the Greek 'radical left' political party Syriza. John Bourdouvalis builds on this theme by arguing that the challenges young generations face cannot be understood solely through the frame of financial crisis management: 'this approach presumes that the problems can be situated at a regulatory or policy level, and can be overcome with more efficient economic management'. The problems young people face are far more nuanced and location-specific as Ken Roberts discusses in his discussion of the Arab Spring and its consequences.

In the first contribution in Part Three, Judith Bessant and Kerry Montero examine the role of new media in allowing young people to engage directly with political processes rather than through more traditional institutional means. Judith and Kerry draw on interviews and a survey of young people in Victoria, Australia, to argue that traditional forms of political engagement privilege consensus and rational deliberation over what they call 'dissensus'. As a result, human action that does not fit this classification is not seen as political. They see this conception of politics as limiting in that it 'excludes a full range of motives and actions that are deeply political', and contributes to the widely held view that young people are disengaged from politics. Judith and Kerry see this as problematic because this traditional view of politics fails to fully take into account changes brought about by new media. Drawing on their recent research they demonstrate that young people are not disinterested in politics, and in so doing contribute to the wider body of literature that is concerned with young people and new forms of political engagement.

In their chapter, Anita Harris and Josh Roose examine young Muslims' everyday political practice using a DIY citizenship approach which can be characterised by fluid, unstructured, localised, immediate, and personally relevant forms of political participation. Drawing on their research involving in-depth peer interviews with 80 young Muslims in Melbourne and Brisbane, Australia, they found that 'cultural production and consumption, engagement in personal networks and local projects, and politico-religious work on the self as an ethical citizen in the present' constitute important forms of participation for those who are outside both radical and mainstream politics. Their research parallels some of the practices identified in the previous chapter, in that a majority of these Muslim research participants viewed social, and non-mainstream, media and creative culture as ways that they could best have their voices heard on issues. As well as activities such as 'blogs, online forums, rap, dance, independent radio, and fashion design' they also used social networks and community engagement as part of their participatory practice. Anita and Josh argue that these young people's experiences raise interesting questions about political practice and citizenship for both youth studies and migration studies in the context of 'changing opportunities for youth engagement and expression, and generational shifts in the multicultural politics of representation'. Here they are concerned with how a DIY citizenship approach relates to migrant background Muslim young people who are frequently the object of forms of regulation that promise to develop appropriate forms of both youth and ethnic participation.

In the following chapter, Michael Hatherall investigates how a group of young Indonesian citizens has engaged with one of the country's most unpopular political institutions, the national parliament. WikiDPR are an activist organisation staffed by young people, who use a combination of social media and youthful energy to engage with politicians. Although he describes the group as only a small piece of the puzzle in such a large country, Michael's findings make a contribution to those who wish to challenge established ideas regarding the political roles and behaviours of young people. He argues, as others have done in relation to other national contexts such as the US, UK and Australia, that national voting rates are only one measure of young people's political engagement and that we need to also look at their involvement in local politics, in neighbourhood organisations, in social movements, and indeed in inventive groups like WikiDPR. He argues that a focus on these forms of engagement will provide a more nuanced and complete picture of the role of young Indonesians in their society.

In his chapter, John Bourdouvalis' examines the rise of the 'radical left' political party Syriza who were elected to power in Greece in 2015 on a platform of pushing back against neo-liberal austerity measures imposed by previous governments, and the European Union and the International Monetary Fund. These measures made the economic crisis more severe, and contributed to the mobilisation of groups demanding a more participative democracy. However, John argues that framing these mobilisations as a 'question of financial crisis management is a one-dimensional interpretation of a more entrenched problem'. This approach presumes that the problems can be situated at a regulatory or policy level, and can be overcome with more efficient economic management. He argues that this solution relies on top-down prescriptions that ignore the ability of young people and other marginalised groups to contribute to viable alternatives. Bourdouvalis' analysis points to the complexity and social heterogeneity of recent social movements across Europe and the ways in which they may contribute to more innovative forms of democratic practice outside traditional forms of political participation.

Ken Roberts' contribution in Chapter 16 continues the focus on young people and forms of resistance in his critique of the term 'Arab Spring' as a catch-all phrase to characterise pro-democracy movements across Arab North Africa in 2011. He argues that the European Union was largely responsible for framing these movements in this way, which tended to obfuscate differences in strategies and outcomes from country to country. He notes for example that Tunisia in 2016 is more democratic but less secure for foreigners than in 2011, while in

Egypt the 'reforms' have turned full circle with a military backed government once again in control. In other countries, the protests died down or were suppressed, and in others civil wars are ongoing. We have also witnessed the rise of the Islamic State (IS or ISIS). Ken argues that 'we now have evidence that enables us to eliminate some postulated causes, to focus on those that remain credible, and thereby better understand why the outcomes up to now have varied so remarkably'. He provides a nuanced analysis by separating relatively enduring contexts from more recent pre-2011 developments, in order to better understand the motivations and worldviews of key actors in 2011. He argues that although some regimes have become less oppressive none of these developments have impacted on young people's employment and housing prospects, with the events of 2011 damaging economies in all countries involved.

In Chapter 17 Madeleine Fox and Brett Stoudt present exploratory findings from a New York City survey on young people's interpretations of income inequality in the Polling for Justice (PFJ) Study. This chapter is set against the backdrop of the US Black Lives Matter movement against structural racism, and the political turmoil that has greeted the Donald Trump presidential campaign and subsequent presidency. In addition, as Madeleine and Brett attest, wealth inequality in the United States as a whole continues to be stark, racialised and on the increase. In this chapter, they explore how we might listen to, and harness, young people's experiences of the injustices that accompany wealth inequality in a time of social and economic uncertainty and upheaval. Madeleine and Brett argue for a better understanding of young people's experiences and attitudes towards the interconnections between 'inequalities, policies and practices' under neo-liberalism in order to work for transformative structural change. This research project was participatory in nature with the aim of co-generating viable strategies to engage structural change. The PFJ study results revealed that these young people were frequently subject to brutal police treatment and this provided an impetus for further research and campaigns for change. The researchers continue to seek ways to produce counter-stories of these young people's lives in order to speak back to what is described as 'the hydra of neo-liberalism'. They argue for participatory action research methodologies to enable young people's voices and generate a collective sense of outrage, and hope for structural change.

In the final chapter Freg J Stokes continues the focus on young people's political engagement. He draws on the various protest movements in what has been called the 'Year of the Protester', to examine how these various protests across Europe and the United States have impacted on the 'methods, goals and viewpoints' of Australian activists. Freg examines the 'Occupy Melbourne' and 'Occupy Sydney' protests as well as strategies such as 'horizontal organisation' that occurred after 2011. He cites two recent examples of this: the campaign against unconventional gas extraction in the state of Victoria, and the continued campaign against companies associated with the offshore detention of refugees by Australian governments on Manus island (PNG) and Nauru. This chapter focuses on the direct links between the local iterations of Occupy and the climate and refugee movements, and, more broadly, links between the local and the international wave of post-2011 militancy. Freg is interested in how these new social movements differ from those of previous generations in their 'concerns, strategies, constraints and opportunities'. He first provides some historical context using World Systems theory and Italian Autonomist Marxist analyses of social struggle. He then draws on interviews carried out with young people aged in their 20s, focusing, in particular, on the organisations involved in the campaigns against unconventional gas extraction and refugee detention, in order to assess both the direct and indirect effects of the Occupy and 2011 uprisings on the politics of the refugee and climate action movements.

References

Anderson, L. (2011) 'Demystifying the Arab Spring: Parsing the Differences Between Tunisia, Egypt, and Libya', *Foreign Affairs*, Vol. 90, No. 3, pp. 1–7 (May/June).

Beck, U. (1992), *Risk Society*, Sage Publications, London.

Beck, U. (2016) *The Metamorphosis of the World*, Polity Press, Cambridge.

Berlant, L. (2011) *Cruel Optimism*, Duke University Press, London.

Braidotti, R. (2013) *The Posthuman*, Polity Press, Cambridge.

Braidotti, R. (2014) 'Punk women and Riot Grrls', paper presented at The First Supper Symposium, Storsalen Oslo, 12 May 2014. Available from: http://www.m.youtube.com/watch?v=i5J1z-E8u6o.

Butler, J. & A. Anathasiou (2013) *Dispossession: the performative in the political*, Polity, Cambridge.

Campbell, P. (2015) *Digital Selves: Iraqi Women's Warblogs and the Limits of Freedom*, Illinois: Common Ground.

Campbell, P. (2018) 'Occupy, Black Lives Matter and suspended mediation: young people's battles for recognition in-between digital and non-digital spaces', *Young*, 26(2): 145–160.

Castells, M. (2012) *Networks of Outrage and Hope: Social Movements in the Internet Age*, Polity: Cambridge.

Castells, M. (2013) 'Manuel Castells: how modern political movements straddle urban space and cyberspace', *The Guardian,* 25 March, https://www.theguardian.com/commentisfree/series/people-and-power-hay/2013/mar/25/all

Collin, P. (2015) *Young Citizens and Political Participation in a Digital Society Addressing the Democratic Disconnect*, Palgrave Macmillan: New York.

Crowley, J. (1999) 'The politics of belonging: some theoretical considerations', in A. Geddes and A. Favell (eds), *The Politics of Belonging: Migrants and Minorities in Contemporary Europe*, Aldershot: Ashgate, 15–41.

Gaonkar, D.P. (2007) 'On Cultures of Democracy', *Public Culture*, 19: 1, 1–22.

Ghonim, W. (2012) *Revolution 2.0*, Harcourt Publishing Company, New York.

Gould-Wartofsky, M.A. (2015) *The Occupiers: the Making of the 99 Percent Movement*, Oxford University Press, New York.

Honwana, Alcinda (2014) '"Waithood": Youth Transitions and Social Change', in: Dick Foeken, Ton Dietz, Leo Haan, and Linda Johnson (eds), *Development and Equity: An Interdisciplinary Exploration by Ten Scholars from Africa, Asia and Latin America*, Leiden: Brill, 28–40.

Hounshell, B. (2011) 'The Revolution will be Tweeted', Foreign Policy, June 20 2011. URL: http://foreignpolicy.com/2011/06/20/the-revolution-will-be-tweeted/.

Howie, L. and P. Campbell (2017a) 'Wear a necklace of h(r)ope side by side with me': Young people's neoliberal futures and popular culture as political action, in P. Kelly and J. Pike (eds.) *Neo-Liberalism, Austerity and the Moral Economies of Young People's Health and Well-being*, UK: Palgrave.

Howie, L. and P. Campbell (2017b) *Crisis and Terror in the Age of Anxiety: 9/11, the Global Financial Crisis and ISIS*, Palgrave Macmillan: London.

Hughes, S. (2015) In debt, out of luck: why Generation K fell in love with The Hunger Games, *The Guardian*, http://www.theguardian.com/film/2015/oct/31/hunger-games-mockingjay-teenage-anxiety.

Huntington, S.P. (1993), 'The clash of civilisations?', *Foreign Affairs*, 72(3), 22–49.

Kelly, P. (2006) 'The entrepreneurial self and "youth at-risk": Exploring the horizons of identity in the twenty-first century'. In, *Journal of Youth Studies* 9, 1, 17–32.

Kelly, P. (2017) Growing up After the GFC: Responsibilisation and Mortgaged Futures, *Discourse*, 38, 1, 57–69.

Manson, P. (2013) 'From Arab Spring to Global Revolution', *The Guardian*, Wednesday, 6 February 2013. Available from: http://www.guardian.co.uk/world/2013/feb/05/arab-spring-global-revolution.

May, V. (2011) Self, Belonging and Social Change, *Sociology*, 45, 3, 363–378.

Occupytogether (2015) Occupy Together. Available from: http://www.occupytogether.org/.

Pollock, J. (2011) 'Streetbook: How Egyptian and Tunisian youth hacked the Arab Spring', Technology Review, September/October 2011, Available from: http://www.technologyreview.com/featured-story/425137/streetbook/.

Rosen, R.J. (2011) 'So, Was Facebook Responsible for the Arab Spring After All?' The Atlantic, September 03, 2011. Available from: http://www.theatlantic.com/technology/archive/2011/09/so-was-facebook-responsible-for-the-arab-spring-after-all/244314/.

Stengel, R. (2011) '2011 person of the year: the protester'. In, *Time Magazine*, vol. 178, no. 25: 29.

Taylor, C. (2007) 'Cultures of Democracy and Citizen Efficacy', *Public Culture*, 19:1, 117–150.

Threadgold, S. (2015), '(Sub)Cultural Capital, DIY Careers and Transferability: Towards Maintaining "Reproduction" When Using Bourdieu in Youth Culture Research', In S. Baker, B. Robards, & B. Buttigieg (eds.), *Youth Cultures and Subcultures: Australian Perspectives*, Farnham: Ashgate, pp. 53–64.

Time (2011) *Time Magazine*, vol. 178, no. 25: 29.

Wellington, D.L. (2015) 'The Power of Black Lives Matter', Crisis Magazine, January 1, 2015.

Wulf, V., K. Misaki, M. Atam, D. Randall, & M. Rohde (2013, February). 'On the ground' in Sidi Bouzid: investigating social media use during the tunisian revolution. In Proceedings of the 2013 conference on Computer supported cooperative work (pp. 1409–1418). ACM.

Yuval-Davis, N. (2011), *The Politics of Belonging: Intersectional Contestations,* London: Sage Publications.

Žižek, S. (2010), *Living in the End Times*, London: Verso.

PART 1

Neo-Liberal Capitalism and the Politics of Outrage

∴

CHAPTER 1

Neoliberal Violence against Youth in the Age of Orwellian Nightmares

Henry A. Giroux

1   Introduction

George Orwell's nightmarish vision of a totalitarian society casts a dark shadow over both Canada and the United States. We live at a time in which institutions that were meant to limit human suffering and misfortune and protect the public from the excesses of the market have been either weakened or abolished.[1] The consequences can be seen clearly in the ongoing and ruthless assault on the social state, workers, unions, higher education, students, poor minorities and any vestige of the social contract. Free market policies, values, and practices with their emphasis on the privatization of public wealth, the elimination of social protections, and the deregulation of economic activity now shape practically every commanding political and economic institution in both countries. Public spheres that once offered at least the glimmer of progressive ideas, enlightened social policies, non-commodified values, and critical dialogue and exchange have been increasingly commercialized—or replaced by private spaces and corporate settings whose ultimate fidelity is to increasing profit margins. Under such circumstances, it becomes more difficult to reclaim a history in which the culture of business is not the culture of education.

Increasingly, Americans and Canadians, and citizens of the EU and OECD economies, live in neoliberal or market-driven societies in which people often participate willingly in their own oppression mostly because of a deep insecurity about their freedom and the future. This is a mode of governance in which individual and social agency are in crisis and begin to disappear in a society in which 99 percent of the public, especially young people, low income groups, the unemployed, and minorities of class and color are considered disposable.

---

[1] This theme is taken up powerfully by a number of theorists. See C. Wright Mills, *The Sociological Imagination* (New York: Oxford University Press, 2000); Richard Sennett, *The Fall of Public Man* (New York: Norton, 1974); Zygmunt Bauman, *In Search of Politics* (Stanford: Stanford University Press, 1999); and Henry A. Giroux, *Public Spaces, Private Lives* (Lanham: Rowman and Littlefield, 2001).

We live at a time when politics is nation-based and power is global. That is, the financial elite now float beyond national borders and no longer care about the social contract. Hence, they make no concessions in their pursuits of power and profits. The social contract of the past, especially in the United States, is now on life support as social provisions are cut, pensions are decimated, and the certainty of a once secure job disappears. Many neoliberal societies are now governed by politicians and financial elites who no longer believe in social investments and are more than willing to condemn young people and others – often paralyzed by the precariousness and instability that haunts their lives and future – to a savage form of casino capitalism.

The basic elements of casino capitalism are now well known: dismantle the welfare state; privatize public schools, transit and other public resources; make consumption the only obligation of citizenship; claim government is the problem when it taxes the rich; invest in prisons rather than schools; model education after the culture of business; insist that market ideology is the template for governing all of social life; maintain that exchange values are the only values that matter, and that the yardstick of profit is the only viable measure of the good life.

With the return of the new Gilded Age, not only are democratic values and social protections at risk in many countries, but the civic and formative cultures that make such values and protections central to democratic life are in danger of disappearing altogether. Poverty, joblessness, low wage work, and the threat of state sanctioned violence produce among many Canadians and Americans the ongoing fear of a life of perpetual misery and an ongoing struggle simply to survive. Insecurity coupled with a climate of fear and surveillance dampens dissent and promotes a kind of ethical tranquilisation fed daily by the mobilisation of endless moral panics, whether they reference the violence of individual domestic terrorists, ISIS thugs blowing up malls, or Ebola spreading through the homeland like a mad, out-of-control virus. Such conditions more often than not produce withdrawal, insecurity, paranoia, and cynicism rather than rebellion among the populace in both Canada and the United States.

Underlying the rise of the authoritarian state and the forces that hide in the shadows is a hidden politics indebted to promoting the fog of historical and social amnesia. The new authoritarianism is strongly indebted to what Orwell once called a "protective stupidity" that corrupts political life and divests language of its critical content (Schell, 2007). Neoliberal authoritarianism has changed the language of politics and everyday life through a poisonous public pedagogy that turns reason on its head and normalises a culture of fear, war, and exploitation. Even as markets unravel causing increased misery, "the broader political and social consensus remains in place" suggesting that the economic crisis is not matched by a similar crisis in consciousness, ideas, language, and values (Hall, Massey & Rustin, 2013).

Dominant cultural apparatuses extending from schools to print, audio, and screen cultures now serve as disimagination machines attacking any critical notion of politics that makes a claim to be educative in its attempts to enable the conditions for changing "the way in which people might think critically" (Williams, 2012). One recent example of this was on full display in Canada when mainstream media uncritically quoted then Prime Minister Stephen Harper who mockingly attacked intellectuals and journalists for what he termed "committing sociology" by which he meant those critics who are brave enough to hold power accountable and take seriously their role as engaged public intellectuals (see, for example, Fitzpatrick 2013). To be sure, Harper's attack on "committing sociology" is synonymous with the call to remove critical reasoning from both the university and broader public discourse while promoting the assumption that any act of critical thinking is a form of stupidity. Under such circumstances, material violence is now matched by symbolic violence and can be seen in the proliferation of images, institutions, and narratives that legitimate not only the manufactured idiocy of consumer and celebrity culture but also what might be called an expanding politics of disposability.

Rendered redundant as a result of the collapse of the welfare state, a pervasive racism, a growing disparity in income and wealth, and a take-no-prisoners market-driven ideology, an increasing number of individuals and groups – especially young people, low income groups, and minorities of class and color – are being demonised, criminalised or simply abandoned either by virtue of their status as immigrants or because they are young, poor, unemployed, disabled, homeless, or confined to low paying jobs. What Joao Biehl (2005) has called *zones of social abandonment* now accelerate the disposability of the unwanted. For example, poor minority and low-income youth, especially, are often warehoused in schools that resemble boot camps, dispersed to dank and dangerous work places far from the enclaves of the tourist industries, incarcerated in prisons that privilege punishment over rehabilitation, and consigned to the increasing army of the permanently unemployed.

People who were once viewed as facing dire problems in need of state intervention and social protection are now seen as a problem threatening society. This becomes clear when the war on poverty is transformed into a war against the poor; when the plight of the homeless is defined less as a political and economic issue in need of social reform than as a matter of law and order; or when government budgets for prison construction eclipse funds for higher education. Indeed, the transformation of the social state into the corporate-controlled punishing state is made startlingly clear when young people, to paraphrase W.E.B. DuBois, become *problem people* rather than *people who face problems*.

Already disenfranchised by virtue of their age, young people are under assault today in ways that are entirely new because they now face a world that is far more dangerous than at any other time in recent history. Not only do they live in a space of social homelessness in which precarity and uncertainty lock them out of a secure future, they also find themselves inhabiting a society that seeks to silence them as it makes them invisible. Victims of a neoliberal regime that smashes their hopes and attempts to exclude them from the fruits of democracy, young people are now told not to expect too much. Written out of any claim to the economic and social resources of the larger society, they are increasingly told to accept the status of "stateless, faceless, and functionless" nomads, a plight for which they alone have to accept responsibility (Bauman, 2004:76–77). Increasing numbers of youth suffer mental anguish and overt distress even, perhaps especially, among the college bound, debt-ridden, and unemployed whose numbers are growing exponentially. Many reports are now available to support claims that, "young Canadians are suffering from rising levels of anxiety, stress, depression and even suicide. Close to 20 per cent – or one in five – have a mental health issue" (Vuchnich & Chai, 2013). According to a Sun Life financial Canada survey, "ninety per cent of Canadians aged 18 to 24 say they are excessively stressed" (Luke, 2014). One factor may be that there are so few jobs for young people. In fact the jobless rate for Canadians aged 15 to 24 stands at 13.6 percent, almost double the unemployment rate of 6.9 per cent for all ages, according to Statistics Canada (Luke, 2014).

2   Young People and the Politics of Disposability

The politics of disposability with its expanding machineries of civic and social death, terminal exclusion, and zones of abandonment represent a new historical moment and must be addressed within the context of a market driven society that is rewriting the meaning of common sense, agency, desire, and politics itself. The capitalist dream machine is back with huge profits for the ultra-rich, hedge fund managers, and major players in the financial service industries. In these new landscapes of wealth, exclusion, and fraud, the commanding institutions of casino capitalism promote a winner-take-all ethos and aggressively undermine the welfare state and labor unions, and wage a counter revolution against the principles of social citizenship and democracy. In this instance, the war on labor is part of the war on democracy, and signifies a new thrust toward what might be called the authoritarian rule of corporate sovereignty and governance.

Politics and power are now on the side of lawlessness as is evident in the state's endless violations of civil liberties, freedom of speech, and most constitutional rights, mostly done in the name of national security. Lawlessness wraps itself in government dictates. In Canada, it was evident in former Prime Minister Harper's support for Bill C-51, an anti-terrorist bill that further limits civil rights through a pedagogy of fear and racist demonisation. It is also evident in the United Sates in such policies as the Patriot Act, the National Defense Authorization Act, the Military Commissions Act, and a host of other legal illegalities. These would include the right of the president "to order the assassination of any citizen whom he considers allied with terrorists," (Turley, 2012) to use secret evidence to detain individuals indefinitely, to develop a massive surveillance apparatus to monitor every audio and electronic communication used by citizens who have not committed a crime, to employ state torture against those considered enemy combatants, and block the courts from prosecuting those officials who commit such heinous crimes.[2] The ruling corporate elites have made terror rational and fear the modus operandi of politics.

Power in its most oppressive forms is now deployed not only by various repressive intelligence agencies but also through a predatory and commodified culture that turns violence into entertainment, foreign aggression into a video game, and domestic violence into a goose-stepping celebration of masculinity and the mad values of militarism. Under the neo-Darwinian ethos of survival of the fittest, the ultimate form of entertainment becomes the pain and humiliation of others, especially those considered disposable and powerless, who are no longer an object of compassion, but of ridicule and amusement. This becomes clear in the endless stories we are now hearing from the U.S. about the near epidemic of young women being sexually assaulted at fraternity parties or by college football players. Under such circumstances, pleasure loses its emancipatory possibilities and degenerates into a pathology in which misery is celebrated as a source of fun. High octane violence and human suffering are now considered entertainment designed to raise the collective pleasure quotient. Brute force and savage killing replayed over and over in various

---

2 For a clear expose of the emerging surveillance state, see Glenn Greenwald, No Place to Hide (New York: Signal, 2014); Julia Angwin, Dragnet Nation: A Quest for Privacy, Security, and Freedom in a World of Relentless Surveillance (New York: Times Books, 2014); Heidi Boghosian, *Spying on Democracy: Government Surveillance, Corporate Power, and Public Resistance*, (City Lights Books, 2013).

media platforms now function as part of an anti-immune system that turns the economy of genuine pleasure into a mode of sadism that saps democracy of any political substance and moral vitality, even as the body politic appears engaged in a process of cannibalising its own young.

Needless to say, extreme violence is more than a spectacle for upping the pleasure quotient of those disengaged from politics; it is also part of a punishing machine that spends more on putting poor minorities in jail than educating them. As Canadian and American societies become more militarized, "civil society organises itself for the production of violence" (Lutz, 2002: 723). As a result, the capillaries of militarisation feed and mold social institutions extending from the schools to local police forces. In the United States, local police forces, in particular, have been turned into soldiers who view the neighbourhoods in which they operate as war zones. Outfitted with full riot gear, submachine guns, armoured vehicles, and other lethal weapons imported from the battlefields of Iraq and Iran, their mission is to assume battle-ready behaviour. Is it any wonder that violence rather than painstaking neighbourhood police work and community outreach and engagement becomes the norm for dealing with alleged "criminals," especially at a time when more and more behaviours are being criminalised?

In the advent of the recent display of police force in Ferguson, Missouri, it is not surprising that the impact of the rapid militarization of local police on poor black communities is nothing short of terrifying and symptomatic of the violence that takes place in authoritarian societies. For instance, according to Celisa Calacal, writing in Think Progress, "In the first half of 2016, police have killed 532 people—many of whom were unarmed, mentally ill, and people of color".[3] Michelle Alexander adds to the racist nature of the punishing state by pointing out that,"There are more African American adults under correctional control today - in prison or jail, on probation or parole – than were enslaved in 1850, a decade before the Civil War began" (Alexander, 2012).

Meanwhile the real violence used by the state against poor minorities of color, women, immigrants, and low income adults barely gets mentioned, except when it is so spectacularly visible that it cannot be ignored as in the case of Eric Garner who was choked to death by a New York City policeman after he was confronted for illegally selling untaxed cigarettes. For many blacks, the police have turned their neighborhoods into battlegrounds. In Canada, the war on terror takes a deadly turn when minorities, particularly black Canadians

---

3 See Celisa Calacal, "This Is How Many People Police Have Killed So Far In 2016," *Think Progress*, [(July 5, 2016). Online: https://thinkprogress.org/this-is-how-many-people-police-have-killed-so-far-in-2016-7f1aec6b7098#.esr4ys3p5.

and aboriginals, are experiencing huge increases among the incarcerated. For example, "While aboriginals make up only 4% of Canada's population, they represent 21.5% of those serving time in federal prisons". Surprisingly, black Canadians have the highest incarceration rate of any ethnic group in federal prisons—a 69% increase over the past ten years.[4]

As the claims and promises of a neoliberal utopia have been transformed into a Dickensian nightmare, the United States, and increasingly Canada, continue to succumb to the pathologies of political corruption, the redistribution of wealth upward into the hands of the one percent, the rise of the surveillance state, and the use of the criminal justice system as a way of dealing with social problems. At the same time, Orwell's dark fantasy of an authoritarian future continues without massive opposition as students, low income, and poor minority youth are exposed to a low intensity war in which they are held hostage to disciplinary measures in which they are subject to police violence, corporate and government modes of surveillance, and the burden of extreme debt.

3   Young People and the Rise of the Punishing State

Historical amnesia takes a toll. For instance, amid the growing intensity of state terrorism, violence becomes the DNA of a society that not only has a history of forgetting, but also refuses to deal with larger structural issues such as massive inequality in wealth and power, a government that now unapologetically serves the rich and powerful corporate interests, and elevates the power of money to an organising principle of governance.[5] One of the worst examples of inequality is the United States, yet, the inequality in Canada is growing at a rate faster than the U.S. (McKenna, 2014).

No democracy can survive the kind of inequality in which "the 400 richest people…have as much wealth as 154 million Americans combined, that's 50 percent of the entire country [while] the top economic one percent of the U.S. population now has a record 40 percent of all wealth and more wealth than 90 percent of the population combined," (DeGraw, 2011). On a global scale, according to a study by anti-poverty charity Oxfam, it reports that it expects "the wealthiest 1% to own more than 50% of the world's wealth by 2016" (Peston,

---

[4] See, http://www.winnipegsun.com/2013/03/11/69-increase-in-black-population-in-federal-prisons.

[5] See, especially, Radley Balko, *Rise of the Warrior Cop: The Militarization of America's Police Forces* (New York: Public Affairs, 2013), Michelle Alexander, *The New Jim Crow* (New York: The New Press, 2010), and Jill Nelson, ed. *Police Brutality* (New York: Norton, 2000).

2015). Higher education will not fare well as a public good under such massive inequities in wealth and power. Reduced to consumers, students will fare no better and will be treated as either clients or as restless children in need of high-energy entertainment. Within such iniquitous conditions of power, access, and wealth, education will not foster a sense of organised responsibility fundamental to a democracy. Instead, it encourages a sense of organised irresponsibility–a practice that underlies the economic Darwinism and civic corruption at the heart of a debased politics.

What is not so hidden about the tentacles of power that now hide behind the euphemism of democratic governance is the rise of a punishing state and its totalitarian paranoiac mindset in which everyone is considered a potential terrorist or criminal. How else to explain the increasing criminalisation of social problems from homelessness and failure to pay off student loans to trivial infractions by students such as doodling on a desk or violating dress code in the public schools, all of which can land the public and young people in jail. The turn towards the punishing state is especially evident in the war on young people taking place in many schools, which now resemble prisons with their lockdown procedures, zero tolerance policies, metal detectors, and the increasing presence of police in the schools. One instance of the increasing punishing culture of schooling is provided by Chase Madar (2013) who argues that:

> Though it's a national phenomenon, Mississippi currently leads the way in turning school behavior into a police issue. The Hospitality State has imposed felony charges on schoolchildren for "crimes" like throwing peanuts on a bus. Wearing the wrong color belt to school got one child handcuffed to a railing for several hours. All of this goes under the rubric of "zero-tolerance" discipline, which turns out to be just another form of violence legally imported into schools.

There are also other forms of violence waged against young people. A more subtle form of repression burdens them with a life time of debt and does everything possible to depoliticise them and remove them from being able to imagine a more just and different society. In Canada the average student graduates with a $25,000 debt while in the United States the average student loan debt is $27,000. These figures point to a form of indebted citizenship. Debt bondage is the ultimate disciplinary technique of casino capitalism to rob students of the time to think, dissuade them from entering public service, and reinforce the debased assumption that they should simply be efficient cogs serving a consumer economy and a punishing society.

Underlying the carnage caused by neoliberal capitalism is a free market ideology in which individuals are cut off from the common good along with any sense of compassion for the other (Buchheit, 2014). Under casino capitalism, acts of translation become utterly privatised and removed from public considerations. Public issues now collapse into private problems. One consequence is not only the undoing of the social contract, but also the endless reproduction of the narrow register of individual responsibility as a substitute for any analyses of wider social problems, making it easier to blame the poor, homeless, uninsured, jobless, and other disadvantaged groups for their problems while reinforcing the merging of a market society with the punishing state. Put differently, all problems are now defined as a problem of faulty character and a lack of individual resilience and responsibility. At the same time, freedom is reduced to consumerism and self-interest becomes the only guiding principle for living one's life. Power and politics can lead to cynicism and despair if casino capitalism is not addressed as a system of social relations that diminishes the capacities and possibilities of individuals and groups to move beyond struggling to merely survive, to where they can more fully participate in exercising some control over the myriad forces that shape their daily lives.

What all of this suggests is that the real crisis is not simply around the growing inequality in wealth and power accompanied by the more visible use of state violence and an arrogant display of hatred for both democracy and the disadvantaged, but also a dismantling of what Hannah Arendt called "the prime importance" of the very nature of politics itself (Arendt, 2013:33–34).

4   Neoliberal Authoritarianism and the Need for a New Politics

What exists in the United States today and increasingly in Canada is fundamentally a new mode of politics, one wedded to a notion of power removed from accountability of any kind, and this poses a dangerous and calamitous threat to democracy itself, because such power is difficult to understand, analyze, and counter. The collapse of the public into the private, the de-politicisation of the citizenry in the face of an egregious celebrity culture, the surrender of mainstream media to corporate power, and the disabling of education as a critical public sphere makes it easier for casino capitalism to render its ideologies, values, and practices as a matter of common sense, removed from critical inquiry and dissent.

If neoliberal authoritarianism is to be challenged and overcome it is crucial that intellectuals, unions, workers, young people, and various social movements unite to reclaim democracy as a central element in fashioning a radical imagination. This means interrogating and rupturing the material and symbolic forces that hide behind a counterfeit claim to participatory democracy. This means rescuing the promises of a radical democracy that can provide a living wage, decent health care, public works, and massive investments in education, child care, housing for the poor, along with a range of other crucial social provisions that can make a difference between living and dying for those who have been cast into the ranks of the disposable.

The growing global threat of neoliberal authoritarianism signals both a crisis of politics and a crisis of beliefs, values, and agency itself. Put differently, the economic crisis has not been matched by a crisis of ideas. Matters of education must be at the heart of any viable notion of politics. This means that education must be at the center of any struggle that is attempting to change consciousness, the ways in which people think, act, and view themselves and their relationship to the larger world. This is an imminently educative, moral, and political task and it is only through such a recognition that initial steps can be taken to challenge the powerful ideological and affective spaces through which market fundamentalism produces the desires, identities, and values that bind people to its forms of predatory governance. The fog of historical, social and political amnesia must be eliminated if there is any hope of creating meaningful alternatives to the dark times in which we live. More specifically, young people need to create their own narratives about their role in a democracy, what it means to sustain public connections, develop a sense of compassion for the other, and what it might mean to think otherwise in order to act otherwise. Moreover, the machineries of oppressive power must be made visible and subject to both critique and collective forms of resistance. A politics of heightened consciousness must translate into both a politics of outrage and a broad-based social movement aimed at restructuring rather than reforming neoliberal societies. This is both a pedagogical and a political task.

But the question remains regarding how a public largely indifferent to politics and paralyzed by the need to just survive while caught in a crippling cynicism can be moved from "an induced state of stupidity" to a political formation willing to engage in various modes of resistance extending from "mass protests to prolonged civil disobedience." (Arendt, 2013: 33–34, and Hedges, 2014). Chris Hedges (2014) is helpful in arguing that the terrifying intellectual and moral paralysis produced by the ruling elite must be offset by the development of alternative public spheres in which educators, artists, workers, young people and others can change the terms of the debate in Canadian and American culture and politics. Ideas matter but they wither without institutions in which they can be nourished, debated, and acted upon. Any viable struggle against casino capitalism must focus on those forms of domination that pose a threat to those public spheres – such as public and higher education and the new media – that are essential to developing the critical, formative cultures that nourish modes of thinking, that are necessary for the production of critically engaged citizens.

For too many liberals and progressives this means simply understanding the economic forces that drive neoliberal global capitalism. While this structural logic is important, it does not go far enough. As Stuart Hall has insisted: "There's no politics without identification. People have to invest something of themselves, something that they recognize is meaningful to them, or speaks to their condition and without that moment of recognition" (Hall & Back, 2009:680–681). Pierre Bourdieu takes this logic further in arguing that progressives have often failed to recognize "that the most important forms of domination are not only economic but also intellectual and pedagogical, and lie on the side of belief and persuasion" (Bourdieu & Grass, 2002: 2). He insists, rightly, that it is crucial for educators, in particular, to recognize that intellectuals bear an enormous responsibility for challenging this form of domination by developing tactics "that lie on the side of the symbolic and pedagogical dimensions of struggle" (Bourdieu, 1998: 11).

If such a politics is to make any difference, it must be worldly; that is, it must incorporate a critical understanding of a politics that both addresses social problems and tackles the conditions necessary for modes of democratic political exchange that enable new forms of agency, power, and collective struggle. Until politics can be made meaningful in order to be made critical and transformative, there will be no significant opposition to casino capitalism. These are only a few of the issues that should be a central goal for the development of a broad-based radical social movement. At the same time, I want to emphasize that if there is to be any move towards a genuine democracy, such a task necessitates not only critical modes of inquiry, but it must also sustain public connections and promotes strategies and organizations that are systemic and long standing. Demonstrations are important because they are the events that can make the abuses of power visible, but they are not enough. A number of theorists, such as Stanley Aronowitz (2014), have recently argued that progressives need to develop new political narratives and a broad-based political movement that can provide real alternatives to the established money and power of the authoritarian state. But for that to happen progressives have to develop narratives that capture the imagination of the public so that they can willingly invest in the struggle for a more just and equal democratic social order.

5   Conclusion

I want to conclude by recommending five initiatives, though incomplete, that might help young people and others challenge the current oppressive historical conjuncture in which they along with other oppressed grounds now find themselves (Aronowitz, 2014).

In the first instance, there is a need for what can be called a revival of the radical imagination. This call would be part of a larger project:

> to reinvent democracy in the wake of the evidence that, at the national level, there is no democracy – if by "democracy" we mean effective popular participation in the crucial decisions affecting the community.
> ARONOWITZ, 2014

Democracy entails a challenge to the power of those individuals, financial elites, ruling groups, and large-scale enterprises that have hijacked democracy. At the very least, this means refusing to accept minimalist notions of democracy in which elections become the measure of democratic participation. Far more crucial is the struggle for the development of public spaces and spheres that produce a formative culture in which the Canadian and American public can imagine forms of democratic self-management of what can be called "key economic, political, and social institutions" (Aronowitz, 2014).

One step in this direction would be for young people, intellectuals, scholars and others to go on the offensive in defending higher education as a public good. This means fighting back against a conservative led campaign "to end higher education's democratizing influence on the nation" (Nichol, 2008). This means defending higher education as a public good in order to reclaim its egalitarian and democratic impulses. Higher education should be harnessed neither to the demands of the warfare state, nor to the instrumental needs of corporations. Clearly, in any democratic society, education should be viewed as a right, not an entitlement.

Second, young people and progressives need to develop a comprehensive educational program that would include a range of pedagogical initiatives: from developing a national online news channel, to creating alternative schools for young people in the manner of the diverse workers' socialist schools that existed in the 1930s and 1940s throughout North America. Such a pedagogical task would enable a sustained critique of the transformation of a market economy into a market society along with a clear analysis of the damage it has caused both at home and abroad. This task suggests developing alternative public spheres such as online journals, television shows, newspapers, Zines, and any other platform in which alternative positions can be developed. It also means working with one foot in existing cultural apparatuses in order to promote alternative ideas and views that would challenge the affective and ideological spaces produced by the financial elite who control the commanding institutions of public pedagogy in North America.

Third, academics and particularly young people, such as those who conducted strikes at York and the University of Toronto during 2014 and 2015, must be engaged in an ongoing struggle for the right of students to be given a formidable, and critical education not dominated by corporate values, and to have a say in the shaping of their education and what it means to expand and deepen the practice of freedom and democracy. Young people have been left out of the discourse of democracy. They are the new disposables who lack jobs, a decent education, hope, and any semblance of a future better than the one their parents inherited. Facing what Richard Sennett (2007) calls the *spectre of uselessness*, they are a reminder of how finance capital has abandoned any viable vision of the future, including one that would support future generations. This is a mode of politics and capital that eats its own children and throws their fate to the vagaries of the market. This is a culture of cruelty and an ecology of finance capital that only believes in short term investments because they provide quick returns. Under such circumstances, young people, who need long term investments, are considered a liability. If any society is, in part, judged by how it views and treats its children, Canada and the United States by all accounts are failing in a colossal way. How else to explain the fact that too many young people in both countries live in poverty, are unemployed, and will not have access to higher education because of rising tuition costs? One solution to this problem is to abolish student debt and to make higher education free.

Fourth, casino capitalism is so widespread that progressives need to develop a comprehensive vision of politics that "does not rely on single issues" (Nichol, 2008). Following Herbert Marcuse, it is only through an understanding of the wider relations and connections of power that the young people and others can overcome uninformed practice, isolated struggles, and modes of singular politics that become insular and self-sabotaging. This means developing modes of analyses capable of connecting isolated and individualised issues to more generalized notions of freedom. It also means developing theoretical frameworks in which it becomes possible to translate private troubles into broader more systemic conditions. In short, this suggests developing modes of analyses that connect the dots historically and relationally. It also means developing a more comprehensive vision of politics and change. The key here is the notion of translation. There is a need to translate private troubles into broader public issues, and understand how systemic modes of analyses can be helpful in connecting a range of issues so as to be able to build a united front in the call for a radical democracy.

This is a particularly important goal given that the fragmentation of the left has been partly responsible for its inability to develop a wide political and ideological umbrella to address a range of problems extending from extreme poverty, the assault on the environment, the emergence of the permanent warfare state, the roll back of voting rights, the assault on public servants, women's rights, and social provisions, and a range of other issues that erode the possibilities for a radical democracy. The dominating mechanisms of casino capitalism in both their symbolic and material registers reach deep into every aspect of American and Canadian society. Any successful movement for the defense of public goods and democracy itself will have to wage a struggle against the totality of this new mode of authoritarianism rather than isolating and attacking specific elements of its anti-democratic ethos.

Fifth, another serious challenge facing advocates of a new democratic social order is the task of developing a discourse of both critique and possibility. Critique is important and is crucial to break the hold of commonsense assumptions that legitimate a wide range of injustices. The language of critique is also crucial for making visible the workings of unequal power and the necessity of holding authority accountable. But critique is not enough and without a discourse of hope can lead to a paralyzing despair or, even worse, a crippling cynicism. Hope speaks to imagining a life beyond capitalism, and combines a gritty sense of limits with a lofty vision of demanding the impossible. As Ernst Bloch once insisted, reason, justice, and change cannot blossom without hope, because educated hope taps into our deepest experiences and longing for living a life of dignity with others, a life in which it becomes possible to imagine a future that does not mimic the present. I am not referring to a romanticized and empty notion of hope, but a notion of educated hope that faces the concrete obstacles and realities of domination but continues the ongoing task of "holding the present open and thus unfinished" (Benjamin, 1997:10).

The discourse of possibility not only looks for productive solutions. It is also crucial in defending those public spheres in which civic values, public scholarship, and social engagement allow for a more imaginative grasp of a future that takes seriously the demands of justice, equity, and civic courage. Democracy should be a way of thinking about education, one that connects equity to excellence, learning to ethics, and agency to the imperatives of social responsibility and the public good. Casino capitalism is a toxin that has created a predatory class of ethical zombies, who are producing dead zones of the imagination while waging a fierce fight against the possibilities of a democratic future. The time has come to develop a political language in which civic values, social responsibility, and the institutions that support them become central to invigorating and fortifying a new era of civic imagination, a renewed sense of social agency, and an impassioned international social movement with a vision, organization, and set of strategies to challenge the neoliberal nightmare engulfing the planet.

I realise this sounds a bit utopian. However, we have few choices if we are going to struggle for a future that does a great deal more than endlessly repeat the present. Given the urgency of the problems faced by those marginalised by gender, class, race, age, and sexual orientation, I think it is all the more crucial to take seriously the challenge of Jacques Derrida's provocation that "We must do and think the impossible. If only the possible happened, nothing more would happen. If I only I did what I can do, I wouldn't do anything" (Derrida, 2001). We may live in dark times, as Hannah Arendt reminds us, but history is open and the space of the possible is always larger than the one currently on display.

References

Alexander, M. 2010. *The New Jim Crow*. New York: The New Press.
Alexander, M. 2012 "Michelle Alexander, The Age of Obama as a Racial Nightmare." In *Tom Dispatch*, http://www.tomdispatch.com/post/175520/best_of_tom dispatch%3A_michelle_alexander,_the_age_of_obama_as_a_racial_nightmare/.
Angwin, J. 2014. *Dragnet Nation: A Quest for Privacy, Security, and Freedom in a World of Relentless Surveillance*. New York: Times Books.
Arendt, H. 2013. *Hannah Arendt: The Last Interview and Other Conversations*. Brooklyn, NY: Melville House Publishing, 33–34.
Aronowitz, S. 2014. "What King of Left Does America Need?" In *Tikkun*, http://www.tikkun.org/nextgen/what-kind-of-left-does-america-need.
Balko, R. 2013. *Rise of the Warrior Cop: The Militarization of America's Police Forces*. New York: Public Affairs.
Bauman, Z. 1999. *In Search of Politics.* Stanford: Stanford University Press.
Bauman, Z. 2004. *Wasted Lives.* London: Polity Press, 76–77.
Benjamin, A. 1997. *Present Hope: Philosophy, Architecture, Judaism*. New York: Routledge.
Biehl, J. 2005. *Vita: Life in a Zone of Social Abandonment.* Berkely: University of California Press.
Boghosian, H. 2013. *Spying on Democracy: Government Surveillance, Corporate Power, and Public Resistance*. City Lights Books.
Bourdieu, P. 1998. *Acts of Resistance*. New York: Free Press.

Bourdieu, P. and G. Grass 2002. "The 'Progressive' Restoration: A Franco-German Dialogue." In *New Left Review 14*.

Buchheit, P. 2014. "The Carnage of Capitalism," In *AlterNet* http://www.commondreams.org/views/2014/08/18/carnage-capitalism.

DeGraw, D. 2011. "Meet the Global Financial Elites Controlling $46 Trillion in Wealth." In *Alternet* http://www.alternet.org/story/151999/meet_the_global_financial_elites_controlling_$46_trillion_in_wealth.

Derrida, J. 2001. "No One Is Innocent: A Discussion with Jacques about Philosophy in the Face of Terror." In *The Information Technology, War and Peace Project* http://www.watsoninstitute.org/infopeace/911/derrida_innocence.html.

Fitzpatrick, M. (2013) Harper on terror arrests: Not a time for "sociology," CBC News, April 25, 2013, http://www.cbc.ca/news/politics/harper-on-terror-arrests-not-a-time-for-sociology-1.1413502.

Giroux, H.A. 2001. *Public Spaces, Private Lives*. Lanham: Rowman and Littlefield.

Greenwald, G. 2014. *No Place to Hide*. New York: Signal.

Hall, S. and L. Back 2009. "In Conversation: At Home and Not at Home." In *Cultural Studies, Vol. 23, No. 4*, 680–681.

Hall, S. Massey D. and M. Rustin 2013. "After neoliberalism: analysing the present." In *Soundings (Spring 2013)*, http://www.lwbooks.co.uk/journals/soundings/pdfs/s53hallmasseyrustin.pdf.

Hedges, C. (2014) "The Last Gasp of American Democracy," truthdig, January 5, 2014, https://www.truthdig.com/report/item/the_last_gasp_of_american_democracy_20140105.

Luke, P. 2014. "Seriously stressed-out students on the rise on post-secondary campuses burdened by debt and facing a shaky job market, many students feel overwhelmed." In *The Province*, http://www.theprovince.com/business/Seriously+stressed+students+rise+post+secondary+campuses/9756065/story.html.

Lutz, C. 2002. "Making War at Home in the United States: Militarization and the Current Crisis." In *American Anthropologist*.

Madar, C. 2013. "Everyone Is a Criminal: On the Over-Policing of America." In *Huffington Post*. http://www.huffingtonpost.com/chase-madar/over-policing-of-america_b_4412187.html.

McKenna, B. 2014. "What growing income inequality is costing Canada's future generations." In *The Globe and Mail*, http://www.theglobeandmail.com/news/national/time-to-lead/the-wealth-paradox-what-growing-income-inequality-is-costing-canadas-future-generations/article15350903/?page=all.

Nelson, J. ed. 2000. *Police Brutality*. New York: Norton.

Nichol, G.R. 2008. "Public Universities at Risk Abandoning Their Mission." In *The chronicle of Higher Education*. http://chronicle.com/weekly/v54/i30/30a02302.htm.

Peston, R. 2015. "Richest 1% to own more than rest of world, Oxfam says." *BBC News*. http://www.bbc.com/news/business-30875633.

Schell, O. (2007). "Follies of Orthodoxy," *What Orwell Didn't Know: Propaganda and the New Face of American Politics*, Perseus Books Group, New York, p. xviii.

Sennett, R. 1974. *The Fall of Public Man*. New York: Norton.

Sennett, R. 2007. *The Culture of the New Capitalism*. New Haven: Yale University Press.

Turley, J. 2012 "10 reasons the U.S. is no longer the land of the free." In *The Washington Post*, http://articles.washingtonpost.com/2012-01-13/opinions/35440628_1_individual-rights-indefinite-detention-citizens.

Vuchnich, A. and C. Chai 2013. "Young Minds: Stress, anxiety plaguing Canadian youth." In *Global News*. http://globalnews.ca/news/530141/young-minds-stress-anxiety-plaguing-canadian-youth/.

Williams, Z. 2012. "The Saturday Interview: Stuart Hall." In *The Guardian*, http://www.guardian.co.uk/theguardian/2012/feb/11/saturday-interview-stuart-hall.

Wright Mills, C. 2000. *The Sociological Imagination*. New York: Oxford University Press.

CHAPTER 2

Channelling Hope through Peer to Peer Technology: Education and Participatory Practice

Judith Bessant

1   Introduction

This chapter is framed by the intersection of two problems: one new and the other old. The new problem is a radical transformation already underway that promises the end of a four-hundred year-old industrial work-based social and economic order. It is a transformation based on recent developments in artificial intelligence, the 'Internet of Things' and new bio-technology. As Harari observes while human power historically relied primarily on improving our external tools, now it is coming to 'rely more on upgrading the human body and mind, or on merging directly with our tools' (2015, 43). This change process raises questions about what we mean by intelligence, what it means to be human and how we will live.

The old problem is the continuing authority and appeal of a state-sponsored educational paradigm based on the transmission and reproduction of approved modes of knowledge and skills like reading, writing and counting. For much of the twentieth century it has been applied to civilising or socialising young people and preparing them for 'work and life', a project recently redacted through the lens of human capital theory.

Each problem is serious enough in itself but in combination they constitute a major crisis. In this chapter I focus on the challenge the intersection poses to the capacity of contemporary institutions such as schools and universities to enable young people to make informed choices about what they value, who they wish to be and how they will live in a time when the practices, and intentions of those institutions are increasingly out of kilter with the world which they will enter as adults.[1]

---

1   I note that education is not alone in failing to recognise what is happening: governments, non government organisation, businesses across all sectors face the same challenges, with some trying to establish what is happening and working out the implications better than others.

I begin by outlining the emergent crisis drawing on what Michel Serres refers to as the convergence of two tectonic plates. As he argues, there is nothing riskier than living across such a gap that 'strangely resembles the tension between two tectonic plates'. It is one that 'silently prepares' for an 'upheaval whose intensity will be proportionate to the length of the wait' (2015, 20). Turning back to one of the metaphoric origins of 'crisis', Serres uses a medical metaphor to explain the nature of 'the crisis' we face, describing it as a critical condition, the point at which the body itself takes a decision (2015, xii). In this way the capacity to make choices about the options and even to prepare for and shape what lies ahead is taken out of one's hands. Moreover, as Serres notes, once a critical point is reached we can never go back to the previous state, because doing so requires us returning to that critical situation (2015, xii–xiii).

I then consider likely obstacles to change in the form of inertia and resistance. If the history of previous major crises is anything to go by, it is likely we will see governments and educational institutions adopting a 'head in the sand' approach reliant on old but failed paradigms of policy and practice punctuated by rare moments of innovation. The risks this denial approach now poses to young people and their communities are too high to be ignored.

Drawing on Bourdieu's theory of practice helps explain the persistence of traditional educational practice. And while Bourdieu helps explain inertia he also clarifies how and why change also occurs. Attention is then given to the intuition informing this chapter. It is one shared with others who have documented the changing patterns of work, and social life courtesy of accelerating technological innovation arguing for an approach that promotes 'a greater life for the ordinary individual' (Unger 2014, 295). As Unger argues a free society exists when everyone has the educational equipment and economic political occasions to traverse the frontier between taking things-for-granted and challenging the taken-for-granted (2014, 295). A free society benefits from disagreement with and opposition to its most basic and pervasive intentions (Unger 2014).

To take advantage of the momentous changes already underway, we require people willing and able to engage in free and open critique, collaboration and experimentation. This requires higher forms of cooperation that can now be bought forth courtesy of new peer-to-peer technologies. Achieving this also rests on an interest in promoting and reimagining older ideas like democratic education and inclusive deliberative practices in ways that appreciate how using these technologies can connect people for those purposes, in ways that overcome 'their place in the scheme of social divisions and hierarchy' (Unger 2014).

2   Change and a Sense of Crisis

It is now generally acknowledged that digital and robotic information technology promises -or threatens- to transform the forms of, and need for, human labour across the full range of skill and knowledge levels (Fuchs 2015). The 2016 World Economic Forum provided evidence of the 'digital disruption' predicting that 47% of current jobs *across all skill levels* will be displaced between 2016 and 2025.

Indicators of the change taking place were already evident in the early 1980s as automated teller machines in the banking systems and desktop computers in offices extinguished typing pools. This suggests something of what is to come: entire industries and classes of jobs disappeared while new ones will appear. Added to this was the fact that such early technological innovations also occurred in the context of broader restructuring processes related to state policy-making (e.g., industrial and financial deregulation, privatization, tax cuts, tariff reduction) and economic and market practices (e.g., financialisation and new trading patterns). They were policy processes that had serious and lasting unemployment effects in different labour markets like the male industrial and manufacturing sector and the collapse of the full-time youth labour market.

However, the scale and speed of change now taking place is of a different order than any previous period of major change. The old industrial work-based order is disappearing while many service sector occupations and professional activities are undergoing fundamental change (Brown et al. 2011; Micklethwait & Wooldridge 2014). The significance of this becomes evident when considering Kurzweil's claim that we are approaching a point of 'singularity'. By 2025 Kurzweil argues we will have personal computers that match the computational and information-retention capacity of any human. By 2029 machines will be a thousand times smarter than a human brain, that may conform with certain ethical ideas and will be fully autonomous – in that they will not be programmed by humans (Kurzweil 2005). Amongst other things, by 2045 Artificial Intelligence will surpass human intelligence. Researchers like Brynjolfsson and McAfee (2011) similarly argue that the speed and scale of change is eliminating jobs faster than it is creating them and this will continue. Susskind and Susskind (2015) also document a 'picture of radical change' identifying substantive developments across all areas of professional workplaces. They point to 'capable machines' operating autonomously and alongside professional operators, high speed and powerful algorithms that can be used to assess financial reports, and to write articles traditionally the work of journalists. Robots also can work in performing arts, in film making where creative technologies can be used to develop scripts, and in minding and shepherding actors with costumes, props, refreshments etc., on the set. Legal disagreements can be resolved without lawyers. Technologies like 'Legalzoom.doc provide automated legal document drafting services. According to Susskind and Susskind all domains of professional practices will be affected. Moreover, given the reduced need for human labour many industries that are currently in developing countries where human labour is cheap will be re-shored (back to western nations), a change likely to alter the lives of many in developing nations.

Not surprisingly considerable disagreement exists about the possibilities of utopian promises (Dunlop 2016; Unger 2014) and dystopian threats this presents (Morozov 2011; Turkle 2011; Bartlett 2014). What is clear is that around two-thirds of adults support themselves and their families through employment and a wage, and that any significant technology-driven unemployment will have widespread socio-economic effects on living standards. Equally the same technologies may also have significant beneficial consequences for institutions and practices like accessing and use of information in public opinion formation, leisure activities, scientific research and cultural expressivity. It's a disruption characterised by uncertainty and the prospect that innovations may be more of a problem than a solution, no such uncertainty however characterises the dominant education paradigm.

The older education paradigm relies on a centuries old transmission model of educational practice. It's an approach reliant on the idea of the teacher as central to education, as the conduit between the socially valued intellectual and the student. According to this model the teacher is the gatekeeper, the one who determines what is learned, and when and who achieves learning credentials. The design and assessment of curriculum is also the responsibility of the teacher. As such they are responsible for the transmission of knowledge and valued cognitive skills. They also transmit the socially approved conventions about good behaviour by maintaining discipline and order through systems of punishment and reward.

In this field the student is rendered a passive subject on whom the active subject teacher acts, by motivating, inscribing, surveilling, measuring and punishing the student against measures of progress.

These practices have relied on a range of common sense assumptions about the nature of knowledge, the best methods for transmitting knowledge and for assessing learning. This is a paradigm that regards knowledge as information and as a bank of true facts and valuable skills. It's a tame solution model that assumes answers are clearly true or false. The authority of the teacher rests on their mastery of the relevant information and skills. The idea that learning is memory and therefore most suited to memory tests has proved irresistible. It's an approach in which knowledge and skills were defined and imparted by experts to generation after generation of children and young people. Informing this was the assumption that competition and objective rigorous assessment would identify the naturally brightest, the academically superior and weed out the rest while sorting and assigning everyone to places in the social order for which they were best suited.

This paradigm has relied on a set of intentions and social functions that stipulate the purpose of education and thus legitimate the entire exercise. Some of these related to the value of education for the individual traditionally framed in terms of intellectual or social capital or economic capital. It was a legitimation exercise that also stated what the value of education was to the community. Since the mid twentieth century this paradigm characterised the value of education as an aid to social mobility, and investment in human capital designed to meet the needs of the economy while securing individual prosperity.

While the teacher was traditionally the central figure in education, the last few decades have seen governments in most western nations make significant interventions promoting centralised models of national curriculum design or national assessment practices, moves that rendered teachers' subject within managerialist systems of control. As a result, and somewhat paradoxically given the capacities of new technologies and all the neoliberal talk of freedom, educational institutions have become more authoritarian organisations committed to settled, typically instrumentalised and vocationally oriented bodies of knowledge to be imparted to students, but also to the management of the emotional, ethical and social well-being of children and young people. All this is now directed towards the task of ensuring education retention rates increase and that graduates are 'job ready'.

Whether they were advocates for the ostensibly egalitarian idea that increased education access would erode class or gender barriers, or advocates for a neoliberal model of education as an investment in human capital, few educationists and policy-makers queried the popular claim that more education benefited everyone. From 1945 the conventional wisdom was that education would help secure a more just and democratic society as people were rewarded according to individual merit and job growth that offered opportunities for social mobility and 'improvement' (Brown et al. 2011).

It was a conception of education revised in the early 1980s courtesy of a neoliberal worldview, which included commitments to business models and the 'virtues of efficiency'. The resurgence of neoliberal policy also reinforced the idea that education was an investment in 'human capital', that private investment by individuals in their own education would improve their future employment options, income and help secure a good life (Berlant 2011).

Generations of critics have not been persuaded about the merits of this paradigm. Critics from Rousseau through Dewey and Montessori to Neill, Freire, Bourdieu and Giroux have expressed concern with this arrangement. They pointed to the authoritarian nature of our education institutions, their undemocratic teacher-centric ethos and reliance on a transmission model of knowledge oriented to integrating young people into prescribed economic, social and civic roles.[2] As critics like Bourdieu, Giroux and Connell have argued more recently, this transmission approach was committed to reproducing a social and economic order legitimised by the idea that education is a meritocratic process and preparation for life and work. To this end, its failures are becoming clear.

One failure relates to the fact that for the second half of the twentieth century many people and governments invested faith, hope and money in the idea that more education assured a prosperous future. Based on what became a common-sense policy, governments in western societies expanded access to secondary schooling and to their higher education systems. By 2000, 51 million 25–34 year olds in OECD countries had a university degree. Ten years later this figure rose to 66 million. In 2015 OECD had 64 million 25–34 year-olds with a tertiary education and 64 million in non-OECD G20 countries (OECD 2014). Soon after the 2008 Global Financial crisis, writers like Brown et al. argued that the implied intergenerational contractual promise that society and the individual would be rewarded if they invested in higher education had been broken (2011).

While many societies increased tertiary education enrolments and many young people especially in countries like Britain, America and Australia incurred increasing debt to fund their higher education or technical training in colleges, on graduation they faced increasing levels of unemployment and underemployment. The collapse of the 'opportunity bargain' implied in mass university education was highlighted by the growing disparities in access to quality education and resources needed for all young people to succeed academically. What we saw were increasing numbers of university-educated workers competing against each other for a diminishing number of jobs courtesy of what Brown et al. (2011, 1–5) described as 'digital Taylorism', as businesses outsourced work at a cheaper rate across the globe.

---

[2] The advent of new technologies has done little to alter teacher-centric practices and hierarchical modes of knowledge transmission which tend to be transferred into technological innovations (e.g. MOOCs) that continue to reproduce traditional top-down teaching, thereby missing opportunities for learning and for more inclusive cooperative practices that reap the benefits of taking participation of young people seriously.

The growing joblessness rates amongst highly educated young people, undermines the credibility of human capital theory. As the International Labour Organization (ILO) explains, while increased access to education over the past decade produced more young people aspiring to jobs in professional occupations, there are 'not enough jobs available in this category to meet the supply of graduates' (2016:30). In short 'graduate unemployment' is a serious problem and tertiary-educated people are at risk of unemployment' (OECD 2014, 13).

After two decades of sustained investment in their 'human capital' wherein young people are more educated and more qualified than ever before, many remain un(der)employed. They also earn comparatively less than did earlier generations. While individual young people made costly investments of time, effort and money in their education, collectively, young people are not benefitting (Gardiner 2016a and b). In most western nations most young people now have far less opportunity than their parents' generation in terms of income quantum, have fewer employment opportunities, and a reduced likelihood of home ownership – all of which exposes how promises of investment and hard work will produce the good life no longer hold true (Gardiner, 2016b). The problem of unemployment and stagnating wages is not due to shortfalls in particular skills and knowledge on the part of the workforce, something that better and more education will fix. Nor is it that they are work-shy. The problem is the absence of jobs, and this is not a short-term problem. This signals the emergence of a new economy.

In short, students continue to be prepared for an industrial work order world within institutions committed to assumptions and intentions that are now far more problematic than they ever were at the height of modernism and the boom years of industrial capitalism – 1945–1975.

3   Bourdieu: Inertia and Change

Bourdieu might help explain the persistence of educational practice and the reluctance to recognize the significance of the changes taking place through his theory of practice and his concept of habitus (1977). His theory proposes that human *practice* is *habitus* operating in a *field* consisting of unequally distributed *capitals* (or powers characterised by inequality and continual conflict (Bourdieu, 1991a). By practice he refers to all the activities and relationships we engage in (such as, talking, thinking or attending school etc.). According to Bourdieu, most of our practice is habitual hence his use of the term *habitus*. Our *habitus* is what we use to perceive, understand, evaluate and act in the social world. It refers to a system of 'generated dispositions integrating past experiences, which functions at every moment in a matrix of perceptions, appreciations and actions and makes possible the achievement of infinitely diversified tasks (Bourdieu 1977, 83). In short, h*abitus* is the person including our emotions, ethical and cognitive life, taste, and how we use our body. Within this construct our practices and knowledge are bound together *in and by* the body. As such our *habitus* is the product of our particular histories or trajectory through life.

Our reliance on *habitus* when engaging in *practices* always occurs in what Bourdieu refers to as *fields*. By *fields* he means social spaces like family, education, work, sports and the arts etc. All societies are ensembles of these different fields, each with its own social positions and relations based on power and struggles over various *capitals* (Bourdieu & Wacquant 1992). We compete in fields to multiply our economic, social, or cultural capital. Thus everyday life is the continuous contest in a conglomeration of organised fields.

Field and *habitus* also entail a two-way relationship. Fields only exist if social agents have the *habitus* necessary to maintain them and, reciprocally, by participating in the field, actors incorporate into their *habitus* the specific rules that will allow them to constitute the field. For this reason, habitus enacts the field, and the field mediates between *habitus* and *practice* (Bourdieu 1977).

We deploy our *habitus* in *fields as* spaces comprising relationships dependent on *capitals*. We also have many relational positions we occupy for example, as a parent *and* child, as a student or teacher, or as a worker or employer/manager. Unlike Marx, who saw society in terms of the dominant economic mode of production, Bourdieu saw the world in terms of many and different fields and different capital. For Bourdieu 'capital' refers to different valued resources found in each field because they have an exchange value in these fields (Bourdieu 1977). Moreover, each field tends to have a distinctive form of capital that agents seek to accumulate, bound by rules of competition that give the field a bounded integrity and relative autonomy.

A *capital* is hierarchically arranged according to 'the structure of the distribution' of the particular kind of power, social resource or 'species of capital' in a given field (Bourdieu 1990, 119). The field of educational cultural capital, which includes various knowledges and cognitive or aesthetic skills, is located in the hands of the powerful (the teachers, managers etc.) and which in the traditional model is given out to those students who 'play the game'. Participating in a field like education entails abiding by 'the rules of the game' and incorporating them into our habitus. This points to the political process and to the value of upholding and reproducing a tradition – this is the way the old order is made over as if it were new.

Such an account of practice may seem to foreclose on the possibility of reflexivity or critique, or indeed change. Bourdieu's emphasis on *habitus* implies that we tend to act 'unknowingly' which thwarts the prospect of reflexivity because such action is highly conscious. Indeed, Bourdieu pays considerable attention to the 'unconscious' and the many actions that are 'not conscious' (1977, 78–79). Given all of this, one might reasonably think that Bourdieu is better at explaining why change is difficult rather than how it is possible. Yet, while he was interested in habitus and reproduction he was also interested in reflexivity (Bourdieu and Wacquant 1992).

For Bourdieu, critical reflexivity is possible and crucial for change. This can be achieved by assuming the position of an 'outsider'. Certain groups like academics and intellectuals engage in various research that most would see as being well beyond the realm of the 'common-sense' life-world for the purpose of making sense of it scientifically (Bourdieu 1977, 65). Such scientific research turns the researcher into an outsider as they attempt to 'discover' the social codes, regularities and power plays that shape particular ways of being and knowing. In this way scientific work can provide an alternative more critical point of view to the taken-for-granted and unconscious understandings that form our habitus. The possibility that there are other, more 'conscious' and intellectual modes of practice than the normal lives bound by unconscious rules, rituals or customs, offers another path to reflexivity. Bourdieu also recognises how some people become critics due to 'alienation', or by being an outsider. Being an outsider is thus a critical enabler of reflexivity. This is what anthropologists do as 'outsiders' looking 'into' a society.

Finally, Bourdieu claims that a crisis in a field can become a source of critical reflexivity. It is what makes politics possible because 'politics begins... with the denunciation of this tacit contract of adherence to the established order which defines the original *doxa* [or collective commonsense] in other words, political subversion presupposes cognitive subversion' (Bourdieu 199, 127–128). Breaking with the established order is possible when a crisis that is too big or obvious to avoid erupts, and people already disposed to be critical seize on it. Consider, for example, how the 2008 recession encouraged a critique of neoliberalism which caused others to query the disparities between promises made and the ways things actually were, thus causing some to suspend their adherence to the established order. This could point to the likelihood that as the broken promises become more apparent they become more clearly recognised, and that young people in particular will become more reflexive. Novel situations like those created by crises create a dissonance or mis-alignment between our *habitus* and the practices reproduced in various fields in part because the repertoires of practices we have, courtesy of our past (habitus), are no longer appropriate in the new context.

If Bourdieu is correct then the novelties we now face in the social transformations taking place give reason for hope. Such novelty can produce a disjuncture in the field of education between our experience and our stock of common sense understandings (habitus), creating fissures or 'radical doubts' that encourage critical awareness or reflexivity about the suitability of our habitual practices for navigating novel territory that clearly requires a quite different compass.

4 The Question of Technology: Peer-to-Peer or Open Source Platforms

Whatever the conventional idea that schools and universities are obvious or natural sites of innovation and creativity this is not generally true for the reasons mentioned above. Nor can the crisis referred to above be sufficient by itself to produce a general change of direction.

What can be expected is that some spaces might open up within schools and universities because some intellectuals and academics are already documenting the changing patterns of work and social life courtesy of accelerating technological innovation, or suggesting normative 'programs' for change that 'promote a greater life for the ordinary individual' by enlarging on the idea of justice-as-freedom (e.g. Brown et al 2010; Sen 2009; Nussbaum 2011; Unger 2014). These and other 'thought leaders' are calling on those able and willing to engage in free and open collaboration, experimentation, innovation and critique to do so. This raises questions about leadership and subsidiarity. While leaders play a critical role, collectives also act as innovation agents. In this way transformation, which is always piecemeal and fragmentary ceases to be the vocation and the prerogative of small groups of visionaries and can become instead the 'common possession of ordinary men and women' (Unger 2014, 429). As I argue here, emerging technologies are now available that can be used to create policy, practice and laws through processes of inclusive co-operation, from the bottom-up.

One exceptionally practicable innovation draws on an old idea of democratic education and inclusive deliberative practice that positions educators as transformative agents with the capacity to encourage self-determination in a community of equals. This is an old idea with direct contemporary relevance. It can be enacted by using recently developed peer-to-peer technology that promotes or enhances higher forms of cooperation as it connects 'people regardless of their place in the scheme of social divisions and hierarchy', while also enabling cooperative alliances and competition to combine in the same activities (Benkler 2013, 288–307).

It has design features ideally suited to the purpose of developing a collaborative educational-political project of the kind just mentioned. It can be used to enable multi-generational projects with a diversity of participants. It has the capacity to foster openness, to facilitate higher forms of co-operation, and to actively encourage forbearance and innovation. Its capacity to achieve this has already been demonstrated in a number of fields. It presents the technical means for developing creative projects that can inform the conception and design of educational and other institutional arrangements in ways that enhance our capacity to thrive and preserve what is valuable about our humanity in this context of major change.

The architecture of distributed innovation technology like peer-to-peer platforms subverts traditional expert status and power in ways that prevent the 'cruelty of subjugation' and enable the views of non-experts (e.g., young people as students) to access a field of deliberation, that provides space to think, deliberate, articulate, edit and create alternate policies and practices. This design feature also encourages forbearance as it weakens those distinctions that mark conventional power relationships and responsibilities between those who define tasks (the manager, teacher, *the* designer or creator) and those who simply implement them (the drone, the automaton, the obedient student or worker) (Unger 2014).

While open source platforms come in various forms, they share a common capacity to enable multiple and diverse groups of people to work collaboratively. It is one example of a technology that relies on collaborative practices with a history of success like creating popular web server software like Apache server and Free and Open Software (FOSS). Another well-known example of this 'open source' practice was that initiated by Jimmy Wales in 2001: the wiki project. Within a short period Wikipedia came to replace conventional reference sources like Britannica, putting many encyclopaedias out of business.[3] It was a project started with a series of access points on the web that anyone at

---

3 While there are many advantages with this technology there are problems like the reliability and nature of the information provided. The unregulated nature of this approach means anyone can contribute. This opens up the prospect of factually incorrect information and deeply objectionable material being included. The flexible and collaborative nature of this practice also means a project can quickly become whatever the creators wish it to be. Thus while it can be a highly creative process, it can also present challenges for those wanting to achieve a specific end purpose.

any time could use to enter for the purpose of adding to and editing (Benker 2013).

It is a decentralised networking technology designed to enable a range of people to have access to information and applications and to interact and swap ideas through a single coherent 'user environment'. Peer-to-peer practices make a project directly available to participants within its networks and other networks without central control of coordination. In this way participants become user-creators and do more than consume and share resources.

It contrasts with more traditional teacher-student or customer-client practices where power tends to be located above or centrally. Open access or peer-to-peer technology can work to ensure the supply and use of material, and intellectual and symbolic capitals are divided and dispersed creating new fields of practice very different to that of education or politics as we have traditionally known them. Such technology can help operationalize projects that actively encourage subsidiarity and bring together a diversity of unique resources and talents to alternate creative deliberative spaces giving participants the power to engage in 'higher forms of cooperation' in ways that go well beyond more traditional modes of participatory projects.

A participatory project using such peer-to-peer technology can expose educational institutions to new imaginary schemes that are generative and can be the source of change. They provide the capacity for young people to engage in redesigning education and other institutions in the light of the transformation taking place. The architecture built into this technology follows democratic principles in the sense that it is open and enables all participants (including young people) access on their own terms, and provides opportunities for creativity and deliberation free from the normal constraints (prejudice, power differences, etc.,) that typically mark the public sphere.

Such a project can work along the same lines as successful peer-to-peer initiatives like the 'Apache server' and 'Free and Open Software' projects that involved non-experts working outside and within formal organisations developing software that was then passed on to others allowing a plurality of recipients to copy, modify and redistribute it to others who then did the same.

I suggest the same design principles used in these highly effective participatory projects can be applied to develop 'sharing platforms' or 'peer-to-peer' software initiatives that enable young people (as students), and others to work creatively and collaboratively for the purpose of developing greater clarity about what is happening in respect to the transformation taking place. It could also enable them to identify the kinds of education and other institutional arrangements that will help encourage the emergence of a just society in which all may thrive.

The same principles embedded in 'free and open software' like the 'Apache server' or Wikipedia, that enable permanently open access, can be used to enable an open access policy-making process with large scale cooperation that is inclusive of a wide range of participants, including students. Setting up such a space can begin in education settings either at the behest of education and policy experts, or young people themselves.[4] In this way it is technically possible to design and develop a participatory project that changes the ways young people engage. This would be done in ways that bypass conventional and largely perfunctory and minimally effective consultative practices.

The technical means are now available to realize political freedom hitherto not enjoyed by most young people and to encourage the inclusion of a diversity of participants to deliberate, engage and create. Moreover, this could be done in an ongoing way directed towards changing our institutions and practices not just through the occasional one time adjustment, but through a continuous practice able to reimagine the character of education and indeed the institutional order of society (Unger 2014). Such a model could be adapted to allow for more fluid and rapid flow of information, talents and projects that run across and amongst many organisations. It is what Blenker refers to as social production within the commons, which can occur through experimentation and under conditions characterized by uncertainty and complexity like those that mark our current context (2013).

Moreover, to help ensure the practical efficacy of such a cooperative project, algorithms designed to channel the 'public opinion' derived from such open and ongoing deliberative processes to inform various political processes could also be embedded into such a program. Interactive creative practice like that proposed here contrasts with the more exclusive traditional 'closed system' methods of decision, knowledge and product making that are too slow and too rigid to serve their environment and invigorate change – and which typically exclude young people as students (Blenker 2013, 293).

Such peer-to-peer platforms have already been successful in facilitating other collaborative projects, in bringing together a diverse range of people and in creating new approaches to innovative practice. They have enabled the emergence of what are now described as 'social production in commons', 'exchange cultures', or sharing societies or economies (Blenker 2013; Sundararajan 2016).[5]

---

4 I note that while this is an idea that lends itself to the prospect of being initiated from below e.g. by students, it is more likely to get immediate traction if it is initiated by the elders.
5 Peer-to-peer technologies have been developed and used by ordinary people to create a range of new transport options like 'Lyft' and 'Uber' which connect passengers to drivers through software designed to locate and connect people wanting a ride with people wanting to provide one. Apps like China's 'Kuaidi' or 'Ola' move millions of people around.

In these ways emerging peer-to-peer or 'social production in commons' technology, which rely on collaboration and sharing, are ideal for creating the kind of innovation now needed in education and in other social institutions. It encourages inclusive large scale collaboration that taps the ideas, talents and energies of young people, many of whom are themselves at the cutting edge – and bearing the brunt of the technological and policy changes now taking place.

5   Conclusion

Developing this project requires more than transferring existing educational and youth participatory practices on to new technology. It requires more than purchasing the latest technologies and furnishing each student with a laptop. It requires recognising that education, like all organisations, faces the challenge of clarifying their end purpose, of creating new methods of operating, and new ways to identify, attract and foster the talent needed for that task (WEF 2016). Importantly, this includes ensuring that a plurality principle informs such a project, and that divergent views are encouraged so that we have generational diversity.

All this matters because young people can and ought to play a role in decision making about matters in which they have a direct interest. Indeed, a principle central to ethical and democratic practice says that for any decision to be legitimate everyone affected by it ought to have a say about its adoption. Thus, if any decision about shaping the present and the future is to be considered legitimate, and if we are to optimize the prospect of 'sourcing' good ideas that are relevant to the lives of young people and that draws on their talents and experiences, then young people need to be included.

Peer-to-peer platforms have also been used to create new swapping, hiring, lending, renting practices providing a raft of communication and exchange opportunities and resources from clothes to tools, (local asset libraries), clothes swaps (e.g., 'stylelend'). Such technology has also bought forth e-farming ('rushce') allowing farmers to post their availability, goods and prices in advance, buyers place their orders and then meet in a physical space (market) for collection (Sundararajan 2016). The emergence of private car sharing 'communities' is a further example (e.g.,'Turo', 'Getaround', 'Drivy', 'Snapp Car', 'Easy Car' and 'Your drive'). Likewise dining platforms (Feasty, VizEat) give people who like cooking, dining and meeting people the ability to connect and share meals. Peer to peer lending or 'finding circles' also allow people to invest in each others' projects. While those needing jobs to be done can be connected to those who can provide the service (e.g. 'Thumbtack', 'Hand', and 'Task Rabbit') (Sundararajan 2016). And of course there are many other highly popular internet enabled exchanges like Airbnb or EBay – and the list goes on.

As the examples cited above indicate, the technical means are now available to seriously renovate various social practices, beginning with education. As Blenker observes, 'For the first time since the industrial revolution, the most important inputs, into some of the most important economic sectors' are the result of distributed social production in the commons (Blenker 2013, 291).

References

Bartlett, J. 2014. *The Dark Net Inside the Digital Underworld*. Random House, NY.
Berlant, L. 2011. *Cruel Optimism*. Duke University, Durham.
Blenker, Y. 2013. 'Distributed Innovation and Creativity, Peer Production, and Commons in Networked Economy'. In, *Change:9 Key essays on how the Internet is changing our Lives*, (ed) F Gonzales. Bilbao, BBVA.
Bourdieu, P. 1990. 'A lecture on the lecture'. In, *Other Words: Essays towards a Reflexive Sociology*, Stanford: Stanford University Press: 177–198.
Bourdieu, P. 1991a. *Language and Symbolic Power*. (ed) J. Thompson Cambridge, Polity.
Bourdieu, P. 1991b. *Language and Symbolic Power*. (ed) J. Thompson Cambridge, Polity.
Bourdieu, P. 1977. *Outline of a Theory of Practice*, (trans) R Nice. Cambridge University Press, Cambridge.
Bourdieu, P. 1999. *The Logic of Practice*. (trans) R Nice. Stanford University Press, California.
Bourdieu, P. & L. Wacquant 1992. An Invitaiton to Reflexive Sociology. Chicago, University of Chicago Press.
Brown, P., H. Lauder, D. Ashton 2011. *The Global Auction: The Broken Promises of Education, Jobs and Incomes*. New York, Oxford University Press.
Fuchs, C. 2015. Culture and Economy in the Age of Social Media, New York: Routledge.
Gardiner, L. 2016a. *Stagnation Generation: the case for renewing the intergenerational contract*. London, The Intergenerational Commission/Resolution Foundation.
Gardiner, L. 2016b. *Stagnation Generation: the case for renewing the intergenerational Contract*. London, The Intergenerational Commission/Resolution Foundation.
International Labour Organization. 2016. *World Employment and Social Outlook – Trends 2016*. Geneva, International Labour Office.
Kurzweil, R. 2005. *The Singularity is Near: When Humans Transcend Biology*. Penguin Books.
Michlethwait, J. & A. Wooldrifge 2015. *The Fourth Revolution: the Global Race to Reinvent the State*. Penguin Random House.
Morozov, E. 2011. *The Net Delusion: The Dark Side of Internet Freedom*. New York, Public Affairs.

Nussbaum, M. 2011. *Creating capabilities: The Human Development Approach*. Cambridge, Belknap Press, Harvard University Press.

OECD. 2014. *Education at a Glance OECD Indicators*, http://www.oecd.org/edu/Education-at-a-Glance-2014.pdf.

Serres, M. 2015. *Times of Crisis: What the Financial Crisis Revealed and How to Reinvent Our Lives and Future*. New York, Bloomsbury.

Sundararajan, A. 2016. *The Sharing economy: The end of Employment and the Rose of Crowd Based Capitalism*. London, MIT Press.

Susskind, R. & D. Susskind 2015. *The future of the Professions: How Technology Will Transform the Work of Human Experts*. Oxford, Oxford University Press.

Turkle, S. 2011. *Alone Together: Why We Expect More From Technology and Less from Each Other*. New York, Basic Books.

Unger, R. 2014. *A Religion of the Future*. Cambridge, Harvard University Press.

World Economic Forum (WEF) 2016. White Paper Digital Transformation of Industries: Digital Enterprise. January 2016. http://reports.weforum.org/digital-transformation/becoming-a-digital-enterprise/

CHAPTER 3

Performing Dispossession: Young People and the Politics of the Guerrilla Self

Perri Campbell and Luke Howie

1   Introduction

> The future ain't what it used to be.
>
> GOULD-WARTOFSKY 2015, 20

In 2011, *Time* magazine declared 'the Protester' its 'Person of the Year' (Stengel 2011, 29). The protester was heralded as someone possessing incredible talents that could capture and highlight, '...a global sense of restless promise...', upend '...governments and conventional wisdom...', and was able to combine '...the oldest techniques with the newest technologies...', in order to do no less than, '...shine a light on human dignity...' and steer '...the planet on a more democratic though sometimes more dangerous path'.

When we spoke to young people in a West Coast, US college town in 2014 and 2015, we were told that they fight for equality, justice and democracy, and do so 'with love and rage' (Howie & Campbell 2017). They understood that their protests could not be born only of anger. They also believed that things could improve. Despite their struggles they were full of hope that they could change the world.

In 2016, riding a wave of right-wing populism, dubious news, and aggressive social media supporters, Donald Trump became President-elect of the United States. This happened despite most political scientists, pollsters and journalists declaring it unlikely, if not impossible. Yet it was Trump supporters that captured a sense of restless promise, upended the political establishment, and displaced conventional wisdom by deploying the newest techniques with the oldest techniques, possibly steering the planet towards a more dangerous path.

In our recent works, we have developed a figure that we call the *guerrilla self* (Howie & Campbell 2016, 2017). It is our way of making sense of the accounts of young people we interviewed who were significantly impacted by the Global Financial Crisis (GFC), but had not lost hope. Indeed, they had found a deep reservoir to draw from, and did not fail when the odds were heavily stacked against them. They exhibited an incredible amount of what psychologists and social scientists would call *resilience*. We do not use the word *figure* lightly in describing the guerrilla self. For Haraway (2008, 4) figures are 'material-semiotic nodes or knots' and 'performative images' that we 'inhabit and are inhabited by'. As such, figures are 'condensed maps of contestable worlds' that 'map universes of knowledge, practice and power'. As a figure, the guerrilla self becomes a marker for the convergence of complex social, cultural and political forces: economic disaster; powerful social movements that have arisen as a consequence; austerity measures rolled out by neoliberal governments across Western democracies; an explosion of citizen and alternative media, much of it found on social media accounts; a return of far-right values and beliefs, for which a major grievance has been the rise of ISIS and its homegrown agents found in the world's cities; and precarity, marginalisation and inequality combined with a widespread distrust of politicians, corporate leaders and the mainstream media.

In this paper these global events form the backdrop for our understanding of the experiences of young people in these times of dangerous dreaming – times of protest, uprising and deep questioning of the current social and economic conditions and futures on offer (Žižek 2012). This dreaming has given way to 'an emerging attitude and desire to thrive in the "interstices" of neoliberalism – sometimes for personal financial well-being, sometimes for social advantage, often for both' (Howie & Campbell 2016, 907). Young people, in the year of the protester and after, have certainly shown themselves capable of imagining the future in other terms. Indeed, we argue in these pages that young people can do quite a bit more than that. We argue that adopting entrepreneurial and guerrilla positions of selfhood are changing the nature of youthful futures. In the aftermath of the GFC, Occupy, Black Lives Matter, and the rise of ISIS and Trump, many young people are developing a sense of social connectedness by drawing on an ethos of survival and responsibilisation for their well-being and socio-economic future. We have dubbed this *the politics of the guerrilla self*. It is a politics that attempts to capture the hope inspired by these movements and how this hope was, and is, lived by young people as they plan their futures in relation to neoliberal ways of being or technologies of the self. By living an entrepreneurial, guerrilla self – everyday, one moment at a time – young people carve out and/or imagine alternative futures. We give this claim substance by analysing a body of literature that has become influential for understanding young people in neoliberal times and interviews we conducted with two young men in 2014 and 2015 in a West Coast college-town in the US.

2   From Guerrilla Selfhood to Dispossession

We first used the term 'guerrilla self' to explain the stories we were told in interviews conducted in 2014 and 2015 with young people in a college town on the US West Coast[1] (see Howie & Campbell 2016, 2017). We asked these young people to describe the challenges they had faced in attaining their education, and their aspirations for the future in a post-GFC world. Many of our respondents had been high school seniors during the GFC. Our respondents had faced extraordinary social and financial dilemmas in transitioning from secondary schooling to college in this time, but had thrived by turning supposed disadvantages into relative advantages. We drew an analogy from counter-terrorism studies and the figure of the widely misunderstood *guerrilla* freedom fighter. The intelligent wager of a guerrilla war does not wish to remove or replace the system they resist. They wish to turn the weapons of that system to their advantage, find weakness in the incredible power of the oppressor, and turn that weakness into personal advantage (Howie & Campbell 2016).

We intend on expanding this allegory here to show that the cultivation of a guerrilla self not only allows young people to *do* certain things or *achieve* certain outcomes, it also changes their relationships to society, people and their place in the world in the process. Our participants cultivated a way of being that we imagined as both drawing on and shaping a *politics of guerrilla selfhood*. This politics seeks to reap what young people sow, and is the process through which being part of a social justice or protest movement is far from the end of the story. These young people did not wish to return to their lives as they were before they became *involved*. They want their lives, their own sense of self and their relationship with their community, to be different in the aftermath, to be connected and transformative.

The challenges they faced are well accounted for in the youth studies literature. Rapid economic and social change has dramatically altered many of the customary markers of adulthood, such as transitioning from education to employment, building a family, and owning a home (Wyn & Woodman 2006). A number of youth studies scholars also argue that transitions are now more fragmented and precarious. Young people are working in temporary jobs, living in debt, and unable to imagine a desired future with the choices available (Walsh 2016; Standing 2014). These conditions mean that in many instances young people are *denied full participation or meaningful engagement* in

---

[1] This research was funded in part by Deakin University through an Alfred Deakin Postdoctoral Fellowship undertaken by Campbell between 2014 and 2016.

'settings that traditionally identified someone as an adult, as a citizen' (Kelly 2017, 60 and Bessant & Montero 2015).

In replacing these meaningful engagements young people have been encouraged to act and behave in particular ways, to achieve success through entrepreneurialism, to see challenges as opportunities, and to demonstrate their *resilience*. Drawing on the work of Foucault (2008), Kelly (2006, 17) argues that particular forms of subjectivity have emerged within neoliberal societies, which he calls the 'entrepreneurial self' and 'self as enterprise'. Young people are expected to become 'rational, autonomous, choice making, risk aware, prudential, responsible and enterprising' (Kelly 2017, 57 and Kelly & Harrison 2009). These forms of selfhood are evidence of an innovative, creative attitude to crafting a self and a life amidst social conditions which encourage rampant individualism through the realisation of the self-as-a-business. Such entrepreneurial forms of selfhood are crucial for supporting the constant reinvention of the self in response to a fast-paced, so-called 'liquid life' – 'a precarious life, lived under conditions of constant uncertainty' (Bauman 2005, 2). Kelly's entrepreneurial self enables an exploration of how the self is *responsibilised* through neoliberal modes of transition from *childhood* to apparent adulthood, how the unpredictable life course is managed, and who is, and is not, responsible for individual failures and successes. The entrepreneurial self and the self imagined as an enterprise, provide the building blocks for our figure of the guerrilla self. We view the guerrilla self as something of an *Entrepreneurial Self 2.0*. The guerrilla politics we wish to develop here cling to the bodies, experiences and stories of those who live them. Guerrilla selfhood is inherently suspicious and critical of current social and economic conditions but,

> ...manifests as an attempt not to replace the existing system, but to gain unexpected benefits within it, all the while playing by the 'rules', or an interpretation of them ... The key ingredient is something that perhaps all young people can possess – imagination. Or so the neoliberal logic goes.
> emphasis in original. HOWIE & CAMPBELL 2016, 918.

We argue here that in living a politics of guerrilla selfhood, we need a further ingredient that goes beyond entrepreneurialism and embracing the potential of 'the precariat' (Standing 2014, 1). We need to, as Butler and Athanasiou (2013, x–xi) urge, be *dispossessed* of our individualism, *dispossessed* of our neoliberal tendencies, and *dispossessed* of the belief that we are surrounded by enemies, competitors and rivals.

Butler and Athanasiou (2013, 1) use the word 'dispossession' to describe the conditions faced by young people after the GFC, particularly those involved in protest movements such as the Arab Spring, Occupy and Black Lives Matter. An understated but key grievance of these movements, they argue, is the lack of community brought about by consecutive decades of neoliberal economics, and the associated un- and underemployment and reduced opportunities for work and family-building (such as gaining a mortgage to buy a home, affording children amid economic insecurities) which have, in turn, had significant consequences for happiness, health and well-being, and the ability to hope for a liveable future. People crave 'passionate attachments', they argue, in order to become subjects of a particular social order (Butler & Athanasiou 2013, 1). Instead, young people in the liberal democracies of the West have been effectively 'dispossessed' of their social intuitions and severed from possibilities for social and cultural belonging (Butler & Athanasiou 2013, 7–8). These are intuitions that seek to share risk, form social bonds, negotiate for collective rights and benefits, and organise their life-worlds around the forms of culture and society that ensure amicable, and democratic, social bonds and relations. But young people have instead faced casualised work and under-employment; the degeneration of working conditions, medical benefits, mental health and well-being; the unsuitability or unavailability of social and relationship opportunities; and the incurring of debt for education and consumption (Brown 2015).

But some young people have dared to imagine their future in other terms, probably because the future they saw for themselves was *unimaginable*. These young people have taken up the

> ...question of how to become dispossessed of the sovereign self and enter into forms of collectivity that oppose forms of dispossession that systematically jettison populations from modes of collective belonging and justice.
> BUTLER & ATHANASIOU 2013, xi

In doing so, they practice a form of responsiveness that seeks to recognise injustice and resist the everyday, almost unacknowledged, realities of 'forced migration, unemployment, homelessness, occupation, and conquest'. Stated differently, *learning to resist how one is dispossessed from ones' rightful future is also to resist other forms of injustice*. By engaging in activism and 'public demonstrations', young people intervene in 'induced conditions of precarity', of their own disposability (Butler & Athanasiou 2013, 102).

In true Butlerian style, this inevitably becomes a question of how the everyday *performance* of precarity[2] is carried out by the fleshy, vulnerable human body. In fields shaped by neoliberalism this becomes a project involving the 'responsibilisation' of everyday life through the 'social therapeutics' of personal decision making (Butler & Athanasiou 2013, 102–103). While *responsibilisation* is at the core of the neoliberal project, Butler and Athanasiou argue that it can be differentiated from *responsibility* as a 'responsive disposition that can make possible a politics of social transformation, in ways that cannot be reduced to a mere calculus of interests', for instance, neoliberal moralities. Here, the ethical formation of the self – what Foucault described as a 'care or ethic of the self' (Foucault 1990) – is envisioned as a way of 'rethinking and remaking sociality itself' (Butler & Athanasiou 2013, 103). Butler and Athanasiou (2013, 214) encourage us to view the body of the person who chooses to resist – a person who may dare to imagine their future in other terms – as a 'vector for change'. We might, in this way, view seeking dispossession *as a performance of selfhood*. The question for us, and other youth studies scholars, is how young people imagine themselves as 'vectors for change' given these conditions.

In the section that follows we share stories that were told by two young people – Harris and Clifton – in a college town on the US West Coast. While the guerrilla self collects up broad and complex issues, we have chosen to share these two short stories because they are illustrative of particular issues and ethical dilemmas shared by other participants we interviewed. Building on our accounts of these and other stories in our earlier work (Howie & Campbell 2016 and 2017), we argue that these young people work responsively in relation to neoliberal conditions to forge a future with hope. They have few designs on replacing the political or social order. Rather, they want to reshape it and stamp their experiences on it. This is their ethos, their politics of everyday life and how they practice and perform their 'dispossession' with entrepreneurial flair.

3 Performing a Politics of Guerrilla Selfhood

> Harris and I sit in a park where many homeless people have taken up residence just near the campus and talk about the challenges Black students face. As a white woman, I was told to avoid this park area, but Harris says he wasn't given that warning – 'maybe because of who I am',

---

2 'Precarity is differently distributed as a condition of social ontology' (Butler & Athanasiou 2013, 102).

he laughs. Harris is a Black man, highly educated and the recipient of a scholarship, which allows him to study at this elite university. This is who he is. Who I am is the recipient of a warning to avoid the area. This hints at the complex narratives and embodied politics that shape our encounter, and the encounters of people throughout the US. They are narratives that Harris is acutely aware of. Black and white histories, histories of slavery and oppression, and contemporary stories of police brutality against Black people form the backdrop for this research encounter.

Harris is a young Black man undertaking Graduate studies at an elite US college. He shares his history of marginalisation, his pathway out of his disadvantage and his involvement in several chapters of the Black Lives Matter movement across California. Black Lives Matter has been wrongly described by some as a terrorist organisation (Flores 2016), but Harris has no desire for a violent uprising. Indeed, he wants to work within systems of inequality to show marginalised young people how to make these systems work for them. One of his main tasks is to 'push thinking': 'how are we re-centring all Black lives here, are we keeping the Black poor in the conversation, are they represented in this circle, because most of us are college educated. And even though I came from poverty doesn't mean I'm still there' (Harris, California, interviewed 23 March 2015). His activism extended well beyond particular protests, events or rallies. He wanted to live the change he desired.

Harris was an active member of the social justice community in California. He ran a social justice institute that was employed by a high school in the South-Central district of Los Angeles to teach social justice principles to mostly Black and Hispanic teenagers. It was also the area where he had grown up, where he shared personal and community connections. His classes were 'all about light mobilising youth of colour, specifically Black and Latino males, on how to do research for change'. Harris organised several 'youth participatory action research' projects and it was not long before students were engaging in 'advocacy on behalf of those projects'. Soon the program encountered several problems as these marginalised young people found their voice and began to understand that they could imagine their futures in other terms, that they could hope for something different. Harris says:

> The problem was that the students became too vocal, when they started doing things for themselves and advocating for themselves, they weren't docile anymore. When the school wanted to fire the principal, the students walked out and occupied [the school] for 3 days straight until they promised that they weren't going to fire anyone.
>
> HARRIS, California, interviewed 23 March 2015

With pride Harris recounts how *his students* led that activism. He had seen how 'social transformation' was possible first hand. But since the entrepreneurial activism he had inspired was not the kind that was 'going to benefit the State' his program was cut from the school's curriculum: 'They kicked us out and they knew why – because these young people were becoming political and engaging in things they had never engaged in'.

Harris knew that he would never make much money working in social justice, but that wasn't his goal. He has become committed to the types of 'identity work' he achieved in that school. It was work that,

> ...meant so much more to me because I was doing it in my own neighbourhood, not only with people who looked like me, but had similar experiences to me.

He had witnessed lives change, for instance he had begun to see ways that cycles of violence might be disrupted. Harris saw that it was possible for people to find supportive and active communities amidst the individualised competition and economic order of major US cities. Harris' politics extended well beyond a desire for personal gain or achievement. He felt certain that such a path would deliver little satisfaction, at least not by itself. His concern became how to build this work into his life in a sustainable way, in a way that would enable him to develop his own skills and shape a different future, not only for himself but for the young people he had worked with. 'We can get to an answer together, but first we need to know what questions to ask. And that's my role' (Harris, California, interviewed 23 March 2015).

> Clifton enters the office where I have been conducting interviews. It is a social justice research institute at an elite West Coast college in the US. He looks strong, rugged ... clearly a tough guy. He has an elaborate tattoo on his neck that he wears to represent his hometown – a large, artistic

> It marks him as a resident of Detroit. He smirks when I tell him our interview will be about the Global Financial Crisis or, as Clifton considers it, 'business as usual' in Detroit.

Clifton was born and raised in Detroit, Michigan. He 'grew up poor' in a city so devastated by economic inequality and failure that it barely felt any different during and after the GFC (Clifton, Detroit, interviewed 27 February 2014). But he was proud of his city. It was 'for a lot of people ... the model for self-determination among the Black community in America'. Despite its problems, he saw Detroit as a city that belonged to Black Americans: 'We set the terms as far as the culture. This is our community'. In a tale we heard regularly in our interviews in the US, Clifton was able to attend college as a result of his mother's position in the military affording a transferable college scholarship for an immediate family member. Clifton did not intend to waste his opportunity, especially since he had left behind siblings who would not be as lucky (Howie & Campbell 2016).

To Clifton's dismay, he has watched his city disintegrate before his eyes. He explained that since his birth in 1990 Detroit had undergone rapid social and economic change, mostly as a result of a collapse of the automotive industry:

> In 1990 Detroit had over, I think it was like 1.5 million people, or something like that. It was one of the largest cities in America. Now we're at about 750000. 23 years later. From 2000–2010 we lost 25% of our population ... Detroit is a really hard place to live in ... It's really hard to find a job. The crime rate is skyrocketing. It is getting really insecure.

Like Harris, Clifton believed that his future would involve the town that made him the person he is. His story is interwoven with the future of his community. Clifton had told a friend that he hoped he could play a role in politics during his career. Should he pursue political office in the elite city where he had moved? Certainly not. He believed he would 'have a much bigger shot of making it politically in Detroit. *You could sell your story a lot better there* ... Maybe' (our emphasis. Clifton, Detroit, interviewed 27 February 2014). He was motivated to this end by his family. One of his brothers was in the military, and 'He's getting to see the world too but not in the same way [nervous laugh]'. At the time we interviewed Clifton, his brother was about to be deployed to Afghanistan. Another one of his brothers had never left Detroit: 'he is just working, struggling, trying to pay the rent, these little manual labour jobs'.

Clifton's politics involves using his education and experiences to intervene in 'precarious' futures in and stories of hopelessness in Detroit where,

> ...anything can be taken away just like that *clicks* because of the financial situation. The city filing for bankruptcy. A lot of workers, their pensions are literally getting cut that they were promised.

Injustices like that, Clifton believed, cannot and should not be tolerated.

4   Conclusions: 'Thank you for nothing'

We want to conclude with a segue into the story of the two-member, pop-music group called MKTO (made up of members Malcolm Kelley and Tony Oller, the band's name an amalgamation of their initials) and, in doing so, draw together the themes explored in this chapter – resistance, defiance and hope. Kelley and Oller got their start on the Nickelodeon teenage-themed television show called *Gigantic* (Scott et al. 2010–2011). *Gigantic* told the tales of the teenage children of Hollywood celebrities – their trials and tribulations, their struggles and efforts to rise above the dilemmas of a life lived in the limelight. The twist of guerrilla selfhood and its political practice arises in everyday situations which are rarely well-hidden. These are some of the lyrics of MKTO's highly subversive song titled 'Thank you'. It is sung to a high-spirited and wholesome tune, drawing comparisons to the boy-bands of the 1990s:

> Yo, this one right here is for all the drop out-of-schoolers.
> The future cougars, the Mary Jane abusers.
> The ones that chose to be losers, for all the Misfit Kids and total outcasts...
> This one's for you role models...
> [to baby boomers] Thank you for feeding us years of lies.
> Thank you for the wars you left us to fight.
> Thank you for the world you ruined overnight.
> But we'll be fine, yeah we'll be fine.
> Thank you for the world you broke, like yolk and it ain't no joke.
> So cold and there ain't no coat, just me, my friends, my folks and we better do what we like.
> So raise that bird up high and when they ask you why.
> Just stand there, laugh and smile...
> We are the ones, the ones you left behind (Google Play Music, n.d.)

There are several tribute videos featuring this song on YouTube, created seemingly in earnest by young people thanking their parents for raising and loving them. Perhaps some do so with a strong sense of irony, especially in the context of widespread criticism of the supposed laziness of Gen Y (Hobart & Sendek 2014). But these lyrics contain a form of resistance, defiance and resilience. If young people are to be criticised for being unemployed, disadvantaged or without hope *then own it! Raise that bird up high!* Just stand there ... laugh and smile. There is an ethos at the heart of this defiance, and defiance isn't possible without *hope*. The defence of the self and of one's dignity amidst unjust social and economic conditions shapes MKTO's particular brand of hopelessness. As Braidotti (2006, 277) argues:

> Hope constructs the *future* in that it opens the spaces onto which to project active desires; it gives us the force to emancipate ourselves from everyday routines and structures that help us dream ahead. Hope carves out active trajectories of becoming and thus can respond to anxieties and uncertainties in a productive manner (our emphasis).

As devastating as the GFC was for many, it has produced the seeds of hope and change. However, this will not always occur in a way of our choosing, as the election of Trump has demonstrated for many in the US. But it would be disingenuous to suggest that Trump's election has not produced tremendous hope for many.

The economic disasters of the 21st century seem to have washed over many of us – we watched, we witnessed, some struggled a little, some struggled a lot. But more than anything we continued living our lives albeit with a new understanding of the impermanence and uncertainty inherent in our economies. The threat of economic uncertainty is everyday and mundane, and references to it can often pass unnoticed. It almost seems a matter of common sense that young people will struggle to find their futures with limited opportunities for work, relationships and well-being. Yet as Harris, Clifton and the young men in MKTO demonstrate, hope in its many different forms, is far from lost.

The ambivalence of hope is mobilised and bought to life through major events, disasters and crises. The young people we encountered in a West Coast college town pose questions about hope – about what hope is, who it belongs to, how it is framed and constructed as options and choices available to a select few. This is their way of questioning the kinds of futures that are on offer, the world they will live in, how aspirations are influenced and structured, and how they are able to imagine their lives. Through self-shaping practices which draw on entrepreneurialism, collectivity, responsiveness, and the disruptive potential of dispossession, young people are contesting imagined futures of isolation and competitive individualism in the pursuit of shared risks and benefits. This embodiment of the tension between *responsibilisation* and *responsiveness* is an ongoing project of the self that grasps at a life beyond neoliberalism. The young people we spoke to are doing some dangerous dreaming and perhaps they will soon be able to, in a sense, imagine and *demand the impossible* (Žižek 2013, 144).

References

Bauman, Z. 2005. *Liquid Life*. Cambridge, Polity Press.

Bessant, J. and K. Montero 2015. 'Situational Justice and New Political Subjectivities', paper presented at the Young People and the Politics of Outrage and Hope Conference, Deakin University City Centre, Melbourne, December 7–8, 2015.

Braidotti, R. 2006 *Transpositions: On Nomadic Ethics*. Cambridge, Polity.

Brown, W. 2015. *Undoing the Demos: Neoliberalism's Stealth Revolution*. Brooklyn, Zone Books.

Butler, J. and A. Athanasiou 2013. *Dispossession: the Performative in the Political*. Cambridge, Polity Press.

Flores, R. 2016. *White House responds to petition to label Black Lives Matter a 'terror' group*. CBS News, 17 July, available at http://www.cbsnews.com/amp/news/whitehouse-responds-to-petition-to-label-black-lives-matter-a-terror-group/, retrieved on 15 December 2016.

Foucault, M. 1990. *The Care of the Self: History of Sexuality: 3*. London, Penguin Books.

Foucault, M. 2008. The Birth of Biopolitics; Lectures at the Collège de France, 1978–79, translated by Graham Burchell. New York: Palgrave Macmillan.

Google Play Music. No Date. '*Thank you. MKTO*', available at https://play.google.com/music/preview/Tanrq7dzfn7qwiuuxgh5pwc2b24?lyrics=1&utm_source=google&utm_medium=search&utm_campaign=lyrics&pcampaignid=kp-lyrics, retrieved on 12 January 2017.

Gould-Wartofsky, M.A. 2015. *The Occupiers: the Making of the 99 Percent Movement*, New York, Oxford University Press.

Haraway, D.J. 2008. *When Species Meet*. Minneapolis, University of Minnesota Press.

Hobart, B. and H. Sendek 2014. *Gen Y Now: Millennials and the Evolution of Leadership*, 2nd Edition. San Francisco, Wiley.

Howie, L. and P. Campbell 2016. 'Guerrilla selfhood: Imagining young people's entrepreneurial futures'. In, *Journal of Youth Studies* 19(7): 906–920.

Howie, L. and P. Campbell 2017. *Crisis & Terror in the Age of Anxiety: 9/11, the Global Financial Crisis and ISIS*. London, Palgrave Macmillan.

Kelly, P. 2006. 'The entrepreneurial self and "youth at-risk": Exploring the horizons of identity in the twenty-first century'. In, *Journal of Youth Studies* 9(1): 17–32.

Kelly, P. 2017. 'Growing up after the GFC: Responsibilisation and Mortgaged Futures'. In, *Discourse: Studies in the Cultural Politics of Education* 38(1): 57–69.

Kelly, P. and L. Harrison 2009. *Working in Jamie's Kitchen: Salvation, Passion and Young Workers*. Hampshire, Palgrave Macmillan.

Scott, J., A. Robinson, R. Rosenthal, F. Savage, J. Babbit, M. Grossman, B. Kellman and S. Smolan 2010–2011. *'Gigantic* (2010–2011): Full Cast & Crew', *IMDb*, available at http://www.imdb.com/title/tt1501515/fullcredits?ref_=tt_ov_st_sm, retrieved on 20 September 2016.

Standing, G. 2014. *The Precariat: The New Dangerous Class*. London, Bloomsbury.

Stengel, R. 2011. '2011 person of the year: the protester'. In, *Time Magazine*, vol. 178, no. 25: 29.

Walsh, L. 2016. *Educating Generation Next: Young People, Teachers and Schooling in Transition*. Hampshire, Palgrave Macmillan.

Wyn, J., & D. Woodman (2006) 'Generation, Youth and Social Change in Australia', *Journal of Youth Studies*, 9 (5): 495–514.

Žižek, S.. 2012. *The Year of Dreaming Dangerously*. London, Verso.

Žižek, S. 2013. *Demanding the Impossible*. Cambridge, Polity Press.

CHAPTER 4

New Politics: The Anonymous Politics of 4chan, Outrage and the New Public Sphere

Rob Watts

1   Introduction

In September 2015 users of the Internet site 4chan started a campaign against Islamic State. This began when one 4chan user changed the battle cry of ISIS soldiers from 'Allahu Akbar' to 'Allahu Quackbar'. Another user then suggested, 'How about replacing the faces on ALL the propaganda photos with bath ducks?' Following the Paris attacks of 13 November 2015, Anonymous used 4chan to mount a digital attack on thousands of ISIS Twitter accounts labeling them '#daeshbags'. This online campaign was typical of both 4chan and Anonymous trademark qualities like humour, vulgarity, offensive trolling, and distributed denial of service activity.

4chan itself was the bright idea of a 15 year-old New Yorker initially identified only as 'moot' who claimed he had only set it up in 2003 to download porn without his parents' permission. By 2008 when he was outed as Christopher Poole, 4chan was famous and notorious for its Manga-style porn and for its politics. In 2016 4chan claimed 22 million unique users per month. 'Anonymous' is the name adopted by a decentralized network of mostly young people who have developed some important forms of political communication and intervention promoting Internet freedom and freedom of speech (Coleman 2014, 54). Since 2007–8 'Anonymous' has staged some of the most spectacular collective interventions in the history of the Internet, targeting governments, corporations and high profile individuals. Anonymous relies on several of Poole's design features. One is the idea that all users are to be anonymous. The other is that anything posted on 4chan does not last long before it is removed: as Poole put it 'This site has no memory' (Herwig, 2010). Poole defends both design features on the grounds that they promote increased rationality and freedom of expression (Sutter 2010).

This minimal description of 4chan, Anonymous and the reliance on anonymity and planned amnesia raise a number of important intellectual and practical problems. One central problem it raises is what is the political and how should we think about the political today?

In the late 1980s Zygmunt Bauman (1989, 471) took his fellow sociologists to task for their failure to pay attention to the attempt by the Nazi state to murder Europe's Jews after 1939. Having documented the paucity of attempts by sociologists to engage with the 'Final Solution', Bauman then posed a provocative question, which he said was not 'what we sociologists can say about the Holocaust' but rather, 'what does the Holocaust ... [say] about us the sociologists and our practice?' (Bauman 1989, 473). In a similar spirit of provocation we need to ask what does 4chan and Anonymous say about modern political science? The need to address this question is raised by one extremely puzzling feature of contemporary political science. A survey of a sample of eleven major American, British and Australian political science journals (2010–2015) tells us that so far these journals have yet to publish one research paper addressing either 4chan, Anonymous or, related instances of digital activism.[1] What this suggests is that political science as the study of the political, sometimes, perhaps often has trouble acknowledging the political. Other social sciences like sociology, media studies or anthropology have had no such trouble (See for instance: Coleman 2011; Fuchs 2013; and Goode 2015).

That these are important problems is suggested in the first instance by the way mainstream political science has managed so far to avoid engaging 4chan and the politics of Anonymous. Rather than asking what does political science have to say about 4chan and Anonymous (to which the answer so far is nothing), we need to ask what does 4chan and Anonymous have to say about political science? This question is directly relevant to the way conventional political science frames problems. I address three of those questions here, namely the idea that democracy is in crisis, that young people are politically disengaged, and that the Internet promises to renew democracy by reinvigorating what Habermas (1989) called the 'public sphere'. I clarify a number of conceptual issues raised by asking how well does Habermas's account of the 'public sphere' and 'communicative action' make sense of something like 4chan? What should we think about the all-too-obvious discrepancies? I argue that framing 4chan and Anonymous as political requires a reframing of what 'the political' is and how young people engage in politics.

---

[1] I surveyed the journals below between January 2010 and the end of 2015: the *Journal of Political Science, Political Studies, Political Studies Review*, the *British Journal of Politics* and *International Relations, Political Science Quarterly, American Journal of Political Science*, the *American Political Science Review*, the *Australian Journal of Political Science, British Journal of Political Science, Journal of Politics*, and *Comparative Political Studies*. I acknowledge the work of political scientists like Vromen who in Marsh and Vromen (2012) has briefly addressed Anonymous.

2 On the Political

Conventional political scientists are having trouble dealing with political phenomena like 4chan and Anonymous because these kinds of phenomena do not conform with various constructive schemes that constitute contemporary 'political science'. As Danziger stresses, 'constructive schemes' 'are not just cognitive frameworks for the *interpretation* of empirical data, but involve practical rules for the *production* of such data' (Danziger 1990, 4). 'Constructive schemes' refers to the way people working in disciplines like political science, criminology, sociology, psychology, or economics establish over time certain basic discipline-defining narratives and 'theoretical' frames. When we examine the history of a discipline like political science we will discover that far from being a simple 'reflection' of reality, we see rather as Sandywell (1996) has shown, a constructive process that has its own history dependent on narrative schemes and constitutive metaphors that cohere into 'constructive schemes'. Constructive schemes rely on interpretations both of the stuff of the world the discipline inquires into, as well as the rules required to produce the data and to make sense of it.

If there is no single constructive scheme in modern political science, there are certainly a number of leading traditions and approaches. Each makes assumptions both about the nature of what is properly political and how 'proper' politics works. Leftwich (2004) for example, highlights the dominance of an 'institutionalist' approach which suggests 'politics' is only found in societies possessing certain institutions like governments, parties and parliaments and focuses on formal political actors, institutions or governments (Leftwich 2004).

Running alongside the institutionalist tradition has been a 'behaviourist' tradition often privileging quantitative methods and committed to scientism. Enthusiasm for this positivist 'science of politics' began in the 1940s and 1950s with the emergence, especially in the USA, of a form of political analysis that drew heavily on behaviourism. Influential figures like Easton (1965) argued that political science could or should adopt the methods of the natural sciences. This saw a proliferation of studies of issues such as voting behaviour, the behaviour of legislators, and the behaviour of municipal politicians and lobbyists, all deploying the use of quantitative research methods.

In the 1980s a 'new institutionalism' emerged. While remaining faithful to the core institutionalist premise that 'institutions matter' because political structures shape political behavior, 'new institutionalism' revised an understanding of what constitutes an 'institution' in a number of respects. Political institutions were no longer equated with political organizations *per se* and were instead treated as 'rules' either formal or informal, which guided or constrained the behaviour of individual actors.

Other traditions in political science have favoured technically, even mathematically expressed, complex forms of 'normative' argument like 'rational-choice theory' or 'public-choice theory' that draws heavily on neo-classical economic theory (Becker 1976). This body of work builds models based on procedural rules, usually premised on the notion that political actors are rationally self-interested (Amadae 2003) and is applied to the actions of voters, lobbyists, bureaucrats and politicians, and even to the international relations of states (Dunleavy 1991).

Another body of work has integrated elements of normative and political theory with elements of communications theory to produce a theory of 'deliberative democracy'. The 'deliberative turn' involves writers like Habermas (1996) Bohmann (1996) and Benhabib (1996) who argued that a healthy democracy involves citizens deliberating about those matters that affect them. This body of work stresses an austere capacity for political deliberation set against some sophisticated, often highly technical criteria for public reasoning.

An implicit understanding of what is properly political operates in each of these 'traditions'. For any action to be 'political', political science assumes there needs to be a regularised, socially-accepted, and repetitive institutionalised framework for instance, in which political activity takes place. In that space, for language to be political it needs to be rationally articulated and to inform actions taken within legitimate institutions. Legitimacy is afforded by the state.

The focus on repetitive routinised practice and the emphasis on rationality are telling. They point to the way a discipline like political science legitimates only particular forms of activity as 'political' by relying on tacit premises like the idea that 'rationality' is co-terminous with conventional forms of strategic political action (Akram 2014: 382). This is why conventional political science has had and will have trouble acknowledging, let alone engaging with, practices and interventions that do no conform to these expectations.

This is also why even those who claim to work from a 'left' or 'critical' perspective continue to assume that 'real politics' has nothing to do with what Srnicek and Williams contemptuously dismiss as 'folk politics' of the kind represented 'by Occupy, Spain's 15M, student occupations, ...Tiqqun and the Invisible Committee ... the Zapatistas and contemporary anarchist-tinged politics' (Srnicek and Williams 2015, 11). This is also why the practices of 4chan or the hacktivism of Anonymous works to strengthen the refusal by conventional political science to engage with these interventions: political science expects political speech and action to be evidence of the 'non-emotional' or 'rational'.

If we turn to recent research and commentary about the 'crisis of democracy' and 'youth participation' we see how the constructive schemes that define political science have shaped the research while leaving undisturbed certain basic assumptions about the political.

3 A Crisis of Democracy and Youth Participation?

For the past few decades, political scientists in countries like Britain, the USA and Australia have been collecting evidence of political disengagement especially on the part of the young. This research can point to abundant evidence of a dramatic decline in voting, formal political party membership, low levels of respect for or trust in the political representatives and 'politics', and declining membership in important NGOs like trade unions (Skocpol 2003; Furedi 2005; Hilton et al. 2010). A large body of research indicates that young people are disengaging from political life and civic participation (Kimberlee 2002; Henn et al. 2007; Manning 2009; Furlong and Cartmel 2012). It represents young people as the most apolitical generation ever and a serious threat to the future of liberal democracy (Bauerlein, 2009).

There is of course an alternative view, which says that some young people are engaged in new forms of political activity especially in on-line spaces (Vromen and Collin 2010; Vromen and Xenos 2010; Martin 2012; Xenos et al. 2014). What this sharp binary points to, is a problem with the way in which the political is conceptualised. As writers like Bessant (2003, 2004), Manning (2009), Harris et al. (2010), Farthing (2010) and Gordon and Taft (2011) have pointed out the contradictory stories about young people and politics indicate important underlying differences about how we conceptualise the political. Without understanding how young people define 'politics', it is difficult to demonstrate that young people are actually 'disengaged'. This is why McCaffrie and Marsh (2013, 116) say 'a pervasive problem with the mainstream participation literature [is that] a restrictive conception of politics forces a restrictive understanding of participation'. We need to understand how young people understand 'politics' and which of their activities they see as 'political'. This suggests that an overly restrictive concept of the political tends to produce restrictive understandings of politics and political activity.

Let me turn now to the way discussion about the Net and new politics has so far worked out. Though there are a number of ways the discussion that needs to be had could be framed, I use Habermas's very influential account of 'deliberative democracy' as a starting point. Again the point is to emphasise the silent (and silencing) effects of some long-standing assumptions about the political, and how these shape the sense people make of the new digital world.

4 The Net: New Politics, New Public Sphere?

A good deal of the discussion about 'new politics' has relied heavily on Jurgen Habermas's (1989, 1991) much admired, if often criticised account of the 'public sphere', and the idea that the Net now provides young people with a new platform for a new politics. Habermas's influential account tells how a bourgeois 'public sphere' devoted to rational discourse, debate and democracy emerged in late seventeenth and eighteenth century European salons, coffee houses and newspapers. He tells too of the collapse of that space as modern media conglomerates dedicated to shaping, constructing, and limiting public discourse destroyed the public sphere. For Habermas, the struggle to reclaim the 'public sphere' was about an attempt to make 'publicity' a source of reasoned consensus formation instead of a site for manipulating popular opinion. Even his many critics like Nancy Fraser (1990) have said that 'something like Habermas's idea of the public sphere is indispensable to critical social theory and to democratic political practice'.

Habermas's work has provided an 'obvious' interpretative framework for commentators eager to make sense of digital technologies and to argue that the Net has regenerated the 'public sphere' and reinvigorated democratic politics. Dahlberg (2001, 1) claims that:

> ...a cursory examination of the thousands of diverse conversations now taking place everyday online and open to anyone with internet access, seems to indicate the expansion on a global scale of the loose webs of rational-critical discourse that constitute what is known as the public sphere.

In effect the Net is a network of 'virtual coffeehouses' enabling a radically egalitarian process of rational will-formation and democratic participation. Westling (2007, 12) argues that sites like Facebook 'have the potential to actually exceed Habermas's expectations of a public sphere and become a major hub for political action among community members'. Castells claims that:

> ...to harness the power of the world's public opinion through global media and Internet networks is the most effective form of broadening political participation on a global scale.
> CASTELLS 2008, 90

Karatzogianni et al. (2016) talk up the transformative effect of digital politics. Yet there are some problems with this and they signal the highly restrictive conception of the political and political rationality, which Habermas takes for granted. These are implied when Habermas says the Internet has not had many positive benefits which emphasises the fragmenting effects of the Net:

> ...computer-mediated communication in the web can claim unequivocal democratic merits only for a special context: It can undermine the censorship of authoritarian regimes that try to control and repress public opinion. In the context of liberal regimes, the rise of millions of fragmented chat rooms across the world tend instead to lead to the fragmentation of large but politically focused mass audiences into a huge number of isolated issue publics.
> HABERMAS 2006, 423

Habermas belongs to a recognisably 'liberal' tradition and one that relies on normative ideas about what is properly political. Western liberals from Locke and Kant through to Kelsen and Rawls have insisted that constitutional norms undergird all political decisions and that the law provides the state with its ultimate legitimacy. The state is understood as bound to the rule of law – which in Kantian terms, is the rule of the rule. What makes Habermas interesting and appealing to liberals is his efforts to secure legitimacy for liberal democracy. Rather than simply seeking to ground the ultimate justification or legitimacy of liberal-democratic order in the fact of a constitution, Habermas has developed a model of deliberative rationality, which involves deriving or making a rule using reason itself. This account of democracy represents the operationalisation of popular sovereignty (or rule by the people) by pointing to the role played by both institutionalized procedures of parliamentary decision-making *and* the deliberative public opinion forming role of the public sphere. Together the legal and deliberative elements that make up modern constitutional parliamentary government run alongside the more direct communicative processes of civil society and the public sphere (including the media) to provide the institutional foundations of democracy. As Critchley (2012, 106) notes, there is here an absolute conviction that 'all political decisions have to be derived from norms, and that the procedure for decision-making is rational deliberation'.

Many have been persuaded that the discourse that constitutes the public sphere, namely austere rational deliberation, is functional, and that as Gimmler says, 'there is no plausible alternative model to rational and un-coerced discourse as the normative basis for democracy' (Gimmler 2001, 23). This is because collective rational deliberation creates a new space 'where the authority of the better argument' could 'be asserted against the established order' (status quo). This in turn 'holds out the possibility of reforming the asymmetrical relations of force' (Tsekeris 2008, 13). This entails an 'idealised form of public reasoning'. Habermas has argued that all communication involves 'communicative action' oriented to *understanding* or agreement and is based on the 'intersubjective redemption of validity claims'. 'Understanding' (*verstandigung*) is a key word here representing several nested ideas. At its most basic it simply means that people are using the same words with the same meanings so as to achieve a degree of shared meanings and mutual comprehension. At its most elevated, 'understanding' means a shared consensus about the universal validity of claims people make to speak the truth or to know the good. This accomplishment says Habermas, seems to require that participants need to believe that a: 'rationally motivated agreement could in principle be achieved … provided e.g. that the argumentation could be conducted openly enough and continued long enough' (Dahlberg 2000, 6).

This looks a lot like a Kantian exercise in rule-bound reasoning. As Dahlberg (2000, 5) says, it is possible to formally specify the nature of 'communicative action'. This will involve:

> …a formal method in the Kantian sense of attempting to reconstruct the conditions of possibility of communicative interaction … and is pragmatic to the extent that it focuses on the use of language and hence on speech acts or utterances.

This is because communicative action relies on presuppositions that are said to be the general or formal structures of action and understanding that are intuitively drawn on by all of us in our people in everyday communications.

Dahlberg (2000) has identified six characteristics of communicative action, which are understood as an, 'ideal-speech situation' able to ensure that truth claims are subject only to the 'revisionary power of free-floating reasons' (Habermas 2001, 34). First, rational communicative action involves the identification of themes open to the reciprocal testing of problematic truth claims and requires that the conversation take place as if everyone potentially affected by the claims being discussed is being taken into account. Second, reflexivity is a critical condition, which means that people are prepared and willing to change their minds by critically examining their own assumptions, prejudices and beliefs. Third, the ideal speech setting requires the assumption of impartiality and respectful listening because participants seek to understand rather than to aggravate disagreements or ignore difference (Habermas 2001, 34).

Fourth, the ideal-speech situation requires everyone to bring good will to bear as all participants aim at being honest and sincere. Fifth, communicative action presupposes formal and discursive equality between participants. This is presumed on the grounds that argumentation is and needs to be open to anyone potentially affected by the claims being discussed. Equally this turns into the idea that each participant is to be given equal opportunity to introduce and question any assertion whatsoever (Habermas 1996, 308). Finally, communicative action requires autonomy from the power exercised by states and corporations. The suggestion is that both states and corporations seem to be characterised by a will to dominate using techniques of instrumental rationality (for example, corporations treat people as consumers rather than as citizens). Habermas envisages that the public sphere should be as free from influence by the state or the market as possible.

It is not surprising that critics have said this account is odd. To the extent it claims to be descriptive this is puzzling since so much mundane communication fails to meet most of the elements said to descriptively characterise it. It also seems to convert politics into the kind of thing a professor running a seminar in logic does. Certainly one effect of treating politics as a deliberative process informed by an austere set of protocols is to treat the kinds of exchanges found on 4chan as beyond the pale.

5   4chan as Political

4chan clearly affronts conventional conceptions of civility and what counts as 'proper' deliberative practice. Several features stand out including the transience of the site, the principle of Anonymity and the use of offensive language. 4chan is a simple site – spartan by today's Web 2.0 standards. It was designed for transient conversation and image sharing and the site still does this. 4chan is a highly transient website. Threads generally '404' (or die) typically after an hour, and there are approximately 700,000 posts a day.

Users are anonymous. 4chan users are not required to register to post and people aren't required to identify themselves. /b/ has no rules about what can be posted other than requiring users to be compliant with local and/or US law. However, Rule Number 4 says clearly: 'The posting of personal information … is prohibited' (4chan x.x.2016). Like the rest of the 4chan website, the users of /b/ mostly choose anonymity. 'Moot' has vigorously defended the principle of anonymity. Speaking publicly in February 2010 Poole claimed that anonymous speech promoted rational discourse and that it was more thoughtful than speech 'attached to a name'.

> When you've got a community with identity, the discussion is mostly revolving around who is saying what and not what they're saying ... with the anonymous system you've got a place where people are uninhibited ... You're getting very truthful conversation ... you judge somebody by the content of what they're saying and not their username, not their registration date.
>
> SUTTER 2010

In this respect 4chan represents a counter-movement to the current preoccupation with personal identity and full disclosure of personal details that has come to characterise websites like Facebook and Twitter. The result is an exuberantly open-minded website where almost anything goes.

Much of what is found on 4chan is vulgar, emotional, exuberant, energetically disrespectful and prone to ridicule rather than seeking to rationally persuade in the kind of hushed and respectful tones Habermas would have us adopt. The protection afforded by anonymity supports a mode of expression which specialises in ridicule, vulgarity and offensive speech exemplified in the practice of 'trolling'. Trolling is a semiotically rich term describing provocative posts on the Internet. Trolling, also referred to by 'Anonymous' as 'chemo', seems to aim at being maximally offensive. One post by Anonymous advises that:

> ...the Holocaust is completely irrelevant. Bring this up frequently in the company of Jews. After all it's hard to stay angry at someone who had just made you laugh.
>
> in BAIR 2008, 43

A recent post commenting on the Trump-Clinton debates calls on Mexicans to get rid of drug cartels because:

> Honestly I just wanna bang some Mexican hotties but I fucking can't because I'm scared I'll be kidnapped by the cartel and get my face peeled off for stepping into the wrong village. How do the fuck did you let them become so powerful Mexicans like seriously remove them so I can visit your fucking shithole.
>
> 4chan 10.23.2016

4chan does not conform to Habermas's protocol ideas about 'communicative action' or democratic politics. The Net has allowed not just new styles of civic discourse which are not all that civil, but it has also facilitated quite vigorous forms of direct political action which use the interconnectedness of the Net to launch political attacks at organizations deemed to be subverting the principle of freedom of speech. /b/ also hosts a vigorous culture of mass on-line interventions called 'raids' or Distributed Denial of Service actions in which hundreds of thousands or millions of internet users flood a targeted website causing it to freeze or crash. Anonymous have staged some of the most spectacular collective interventions in the history of the Internet. For example, in December 2010, Anonymous launched a series of attacks against PayPal, Mastercard and Visa in retaliation for their response to the release by Wikileaks of US diplomatic cables. What makes Anonymous interesting is their use of these raids to defend democracy and free speech. When the *Anonymous Iran* project was launched in late 2009 to protest the botched Iranian election, Anonymous declared to the people of Iran: 'We are Anonymous. We are Legion. We do not forgive. We do not forget. Expect us'. Agamben may well be right when he sees here a new kind of political speech created by a new kind of political community:

> It is neither apathy nor promiscuity nor resignation. These pure singularities communicate only in the empty space of the example, without being tied by any common property, by any identity. They are expropriated of all identity, so as to appropriate belonging itself, the sign ... Tricksters or fakes, assistants or 'toons, they are the exemplars of the coming community.
> AGAMBEN 1993

To cut to the chase, writers like Habermas, Gimmler and Tsekeris claim there is a link between rational deliberation, the public sphere and the democratic order. These claims notwithstanding, no particular reasons however have been advanced to say why we can believe that rational arguments will transform asymmetrical power relations, or that rational deliberation can challenge a status quo. Nor are we shown why there is some inherent relationship between rational deliberation, the public sphere and a democratic order. This is the point first made by Carl Schmitt in the 1920s.

6   After Rational Consensus

Agamben (2005) has reminded us of the subversive value of Carl Schmitt, the black prince of German political theory. Schmitt (1985, 1996) argued that the condition of possibility for legality and legitimacy is always susceptible to being undone by the political act that suspends it. This is Schmitt's (1985, 1) account of sovereignty as the state of exception (*iustitium*): 'sovereign is he who decides on the state of exception'. In effect Schmitt undoes the point and purpose of the liberal tradition which ostensibly renders the state subject to law reminding us that the state is both the source of law *and* above the law. A truly political decision is what breaks from any norm, indeed frees itself from normative justification and becomes the expression of pure political will. This formulation depends on Schmitt's radical reduction of the 'political' to the ways we deal with our friends and our enemies to produce a decisionist account of the political. As Critchley reminds us, the core of Schmitt's theory of the political shows us 'that the true subject of the political is the state, and that the state must always stand higher than the law' (Critchley 2012, 105). Critchley points to very large problem by showing how this proposition creates profound problems both for those who argue for popular sovereignty, that is sovereignty grounded in the people, and for those who argue for deliberative democracy. Critchley goes back to the question of how the people are to assert their sovereignty and points as Olson (2007, 3) says to a basic paradox: 'democratic lawmaking becomes paradoxical when it must establish the very conditions for its own institutionalization'.

There is of course no problem in creating a polity, or a system of laws or a constitution or a political order by simply declaring that it be brought into being by force: 'obey these laws or suffer the consequences'. Schmitt's decisionism reflects the unilateral political will of a personal dictatorship, or an army. However, given the liberal wish to ground legitimacy in something other than violence or political will, any such unilateral decisionism is deemed to be procedurally invalid because it is not the fruit of the rule of the rule.

What does this signify about the role of ethical ideas? Critchley (2004), who properly emphasises the ethical grounding of politics. If ethics without politics is empty, then politics without ethics is blind. Critchley's (2004, 1) conception of politics requires 'an experience of empowerment that is irreducibly *ethical*'. For Critchley this ethics involves the:

> anarchic disturbance of the political status quo, a meta-political disturbance of established politics for the sake of politics, that is, for the sake of a politics that does not close over into itself, becoming a whole, a state, the fantasy of the One, or what Levinas will call a totality.

7   ...and the Problem with Consensus

Critchley is part of a diverse approach to rethinking the nature of the political. Contemporary radical democratic theorists point to deep, non-remediable problems in the excessive individualism, rationalism and universalism characterizing the liberal framework and its preoccupation with treating politics as the task of creating consensus using institutions like elections, political parties and parliaments (Mouffe 2005; Žižek 2014; Unger 2014). This body of work identifies why and how we can begin to reconceptualise 'the political' by by-passing the tacit liberal promotion of an ideological consensus that treats the market and the neoliberal state as either the natural or inevitable organisational foundations of any society. As Mouffe (2005, 3) argues, democratic theorists and politicians should aim for the creation of a vibrant 'agonistic' public sphere of contestation 'where different hegemonic political projects can be confronted'.

Evans and Reid (2014) have called for a new ethics, which goes beyond clinging to life in decreasingly liveable conditions requiring of us that we be 'resilient'. As they argue a concept like 'resilience' is quickly universalised and moralised into a narrative of heroic adaptation against endemic risks, threats, and dangers that become naturalised as normative expectations. In effect, resilience becomes an ideological-political concept and 'a key strategy of contemporary regimes of power that hallmark vast inequalities in all human classification' (Evans & Reid 2014,10). Rather, what is needed is a new ethos skeptical about all claims to universalism in which we again speak with confidence about our capacity to transform the world, 'not for the better, but for the sake of it' – and for the people to come. They counsel using provocation as a political tool.

Habermas may well be proposing some entirely worthy prescriptive intentions about how 'good' political speech should look and work. It may also be nothing more than the modern philosopher's tendency to look at the world through pursed lips. What we see in Anonymous and 4chan is a challenge to the liberal idea that the political relies on rational and un-coerced discourse and deliberative practices oriented to consensus. Don't we see in the sarcastic laughter of Anonymous, directed at ISIS, such a politics. The point of 4chan is that it points to new conceptions of the political. This is not grounded in an austere conception of deliberative rationality. Rather it invokes the imaginary, the poetic, the capacity to ridicule, the ethical and the emotional in striking new ways.

References

Agamben, G. 1993. *The Coming Community*, trans. Michael Hardt, Minneapolis: University of Minnesota Press.

Agamben, G. 2005. *State of Exception*, Chicago: University of Chicago Press.

Akram, S. 2014. 'Recognizing the 2011 United Kingdom Riots as Political Protest: a Theoretical Framework Based on agency, habitus and the Preconscious'. In, *British Journal of Criminology, 54*: 375–92.

Amadae, S. 2003. *Rationalizing Capitalist Democracy: The Cold War Origins of Rational Choice Liberalism*. Chicago: University of Chicago Press.

Bauerlein, M. 2009. *The Dumbest Generation: How the Digital Age Stupefies Young Americans and Jeopardizes Our Future*. New York: Penguin.

Bauman, Z. 1989. *Modernity and the Holocaust*. Ithaca: Cornell University Press.

Becker, G. 1976. *The Economic Approach to Human Behavior*. Chicago: University of Chicago Press.

Benhabib, S. 1996. 'Towards a deliberative Model of democratic Legitimacy'. In, S. Benhabib (ed) *Democracy and Difference: Contesting the boundaries of the Political*. Princeton: Princeton University Press.

Bessant, J. 2003. 'Youth participation: A new mode of government'. In, *Policy Studies, 24,* (2/3): 87–100.

Bessant, J. 2004. 'Mixed Messages: Youth Participation and Democratic Practice'. In, *Australian Journal of Political Science 39*(2)*:* 387–404.

Bair, A. 2008. *'We are legion: An anthropological perspective on Anonymous,' Proceedings in the 2008 Senior Symposium in Anthropology*. Dept. of Anthropology: Idaho State University Press.

Bohmann, J. 1996. *Public deliberation; Pluralism, Complexity and Democracy*. Cambridge: MIT Press.

Castells, M. 2008. "The New Public Sphere: Global Civil Society, Communication Networks, and Global Governance". In, *The Annals of the American Academy of Political and Social Science, 616*: 78–93. http://www.jstor.org/stable/25097995.

Coleman, G. 2011. 'Hacker politics and publics'. In, *Public Culture, 23*(3), 511–516.

Coleman, G. 2014. *Hacker, Hoaxer, Whistleblower, Spy: The Many Faces of Anonymous*. Verso, London.

Critchley, S. 2004. *'*The Problem of Hegemony'*, Political Theory Daily Review*. Available: http://politicaltheory.info/essays/critchley.htm-www.politicaltheory.info/essays/critchley.htm.London: Verso.

Critchley, S. 2012. *Faith of the Faithless*. London: Verso.

Dahlberg, L. 2000. 'The Habermasian Public Sphere: A Specification of the idealised Conditions of democratic Communication'. In, *Studies in Social and Political thought,* www.sussex.ac.uk/cspt/documents/10-1a.pdf.

Dahlberg, L. 2001. *Extending the public sphere through cyberspace: The case of Minnesota E-democracy*. Available: www.firstmonday.org/issues/issue6_3/dahlberg/index.html#note2.

Danziger, K. 1990. *Constructing the subject: Historical origins of psychological research*. New York: Cambridge University Press.

Dunleavy, P. 1991. *Democracy, Bureaucracy and Public Choice: Economic Models in Political Science*. London: Pearson.

Easton, D. 1965. *A Systems Analysis of Political Life*. New York: Wiley.

Evans, B. & J. Reid 2014. *Resilient life. The Art of Living Dangerously*. Cambridge; Polity.

Farthing, R. 2010. 'The politics of youthful anti-politics: representing the "issue" of youth participation in politics'. In, *Journal of Youth Studies, 13 (2)*: 181–195.

Fraser, N. 1990. 'Rethinking the Public Sphere: A Contribution to the Critique of Actually Existing Democracy'. In, *Social Text, No 25/26*: 56–80.

Fuchs, C. 2013. 'The Anonymous movement in the context of liberalism and socialism'. In, *Interface*, 5(2): 345–376.

Furedi, F. 2005. *The Politics of Fear. Beyond Left and Right*. London, Continuum.

Furlong, A. & F. Cartmel. 2012. 'Social change and political engagement among young people: generation and the 2009/2010 British Election Survey'. In, *Parliamentary Affairs, 65 (1)*: 13–28.

Gimmler, A. 2001. 'Deliberative Democracy, the Public Sphere and the Internet'. In, *Philosophy and Social Criticism 27(4)*: 21–39.

Goode, L. 2015. 'Anonymous and the Political Ethos of Hacktivism'. In, *Popular Communication, 13:1*: 74–86, DOI: 10.1080/15405702.2014.978000.

Gordon, H. & J. Taft 2011. 'Rethinking youth political socialization: teenage activists talk back'. In, *Youth & Society, 43 (4)*: 1499–1527.

Habermas, J. 1989. *Structural Transformation of the Public Sphere: An Inquiry into a Category of Bourgeois, Society*, (Trans by T. Burger & F. Lawrence) Cambridge, MIT Press.

Habermas, J. 1991. 'The Public Sphere'. In, *Rethinking Popular Culture: Contemporary Perspectives in Cultural Studies*, editec by C. Muckerji & M. Schedson Berkeley, UCP.

Habermas, J. 1996. *Between Facts and Norms: Contributions to a Discourse Theory of Law and Democracy*. Cambridge, Polity Press.

Habermas, J. 2001. 'From Kant's idea of "pure reason" to the Idealizing Presuppositions of Communicative Action'. In, *Pluralism and the Pragmatic Turn: The Transformation of Critical Theory*, edited by J. Rheg & J. Bohmann Cambridge, MIT Press: 11–39.

Habermas, J. 2006. Political Communication in Media Society: Does Democracy Still Enjoy an Epistemic Dimension? The Impact of Normative Theory on Empirical Research. Communication Theory, 16(4), 411–426. doi: 10.1111/j.1468-2885.2006.00280.x.

Harris, A., J. Wyn & S. Younes 2010. 'Beyond apathetic or activist youth. "Ordinary" young people and contemporary forms of participation'. In, *Young, 18 (1)*: 9–32.

Henn, M., M. Weinstein & S. Hodgkinson. 2007. 'Social capital and political participation: understanding the dynamic of young people's political disengagement in contemporary Britain'. In, *Social Policy and Society*, 6 (4): 467–479.

Herwig, J. 2010. 'The Archive as the Repertoire. Mediated and Embodied Practice on Imageboard 4chan.org'. In, *Mind and Matter,* edited by G. Friesinger & T. Ballhausen Paraflows 10 Symposium, conference proceedings.

Hilton, M., J. McKay, N. Crowson & J-F Mouhot. 2010. '"The Big Society": civic participation and the state in Modern Britain'. In, *History and Policy* http://www.historyandpolicy.org/papers/policy-paper-103.html.

Karatzogianni, A., D. Nguyen & E. Serafinelli 2016. (eds). *The Digital Transformation of the Public Sphere.* London: Palgrave Macmillan.

Kimberlee, R.H. 2002. 'Why Don't British Young People Vote at General Elections?' In, *Journal of Youth Studies 5 (1):* 85–98.

Leftwich, A. 2004. *What is politics? The activity and its study.* Cambridge: Polity.

Manning, N. 2009. *Young people and politics: apathetic and disengaged? A qualitative inquiry.* Koln, Lambert Academic Publishing.

Marsh, D. and A. Vromen 2012. 'Everyday Makers with a Difference?: Contemporary Forms of Political Participation, *Tasa Conference,* Available: https://www.tasa.org.au/wp-content/uploads/2012/11/Marsh-David-Vromen-Ariadne.pdf.

Martin, A. 2012. 'Political Participation among the Young in Australia: Testing Dalton's Good Citizen Thesis'. In, *Australian Journal of Political Science, 42*: 211–26.

McCaffrie, B. & Marsh, D. (2013). *Beyond mainstream approaches to political participation: A response to Aaron Martin.* Australian Journal of Political Science. *48 (1):* 112–117. DOI: 10.1080/10361146.2012.759903.

Mouffe, C. 2005. *On the Political.* London, Routledge.

Sandywell, B. 1996. *Logological Investigations, Vol 1, Reflexivity and the Crisis of Western Reason.* London: Routledge.

Schmitt, C. 1985. *Political theology: Four Chapters on the concept of Sovereignty.* (Trans G. Schwab). Chicago, University of Chicago Press.

Schmitt, C. 1996. *The Concept of the Political* (Trans G. Schwab). Chicago, University of Chicago Press.

Skocpol, T. 2003. *Diminishing Democracy – From Membership to management in American Civic Life.* Cambridge, Harvard University Press.

Sutter, J. 2010. '4Chan founder: Anonymous speech is endangered'. In, *CNN SciTech Blog* http://scitech.blogs.cnn.com/2010/02/12/4chan-founder-anonymous-speech-is-endangered/.

Tsekeris, C. 2008. 'Sociological Issues in Culture and Critical Theorizing'. In, *Humanity and Social Sciences Journal, 3(1):* 18–25.

Unger, R. 2014. *The Religion of the Future.* Cambridge, Harvard University Press.

Vromen, A. & P. Collin 2010. 'Everyday youth participation? Contrasting views from Australian policymakers and young people'. In, *Young, 18 (1):*97–112.

Vromen, A. & M. Xenos 2010. *Civic networking in comparative perspective: young people, civic engagement and social media in Australia and the USA*. Sydney, University of Sydney.

Westling, M. 2007. *Expanding the Public Sphere: The Impact of Facebook on Political Communication*. Madison: University of Wisconsin-Madison.

Xenos, M., A. Vromen & B Loader. 2014. 'The great equalizer? Patterns of social media use and youth political engagement in three advanced democracies'. In, *Information, Communication & Society*, 17 (2): 151–67.

Žižek, S. 2014. *Trouble in Paradise*. London, Allen Lane.

Websites

Anonymous, available from: https://anonofficial.com/.
4chan, available from: http://boards.4chan.org/pol/10/23/16.
Google. 2009. 'Google Privacy Policy'. Last modified March 11.
http://www.google.com/intl/en/privacypolicy.html.

CHAPTER 5

Hacking the Future: Youth, Digital Disruption and the Promise of the New

Shane B. Duggan

1   Introduction

In May of 2016, Australian Federal Education Minister Simon Birmingham held a press conference at a small primary school in regional New South Wales to laud the 'wonderful coding programme' operating at the school. The press conference, just days into a lengthy election campaign by Australian standards, followed a fortnight of education and training announcements by the Minister foregrounding innovation, and the leveraging of science, technology, engineering, and mathematics (STEM) skills in a rapidly evolving digital economy. Just days later, Opposition Leader Bill Shorten announced a multi-million-dollar plan to establish a National Coding in Schools centre to support primary and secondary school teachers across the country to upskill their teaching in the use of coding in the classroom. These moves follow a global trend, with similar initiatives in the UK, US, Europe and Asia. Many initiatives are introduced at a school, rather than system level with US-led global initiatives such as Code. org, 'Hour of Code,' and *Galileo* championed by Google, Microsoft, and Intel, respectively, commanding a substantial footprint in STEM training and instruction. Whilst these initiatives differ in their scope, links with industry, and intended outcomes, what is common is a concern for how young people are being prepared, or not, to participate in an economy that increasingly relies on the production and exchange of information through digital platforms. Here, young people are positioned as the vanguard for realising the potential of the future, and educational institutions the key policy apparatus through which that potential might be cultivated.

   As this chapter explores, significant popular and policy attention over the last decade has come to be concerned with the changing notions of the future and the 'new' within the digital information economy and their implications for how young people make a life. I argue that the abstraction of the traditional forms of information and labour have emerged as a key imperative of popular and policy understandings of young people's lives. The chapter traces what McKenzie Wark (2004) calls the 'hacker class' to explore how traditional notions of labour market participation are being abstracted in ways that expose young people to new forms of governance and intervention. This abstraction, what Wark terms 'hacking,' creates both the possibility of the new—and the spoils it brings for the most advantaged—yet displaces the vast majority of young people in material and symbolic ways. To begin, I bring together notions of time and futurity, as these have been taken up in youth scholarship, to frame the substantive contributions of this chapter.

2   Framing the 'new'

There is a long history of engagement with the differential effects of successive shifts in labour market conditions for young people in youth studies research (Thomson and Holland 2010; Furlong, Woodman, and Wyn 2011; Kelly 2006; Thomson and Holland 2010). An underlying concern of this diverse scholarship is a concern for how young people 'move' differently through their engagement with school-based institutions, to interfacing with industry within late industrial capitalism, particularly in the global north. As Carabelli and Lyon (2016, 1110) pithily remind us, 'young people are positioned in linear intergenerational relationships as the bearers of the future hopes of others and 'society' more generally…they are [also] denigrated for not adequately living up to these investments'. This doubling of expectations produces what Walkerdine (2003, 243) terms a constellation of 'defenses and desires' which 'work through popular narratives [and] formal discourses'.

Central to narratives told by and about young people is an imagining of the future within a spatial and linear conception of time and futurity. The compression of time into distinctive periods which must be successfully navigated or 'passed through' produces what Adam (2003, 73) names a 'clash of temporal logics' within modern social conditions in which certainty, stability, and linearity are being displaced by rapid changes in technological capabilities, connectivity, and accompanying shifts in the labour market. She identifies three related conceptions of time that are useful for understanding the ways in which time and futurity are experienced *in* the world, and how they are made sense of in academic discourses: First, in terms of regeneration, rebirth, and other cyclic, biological processes; second, as an ordering of social life through the division of activities into fragments, such as in the timetabling of schools, pay cycles, and social activities such as dining and entertainment or what she calls 'clock' time; and finally, through bringing 'clock' and bodily time together into irreversible, contextual, and contingent social arrangements in which activities are regulated, repeated, and measured in terms of 'process' and 'product'.

McLeod and Thomson (2009, 166) argue that the tension between clock and social time challenges any attempt to 'locate the subject' by instead placing emphasis on the paradoxical situation of attending simultaneously to 'the spatiality of the temporal and the temporality of the spatial'. As they suggest, attention to both positions, along with a refusal to separate them out in social science research, is generative for 'pointing to questions of synchronization as well as sequence; and understanding continuity and change as integral to each other' (2009, 166). The juxtaposition of objective and subjective temporalities is particularly powerful for understanding the ways in which different temporalities are present in the lived experiences of young people. As Coffey and Farrugia (2014, 470) note, such conceptions of time permeate dichotomous debates in youth studies around structure and agency, knowledge and practice, subjectivity and object. In these debates, they suggest, 'the on-going relationship between structures, habitus and the "structured improvisation" of practice contribut[es] a kind of forward looking temporality' which informs the constitution of subjectivities in the present.

Temporal processes are approached in two main ways in contemporary youth sociology that are relevant to thinking about the 'new'. First, they are central to understanding the various markers of transition that young people are said to pass through in the passage from 'youth' to 'adulthood' (Leccardi 2005; Woodman 2011). Second, they are an important dimension for understanding how young people—as well as the institutional and cultural frameworks with which they engage —*understand* and make sense of their orientations toward the future (see, for example, Uprichard 2011; Woodman 2011). Woodman (2011, 112) suggests that there is a 'certain family resemblance…in much contemporary sociological theory on time: a stretching of the present, or forcing more action into the same duration, and a loss of the ability to plan into the future due to a sense of uncertainty'. Indeed, a significant body of literature affirms that, due to myriad factors including technological change and shifts in the youth labour market, the speed of change is accelerating in modern times, accompanied with a significant decline in the certainty of day-to-day life, thus affecting young people's ability to meaningfully plan for the future (Leccardi 2005; McLeod 2017; Rosa 2003). As Rosa (2003) argues, it is primarily the speed at which technological change is taking place which is having the most significant effect on the ways in which people can productively make a life. Along with an unprecedented acceleration of technological and social change, there has been a paradoxical increase in what Rosa (2003) calls the 'pace of life'. That is, despite innovations designed to lower the amount of time taken on mundane tasks, time has become scarcer, and there is a growing urgency and anxiety around decision-making and forward planning. Brannen and Nilsen (2002,

517) disagree; arguing that it is not so much that time has become scarcer but that in the present era 'experience is overtaxed by expectations'. As I show below, both perspectives are embedded in how the future is re/made with the production of emerging forms and flows of capital.

3   The Future as a Roadmap, Not a Road

The future is, either implicitly or explicitly, a core concern of popular and policy attention towards young people. Like many key concepts in youth studies, it has been taken to mean many things in popular, policy, and scholarly discourses. Adam (2010, 47) argues that '[c]ontemporary daily life is conducted in the temporal domain of open pasts and futures…[which are]…projectively oriented toward the "not yet:"'. She usefully suggests a distinction between *future presents* and *present futures*. Future presents guide our anticipation for change, while present futures are useful for taking up the everyday tasks of prediction and enactment. For Adam, future orientation is a necessary precondition for participation in many aspects of social, cultural, and civic life, with both our anticipations and anxieties, as well as our predictions and yearning for certainty, largely making up our ability to meaningfully plan and act in the everyday. These anticipations and anxieties operate in and on young people's activities—in relation to their own ability to meaningfully plan and orient toward the future, and in broader imaginings of young people, particularly in relation to popular 'moral panics' around their activities and identities.

Clegg (2010) notes that embedded in the policy frameworks in many countries in the global north, young people are bound up and projected as 'good' citizens so long as they continually remake themselves within a neoliberal, and 'employable' frame. Neoliberalism is taken up in many of the other contributions to this volume (for example, Peter Kelly) and as such, I will not elaborate on this in detail here. According to Clegg (2010), the ultimate goal of many youth policies in present times is not only that young people are employed as they were in previous generations, but also that they continually remake themselves in an image of the future in which heightened unpredictability is taken as normal. Individual social mobility is given primacy and is bound up in the activities young people engage with in the present, as well as their orientation to future activities. Being active, continual self-improvement, and critical self-reflection are emphasised as necessary attributes that regulate young people's temporal orientations; both the past and the future are coded within 'the discursive and material practices of the present' (Clegg 2010, 346). However, as Carabelli and Lyon (2016, 1111) note, 'whilst many authors make reference to the importance of temporality in navigating the world, the significance of the (imagined) future in the present is not well articulated'.

Highlighting the significance of 'social time' in contemporary life, du Bois-Reymond and López Blasco (2003) note the precariousness of the category of 'youth' and 'adulthood' in modern times, suggesting that young people experience 'yo-yo' transitions which are non-linear, changeable, and potentially reversible. This produces an image of the future that is not only uncertain, but also fraught with danger, and requires responsible dispositions in the present to successfully overcome. McLeod (2014) usefully expands on this, suggesting that research into young people's lives must consider how they are experiencing temporality differently and how this affects their conditions of life. This means understanding the different histories, cultures, and understandings of institutions such as educational providers and industry that young people bring to their own narratives. However, it also means understanding the notion of orientation toward the future differently, as simultaneously reflective and productive of the conditions of life that young people find themselves within. Put another way, there are inequalities in young people's experiences based on gender, race, and class lines, yet the challenges that young people face are not only structural or categorical, they are also comprised of expectations and stereotypes around what it means to achieve 'success', orient themselves in time, and make sense of the future (See: Kehily and Nayak 2013; Matthews 2002).

In popular media, Adam's (2010) notion of the *future present* often takes the form of catastrophising the predispositions and activities of young people, expressed as a loss of the 'proper' means that 'should' make up the future. Such an understanding of the future present resonates with Miller and Rose's (2008) account of governmentality. For Miller and Rose (2008, 7) expressions of the loss of 'proper means' for making a future arise out of an assemblage of 'aims methods, targets, techniques and criteria' upon which popular culture, organisations, and 'individuals judge and evaluate themselves and their lives', as well as seek to 'master, steer, control, save or improve themselves'. Importantly, these 'aims' and 'targets' are designed to remake the present *in* the future, and to condition young people's desires such that they produce a 'good' life. It is to these aims and targets that I now turn, specifically considering how these have been differentially realised within the context of the apparent digital disruption.

4   Hacking the Future

An emerging field of enquiry within youth studies takes up what Côté (2014) terms a *political economy approach* to the study of youth. This approach seeks to examine the relationship of local settings to 'the *totality of social relations* that make up the economic, political, social, and cultural areas of life' (Mosco, 2009 in Sukarieh and Tannock 2016, 1282, emphasis in original). For Sukarieh and Tannock (2016, 1281–82), despite the significant opposition to the term and the narrow ways in which it is employed by Côté, 'there is considerable value to increasing the attention paid to political economy in the field of youth studies, particularly in the current historical conjuncture'. Indeed, the decline in secure economic and social conditions for young people which have accompanied the first decades of the new millennium in many post-industrial economies is increasingly the product of global forces, with localized implications (Ball and Olmedo 2013; Rizvi 2013; Sukarieh and Tannock 2016; Woodman and Threadgold 2011). The combined effects of national policies in relaxing cross-border trade and advances in networked technologies has, for many in the global north, led to what Appadurai (2013, 3) sees as 'the broadening of risk-taking and risk-bearing as properties of human life'.

Networked technologies remain a deep marker for analysing forms of social and economic inclusion and exclusion. The availability, efficacy, and efficiency of networked technologies for directly impacting the lives of the vast majority of those in the global north reflects a profound re-organisation of traditional forms of consumption and production. Similarly, the profound and contingent effects for the extraction, refinement, and manufacture of those technologies on the global south has led to new forms of opportunity for a very small number of elites, and deep exploitation for a new manufacturing class of workers. Young people, positioned as both the vanguard for identifying and benefiting from the 'new,' are also those most likely to feel the detrimental effects of its implications for their participation in a labour market which decreasingly requires their participation in its production. This is not merely a symbolic shift, as France and Threadgold (2016, 622) tell us, but one in which young people face a 'material and ontological reality of lack of options in their actual lives'. In their view, new forms of educational and labour market inequality matter, and sit alongside those which appear remarkably like inequalities experienced by previous generations. As France and Threadgold (2016, 613) note, there is a need to recognise 'not only the complexity of the relationship between the economy and the everyday life of young people but also the processes and practices that are at work in shaping their subjectivities and outcomes'. Thus, what is significant in thinking about young people within the context of *digital disruption* is how young people's lives become open to intervention, or not, by government policies, dominant economic interests, or technological instruments.

Concern for the influence and impact of technological instruments in the everyday practices of young people resonates well beyond youth studies scholarship. For example, economist Yochai Benkler (2006, 2011) has written extensively on the shift toward what he terms 'the networked information economy' over the last two decades. Two related aspects of Benkler's theory are worth elaborating for this discussion. Firstly, advanced economies are seeing 'a radical change in the organization of information production' (2006, 1). For Benkler, this new information environment can be characterised by an increase in the freedom of individuals to actively contribute to global flows of information, and its on-flow effects for economic and ultimately democratic participation. Significantly, the rapid decrease in the cost of producing, transporting, and sharing information on a global scale has spurred an edification of what he considers non-proprietary, nonmarket motivations by an increasingly diverse array of actors. Second, the combined efforts of these actors 'led to the emergence of *coordinate effects*, where the aggregate of individual action...produces the coordinate effect of a new and rich information environment' (Benkler 2006, 4–5). Taken together, for Benkler (2006, p.6), the productive capacity of the networked information economy is 'a new mode of production emerging in the middle of the most advanced economies in the world...for which goods and services have come to occupy the highest-valued roles'.

Whilst there are many who would laud the benefits of networked technologies for opening diverse market and nonmarket activities on a global scale, there exists a significant scholarship that notes their uneven distribution and effects, particularly in relation to young people and education (for example, Appadurai 2013; Leander, Phillips, and Taylor 2010; Rizvi 2013). This is not to suggest that Benkler constructs a naïve or benign portrait of the differential effects of networked technologies. Indeed, he notes how conditions of life for the most marginalized, even in post-industrial economies, have seen a rapid decline in recent times. Yet, his is a thesis which emphasises the productive and distributed capacity of the emerging ecosystem of nonproprietary information. Indeed, what is most significant in Benkler's (2006, 17) understanding of the networked information economy for this chapter is his emphasis on the shifting social ties, and the ways in which 'different kinds of human action and interaction [have become] easier or harder to perform' through their implication in digital technologies.

Thus, whilst there are significant benefits and potential risks to the embedding of digital and networked technologies in people's everyday lives, there is evidence to suggest that these changes have differentially affected the lives of young people. For Côté (2014, 2016), this can be at least partially accounted for by understanding the shift in relations between the conditions of youth as a class and adults over the last three decades. Others, however, are more skeptical of the utility of considering young people as a class for themselves, and instead point to the impact that the emergence of new forms of labour and capital have had on traditional markers of adulthood as a whole. A prominent example of this is what McKenzie Wark (2004) terms the 'hacker class,' who he sees as emerging as a distinct historical unit for analysis with their own impulses, tools, and relations to neighboring or competing classes. For Wark (2004, para. 36), the social and political conditions of the networked economy are such that new kinds of information objects and subjects are formed, in 'new kinds of relation[s], with unforeseen properties, which question the property form itself'. Counter to Benkler's (2006, 3) suggestion that 'nonmarket and radically de-centralised' forms of production make up the core of social and economic conditions of the most advanced economies, Wark (2017) argues that the productive capacity of the networked economy is constantly captured and abstracted in new commodity forms. The key element of this shift, in his terms, is worth quoting at length:

> At one point, it looked like the capacity for information to be the commons, to be shared, would undermine private property in information, and indeed we see ever more restrictive and punitive legal and technical means to enforce it. And yet there is also another and more effective way of generating a surplus out of control of information. This is to let it circulate freely but to control the access points to it or to control the whole aggregate of information generated.
> WARK 2017, 63

This process of control, what Wark has termed 'vectors,' contribute to a refiguring of relations between the production of content and its commodification. It is not that the information itself is commodified, but rather that its circulation is leveraged for the commercial gain of a new form of elite class, which he terms the 'vectoral class'. Thus, there is some merit in Côté's (2014, 531) charge that there has emerged over the last two decades 'significant material differences between [young people] and an older age segment'. However, there is also a broader refiguring of capital that is not captured by simply extending traditional forms of class analysis.

In a recent review of the field of hacker studies, Jordan (2017) argues that despite sustained research into the figure of the 'hacker' over the last two decades, it remains an elusive figure. Noting the emerging distinction between technological and social practices of hacking, he makes a case for an enlarged definition: 'hacking should be understood as practices that express the rationality of information technocultures' (2017, p. 529). This line of argument, drawing on Foucault, echoes that of Wark (2004) and Söderberg (2017) and reflects the growing awareness of what he terms 'computer-mediated practice' that 'reveals the logics of the intersection of information technology and information culture' within the conditions of the present (2017, p. 529). For Jordan, differently than Wark, the hacker is a techno-cultural figure, rather than one which may come to constitute a class in-itself. However, for Wark, two additional elements concerning the emergence of a 'hacker' and 'vectoral' class relation are worth noting. First, Wark (2017, 65) does not suggest these emerging classes encompass every person within advanced economies, or specific locations such as Silicon Valley, or even specific communities of technologically literature workers. Indeed, successful vectors incorporate and leverage 'whole new qualities of social activity'. Forms of information once designated as non-labour, such as social media interactions, playspaces, and leisure activities have been reformed and channeled through 'forms of information, whether of a qualitative sort, such as brands and corporate superheroes or a quantitative sort, such as metrics and big data and the algorithm and so on' (Wark 2017, 64). This echoes recent scholarship in youth studies by Farrugia (2017) and in information studies by Scholz (2013). Social media channels such as Facebook function as amassers of multiple contours of big data that are leveraged as a means of *generating* income on the one hand, and dispensing ever more sophisticated algorithms for targeting news and commercial advertising on the other (O'Neil 2016). Beyond this, as Wark (2017, 65) writes, these new vectoral forms have even come to incorporate 'social production of novelty itself, whether that novelty be aesthetic or technical'. Second, the production, commodification, and control of new social forms of information through the relation works to sediment an idealised form of 'labour' which organises the allocation of value among those considered most suited to leverage information capital. Information capital, to Scholz works to sediment particular forms of identity capital, tending to animate particular 'assets' such as those consistent with an entrepreneurial identity, and suppress or discourage others either explicitly or tacitly. It is to these two points that I now turn in the final section of this chapter.

5   Exploring the Value of the New

Carabelli and Lyon (2016) note four orientations that are useful in thinking about young people's lives within the conditions of the present; reach, shape, resources, and value. I draw on these here to return to the concerns which frame this chapter. I hope to open up each in the spirit of further inquiry, rather than draw specific conclusions here. First, as Benkler (2006, 8) notes, under the technological conditions of the present, there is greater capacity than at any other time in history for young people to 'do more in loose commonality with others, without being constrained to organize their relationship through...traditional hierarchical models of social and economic organization'. As is well regarded within recent youth studies scholarship (for example, Kehily and Nayak 2013; Mitchell 2007; Sukarieh and Tannock 2016), this capacity has seen innumerable benefits in terms of recognition of traditionally marginalised and disenfranchised populations, and is widely credited as a key aspect of many youth-led activist forms such as the Arab Spring and Spanish Indignados to name but a few. However, the effects of this reach are not even, and have also led to new forms of violence, predatory behaviour, and exclusion. In line with rapid changes in labour market conditions, technological advancements and increases in connectivity both locally and globally, these risks have increasingly pervasive and global effects, especially around issues of ethnicity, gender, and class (see, for example, Ahmed 2016).

Second, Carabelli and Lyon (2016, p. 1116) emphasise the importance of the 'micro-temporal projections' and 'entanglements through which young people envisage their lives'. These ways in which seemingly novel aspects of young people's lives are open to organisation and intervention play an increasingly significant role in everyday practices in the networked information economy. To this end, what is 'new' is novel in the sense it enhances an individual's identity capital for making themselves in the present *for* the future. However, a core tenet of successive 'innovation' policy frameworks in many advanced economies has been in shaping these novel aspects of inter- and intra-action into increasingly abstracted and commodified forms. To return to the vignette which opened this chapter, in Australia, as in many countries in the global north, a dominant presumption in successive state and federal education policy frameworks has been to shape young people's growth and development in such a way that they can participate in the economy of the future. As Sukarieh and Tannock (2016, 1287) note, 'the global embrace by economic and political elites of a prominent youth agenda...inevitably works to shape the very terrain on which young people...act, think and live their lives'. This embrace is inherently value-*laden*, and value-*generating* as can be clearly seen in the opening of higher education markets and the corresponding 'pairing down of education to its most functional vocational elements, to the bare necessity compatible with a particular function' (Wark 2004, para. 53). For Wark, the hacker appears as a short-circuit to this narrative, but is also one who may be captured by ever-new forms of commodification, along ever-more pervasive and tightly controlled vectors of information flows.

Third, it is well recognised that opportunities for young people to engage in full-time waged labour have declined almost universally (see, for example, Côté and Bynner 2008; Wyn 2012; Kelly 2015), and indeed, this is a key concern of this volume. Youth unemployment, and more recently under-employment has been well studied, especially in the wake of the global financial crisis of 2008 (Sukarieh and Tannock 2016; Kelly 2015). Much of this work has sought to explore the experiences that young people have of under- and unemployment and their lasting effects on both traditional and emerging forms of adulthood (Woodman and Threadgold 2011). These debates are often framed in terms of broad-scale shifts in political and economic forces on a global scale, and thus tensions emerge in thinking about the relationship between local conditions and larger patterns in economic and policy structures within and between countries (for an extended discussion of these tensions, see Sukarieh and Tannock 2015, 2016). However, whilst these tensions make good sense in framing debates around traditional forms of labour, production, and capital, as Wark (2004) notes, they are less useful for thinking about networked information, which is by its nature ubiquitous. Instead, he notes that it is the processes of abstraction, rather than the production and consumption of information as a resource that organises, to a large extent, the economic and social conditions of the networked economy in which young people live, work, and learn. For Wark (2004, para. 77) 'through the production of new forms of abstraction, the hacker class produces the possibility of the future'. Put another way, a policy focus on preparing young people for the future—and its implication that the future will be dominated by networked technologies—informs both what counts as 'success' for young people's lives in the future, and the reorganization of the information of the present in new, commodified forms.

Finally, the move to a more highly abstracted economy in much of the global north focused on processing information rather than goods has deep implications for the allocation of value among, and between different segments of the youth population. France and Threadgold (2016, 621) hint at this in their assertion of the 'important role that politics has on structuring and forming the world around the young but also how relationships of power and access to resources operate in particular contexts to produce unequal outcomes'. As they note, young people, and especially those from disadvantaged backgrounds are 'reflexively aware of their own position in social space' (2016, 619). As Benkler (2006, 11) argues, 'the networked public sphere enables many more individuals to communicate their observations and their viewpoints to many others, and to do so in a way that cannot be controlled by media owners'. In reality though, the emergence of a networked public and the people who extract value from it also produces, as Wark (2017, 61) notes rather cynically, 'a second set of low-paid humans to service those information processing humans'. Put bluntly, amid changes in the allocation of value both within advanced economies and for those in the global south who provide the material resources to service them, traditional forms of class distinction continue to resonate along familiar lines which shape, and are shaped by labour market opportunities, educational access, and differences of age, gender, and ethnicity. In this context, Appadurai (2013, 40) argues that 'the decisive factors in technological innovation…are often social and political rather than simply technical'. Accounting for changing notions of value (and indeed the positioning of young people in relation to that value), is critical for considering 'new uses of technological discoveries and new forms of political control of the products of such innovations' (2013, p.40). In this sense, beyond the political economy moniker of 'following the money,' there is a need to account for changes in the allocation of value in and around how and where that money emerges, and flows.

6   Conclusion

The article elaborates on the image of the 'hacker' as a refiguring of scientific, technical, and intellectual labour in the present. It argues that the disruptive tendency of this figure provides a generative platform for investigating Côté's (2014) call to consider youth as a *class-for-itself*. This article finds benefit in Côté's suggestion that young people occupying a distinctive position in new networked economies, yet within this, it identifies a gap in accounting for the broader ways in which the capital form has undergone a material, as well as symbolic shift within the continued expansion of the networked economy. I have attempted to bring into conversation contemporary debates concerning the experience and orientation of temporal processes with emerging understandings of new commodity forms and digital informational flows. By introducing the image of the 'hacker'—a technologically savvy subject who engages in ever-further abstracted labour and realises the potential of vast information flows—it highlights the process by which existing and emerging distinctions and relations are being leveraged in ways that have implications for how we think of young people's lives, and their activities in the present. This is nascent work, and several critical questions remain. Most pressingly, there is a need to account for what is left out, displaced, or made redundant by both the 'hacker' and the 'vectoralist'—to use Wark's terms. This includes an interrogation of their subjective, as well as material and symbolic affects. A sensible place for this analysis to begin, to draw on Côté (2014), would be in the structure, allocation, and symbolic attachment to traditional and emerging forms of Higher Education. Here, on Wark (2017, 62–63) reminds us, the hacker is both the product and the target of policy prescriptions which 'tak[e] advantage of changes…and formalize intellectually a series of material transformations in the forces of production'. Read alongside recent scholarship into the making and sedimentation of the entrepreneurial subject (for example, Kelly 2006), an analysis of the emergent hacker class is a powerful analytic for exploring notions of production and commodification in the present, and the ongoing effect of digital disruption and the networked economy on young people's lives.

References

Adam, Barbara. 2003. 'Reflexive Modernization Temporalized.' *Theory, Culture & Society* 20 (2): 59–78.

Adam, Barbara. 2010. 'Future Matters: Challenge for Social Theory and Social Inquiry.' *Cultura E Comunicazione* 1:1 47–55.

Ahmed, Shamila. 2016. 'Reflections on Conducting Research on the "War on Terror": Religious Identity, Subjectivity and Emotions.' *International Journal of Social Research Methodology* 19 (2): 177–90.

Appadurai, Arjun. 2013. *The Future as Cultural Fact: Essays on the Global Condition.* London: Verso.

Ball, Stephen J., and A Olmedo. 2013. 'Care Of the Self, Resistance and Subjectivity under Neoliberal Governmentalities.' *Critical Studies in Education* 54 (1): 85–96.

Benkler, Yochai. 2006. *The Wealth of Networks How Social Production Transforms Markets and Freedom.* New Haven: Yale University Press.

Benkler, Yochai. 2011. *The Penguin and Leviathan.* New York: Crown Business.

Brannen, Julia, and Ann Nilsen. 2002. 'Young People's Time Perspectives: From youth to adulthood.' *Sociology* 36 (3): 513–37.

Carabelli, Giulia, and Dawn Lyon. 2016. 'Young People's Orientations to the Future: Navigating the Present and Imagining the Future.' *Journal of Youth Studies* 19 (8) 1110–27.

Clegg, Sue. 2010. 'Time Future – the Dominant Discourse of Higher Education.' *Time & Society* 19 (3): 345–64.

Coffey, Julia, and David Farrugia. 2014. 'Unpacking the Black Box: The Problem of Agency in the Sociology of Youth.' *Journal of Youth Studies* 17 (4): 461–74.

Côté, James E. 2014. 'Towards a New Political Economy of Youth.' *Journal of Youth Studies* 17 (4): 527–43.

Côté, James E. 2016. 'A New Political Economy of Youth Reprised: Rejoinder to France and Threadgold.' *Journal of Youth Studies* 19 (6): 852–68.

Côté, James E., and John M. Bynner. 2008. 'Changes in the Transition to Adulthood in the UK and Canada: The Role of Structure and Agency in Emerging Adulthood.' *Journal of Youth Studies* 11 (3): 251–68.

du Bois-Reymond, Manuela, and A López Blasco. 2003. 'Yo-Yo Transitions and Misleading Trajectories: Towards Integrated Transition Policies for Young Adults in Europe.' In *Young People and Contradictions of Inclusion: Towards Integrated Transition Policies in Europe*, edited by A Lopez Blasco, W McNeish, and A Walther, 19–42. Bristol: Policy Press.

Farrugia, D. (2017) 'Youthfulness and immaterial labour in the new economy', *The Sociological Review*, p. 3802611773165. doi: 10.1177/0038026117731657.

France, Alan, and Steven Threadgold. 2016. 'Youth and Political Economy: Towards a Bourdieusian Approach.' *Journal of Youth Studies* 19 (5): 612–28.

Furlong, Andy, Dan Woodman, and Johanna Wyn. 2011. 'Changing Times, Changing Perspectives: Reconciling "transition" and "cultural" perspectives on Youth and Young Adulthood.' *Journal of Sociology* 47 (4): 355–70.

Jordan, T. (2017) 'A genealogy of hacking', *Convergence*, 23(5), pp. 528–544. doi: 10.1177/1354856516640710.

Kehily, Mary Jane, and Anoop Nayak. 2013. *Gender, Youth & Culture: Global Masculinities & Femininities*. 2nd ed. Basingstoke: Palgrave.

Kelly, Peter. 2006. 'The Entrepreneurial Self and "Youth at-Risk": Exploring the Horizons of Identity in the Twenty-First Century.' *Journal of Youth Studies* 9 (1): 17–32.

Kelly, Peter. 2015. 'Growing up after the GFC: Responsibilisation and Mortgaged Futures.' *Discourse: Studies in the Cultural Politics of Education* 38 (1): 57–69.

Leander, Kevin M, Nathan C Phillips, and Katherine Headrick Taylor. 2010. 'The Changing Social Spaces of Learning: Mapping New Mobilities.' *Review of Research in Education* 34 (1): 329–94.

Leccardi, Carmen. 2005. 'Facing uncertainty: Temporality and biographies in the new century' *Young* 13 (2): 123–46.

Matthews, Julie. 2002. 'Racialised Schooling, "Ethnic Success" and Asian-Australian Students.' *British Journal of Sociology of Education* 23 (2): 193–207.

McLeod, Julie. 2014. 'Temporality and Identity in Youth Research.' In *A Companion to Research in Education*, edited by A.D. Reid, P.E. Hart, and M.A. Peters, 311–13. Netherlands: Springer.

McLeod, Julie. 2017. 'Marking Time, Making Methods: Temporality and Untimely Dilemmas in the Sociology of Youth and Educational Change.' *British Journal of Sociology of Education* 38 (1): 13–25.

McLeod, Julie, and Rachel Thomson. 2009. *Researching Social Change: Qualitative Approaches*. London: SAGE.

Miller, Peter, and Nikolas Rose. 2008. *Governing the Present: Administering Economic, Social and Personal Life*. Cambridge: Polity Press.

Mitchell, Katharyne. 2007. 'Geographies of Identity: The Intimate Cosmopolitan.' *Progress in Human Geography* 31 (5): 706–20.

O'Neil, Cathy. 2016. *Weapons of Math Destruction: How Big Data Increases Inequality and Threatens Democracy*. New York: Crown.

Rizvi, Fazalı. 2013. 'Equity and Marketisation: A Brief Commentary.' *Discourse: Studies in the Cultural Politics of Education* 34 (2): 274–78.

Rosa, Hartmut. 2003. 'Social Acceleration: Ethical and Political Consequences of a Desynchronized High-Speed Society.' *Constellations* 10 (1): 3–33.

Scholz, T. (2013) *Digital Labor: The Internet as Playground and Factory*. Edited by T. Scholz. New York: Routledge. doi: 10.1080/09518398.2013.816888.

Söderberg, J. (2017) 'Inquiring Hacking as Politics: A New Departure in Hacker Studies?', *Science, Technology, & Human Values*, 42(5), pp. 969–980. doi: 10.1177/0162243916688094.

Sukarieh, Mayssoun, and Stuart Tannock. 2015. *Youth Rising? The Politics of Youth in the Global Economy*. London: Routledge.

Sukarieh, Mayssoun, and Stuart Tannock. 2016. 'On the Political Economy of Youth: A Comment.' *Journal of Youth Studies* 19 (9): 1281–89.

Thomson, Rachel, and Janet Holland. 2010. 'Imagined Adulthood: Resources, Plans and Contradictions,' *Gender and Education* 14 (4): 337–50.

Uprichard, Emma. 2011. 'Narratives of the Future: Complexity, Time and Temporality.' In *The SAGE Handbook of Innovation in Social Research Methods*, edited by Malcolm Williams and W. Paul Vogt, 113–19. London: SAGE.

Walkerdine, Valerie. 2003. 'Reclassifying Upward Mobility: Femininity and the Neo-Liberal Subject.' *Gender and Education* 15 (3): 237–48.

Wark, McKenzie. 2004. *A Hacker Manifesto*. Cambridge, MA: Harvard University Press.

Wark, McKenzie. 2017. 'What If This Is Not Capitalism Any More, but Something Worse? NPS Plenary Lecture, APSA 2015, Philadelphia, PA.' *New Political Science* 39 (1): 58–66.

Woodman, Dan. 2011. 'Young People and the Future: Multiple Temporal Orientations Shaped in Interaction with Significant Others.' *Young: Nordic Journal of Youth Research* 19 (2): 111–28.

Woodman, Dan, and Steven Threadgold. 2011. 'The Future of the Sociology of Youth: Institutional, Theoretical and Methodological Challenges.' *Youth Studies Australia* 30 (3): 8–12.

Wyn, Johanna. 2012. 'The Making of a Generation: Policy and the Lives and Aspirations of Generation X.' *Journal of Educational Administration and History* 44 (3): 269–82.

CHAPTER 6

Neo-Liberal Capitalism and the War on Young People: Growing Up with the Illusion of Choice and the Ambivalence of Freedom

Peter Kelly

1   Introduction

In his *The Future of an Illusion*, a short book that provides a psychoanalytic reading of religions and their attractiveness to humans, the roles that they play in human meaning making, Sigmund Freud (2004 [1927], 38–39) argued that:

> An illusion is not the same as an error, nor is it necessarily an error … In other words, we refer to a belief as an illusion when wish-fulfilment plays a prominent role in its motivation, and in the process we disregard its relationship to reality, just as the illusion itself dispenses with such accreditations …
>
> If, armed with this information, we return to the teachings of religion, we may say again: they are all illusions, unverifiable … Some of them are so improbable, so contrary to everything we have learnt so laboriously about the world, that … they can be likened to delusions.

I encountered Freud's words in John Gray's (2014) *The Silence of Animals: On Progress and Other Myths*. Gray is a prolific author, a former Professor of Politics at Oxford, and a political philosopher who is deeply skeptical about the faith that many of us invest in the possibilities of human progress. In giving expression to this skepticism he suggests that this faith is an illusion, hence his reference to Freud, and that the idea of human progress is mythic, a secular fiction we tell ourselves as we seek a meaningfulness to human existence. His account of this myth-making suggests that post Enlightenment secular humanism – made real in the disciplines we deal in, including philosophy and economics and psychology and sociology and feminism – shares much with many religions. Particularly at the level of making fictions that seem to fly in the face of historical evidence, even historical realities.

Gray (2014) tells a troubling story of a human history that continues to be marked by violence, wars, crises, totalitarianisms, actually existing free markets, democracies and individualisms, and a recent faith in the possibility of human perfectibility promised through the practice of reason. His telling of this history, updated for the particular globalising challenges and crises of the early 21st century embraces Marx's observation that *History repeats itself. First as Tragedy, then as Farce.*

A fundamental concern for Gray is the ways in which we continue to make fictions and elevate them to the level of illusion and myth, and continue to believe in them in the face of often overwhelming evidence to the contrary. As Simon Critchley (2013) writes in an *LA Review of Books* review of *The Silence of Animals*:

> HUMAN BEINGS DO NOT just make killer apps. We are killer apes. We are nasty, aggressive, violent, rapacious hominids, what John Gray calls in his widely read 2002 book, *Straw Dogs*, *homo rapiens*. But wait, it gets worse. We are a killer species with a metaphysical longing, ceaselessly trying to find some meaning to life, which invariably drives us into the arms of religion. Today's metaphysics is called "liberal humanism", with a quasi-religious faith in progress, the power of reason and the perfectibility of humankind ...
>
> Gray's most acute loathing is for the idea of progress, which has been his target in a number of books ... He allows that progress in the realm of science is a fact. (And also a good: as Thomas De Quincey remarked, a quarter of human misery results from toothache, so the discovery of anesthetic dentistry is a fine thing.) But faith in progress, Gray argues, is a superstition we should do without.

Critchley (2013) suggests that Gray, *contra* Descartes, imagines:

> that human irrationality is the thing most evenly shared in the world. To deny reality in order to sustain faith in a delusion is properly human. For Gray, the liberal humanist's assurance in the reality of progress is a barely secularized version of the Christian belief in Providence.

In this chapter I want to argue that 21st century capitalism is increasingly globalised, digitised and bio-genetic. Through myriad processes and developments, that are largely autonomous and reflexive, and which answer to a single logic above all others – privatise, monetise and commodify all that is possible in the pursuit of profit – the neo-Liberal version of capitalism individualises and atomises the person. This type of person is made responsible for the choices they make about all aspects of what we have come to know as a life (Childhood-Youth-Young Adulthood-Adulthood).

I want to suggest that the processes of making individuals responsible for the choices made and not made, and for the consequences of choices made and not made, can be thought about in terms of the *mythic dimensions* of choice, and the *ambivalence* that always accompanies the possibility of choice, the actuality of the practice of freedom, in 21st century neo-Liberal capitalism.

Drawing on the recent political philosophy of Gray, together with the sociological work of Zygmunt Bauman on ambivalence, and the concerns of Michel Foucault with ethics, the care of the self and the practice of freedom, I will argue that choice and freedom are not, as Nikolas Rose (1992) would say, *shams*. But they may well be, as Freud would argue, *illusions*.

In neo-Liberal capitalism choice and freedom are mythic. That is, they structure the dominant stories of what it is to be human, how it is that we have become who it is that we are, what it means to grow up in the first decades of the 21st century, to imagine, to *hope*, what a life is, what a life can be. These powerful illusions, and the ambivalences they produce, then divert our attention from neo-Liberalism's undeclared war on young people. From the consequences of the commodification and privatisation of education. From the possibility of the permanent disappearance and precariousness of work – our main hope for an earthly salvation. From the tragic dance of State, surveillance, in-security and freedom. From the rise of digital machines, networks and systems – the Internet of Things – that make billions of dollars for a very few, promise a version of *togetherness* for many, and spawn autonomous drones, vehicles, other non-human agents and the promise of war without human casualities – at least on 'our' side. And, from the brutality of millions of young people around the globe cast adrift as refugees and asylum seekers, sexually abused, humiliated and exploited, enslaved and forced to labour, criminalised and incarcerated, condemned, as Zygmunt Bauman (2004, p.12) argues, to live *wasted lives*.

2   What is Neo-Liberal Capitalism and Why is at War with Its Young? Or, Why is Neo-Liberal Capitalism Eating Its Young?

In contemporary sociological discourses neo-Liberalism is a much used, possibly little examined concept. In other spaces I have drawn on Foucault's (1991) work on governmentality to suggest that neo-Liberalism can be imagined as a mentality of rule, a moral project, an art of governing at-a-distance, that increasingly makes individuals responsible for the practice of freedom, the exercise of choice, and for the consequences of choices made and not made (Kelly 2013, Pike and Kelly 2014, Kelly and Pike 2017). As an art of government, neo-Liberalism is a vast assemblage, even *apparatus* (Foucault 1980; Agamben

2009), that brings together an array of political rationalities and governmental technologies (Rose and Miller 1992) in order to render 'reality' knowable, in ways that promise to make 'reality' governable.

This idea of apparatus, *dispositif* in the French, is important here because it points to a 'heterogeneous ensemble' (Foucault 1980) of actors, networks, materials and thoughts that are 'assembled', mostly loosely, always strategically, with the purpose to arrange the 'right disposition of things' – whatever those 'things' might be (Foucault 1991, also Law 2000). Foucault clarified his use of the term *dispositif* in a 1977 interview – published in the 1980 collection *Power/ Knowledge*. There he outlined three aspects of what he understood this concept to mean, and what it could do. First, he indicated that an apparatus can be imagined as:

> ... a thoroughly heterogenous ensemble consisting of discourses, institutions, architectural forms, regulatory decisions, laws, administrative measures, scientific statements, philosophical, moral and philanthropic propositions–in short, the said as much as the unsaid. Such are the elements of the apparatus. The apparatus itself is the system of relations that can be established between these elements.
> FOUCAULT 1980, 194.

In the second instance Foucault (1980, 194–195) suggests that it is 'precisely the nature of the connection that can exist between these heterogenous elements' that is of analytical interest:

> Thus, a particular discourse can figure at one time as the programme of an institution, and at another it can function as a means of justifying or masking a practice which itself remains silent, or as a secondary reinterpretation of this practice, opening out for it a new field of rationality. In short, between these elements, whether discursive or non-discursive, there is a sort of interplay of shifts of position and modifications of function which can also vary very widely.

Finally, Foucault (1980, 195) argues that an apparatus, as an assemblage of heterogeneous elements, has

> ... as its major function at a given historical moment that of responding to an *urgent need*. The apparatus thus has a dominant strategic function. This may have been, for example, ... a strategic imperative acting here

as the matrix for an apparatus which gradually undertook the control or subjection of madness, sexual illness and neurosis.

In relation to discourses of youth at risk, for example, I have used Foucault's work to think about such things as: the identification and analysis of systems of thought, systems of relations, that imagine such things as young people, education, sexuality – in their particularity and in their generality – in terms of risk; the nature of the interplay of diverse elements, and the consequences of this interplay; and the strategic function of an apparatus of risk, particularly in the context of neo-Liberal arts of government (Kelly 2006).

From this perspective neo-Liberalism is much more than economics or economic theory, much more than politics or political science. But this is just one way to know neo-Liberalism. In their Introduction to the *Kilburn Manifesto* the late Stuart Hall and Doreen Massey, and Michael Rustin (2013) try to capture and analyse a sense of our neo-Liberal present that is less genealogical. As a colleague and I suggested elsewhere, this more sociological present, a present that is post the Global Financial Crisis (GFC) of 2007–2009, is one that is marked by recession, sovereign debt crises, austerity and the language of *strivers and skivers*, and *lifters and leaners* (Kelly and Pike 2017).

For Hall and the others (Hall et al. 2013, 8–9) the 'current neoliberal settlement has … entailed the re-working of the common-sense assumptions of the earlier, social democratic settlement'. This making of 'common sense' requires the joining together of 'ideas beyond question, assumptions so deep that the very fact that they are assumptions is only rarely brought to light'. The bundle of beliefs we name as neo-Liberalism 'revolves around the supposed naturalness of "the market", the primacy of the competitive individual, the superiority of the private over the public' (see also Kelly 2017).

For hundreds of millions of young people the experience of growing up after the 2007–08 GFC, in the still echoing Great Recession in many of the OECD and EU economies, is one that is characterised by high levels of youth unemployment and precarious employment, student debt accompanying increased costs for higher education, housing costs that lock many out of home ownership, and challenges for physical and mental health and well-being.[1] Young people are being made to bear a heavy burden, to carry significant responsibilities for imagining their lives as an enterprise. An enterprise in which an

---

1 Evidenced, possibly, in the apparent explosions in the rates of anxiety disorders experienced by young people in the liberal democracies (see, for example, https://www.theguardian.com/society/anxiety).

investment in education and training and work increasingly looks like a *mortgaging* of an uncertain future. In mortgaging their future many young people are confounded by the possibility of repaying this debt, or of leveraging it into a life that was promised them if only they stayed in education and training, if only they got a job, if only they studied and worked hard, and had a wary, prudential eye to the future (Kelly 2016).

At the start of the 21st century the advanced neo-Liberal democracies are, argues Henry Giroux (2015, 224), characterised by a violence against the young that has:

> produced a generation without jobs, without an independent life, and without even the most minimal social benefits. Youth no longer occupy the hope of a privileged place that was offered to previous generations. They now inhabit a neoliberal notion of temporality that resembles dead time marked by a loss of faith in progress along with the emergence of apocalyptic narratives in which the future appears indeterminate, bleak, and insecure.

For Giroux (2015, 224) this violence is:

> produced in part through a massive shift in wealth to the upper one per cent, growing inequality, the reign of the financial services, the closing down of educational opportunities, and the stripping of benefits and resources from those marginalized by race and class.

And this, in nation state settings that are vastly over-privileged, both in relation to the majority of nations, and also to the vast majority of humans who struggle to eke out an existence on a planet remade through globalisation – of capitalism, of a commodity fetishism, and of the profit principle. Here neo-Liberalism can become ideological, as well as political, as well as economic. It may also have become mythic. My sense, then, is that we need to imagine neo-Liberalism as a globalising enactment of capitalism. Even if in different spaces and places a globalising neo-Liberal capitalism plays out in different ways, with different consequences. There are winners as well as losers in this war – even if it isn't a zero-sum game (see Kelly and Pike 2017).

Zymunt Bauman's (2004) *Wasted Lives: Modernity and its Outcasts* is still one of the most eloquent and poignant accounts of how an increasingly globalised, neo-Liberal capitalism is productive of waste – human and non-human – on a scale that is mostly beyond our imagining. Bauman (2004, 5–6) argues that this is the 'production of "human waste"', what he terms:

the "excessive" and "redundant", (that is the population of those who either could not or were not wished to be recognised or allowed to stay), is an inevitable outcome of modernization.

These modernisation processes can, largely, be understood in terms of the colonisation of all aspects of life, of all spaces and places, by market forces, practices and processes under regimes of capital accumulation. As Bauman (2004, 5–7) suggests, when processes of modernisation have become truly globalised, when the 'totality of human production and consumption has become money and market mediated', and the commodification 'of human livelihoods have penetrated every nook and cranny of the globe', then the *'crisis of the human waste disposal industry'* has become more acute. A key element to Bauman's argument is that the history of European colonisation is a history characterised by exporting 'redundant humans' to the *pre-modern, under-developed* spaces of the Americas, Africa, Asia and the Pacific. The triumphant globalisation of neo-Liberal capitalism has resulted not only in the continued over production of wasted lives in the *over-developed* West, but also the disappearance of a colonial solution to *waste disposal*. Indeed, the figures of the *immigrant*, the *asylum seeker* and the *refugee* represent the reversal of the flows of waste disposal: a reversal that provokes fear and anxiety in the imaginations of the 21st century inhabitants of the affluent, but increasingly insecure, West.

Being redundant, being surplus to requirements, means that individuals are confronted with a life that does not provide the means to secure a livelihood. Redundancy, the sense that you, or I, or we are of limited or no use – particularly in social, cultural and commercial environments in which *usefulness* not only brings material rewards, but also gives purpose and meaning to a life – can have profound consequences for a sense of self. As Bauman (2004, 12) suggests: 'To be "redundant" means to be supernumerary, unneeded, of no use – whatever the needs and uses are that set the standard of usefulness and indispensability'. Redundancy implies that the 'others do not need you; they can do as well, and better, without you'. What is more, to be redundant suggests that there is no 'self evident reason for your being around and no obvious justification for your claim to have the right to stay around'. To have been made redundant (and not just in the narrow sense of losing your job) 'means to have been disposed of *because of being disposable* – just like the empty and non-refundable plastic bottle or once-used syringe, an unattractive commodity with no buyers ...' (see also Kelly and Harrison 2009).

My suggestion here is that this is a 'war' fought on the ground of freedom, in the logics of choice. We are told, we tell young people: You choose! You should have the choice! A good life is one in which we have choices. In which we are free to choose. But you carry the responsibility for the making of choices, and for the consequences of the choices made!

3   The Illusion of Choice, The Ambivalence of Freedom

As I suggested earlier, the scale of an array of crises at the start of the 21st century, of human suffering and despair, of the exploitation and mass extinctions of non-human organisms and planetary eco-systems, of possibly irreversible climate change, should provide a mass of evidence to unsettle humanism's myth of human progress and reveal this belief as an illusion (Gray 2014). The mountains of data that point to the amassing and hoarding of wealth by a tiny percentage of the planet's human population – extracted via what Rosi Braidotti (2013) calls the *thanato-politics* of global capitalism's endless cycle of destruction and consumption to produce surplus value – should make explicit the mythic dimensions of choice. It should reveal the social, and privatised, ambivalence of the freedom that we tell ourselves that we exercise.

In the remainder of this chapter I want to briefly introduce what it is that I mean by suggesting that young people, under these circumstances, might be growing up with, might be struggling with, the *illusion of choice* and the *ambivalence of freedom*.

There are any number of ways in which this could be approached. I don't particularly want to go down the path of the *ideological*, suggesting that we mis-recognise our true positions, and that our investments in stories of choice and freedom might be falsely conscious. Though I have found Stuart Hall's (1986) work in this space particularly helpful when he suggests that the ideological is the space in which *no necessary correspondence* (between, for example, signifiers such as 'choice' and 'better outcomes' in education) becomes *necessary correspondence*. This is the space in which the possibilities of choice and freedom in neo-Liberal capitalism become unquestioned assumptions, beliefs and myths beyond question. This is an active process of meaning making in which a whole array of often diverse interests, actants and processes are at play in the work of joining things together in ways that make them appear as natural, as self-evident common-sense. The connections to Foucault's concept of a neo-Liberal *dispositif* should be apparent here.

And I also don't want to follow Freud all the way down a psychoanalytic 'rabbit hole' in thinking about illusions and myths in terms of psychic processes. Though, once again, the idea that there are psychic processes, often unconscious, at play in shaping our attachments to ideas that don't seem to stand up to close, critical, intense scrutiny has some attraction. Why do many people, for example, continue to believe in an Almighty? And to do so with increasingly murderous intent and consequences? We want to believe that we are free. We want to hope that we have choices. That we can shape the world we live in. Yet, there may be masses of evidence to the contrary. And we will respond in different ways to that evidence. But why do we continue to hope, to believe in the face of our incapacity to choose, to change the world?

The argument here is not that we do not have choices, that we do not make choices, that we do not live with the consequences of our choices. Even if we make choices under circumstances we do not often choose, and the choices we might make appear, often, insignificant in light of the scale and reach and orders of magnitude of these circumstances.[2] And we mostly don't know in advance what the consequences of our choices will be. It is in thinking through particular choices, in particular circumstances, in imagining what, indeed, a choice might be, might consist of, what alternatives, what other possibilities exist, what happens if I make this choice and not another, that we can see the ways in which ambivalence is such a fundamental part of the human experience (Bauman 1989).

Neo-Liberal capitalism can be said to be energised by, and, indeed, to produce a qualitatively different, spectacularly enhanced ambivalence. And, as Zygmunt Bauman (2001), Ulrich Beck (2016) and others have argued, to leave it to individuals to work through this ambivalence under their own steam, and live with the consequences of their differing capabilities to do so.

With these qualifications and observations in mind I want to briefly return to John Gray and his discussion of human progress and other modern myths. In the first instance I want to trouble the 'faith' invested in the neo-Liberal idea of markets, the neo-Liberal idea of competition, the neo-Liberal idea of choice, and the neo-Liberal idea of freedom. A 'faith' that is made real in such ideas as the 'invisible hand' of a free market that if left to its own devices, will enable individuals, in pursuit of an 'enlightened self-interest', to maximise their choices and the benefits of these choices – not just for themselves, but for other choice making, profit-maximising individuals (Friedman and Friedman 1980, Hayek 1944, 1967a & 1967b, 1989).

This troubling requires the development of a view of freedom and power that does not see in the emergence or presence of one, the disappearance of the other. The back story here comes from Foucault's work on power relations, and the subjects of power. For Foucault (1991, 95), the emergence of modern arts of government are signalled, in part, by the movement of those who

---

2 'Man makes his own history, but he does not make it out of the whole cloth; he does not make it out of conditions chosen by himself, but out of such as he finds close at hand'. Karl Marx, *The Eighteenth Brumaire of Louis Bonaparte*.

govern from a concern with enforcing obedience to sovereign forms of power, to a concern with a 'plurality of specific aims', a 'whole series of specific finalities' as marking the ends of the practice of government. A key element in this framework is the notion of *disposition*. To *dispose* signals a shift from the idea of government as being primarily concerned with a transcendental sovereignty that achieved its end, of obedience to the Sovereign (Law), through 'obedience to the laws'. Law and sovereignty here 'were absolutely inseparable'. In the concern to conceive of the arts of government there is an acknowledgment that government cannot solely be a question of 'imposing law on men'. Rather, in emphasising the *disposition* of things, the art of government becomes more a question of imagining how it might be possible, strategically, 'to arrange things in such a way that, through a certain number of means, such and such ends may be achieved'.

As I have argued elsewhere (Kelly 2013) this is a quite specific characterisation of power in its pastoral form; a characterisation that marks pastoral power off from power as domination, or from a relationship of violence. For Foucault (1983, 220), this form of power relation is defined, not as a 'mode of action' which acts 'directly and immediately on others', as in a relationship of violence which 'forces', 'bends', 'destroys' and/or 'closes the door on all possibilities'. Rather, a power relation, in this sense, is characterised by 'action upon action', on existing actions or on those which may arise in the present or future: 'Power is exercised only over free subjects, and only insofar as they are free'. Here, to speak of freedom suggests that individuals and groups, as the subjects of power, are situated in a 'field of possibilities in which several ways of behaving, several reactions and diverse comportments may be realised'. Imagining power in this manner avoids some of the problems associated with seeing power and freedom as *oppositions*, as being 'mutually exclusive (freedom disappears everywhere power is exercised)'. Foucault (1983, 221) sees the interplay between power and freedom in the 'shepherd game' as being far more complicated:

> In this game freedom may well appear as the condition for the exercise of power (at the same time its precondition, since freedom must exist for power to be exerted, and also its permanent support, since without the possibility of recalcitrance, power would be equivalent to a physical determination).[3]

As we (Kelly and Harrison 2009) suggested in *Working in Jamie's Kitchen* there is a need to develop a vocabulary, a politics that can engage with and trouble,

---

3 These ideas have been more fully developed in Kelly & Harrison 2009 and Kelly 2013.

even unsettle, these powerful illusions, these powerful myths. The task, as we imagined it then, was to explore the processes, forces, tactics, knowledges, self understandings, practices of self transformation and choices that can become evident in a framework that draws on Foucault's work on power, government, the care of the self, and the practice of freedom. And to identify and analyse the consequences – intended or otherwise – of the play of these forces and processes, and the particular forms that freedom takes in particular times and spaces.

Such analyses could be situated in what Nikolas Rose (1992, 3) has called *critical sociologies of freedom*. We suggested that critical or genealogical analyses of freedom of the type envisaged by Rose – the *texture* of which derives from the later Foucault – would explore and analyse the myriad ways in which freedom has informed, and informs, the Liberal and neo-Liberal rationalities of government that have given shape to individual and collective lives in Western democracies since the 18th century. As Rose (1992, 3–4) argues, these 'investigations would not be critical *of* freedom. They would not try to reveal freedom as a sham, or to decry the freedom we *think* we have in the name of a truer freedom to come'. Rather, these analyses would examine the ways in which we 'have come to define and act towards ourselves in terms of a certain notion of freedom'. As Rose suggests, contemporary 'advanced liberal' mentalities of rule are framed by conceptualisations of choice and freedom that rely on, are embedded in, and emerge from certain, *technical*, understandings of the person, and of the aptitudes, the behaviours, the skills, the dispositions that the individual should possess, exhibit and be capable of exercising in order to practise their freedom in appropriate ways in different contexts and relations.

In these formulations of government we are imagined as individuals who are *economic* (prudent, entrepreneurial, choice making) in the conduct of our lives. We are imagined as not only capable but *desiring* of being able to exercise our freedom through a myriad of choices in all realms of our existence. We are imagined as individuals who are, passionate, or *aspirational* in terms of our capacities for betterment, advancement, and the creation of a particular *lifestyle*. None of these are a *sham*, but they emerge from, and give shape to the fields of possibilities in which we contrive to fashion a life – and they should be unsettled in order to explore their limitations and possibilities.

4 Conclusion: *Hope Without Optimism?*

In ways that echo much of the discussion to this point, Terry Eagleton's (2015) *Hope Without Optimism* takes elegant aim at the shallowness and naiveté that, he suggests, characterises an optimistic disposition: a Pollyanna-erish orientation to the ambivalence and irony of the human condition that glosses the evidence of human history, as it invests heavily in the promise of human progress. In his opening chapter – *The Banality of Optimism* – a sometimes withering critique of Matt Ridley's *The Rational Optimist* provides the means for Eagleton to open up the spaces in which to make explicit distinctions between human capacities for optimism and hope. For Eagleton (2015, 24):

> If the past cannot simply be deleted ... it is not least because it is a vital constituent of the present. We can progress beyond it, to be sure, but only by means of the capabilities which it has bequeathed us. The habits bred by generations of supremacy and subservience, arrogance and inertia, are not to be unlearned overnight. Instead they constitute an Ibsenesque legacy of guilt and debt which contaminates the roots of human creativity, infiltrating the bones and bloodstream of contemporary history and entwining itself with our more enlightened impulses.

Some would argue that a lack of faith in a human capacity for progress, a focus on the history of human irrationality, violence, illusion and myth making, a sense that what is 'unique about the human animal' is our capacity to 'grow knowledge at an accelerating rate while being chronically incapable of learning from experience' (Gray 2014, 75), appears to leave little room for the human capacity for hope, for love, for kindness, for struggle, for 'redemption', for some sort of meaning to human existence, that often emerges so powerfully in the moments and spaces of most despair. But, that is, possibly, a misreading of what Gray and others should provoke us to imagine. As Eagleton (2015, 5) argues:

> Only if you view your situation as critical do you recognise the need to transform it. Dissatisfaction can be a goad to reform. The sanguine, by contrast, are likely to come up with sheerly cosmetic solutions. True hope is needed most when the situation is at its starkest, a state of extremity that optimism is generally loath to acknowledge.

The challenge, in terms of young people and a politics of outrage and hope, is to imagine what such a politics would look like if we trouble and unsettle the myth of human progress, the illusion of choice, and the ambivalence of freedom. And do the difficult, never-ending work of imagining and enacting a politics of outrage and hope that might be shaped by such things as Michel Foucault's self-description of his hyper- but pessimistic activism; or Zygmunt Bauman's critical sociological mission that is framed by an embrace of the ambivalence and irony that characterises human experience; or Lauren Berlant's (2011) sense that 'cruel optimism' – the 'condition of maintaining an attachment to a significantly problematic object' – is 'cruel' precisely because it is so fundamental to a 'sense of what it means to keep on living on and to look forward to being in the world' (Berlant 2011, 24); or Sarah Ahmed's (2010) claim that to be a 'killjoy' – to trouble the 'promise of happiness' that shapes so much of what we are told our lives 'should' be – is to 'open a life, to make room for life, to make room for possibility, for chance' (Ahmed 2010, 20); or Rosi Braidotti's (2013) framing of hope as an 'anticipatory virtue' that enables humans to imagine 'possible futures'; or …

In the end, it is this governmental obligation, this moral project of making people responsible for the choices to be made, and the consequences of choices made and not made that needs to be unsettled by claiming that neo-Liberal capitalism is 'eating its young', is confounding large numbers of young people as they grow up with the illusion of choice and the ambivalence of freedom.

Resilience. Aspiration. Choice. Freedom. These are key words in contemporary governmental rationalities shaping an array of programs and interventions with young people. It is how these sorts of ideas are joined up, articulated as Stuart Hall (1986) would have said, to an array of moral projects of government that needs troubling. It is the processes of meaning making, the cultural politics, that form ideas such as these into powerful contemporary myths that come to appear as self-evident common-sense that we need to unsettle.

References

Agamben, G. (2009) *What is an Apparatus?* Stanford University Press. Stanford.
Ahmed, S. (2010) *The Promise of Happiness*. Duke University Press. Durham and London.
Bauman, Z. 1989. *Modernity and the Holocaust*. Cambridge: Polity Press.
Bauman, Z. 2001. *The Individualized Society*. Cambridge: Polity Press.
Bauman, Z. 2004. *Wasted Lives: Modernity and its Outcasts*. Cambridge: Polity Press.
Beck, U. (2016). *The Metamorphosis of the World*. Polity Press. Cambridge.
Berlant, L. (2011) *Cruel Optimism*. Duke University Press. Durham and London.
Braidotti, R. 2013. *The Posthuman*. Cambridge. Polity Press.
Critchley, S. (2013) John Gray's Godless Mysticism: On "The Silence of Animals", *LA Review of Books*, https://lareviewofbooks.org/review/john-grays-godless-mysticism-on-the-silence-of-animals, accessed 19 November 2015.

Eagleton, T. (2015) *Hope Without Optimism*. Yale University Press. New haven and London.

Foucault, M. (1980) The Confession of the Flesh. In Colin Gordon (ed) *Power/Knowledge Selected Interviews and Other Writings* 1980: pp. 194–228. This interview was conducted by a round-table of historians.

Foucault, M. (1983). The Subject and Power. In H.L. Dreyfus & P. Robinow, *Michel Foucault: Beyond Structuralism and Hermeneutics*, University of Chicago Press, Chicago, pp. 208–226.

Foucault, M. 1991. Governmentality. In G. Burchell, C. Gordon & P. Miller (eds) *The Foucault Effect: Studies in Governmental Rationality*. Hemel Hempstead, Harvester Wheatsheaf, pp. 87–104.

Freud, S. [1927](2004) *The Future of an Illusion*, Penguin, London.

Friedman, M. and R. Friedman (1980) *Free to Choose*, Macmillan, Melbourne.

Giroux, H. (2015) Resisting youth and the crushing State Violence of Neoliberalism. In P. Kelly and A. Kamp (eds) *A Critical Youth Studies for the 21st Century*, Brill, Amsterdam/Boston, pp. 223–241.

Gray, J. (2014) *The Silence of Animals: On Progress and Other Modern Myths*. London. Penguin.

Hall, S. 1986. On Postmodernism and Articulation. *Journal of Communication Inquiry*. 10(2), pp. 45–60.

Hall, S., D. Massey, and M. Rustin. 2013. After neoliberalism: analysing the present. In S. Hall, D. Massey and M. Rustin. eds. After neoliberalism? The Kilburn manifesto. Soundings.

Hayek, F.A. (1944) *The Road to Serfdom*, Routledge and Kegan Paul, London.

Hayek, F.A. (1967a) 'The Road to Serfdom after Twelve Years', in F.A. Hayek, *Studies in Philosophy, Politics and Economics,* University of Chicago Press, Chicago, pp. 216–228.

Hayek, F.A. (1967b) The Principles of a Liberal Social Order, in F.A. Hayek, *Studies in Philosophy, Politics and Economics,* University of Chicago Press, Chicago, pp. 178–194.

Hayek, F.A. (1989) *The Fatal Conceit: The Errors of Socialism*, University of Chicago Press, Chicago.

Kelly, P. and L. Harrison. (2009) *Working in Jamie's Kitchen: Salvation, Passion and Young Workers*. Palgrave. London.

Kelly, P. (2006) The Entrepreneurial Self and Youth at-Risk: Exploring the Horizons of Identity in the 21st Century, *Journal of Youth Studies*, 9 (1), pp. 17–32.

Kelly, P. (2013) *The Self as Enterprise: Foucault and the "Spirit" of 21st Century Capitalism* Ashgate/Gower, Aldershot.

Kelly, P. (2016) Growing up After the GFC: Responsibilisation and Mortgaged Futures, *Discourse*, DOI: 10.1080/01596306.2015.1104852

Kelly, P. (2017) Young People's Marginalisation: Unsettling What Agency and Structure Mean After Neo-Liberalism, in P. Kelly and J. Pike (eds) (2016) *Neo-Liberalism and Austerity: The Moral Economies of Young People's Health and Well-Being*, Palgrave, London, pp. 35–52.

Kelly, P. and J. Pike (eds) (2017) *Neo-Liberalism and Austerity: The Moral Economies of Young People's Health and Well-Being*, Palgrave, London.

Law, J (2000) On the Subject of the Object: Narrative, Technology, and Interpellation. *Configurations*, Volume 8, Number 1, pp. 1–29.

Pike, J. and P. Kelly (2014) *The moral geographies of children, young people and food: Beyond Jamie's School Dinners*, Palgrave, London.

Rose, N. 1992. *Towards a Critical Sociology of Freedom*, Inaugural Lecture, 5 May, London: Goldsmiths College, University of London.

Rose, N. and P. Miller (1992) Political Power beyond the State: problematics of government, *British Journal of Sociology*, Vol. 43, No. 2, pp. 173–205.

PART 2

Education, Work and the Promise of Hope

∵

CHAPTER 7

Making the Hopeful Citizen in Precarious Times

Rosalyn Black

1   Introduction: Citizenship and the Project of Hope

Since the Global Financial Crisis or GFC of 2008–2009 and the austerity measures that numerous nations have adopted in its wake, education and citizenship have both become, in different ways, a means by which increasing numbers of young people are encouraged to live in hope. The "politics of aspiration" (Raco 2009:438) is often used to describe the hopes that young people are expected to nurture for educational, economic and other positional goods and forms of security in the face of growing economic precarity. The causes and effects of this precarity on many aspects of young people's lives have been described in numerous recent studies (e.g. Walsh and Black 2015). I don't intend to replicate that account here. Instead, my concern is with the ways in which, in the face of this precarity, young people are increasingly encouraged to engage in a form of optimism that one commentator has described as "magical thinking: believing you can have everything you want if you strategise shrewdly, reinvent yourself, push upscale, stay hungry and keep the faith" (Bidisha 2015). Young people, like the rest of society, are expected to create their own opportunities and, as Cooper (2012, 13) notes, "any notion that the social state should support young people to realise their hopes and ambitions is now derided".

The politics of aspiration could also be used to describe the hopes that many young people have for citizenship. This includes the longing for belonging, and the aspirations for educational and social mobility of a vast and growing number of young migrants, refugees or asylum seekers with marginal or liminal citizenship status. It could also be used to describe the hopes and desires for recognition and influence held by young people who are citizens but who occupy the precarious spaces of socio-geographic disadvantage.

These hopes and desires are also embedded in the notion of active citizenship. A growing body of educational projects, practices and policies purport to produce resilient and hopeful young citizens who can ensure their own meaningful educational, cultural, social, economic and political participation within the precarious contexts of contemporary life. These projects, practices and policies represent a curious combination of purposes, creating deeply ambiguous experiences for young people who are already bearing the brunt of the precarity of globalisation as well as residual forms of localised disadvantage. They encourage these young people to be – or to become – hopeful young citizens who can "make a difference" personally, locally and societally, but they also seek to make them different, to make or remake them as citizens. This includes channelling or containing other responses that they may have to precarity, such as outrage, protest or democratic disengagement.

The question remains as to what purposes are being pursued through this enlistment of young people's active citizenship within a politics of hope. Active citizenship is an idea with a very long history, and there are equally longstanding concerns about its genesis and use. Drawing on data from a small scale study, this chapter examines the way in which hope is employed as a neoliberal strategy for making or remaking active young citizens in economically precarious places. The chapter is informed by Appadurai's ideas about the politics of hope: *Democracy rests on a vision. And all visions require hope* (*Appadurai 2007, 29*). It also draws on work by Isin (2009) which considers the ways in which citizens are made or remade by governmental projects, practices and policies.

2   From Risk to Hope

The vast sociological literature on young people and risk has argued for some time that youth as a construct, and specific groups of young people in particular, are "the focus of the fears, rather than the hopes, of western societies" (Pain et al. 2010, 972). There is little doubt that young people remain subject to deep political concerns about their engagement in the democratic project. Young people living in economically depressed or precarious places are particularly subject to a disturbingly pervasive distrust, accusation and stigmatisation as *"pessimistic disaffected citizen[s]"* (Cammaerts et al. 2014, 646, original emphasis), or as dangerous citizens in need of containment or control (Pickard 2014).

This mistrust of young people as citizens emerges readily from the public discourse at times of social unrest or protest. Events such as the so-called London riots of August 2011 have sparked a fierce public debate about the nature of youth and the social belonging of young people. Where some commentators highlighted the role of entrenched socioeconomic inequality and precarity in seeding the riots, others characterised the young people involved in them as "immoral, disrespectful, criminal, undisciplined, materialistic and hedonistic"

(Cooper 2012,7), "a generation that has no sense of community spirit or social solidarity" (O'Neill 2011).

Even policy documents which acknowledge the role of economic precarity in young people's outrage, protest or democratic disengagement describe it – and, to an extent, young people themselves – as a problem to be solved. This statement by the European Commission is a case in point:

> Europe is facing the risk of the emergence of a new "lost generation" whose life prospects are very uncertain as they have to face a decrease in their well-being and that of their children in a generation's time (2015, 6).

There is also a persistent counter-discourse, however, which establishes young people as the subjects of more hopeful purposes. It could be said that young people carry the symbolic burden of hope for the future, as critical actors and carriers of the hopeful project of national, regional and global democracy and stability. This counter-discourse is fast becoming ubiquitous within education and youth policy. At the same time as they have seen the development of austerity measures with dire consequences for young people, the years since the GFC have also seen the continued development of educational projects, practices and policies that purport to produce active young citizens, young people whose citizenship is constructed in very specific ways. Active young citizens are those who can ensure their own social, economic and political participation within the precarious contexts of contemporary life. They are citizens with the skills to "secure some sort of parlous redemption in the globalised, increasingly precarious labour markets of twenty-first-century capitalism" (Kelly 2015, 2). They are also "aspirational citizens" (Raco 2009, 436) who are able to employ and create hope as a resource – for themselves, their communities and for society as a whole.

3   Imagining a Better World

As Wrigley (2012, 105) and his colleagues have noted, "part of a politics of hope relates to the encouragement of students to imagine other, to imagine a better world". European education and youth policy provides plenty of examples of this encouragement. The Council of Europe's Charter on Education for Democratic Citizenship and Human Rights Education, for example, describes the role of education in enabling young people "to exercise and defend their democratic rights and responsibilities in society, to value diversity and to play an active part in democratic life, with a view to the promotion and protection of democracy and the rule of law" (Council of Europe 2010, 5–6). The main objectives of the European Union's 2010–2018 Youth Strategy, designed to promote young people's economic, political and social participation, is to foster active citizenship and "encourage young people to actively participate in society" (European Commission 2015a). In 2015, it released funding for a new research project, CATCH-EyoU, which seeks to engender a "cutting-edge conceptualisation of youth active citizenship in the EU" (European Commission 2015b).

These and many other similar statements reflect the expectation that contemporary young people act as citizens in the traditional sense of the word: that is, by voting, paying their taxes, abiding by the laws of the nation and, when need dictates, engaging in activities for the public good such as recycling, donating blood or volunteering at times of crisis. They also reflect the expectation that young people act as citizens in ways that improve their own lives and circumstances, as well as support various forms of social and environmental justice. They depict young people as global citizen actors, "self-perfecting cosmopolitans" (Kennelly and Dillabough 2008, 493), who are responsible for fostering their own hopes for a better future (Shiller 2013), but who must also take hopeful action as agents for change, whether to contain the factors contributing to climate change (Ojala 2012), to combat social disintegration in conflict-affected areas (Akar 2014), or, in economically precarious contexts, to be "*the* critical hope" for the future of their communities (Cuervo 2011, 126, original emphasis).

Such expectations constitute young people as a collective symbol of "hopefulness and future aspiration" (Bradford and Cullen 2014, 1), even in the face of political, social and economic precarity and the rapidly escalating unrest and inequality that comes with it. In this way, they also constitute young people as actors in one of the most recent iterations of the "politics of hope" (Appadurai 2007, 29). This equation between young people and a more hopeful democratic future informs the kind of policy I mentioned earlier. It is also woven into the rhetoric and calls to action of protest movements such as Occupy and Fight for 15. In the United States, for example, media coverage of Occupy rallies characterised young people as "prime mover[s] in perhaps the most promising protest movement to sweep the country in decades" (Manson 2011).

A similar equation is also increasingly reflected in the sociological literature. A recent study of young people's democratic attitudes claims that despite their general disenchantment with established representational political systems and processes, young people are also "the most likely, to a significant degree, to hold ambitious and idealist notions about what democratic participation should be like and about how involved they actually say they want to be"

(Cammaerts et al. 2014, 648). This and numerous other studies highlight young people's role as transformative citizenship actors, "co-creators in the political, in their own political socialization and in the creation of society" (Andersson 2015, 14). It describes their engagement in acts and practices of citizenship that include online campaigns (Harris et al. 2010), cloud, swarm and other network initiatives (Tormey 2015), cultural production and consumption (Harris and Roose 2013), the creation of "action camps" for young activists (Juris and Pleyers 2009), volunteering (Smith et al. 2005) and legal graffiti programs (Baker 2015). These acts and practices are credited not only with the potential to generate "more creative and alternative forms of economic, social and political organisation" (Williamson 2014, 15) but with the potential to challenge and change existing forms.

4   The Purpose of Hope

There are concerns that young people's education for active citizenship is chiefly a form of political socialization, a way of engaging their commitment to existing political and social orders, institutions and citizenship practices (see Down 2004, Banaji 2008, Edwards 2009, Harris 2010, Amnå and Ekman 2014). A number of studies (e.g. Kennelly 2009, Gordon and Taft 2011, Boudreau et al. 2015) have described the experience of young people who engage in conscious acts of citizenship that challenge these normative practices and who are warned, through their encounters with police and the justice system, about "the boundaries of permissible citizenship" (Kennelly 2009, 145). Isin (2009, 383) has voiced similar concerns about the project of active citizenship overall:

> In my words, active citizenship has become a script for already existing citizens to follow already existing paths. It is most often used to denote the kinds of behaviour that citizens ostensibly follow. Thus, it is always tied into governmental practices through which conduct is produced.

There are also concerns that active citizenship is chiefly a neoliberal technology, one that is designed to foster the "self-making" of the contemporary young citizen (Aldenmyr et al. 2012, 258) as "an active agent in his or her government" (Miller and Rose 2008). This is part of a wider concern about the use of "citizenship as government" (Rygiel 2011, 11) – that is, as a set of "practices, discourses, technologies, forms of power and political subjectivities" which are mobilised not only to govern groups of young citizens but to encourage and direct the self-governing of the individual young citizen.

Isin suggests that the key question about citizenship in neoliberal times has become not "who *is* the citizen" but "what *makes* the citizen?" (Isin 2009, 383, original emphases). The school remains one of the chief strategies or mechanisms by which young people are "made up – encouraged, incited, directed, educated, trained" (Kelly 2015, 11) as active citizens. Especially in economically precarious places, this process includes the making up of the young citizen into "a unit of human and social capital that can be bound together with other units in a common entrepreneurial project designed to deliver economic productivity, social cohesiveness and individual benefit" (Black et al. 2016, 159).

In order to better understand the way in which this making up takes place in places characterised by precarity, I would like to reflect on my small scale study of two Australian schools that have each implemented a curriculum of active citizenship for their middle-year students: the Student Leader program at what I will call Eastview College and the Making A Difference (MAD) program at what I refer to as Valley High School. The study was conducted in 2010 as part of my PhD research, with ethics clearance from The University of Melbourne.

Each school was selected on the basis of its potential to provide a critical rather than a typical case (Flyvberg 2006; Yin 2013). Both schools are small to medium-sized government schools located in peri-urban or rural communities that are characterized by economic precarity and that are periodically identified as some of the most socio-economically disadvantaged areas in the state. Both schools cater to local young people whose families largely rely on low skilled and poorly paid employment in manufacturing or rural industries that are fluid and uncertain. Where young people are employed, this is often in casual roles in the same insecure workforces. Poor public transport services mean that young people in both areas are subject to a perceived isolation. They are also frequently associated with local vandalism and petty crime.

The recruitment of educators and students for interviews followed the purposive sampling logic of the critical case. It was not my intention in this study to examine what young people and educators collectively believe about education for active citizenship, and my sample size was not designed to permit such an examination. Rather, my intention was to understand the experience of educators and young people who had had consistent or in-depth involvement in an active citizenship curriculum.

Two semi-structured individual interviews were conducted at each school: one with the school principal and one with the teacher or co-ordinator primarily responsible for the implementation of the relevant active citizenship curriculum. These interviews were designed to shed light on the authorising context for the curriculum's creation and introduction, including the school and system priorities that informed it. At each school, one focus group interview was then held with the teachers involved in delivering each curriculum, in order to illustrate their more personal motivations and experiences in its development and delivery as well as their perceptions of their students' experience within the curriculum. These focus groups involved two teachers at Eastview College and three teachers at Valley High School.

Finally, one focus group interview was held at each school with students who had participated in the curriculum. The selection of students was determined by the curriculum co-ordinator at each school, reflecting which cohort was most involved in the curriculum at the time of the interviews. At Eastview College, around half of the students were in Year Eight at the time of interview and half were in Year Nine. At Valley High School, all students were in Year Nine at the time of interview. At both schools, the focus groups comprised almost equal numbers of male and female students.

5   Hope as a Resource

Earlier, I cited the observation by Wrigley and his colleagues that part of the politics of hope encourages young people to imagine a better world. The structure of the active citizenship curriculum differs across the two schools. At Eastview College, the Student Leader program engages a small group of students who have had to compete for selection in the program. At Valley High School, the MAD program is conducted as part of the core curriculum, engaging all Year Nine students over the course of an entire semester.

In each case, the nature and aims of the curriculum are similar. Each curriculum seeks to position students as citizen actors capable of imagining and engineering social or environmental change through practical projects. Some of these have a global focus: they are designed to address large scale issues such as poverty, racism and human rights. Others are focused on and located within the local community. These include campaigns for better youth recreation facilities or to raise local community awareness of issues facing young people such as drink-driving, bullying, drug use and discrimination against LGBTI young people. They also include campaigns for better local public transport and projects to develop the local rail trail, encourage local reforestation, and create productive community gardens.

Another part of the politics of hope is more personal; it encourages young people to imagine a better life. The discursive promise of active citizenship offers young people in economically precarious places the chance to enter a "citizen space" (Arnot and Swartz 2012, 2) from which they may otherwise be excluded. More than this, it offers them "the chance to dream as citizens of better lives" (Arnot and Swartz 2012, 7).

At both schools, educators were deeply concerned about student disengagement and early school leaving in the middle years and what this might mean for students' transition to further education or employment. Valley High School's submission to the state government education authority about the need for the new curriculum highlights the school leadership's concerns about high student absenteeism and a poor sense of connectedness to the school and to schooling, but also decreased levels of student self-esteem, direction and aspiration.

Both schools have implemented their active citizenship curriculum as part of a strategy to address these concerns. At both, the curriculum is constructed as an important educational resource which will prepare young people for success in the final years of schooling and for labour market participation, both of which are strongly associated in educational discourse as markers of a good or successful life. As an extension of this, each curriculum is constructed as a means of making students into "self-regulating, economically autonomous and employable" citizens (Wood and Black 2014, 58). At Eastview College, the school principal describes his hope that the Student Leader program will enable students to become "well informed citizens who've got a job that they're happy with" (2010). At Valley High School, the principal describes similar hopes in relation to the MAD curriculum:

> there's a little bit of hope that this better prepares students for their senior years. [...] now that students are more confident in themselves, more engaged, we then start talking career and future steps (2010).

6 Hope as Prophylactic

This same hope that their experiences of active citizenship will secure a better future also emerges from the narratives of the young people themselves:

> [The MAD program will] help you in life, for the future (student, Valley High School, 2010)
>
> If you have your resume, it's better if you have a leadership role so you can take on board lots of job opportunities (student, Eastview College, 2010).

Miles has criticised the tendency of youth sociologists to romanticise young people's relationship to citizenship and social change: his premise is that young people, at least in the Western context, "are rarely radical and are much more likely to be in the habit of reinforcing the status quo" (Miles 2015, 101). Bronwyn Wood and I have previously noted that the model of citizenship which is promoted and permitted within active citizenship curricula is an *active* citizen model rather than an *activist* one: it is "likely to follow pre-organised scripts that are tightly structured along timelines to meet assessment deadlines and pre-established outcomes" (Wood and Black 2014, 63). At both schools, the active citizenship curriculum is rich with the language of change and transformation, but the change that it promotes is bounded by normative ideas of what constitutes desirable citizenship behaviour: that is, the "responsible pursuit of normative aspirations for a good life in the future" (Zipin et al. 2015, 230).

This recalls the findings of other recent studies such as that of Bryant and Ellard (2015, 489–497). Their interviews with young people in metropolitan Sydney who were subject to "massive uncertainty" in the form of homelessness, incarceration, addiction and suspension or expulsion from school or work, found that those who could envisage a possible future did so in terms of "what they called "normal" life: a job, a safe home and a family". In the face of poverty, family breakdown, abuse and violence, these young people all "managed to generate hope for something better", but this better life was a strictly normative one, one in which they might have "a proper family" with which they could "eat dinner and that".

At Eastview College, this good or better life is set against the past and future socio-geographic risks to which the students are seen to be subject. The teacher conducting the Student Leader program describes her concern for what her students have already experienced:

> A lot of them come from tough family lives, whether that be a broken home or violence or abuse. We have a lot of families with refugees that have come over and haven't been in Australia very long. We have one student for example who spent most of his life in a refugee camp, and so they've seen the worst in the world, and so for them to come here their shoulders are heavy.
> Eastview College 2010

Active citizenship is framed as a kind of palliative treatment for these past experiences of uncertainty, but it is also framed as a prophylactic measure that may allay or ameliorate future precarity, as the same teacher explains:

> So having kids like we do in the Student Leadership group reminds them that there is a reason to be happy here. [...] It's believing in themselves, that just because they come from a poor country or just because they're one of eighteen kids, or just because their family doesn't have a lot of money doesn't mean they can't work hard and develop a certain set of skills or make opportunities available to them when they get older.
> Eastview College 2010

7   The Virus of Hope

Such observations reflect the deep concern of educators at both schools to protect their students from future risk and uncertainty, and their deep commitment to doing so (see Black 2015). These educators are keenly aware of the constrained circumstances and life chances that are likely to face young people in economically precarious communities, the "flawed consumers and unwanted workers" who are "exiled into various dead zones in which they become ... invisible" (Giroux 2010, 1). While the MAD and Student Leader curricula are rich with the language of youth empowerment and social change, of "making a difference", the chief concern that motivates both schools as institutions is the promotion of educational and citizenship attitudes and competencies – including hope, ambition and aspiration – that might better enable their students to ensure their own economic participation in a precarious labour market.

At both schools, the curriculum of active citizenship is consciously utilised to foster hope among the young people who are directly involved in it. There is also a hope that the experience of these young people will influence the educational and citizenship values and aspirations of others. At Eastview College, the Student Leaders are encouraged to foster ambitions for the future both for their own benefit and for the hopes that they may be able to encourage in other students:

> You push them a little bit harder, because I know that if there are students that come from the same background and they've been able to overcome those fears and those hesitations then it's possible for other kids to as well (teacher, Eastview College, 2010).

Other statements from teachers at both schools illustrate the way in which the Student Leader and MAD curricula, and the students who participate in them, are employed as a kind of educational virus to promote similar attitudes in other young people facing the same socio-geographic restrictions:

> So not only have they done something physically good for them, good for other people helping where there was a need, but creating opportunities – future opportunities – for other people to follow in their footsteps if they choose to ... (teacher, Valley High School, 2010)

> They take those skills and they take that attitude back into their own classrooms and back into their groups, and hopefully it spreads like wildfire (teacher, Eastview College, 2010).

Particularly at Eastview College, where the Student Leaders occupy a formal and visible leadership role, the students themselves are conscious of their obligation to foster hope amongst other young people. The Student Leaders are charged with being role models for other students in their own school. This is a responsibility that they take seriously, one that they imbue with an almost paternalistic sensibility:

> Because we're all leaders here and most people look up to us, so we're kind of role models for them. So what we do, they'll follow along (student, Eastview College, 2010).

Their responsibilities also include giving presentations about active citizenship at local primary schools. They regard these presentations not only as a way of encouraging other young people to see themselves as actors for social change, but as a way of spreading optimism:

> Our location isn't that cool, so maybe it's giving a few kids some hope or something like that (student, Eastview College, 2010).

8 Conclusion

For young people, the message from austerity-era Europe and beyond is bleak. In 2012, the Council of Europe's Parliamentary Assembly summed up the situation in the following terms:

> the financial and economic crises, together with underlying structural problems, threaten the effective exercise of rights by the young generation, whose autonomy, dignity and well-being are severely affected by growing economic and social inequalities.
>   Parliamentary Assembly 2012

Circumstances for many young people have only worsened since then. In place of the recognition, membership and belonging that are supposed to attend citizenship, "those old grand narratives of class, ethnicity, gender and indeed geography and nation, the structural forces that shape young people's destinies, are returning with a vengeance" (Williamson 2014, 7). Yet despite these dark realities, young people are still encouraged to hope. The "hope-goading" discourses (Zipin et al. 2015, 232) of the neoliberal polity, with their reflection in education narratives, curricula and policies, urge young people to hope for the positional goods of the education and labour markets, for autonomy and self-determination, for the ability to shape or reshape their communities, their societies, and even the world. They are also expected to engage in new or renewed forms of "hopeful politics" and acts of citizenship that "offer new social and political possibilities" (Newman 2015).

Some of these hopeful acts of citizenship may indeed prompt new possibilities, including challenges to the structural causes of the precarity to which so many young people are subject and challenges to the normative responses which they are encouraged to make to this precarity. Kelly has recently described the ways in which some young people are using social media and other spaces to undertake "a powerful questioning" of the markers of success to which they are expected to aspire as well the processes of hope and anticipation in which they are expected to engage: the processes of "*becoming* an adult, *becoming* a citizen, *becoming* independent, *becoming* autonomous, *becoming* mature, *becomin*g responsible" (Kelly 2015, 6, original emphasis).

For many or even for most young people, however, this questioning and the responses it may provoke – "radicalisation, revolt or retreat" (Williamson 2014, 12) – may be limited or unlikely. It may be "beyond their imagination or contemplation" (Williamson 2014, 12). This leaves them grasping at "toxic straws of hope" (Zipin et al. 2015, 235) with no assurance of any kind that these hopes might be fulfilled.

Certainly within the two schools of my study, such questioning of the status quo is not evident. Rather, the hopefulness embedded in the students' statements suggests an acceptance of the normative aspirations of learning and earning. It suggests an acceptance of the precarious state of the labour and education markets within which they are expected to compete. It also suggests an acceptance of the promises – of citizenship, of membership, of belonging and of fulfilment – which are linked within the educational discourses to labour and education market participation.

This acceptance belies the actual experience of citizenship for many young people who struggle to define and protect their entitlements in a casualised and competitive labour market (McDonald et al. 2014), or who are obliged to conform to specific modes of acting and being in order to gain or maintain a place in that labour market (Harrison and Kelly 2012), yet it appears to be a widespread response, even for young people living in communities where labour market realities are harsh. While some studies have suggested, following Appadurai (2004), that a belief in their ability to shape their own future is largely limited to young people with adequate socioeconomic resources and forms of cultural capital, others have found that young people appear to read the future in hopeful ways even in precarious circumstances (McCarthy et al. 2009, Beadle 2011, Farrugia and Watson 2011, Wierenga and Ratnam 2011, Reid and McCallum 2014).

It may be that such young people are transforming their experience into one that can be addressed with hope. It may also mean that they are misreading the future and their capacity to shape it in what has been described as a "darkly troubled historical era" (Zipin et al. 2015, 243). The unanswered question is whether educational technologies such as active citizenship are inherently enabling because they offer young people important experiences of belonging and influence in the face of precarious or eroding social and economic conditions, or whether they are a form of cruel optimism (Berlant 2011), one that leaves young citizens "wait[ing] in perpetual hope for the "good life" to come" (Sellar 2013, 255).

References

Akar, B. 2014. "Learning active citizenship: conflicts between students' conceptualisations of citizenship and classroom learning experiences in Lebanon." In *British Journal of Sociology of Education*: 1–25. http://dx.doi.org/10.1080/01425692.2014.916603 (Retrieved on 1 July 2014).

Aldenmyr, S.I., U.J. Wigg and M. Olson. 2012. "Worries and possibilities in active citizenship: Three Swedish educational contexts." In *Education, Citizenship and Social Justice* 7(3): 255–270.

Amnå, E. and J. Ekman. 2014. "Standby citizens: diverse faces of political passivity." In *European Political Science Review : EPSR* 6(2): 261–281.

Andersson, E. 2015. "Situational political socialization: a normative approach to young people's adoption and acquisition of political preferences and skills." In *Journal of Youth Studies*: 1–17.

Appadurai, A. 2004. "The capacity to aspire." In *Culture and Public* Action, edited by V. Rao and M. Walton. Palo Alto, California: Stanford University Press.

Appadurai, A. 2007. "Hope and Democracy." In *Public Culture 1*: 29–34.

Arnot, M. and S. Swartz. 2012. "Youth citizenship and the politics of belonging: introducing contexts, voices, imaginaries." In *Comparative Education* 48(1): 1–10.

Baker, A.M. 2015. "Constructing citizenship at the margins: the case of young graffiti writers in Melbourne." In *Journal of Youth Studies 18(8)*: 997–1014.

Banaji, S. 2008. "The trouble with civic: a snapshot of young people's civic and political engagements in twenty-first-century democracies." In *Journal of Youth Studies 11(5)*: 543–560.

Beadle, S. 2011. "The changing nature of civic engagement." In *For we are young and ... ? Young people in a time of uncertainty*, edited by S. Beadle, R. Holdsworth and J. Wyn. Melbourne: Melbourne University Press, 196–214.

Berlant, L. 2011. *Cruel optimism.* Durham and London: Duke University Press.

Bidisha. 2015. "Politicians keep using the word aspiration – but what does it mean?" http://www.theguardian.com/commentisfree/2015/may/27/politicians-aspiration-labour. Accessed?

Black, R. 2015. "Between policy and a hard pedagogical place: the emotional geographies of teaching for citizenship in low socioeconomic schools." In *Pedagogy, Culture & Society 23(3)*: 369–388.

Black, R., E.M. Gray and D. Leahy. 2016. "Zombies, Monsters and Education: The Creation of the Young Citizen." In *Generation Z*, edited by V. Carrington, J. Rowsell, E. Priyadharshini and R. Westrup. Singapore: Springer, 159–172.

Boudreau, J.-A., M. Liguori and M. Séguin-Manegre. 2015. "Fear and youth citizenship practices: insights from Montreal." In *Citizenship Studies 19(3–4)*: 335–352.

Bradford, S. and F. Cullen. 2014. "Youth policy in austerity Europe." In *International Journal of Adolescence and Youth 19(sup1)*: 1–4.

Bryant, J. and J. Ellard. 2015. "Hope as a form of agency in the future thinking of disenfranchised young people." In *Journal of Youth Studies 18(4)*: 485–499.

Cammaerts, B., M. Bruter, S. Banaji, S. Harrison and N. Anstead. 2014. "The Myth of Youth Apathy: Young Europeans' Critical Attitudes Toward Democratic Life." In *American Behavioral Scientist 58(5)*: 645–664.

Cooper, C. 2012. "Understanding the English "riots" of 2011:"mindless criminality" or youth "Mekin Histri" in austerity Britain?" In *Youth and Policy 109(6)*: 6–26.

Council of Europe. 2010. *Council of Europe Charter on Education for Democratic Citizenship and Human Rights Education.* Strasbourg: Council of Europe.

Cuervo, H. 2011. "Young people in rural communities: Challenges and opportunities in constructing a future." In *For we are young and ... ? Young people in a time of uncertainty*, edited by S. Beadle, R. Holdsworth and J. Wyn. Melbourne: Melbourne University Press, 126–141.

Down, B. 2004. "From patriotism to critical democracy: Shifting discourses of citizenship education in social studies." In *History of Education Review 33(1)*: 14–27.

Edwards, K. 2009. "Beyond the Blame Game: Examining 'The Discourse' of Youth Participation in Australia." In *The Future of Sociology: 2009 TASA Conference.* Canberra.

European Commission. 2015a. *Their Future is Our Future: Youth as Actors of Change.* Brussels, European Commission.

European Commission. 2015b. *Youth: Supporting youth actions in Europe.* http://ec.europa.eu/youth/policy/youth_strategy/index_en.htm. Accessed on 17 November, 2015.

Farrugia, D. and J. Watson. 2011. "'If anyone helps you then you're a failure': Youth homelessness, identity, and relationships in late modernity." In *For we are young and ... ? Young people in a time of uncertainty*, edited by S. Beadle, R. Holdsworth and J. Wyn. Melbourne: Melbourne University Press, 142–157.

Flyvberg, B. (2006). "Five misunderstandings about case-study research". In *Qualitative Inquiry* 12(2): 219–245.

Giroux, H.A. 2010. "Zombie Politics and Other Late Modern Monstrosities in the Age of Disposability." In *Policy Futures in Education* 8(1): 1–7.

Gordon, H.R. and J.K. Taft. 2011. "Rethinking Youth Political Socialization Teenage Activists Talk Back." In *Youth & Society* 43(4): 1499–1527.

Harris, A. 2010. "Young people, everyday civic life and the limits of social cohesion." In *Journal of Intercultural Studies* 31(5): 573–589.

Harris, A. and J. Roose. 2013. "DIY citizenship amongst young Muslims: experiences of the 'ordinary'." In *Journal of Youth Studies* 17(6): 794–813.

Harris, A., J. Wyn and S. Younes. 2010. "Beyond apathetic or activist youth: 'Ordinary' young people and contemporary forms of participation." In *Young* 18(1): 9–32.

Harrison, L. and P. Kelly. 2012. "Making the Cut in Jamie's Kitchen: Gender Relations and Young Workers." In *Public sociologies: lessons and Trans-Tasman comparisons*, Citeseer.

Isin, E.F. 2009. "Citizenship in flux: The figure of the activist citizen." In *Subjectivity* (29): 367–388.

Juris, J.S. and G.H. Pleyers. 2009. "Alter-activism: emerging cultures of participation among young global justice activists." In *Journal of Youth Studies* 12(1): 57–75.

Kelly, P. 2015. "Growing up after the GFC: responsibilisation and mortgaged futures." In *Discourse: Studies in the Cultural Politics of Education*: 1–13. doi:10.1080/01596306.2015.1104852

Kennelly, J. 2009. "Good citizen/bad activist: The cultural role of the state in youth activism." In *The Review of Education, Pedagogy, and Cultural Studies* 31(2–3): 127–149.

Kennelly, J. and J.A. Dillabough. 2008. "Young people mobilizing the language of citizenship: struggles for classification and new meaning in an uncertain world." In *British Journal of Sociology of Education* 29(5): 493–508.

Manson, J. 2011. "Occupy Wall Street: A new generation, a new kind of leadership." In *National Catholic Reporter*. October 12, 2011. https://www.ncronline.org/blogs/grace-margins/occupy-wall-street-new-generation-new-kind-leadership

McCarthy, B., M. Williams and J. Hagan. 2009. "Homeless youth and the transition to adulthood." In *Handbook of Youth and Young Adulthood: New perspectives and agendas*, edited by A. Furlong. Oxon and New York: Routledge, 232–240.

McDonald, P., J. Bailey, R. Price and B. Pini. 2014. "School-aged workers: Industrial citizens in waiting?" In *Journal of Sociology 50(3)*: 315–330.

Miles, S. 2015. "Young People, Consumer Citizenship and Protest The Problem with Romanticizing the Relationship to Social Change." In *Young 23(2)*: 101–115.

Miller, P. and N. Rose. 2008. *Governing the Present: Administering Economic, Social and Personal Life*. Cambridge: Polity Press.

Newman, J. 2015. *Austerity, aspiration and the politics of hope*. http://www.compassonline.org.uk/austerity-aspiration-and-the-politics-of-hope/.

O'Neill, B. 2011. "Less political rebellion, more mollycoddled mob." In *The Australian*. August 10, 2011. https://www.theaustralian.com.au/opinion/less-political-rebellion-more-mollycoddled-mob/news-story/1fda762c808e860ea1b794889b25d2a6

Ojala, M. 2012. "Hope and climate change: the importance of hope for environmental engagement among young people." In *Environmental Education Research 18(5)*: 625–642.

Pain, S., R. Panelli, S. Kindon and J. Little. 2010. "Moments in everyday/distant geopolitics: Young people's fears and hopes." In *Geoforum 41*: 972–982.

Parliamentary Assembly. 2012. *The young generation sacrificed: social, economic and political implications of the financial crisis*. http://assembly.coe.int/nw/xml/XRef/Xref-XML2HTML-en.asp?fileid=18918&lang=EN. Accessed 19 November, 2015.

Pickard, S. 2014. "'The Trouble with Young People These Days': 'Deviant' Youth, the Popular Press and Politics in Contemporary Britain." In *Labelling the deviant: othering and exclusion in Britain from past to present. French Journal of British Studies 19(1)*: 91–121.

Raco, M. 2009. "From expectations to aspirations: State modernisation, urban policy, and the existential politics of welfare in the UK." In *Political Geography 28(7)*: 436–444.

Reid, A. and F. McCallum. 2014. "'Becoming your best': student perspectives on community in the pursuit of aspirations." In *The Australian Educational Researcher 41(2)*: 195–207.

Rygiel, K. 2011. *Globalizing citizenship*, UBC Press.

Sellar, S. 2013. "Equity, markets and the politics of aspiration in Australian higher education." In *Discourse: Studies in the Cultural Politics of Education 34(2)*: 245–258.

Shiller, J.T. 2013. "Preparing for Democracy How Community-Based Organizations Build Civic Engagement Among Urban Youth." In *Urban education 48(1)*: 69–91.

Smith, N., R. Lister, S. Middleton and L. Cox. 2005. "Young people as real citizens: Towards an inclusionary understanding of citizenship." In *Journal of Youth Studies 8(4)*: 425–443.

Tormey, S. 2015. "Democracy will never be the same again: 21st Century Protest and the transformation of Politics." In *RECERCA. Revista de Pensament y Anàlisi (17)*: 107–128.

Walsh, L. and R. Black. 2015. "The Ambiguous Mobilities of Young Australians." In *A Critical Youth Studies for the 21st Century*, edited by P. Kelly and A. Kamp. Amsterdam: Brill, 70–86.

Wierenga, A. and S. Ratnam. 2011. "Young people and the future." In *For we are young and ... ? Young people in a time of uncertainty*, edited by S. Beadle, R. Holdsworth and J. Wyn. Melbourne: Melbourne University Press, 214–228.

Williamson, H. 2014. "Radicalisation to retreat: responses of the young to austerity Europe." In *International Journal of Adolescence and Youth 19(sup1)*: 5–18.

Wood, B.E. and R. Black. 2014. "Performing Citizenship Down Under: Educating the Active Citizen." In *Journal of Social Science Education 13(4)*.

Wrigley, T., B. Lingard and P. Thomson. 2012. "Pedagogies of transformation: Keeping hope alive in troubled times." In *Critical Studies in Education 53(1)*: 95–108.

Yin, R.K. 2013. *Case study research: Design and methods*. SAGE Publications.

Zipin, L., S. Sellar, M. Brennan and T. Gale. 2015. "Educating for futures in marginalized regions: A sociological framework for rethinking and researching aspirations." In *Educational Philosophy and Theory 47(3)*: 227–246.

CHAPTER 8

Indigenous Young Australians and Pathways to Hope in the Struggle to 'get real'

Chris Hickey and Lyn Harrison

1   Introduction

Indigenous (Aboriginal and Torres Strait Islander) young people continue to profile amongst the most disadvantaged groups within Australia's education and health systems. The nature of their underachievement expresses itself relatively early in mainstream education settings. By year 10 Indigenous youth are 50% more likely to have dropped out of school than their non-indigenous counterparts. Further, less than 50% of Indigenous youth see University as a possibility following school, compared to over 70% of non-Indigenous respondents (Mission Australia 2012). Educational disadvantage can readily become entrenched, with early school leavers who have no qualifications having greatly reduced opportunity of achieving labour market security (Vinson 2007). Magnified across the community, there is a growing body of evidence depicting the consequences of 'generational disadvantage' encountered in many Indigenous communities (McLachlan, Gilfillan & Gordon 2013). This is expressed through low educational attainment, early parenthood, high rates of crime and drug use and disproportionate levels of incarceration. High level exclusion from the labour market and an over-dependence on social security are preconditions for enduring social exclusion (Campbell et al. 2012).

This chapter reports on a particular dimension of a three-year Australian Research Council funded project undertaken to explore the potential for a social enterprise Transitional Labour Market Program (TLMP) to re-engage disadvantaged Indigenous youth.[1] The social enterprise restaurant at the center of this intervention was conceived as a hospitality based education and training pathway for both front-of-house (customer service) and back-of-house (food preparation) employment. Through its alignments with a number of key stakeholders, including a national community service organisation, registered training organisation and an employment transition agency, the program offers

---

1   Capacity building and social enterprise: Individual and organisational transformation in transitional labour market programs. *Australian Research Council Linkage Project* (Project ID: LP100200153).

an accredited training pathway alongside sustained work experience. The restaurant established within the social enterprise framework, aims to legitimate new ways of being and knowing as a foundation to building hope and 'dreaming up possible futures' for marginalised Indigenous youth (Braidotti 2013). Within this framework it was envisaged that participants would develop transferable labour market skills and knowledge that had currency across the hospitality industry, within a learning environment that was culturally respectful and enabling.

Despite a spirit of hope and goodwill among all stakeholders, the 'wicked problem' associated with mediating the competing tensions between the social and financial goals of social enterprise endeavors quickly raised its head (Paulsen & McDonald 2010; Campbell et al. 2011). In the early phases this tension impacted the recruitment of participants, and the support of the local Indigenous community. As the program progressed it became clear that the intention to create a place of cultural inclusivity was not supported by accompanying values and practices that genuinely embraced and celebrated diverse forms of Aboriginal culture. Rather than entering a program that was culturally sensitive, participants soon found it to be overwhelmingly imbued with the mainstream educational ideologies and methodologies that had failed them in the past. Rather than object and agitate for change, theirs was a different form of protest, in that they merely stopped turning up. Here, their discontent must be read against a history of 200 years of gross injustice and inequity across which the voice of protest has been largely suppressed or ignored (Pearson, 1996, 2011).

Our reference to 'getting real' captures the enduring tension that existed between the perceived need to tailor the program to fit with the cultural needs of the participants, and the commitment to ready the participants for active participation in mainstream employment settings.

As 'hybrid' organisations social enterprises seek to both sustain a social mission and maintain commercial viability. Though it is possible for social and business demands to reinforce one another to benefit the organisation, they are more likely to be associated with contradictory expectations that raise persistent conflicts and challenges. To date there has been little research that has provided in-depth, systematic insight into the nature and management of the competing social and business demands that are commonplace in social enterprise organisations (Gonin et al. 2012).

2   Contextualising the Research

The TLMP in focus was founded on a recognition that marginalised Indigenous youth have specific needs, extending to culture, community, learning styles and social and emotional support. In seeking to reach out to them the program acknowledged the limitations of dominant educational paradigms and the implications for young people who are unsuccessful. Against this backdrop the social enterprise restaurant was strategically developed as an alternative pathway for a particular cohort of young people who, for various personal and systemic reasons, would struggle to successfully complete mainstream offerings.

In targeting members of a particular cultural group (Indigenous Australians) for whom identity is *grounded in place*, the site of the TLMP was significant (Memmott & Horsman, 1991; Sandri, 2016). The social enterprise restaurant was established in a cultural heritage building that held important standing within the local Indigenous community. The site had previously been the venue of an Aboriginal Health Service and as such, had a long history of being a social support hub for the local Indigenous community. Underpinning its selection as the site for the social enterprise was an aspiration for its cultural significance to be a conduit to the Indigenous community. The name of the restaurant also had strong connections to Indigenous culture.

The collection of data associated with the research of the social enterprise TLMP program had two distinct, but intimately related, phases. One involved the implementation of an action learning cycle wherein the key stakeholders met on a regular basis to discuss, review and analyse a range of issues related to the program. These monthly forums were the conduit to the cyclic integration of data gathering strategies, such as issue/problem identification, briefing notes/papers and to facilitate a range of planning, reflection and feedback processes. The methodological underpinnings of the action learning cycle were broadly based on Lewin's (1946) collaborative action research 'spiral' of planning, acting, observing and evaluating. At the heart of this approach is a recognition that the most productive forms of action research are those where the participants accept a shared responsibility for implementing the results of their learning.

The other source of data gathering took the form of a series of qualitative, one-on-one interviews with participants. Included in the interview schedule were key program staff, hospitality educators and, most importantly, the trainees. In collecting data around the trainees, we used a biographical approach. The biographical approach employs a framework for talking about how people shape their sense of 'self', and how we as researchers capture that. Guided by Henderson et al. (2007) we sought to develop participant biographies that could add value to the project through an increased understanding of individual learning experiences, needs and expectations. To achieve this we took into consideration, things like family, school, work, relationships, friends, experiences, training at the restaurant, and future aspirations – and the relationship between these fields. Building a biographical account provides a window into the life of the individual and can record movement and change as it happens, and position this within broader stories about educational success and failure, and culture. The trainees were interviewed at least three times during the course of the project to track their transitions in and out of the TLMP, and to identify key influences that shaped these transitions.

3   Tension, Barriers and Unrealised Hope

For every success story there is a story of another trainee who has exited the program or faces serious health and well-being issues that stand to compromise their progress. During the course of the project numerous trainees spoke to us about personal emotional challenges associated with depression and anxiety and how they impacted on their capacity to meet the demands of the program. At the beginning of our research we were told that many of the trainees wanted and needed to turn their lives around and that for many, each day was a struggle. In their day-to-day struggles the program could not always be given priority, nor was it necessarily the best place for them to be. At times like this they described attending the program as, 'impossible', 'fruitless', 'risky', 'boring' and/or 'aggravating'.

In our conversations with the trainees about life, change, security and their imagined futures, they shared a range of experiences and visions with us. These were not just stories about the challenges they faced in their everyday lives, at home, or with family – but accounts of the expectations they encountered in these discursive fields, and how they could imagine themselves in, and beyond, these spaces. Within the constraints of this chapter, the following narratives are just two examples compiled from the expansive data collected from the trainees.

3.1   *I Can't Believe He Walked Away (James's Story)*
Reflecting on his pathway into the TLMP James conceded that his history as a school student had not been good. School had been difficult for James on account of his experience of being ostracised and bullied, causing him to become increasingly distrustful of people. Even though he had some friends at school he didn't really enjoy it and wanted to leave early on but 'had nothing else to go to'. Rather than formally leaving school, he just drifted away from it and by his own admission would 'take months off at a time, just to bum around'. Eventually, 'sometime in year 9', he just didn't go back.

James' family circumstances played an important role in his life. He moved down from Darwin with his mother four years prior to joining the TLMP and had lived with her and his stepfather in Melbourne. Since taking his place in the TLMP they had recently separated, James' mother had been struggling financially and had fallen behind in her rent payments. James revealed that she often did not have money for food for James and his two brothers and was struggling to pay for day-care for his younger sibling (3 years old). This situation had quickly begun to impact on James' participation in the program.

During the first 12 months of his participation in the TLMP James's attendance was almost perfect. Clearly committed to successfully completing the program he rarely missed training or his shift work. In an early interview with him, he expressed his ambition to make it as a chef and to ultimately go back up to Darwin and open his own restaurant. However, early in his second year his participation in the program had begun to wane.

The demands of James' family situation had grown and he had become more involved in looking after his younger brothers. It became clear that Monday was a day that he was expected to look after them and it was particularly difficult for him to attend his workplace-training program. By the second half of the year James had almost missed the maximum amount of training days that a trainee is permitted to miss across a year. Having been to just 4 out of 13 training classes James was in danger of not completing his traineeship if he didn't attend all of his remaining training classes. A fellow trainee described what he believed was a cycle of disengagement that James had fallen into:

> I think the weekends are particularly bad for him, looking after his brothers and that, which is why he is missing Mondays. It's pretty terrible, I dare say he's getting more depressed and his resilience just isn't there anymore.
> RYAN

Soon after, James' supervisor Cameron called him in and made him aware of just how many training shifts he had missed and the consequences if it were to continue. He explained to James:

> ... this is not about you being in trouble, but if you continue to miss class you won't be eligible for your training and we won't be able to catch you up, but your probably at a point now where we still can.
> CAMERON

Following this discussion, a youth support worker was asked to meet with James and try to establish a personal plan to enable him to give greater priority to his participation in the program. It was explained that he could provide more support to his family in the long run if he could complete his traineeship and build a successful career as a chef. James accepted this and for a short time his engagement with the program did improve. However, this didn't last long and he soon began to struggle to meet the competing expectations that home and the program placed on him.

During this time a number of the program personnel clearly lost patience with him and felt that James was his own worst enemy. The head chef at the time described James as:

> ... a bit of a sissy ... he needs to man up. It sounds a bit harsh but he's a bit of a sissy, a bit of a girl. He'll get a real shock when or if he tries to work in another kitchen. Maybe this experience will wake him up a bit.
> SASHA

A month later James told the Youth Support Worker that he did not want to work or train in the program any more. He told her that he no longer wanted to work in hospitality, that he no longer enjoyed it. Commenting on James's departure, Cameron felt that in the wake of his absences James had become increasingly detached from the workplace, and that he had clearly come to feel on the outer with his colleagues.

> I don't think he lost interest in the job, but he felt a bit left out because he wasn't always here at work to be part of everything and sort of just felt like maybe it's easier if I don't come back. It's a bit sad really.
> CAMERON

James's exit from the program came as a bit of a shock to a number of people. Only five months prior to leaving the program he had publicly outlined his personal goals, indicating his strong interest in hospitality and food service. In a trainee forum he said that his dream job would be to 'be a rock star, but after that it's to be a chef'.

3.2   *The Struggle to 'get real' (Sara's Story)*

In high school Sara was an out-rider and often in trouble. She was suspended for fighting a number of times. Sara's father passed away while she was in year 8 and soon after her family moved. The school in her new neighbourhood would not accept her because of her history of fighting and suspension. They requested she write a thousand word essay detailing why the school should accept her. She decided not to do the essay. She ended up leaving school at the start of year 9 and continuing her studies at a local TAFE. Sara left TAFE when she fell pregnant with her first child. Some three years later she found out about the TLMP program through her involvement with the local community. She joined the program hoping it would offer her a chance to become financially independent so that she could give her young son a good life. She thought that developing skills in the hospitality industry would provide her with a range of employment opportunities, and ultimately perhaps a managerial role.

On one particular morning when we were observing a training session being delivered by the hospitality education provider, as part of our 'field observations', Sara turned up late. The session had been in progress around 35 minutes when Sara burst into the room apologising for her tardiness and moving to take up a seat in the room. The hospitality educator (Yetska, Hospitality Educator) acknowledged Sara's arrival and announced that people who turned up late would have to catch up and that she couldn't be expected to restart the class or go back over what had been covered each time someone turned up late. 'It's your responsibility to be here on time, just as it will be when you are out in the workforce', she explained. In our debriefing interview with the teacher immediately following the session she revealed her general frustration with the group and their apparent lack of personal commitment and organisation toward the course.

> The level of punctuality and attendance is much lower with this group, than my other groups. None of them are particularly good but Sara and Terry are really poor. I mean, Sara's been late to every class ... you can't expect to hold down a job if you can't even be on time!
> YETSKA, Hospitality Educator

The following week we had our regular catch-up interviews with a number of the trainees, including Sara. Ironically, Sara rang ahead to pass a message to us that she was running a little late but was 'on her way'. During her interview, Sara revealed that she was going pretty well with the program and was determined to see it through.

> Chris: So what is your biggest obstacle to getting through the course?
> Sara: The theory stuff, I find the reading and book work the hardest. I'm okay with the hands-on stuff and I'm getting better at taking orders.
> Chris: You mean, like writing down what customer's order in the restaurant?
> Sara: Yeah, I'm not a good writer or speller so at the start the kitchen staff couldn't understand the order. It was really embarrassing if someone had to go back and get the order again. I thought, 'I can't do this'. But now we have these menu sheets and I just have to tick the right one's ... its easier now and I'm much more confident with the customers now.

The proverbial 'elephant in the room' that had not emerged organically through our conversation was about her punctuality and how she felt about her profile as someone who was always running late. Sara made no attempt to combat this perception as unfair, instead acknowledging that it was an ongoing issue for her and one that she felt she was willing to accept. We specifically asked her about her repeated lateness at the hospitality training sessions, euphemistically referring to Yetska's commentary. Sara explained that being a single mum who doesn't drive made it difficult to be across town for the 9.00am start. Her morning routine involved getting her 3 year old son (Alex) up, dressed and giving him breakfast so that they could catch a tram to his childcare facility. She said that Alex was experiencing some separation anxiety that sometimes delayed her exit. 'I feel like it is getting easier though as he gets more used to the people and the place'. Travel between the childcare facility and her hospitality training sessions involved two tram rides and a 5 to 10 minute walk. To Sara this wasn't construed as an excuse for being late or something for which she should apologise. It was simply the reason.

> My family don't help me with child-care. I moved out and since that time I have done everything by myself. It just has to be like that. But I'm fine, I'm happy, Alex is happy. I've got food, he's in day care, that's it.
> SARA

Sara conceded that she had not attempted to explain her personal circumstances to Yetska, questioning what difference it would make. 'I don't want sympathy or special treatment, I want to stand on my own two feet. I want to prove to myself and others that I can do this', she said. The fact that Sara had almost completed a day's work before she even got to class was surely something that would incite a measure of compassion and tolerance that her teacher was currently not affording her. 'She's never asked', said Sara. We asked if she would mind if we, or someone more central to the program, took the liberty of conveying her circumstances to her teacher, as a way of advancing her understanding and tolerance of her circumstances and perhaps those of others in the group. She was agreeable as long as it was not portrayed as 'a bleeding heart story'.

Later on that day we had a scheduled interview with the Restaurant Manager (Paul). Among the many things we discussed with him was the issue of punctuality. Like Yetska, Paul was of the view that the group were generally tardy and that it was something that would undermine their chances of a successful transition into the labour market. The major point of difference between Paul and Yetska was that Paul had knowledge about each of the program participants' life circumstances and their journey into the TLMP. However, rather than this knowledge being a source of compassion or tolerance Paul was inclined to separate the personal from the professional. He felt that it was his role to challenge the participants to rise above their personal circumstances in order to succeed in the program. This is amplified in his comment about Sara:

> Seriously, she's been late to nearly every class. That's not how it works in the real world. You're not going to get a job, or keep a job, if you can't turn up on time. We can piss around with them pretending that it doesn't matter that they're late or didn't turn up at all for some reason. I mean *'get real'*.
>
> PAUL, Restaurant Manager

4 Pathways to Hope: Discussion

A number of key issues, tensions and possibilities can be identified in the trainee's biographical narratives. In the context of this paper we draw attention to the educational model put in place to deliver the program and its limitations in accommodating individual learning needs. As amplified through the biographies of James and Sara, a number of the trainees identified challenging home lives, complicated by personal health and well-being issues as significant factors impacting their progress through the TLMP specifically set up to serve them. Given the complex life circumstances, personal learning profiles, and the challenges that many of the trainees brought with them to the program, it was somewhat alarming that a level of tolerance around incidents of lateness and absenteeism had not been initially built into the program design and implementation. Beneath the program rhetoric to support marginalised and disaffected Indigenous young people, relatively few supports existed to offset key barriers to their sustained participation.

The problem for marginalised young people is that being successful in a mainstream program requires them to act within a very tightly defined understanding of what it takes to make the grade. As Black (2010, 12) has argued: 'Participation may require a similar suppression of young people's identity in ways that sit oddly with the empowerment that it promises'.

For many of the trainees the classroom based learning mode had not been conducive to facilitating their educational success in the past. Indeed, failure to navigate mainstream educational philosophies and practices which produce what it means to be a successful student was identified as a major reason why many trainees had moved away from formal education and training. With the same underpinning pedagogical structures having been put in place within the TLMP program it is not surprising that many were struggling with the program.

Of particular concern here was the partnership it had with the external training organization where there was little attempt to alter the pedagogic paradigm to better suit the needs of its learners. Rather, the trainees were expected to fit into mainstream structures and ways of working the same as all other students. Here, their point of difference, their particular learning needs, were neither acknowledged nor accommodated. Though seemingly being promised something different, there was a sameness about what they were experiencing that aligned with past educational failures.

Corroborating the trainee's narrative accounts of the ways that the program was failing to meet their learning needs was a high attrition rate. Built on a biography of educational failure, James did not rebel against the program, he did not protest the constraints of its structure, nor did he strategise a modified mode of engagement. When the TLMP no longer fitted with his life circumstances he simply walked away. The vestiges of hope that had previously nurtured plausible future scenarios of himself as a successful chef quickly became fragile memories of unrealised hope. Behind its rhetorical claims of a second chance pathway for James, the constraints of the mainstream educational paradigm were omnipresent. In the pursuit to open up and/or expand labour market opportunities for marginalised Indigenous young people there is clearly a need to explore alternative modalities of engagement. It is incumbent on such programs to make explicit links between cultural identity and inclusion.

There are too few pathways through which our young people can find roles and subjectivities in mainstream institutions that do not conflict with their pride in being Aboriginal or Torres Strait Islander. We are suggesting that some young people are forced to suppress their sense of being Aboriginal or Torres Strait Islander as a condition for participation, and others are locked out of wider participation because of the pain and discomfort of racist environments. (Fredericks & Legge 2011, 23)

In similar work with marginalised young pregnant and parenting students Harrison et al. (2004; 2007) drew on Kelly's (2000) formulation of the 'dilemma of difference' to mediate the 'risk' associated with being different. Kelly (2000, 6) describes this as 'the risk of reiterating the stigma associated with assigned difference either by focusing on it or by ignoring it'. Kelly (2000, 6) expands on this arguing that:

> To ignore the differences of subordinate groups, argues legal scholar Martha Minnow, 'leaves in place a faulty neutrality, constructed so as to advance the dominant group and hinder those who are different'. But attending to the differences of subordinate groups can highlight their deviance from the norm.

This dilemma is one that a number of the participants experienced around attempts to name and frame their marginalisation as a category of difference. Sara, for instance, did not want her personal life circumstances to be the basis for reducing the level of achievement expectation placed on her, in comparison to her colleagues. She was however, happy enough for her circumstances to be discussed with her teachers as long as they were not read as a 'bleeding heart story'. For Sara, the dilemma of difference is ever present. While she is proud of her heritage and grateful for targeted support to overcome some of the cultural barriers that confront her, she is vigilant to not let it dilute her sense of agency and position her as a victim.

A turning point for the TLMP emerged when a change of leadership accompanied a review of the structural foundations of participant disengagement. This invoked a range of programmatic changes orientated towards an increased accommodation of cultural differences, needs and sensitivities. Rather than reading the participants as the problem that needed changing, the new program manager began to explore how the program was failing Sara, James and others.

> Looking at their case biographies and the rigidness of some of our expectations, its not surprising that they are struggling. We need to make sure we are a nurturing and supportive environment.
> MARK, Program Manager

The reflexivity embedded in the action learning cycle created the conditions for organisational change to begin to take place. Change would not be without its challenges and along the way to establishing an alternative mode of operation both the trainees and the trainers would struggle to overwrite the known and familiar. As the new Program Manager noted:

> as an alternative pathway we need to provide an alternative model because a lot of the young people that come here will have experienced disenfranchisement from other pathways – education, training and employment.
> MARK, Program Manager

Over the following six months a range of adaptations were implemented across the program to better align its operational practices with its fundamental objectives. At the heart of this was the relocation of the hospitality training program from off-site to in-house. The hospitality education provider continued to be involved but the program was delivered in-house. This offered the trainees increased flexibility through the introduction of make-up classes, revision sessions and alternative assessment practices. According to Mark:

> Bringing the training in-house gives us more flexibility to tailor the program for each individual. It allows us to not have fixed constraints when it comes to timelines. If a young person needs to take some time for themselves they are not all of a sudden really behind the eight-ball. We have more flexibility in the time line, if the young person needs time to go away then that won't set them back so much. That's the real beauty of where we're headed with this.
>
> MARK, Program Manager

In recognition of the complex life circumstances of many of the trainees additional pastoral support was established around them. The employment of a Youth Support Worker (YSW), who had previous experience working with Indigenous young people, greatly enhanced the capability to assist the trainees with their individual learning and training needs. The new YSW was invested in getting to know the trainees and developing an understanding of their individual backgrounds, their current circumstances and their aspirations for the future. The YSW quickly established herself as someone that the trainees could trust and could call on for support and guidance in circumstances where they were struggling to meet the demands placed upon them, both within and outside of the program. As well as supporting the trainees, the YSW was an important resource in ensuring the trainees had a consistent 'voice' in dialogues between program staff and management. In this pursuit, she quickly became a strong source of support for Sara.

5   Conclusion

Just as young people are expected to display a particular attitude at school in order to be successful, so too are a range of appropriate attitudes required in the labour market – for instance, a 'work ethic' measured by characteristics such as turning up on time. In assisting marginalised Indigenous young people to move into the labour market TLMPs need to reconcile the tension between mainstream constructions of what it means to be a good worker, and the particular characteristics of the cohort. With a particular focus on Indigenous young people Palmer (2003) argues that the environment in which the training takes place, and the types of knowledge systems that are privileged, play a significant role in the effectiveness of an intervention.

> Those of us who have been around for as long as I have now know that just about all the old strategies (for working with Aboriginal groups) have been tried and found wanting. We've used training programs, locked

them up, run self-development workshops, and offered counseling. None of these things have worked, so finally we have had to go back to Aboriginal people and ask them what we should do.

PALMER 2003, 15

Here, it becomes increasingly important to question what learning looks like and how it is mobilised, and to be open to new and innovative approaches that seek to function in a more holistic fashion. This is a call for the legitimisation of new learning paradigms that are responsive to the historical and contextual barriers to fulsome access to reasonable educational and labour market participation.

Sandri (2016) argues that knowledge about Indigenous ways of being and knowing can only be developed in dialogue with Indigenous communities. In the absence of such dialogue those charged with supporting marginalised Indigenous young people will be operating in spaces of uncertainty and ambiguity that can, often unwittingly, promote cultural violence. To undertake this work effectively programs need to be structured within dialogic modalities so that the instructors can be constantly learning from the young people they are instructing and, as such, are continuously (re) shaping their ideas about the learners and how they understand themselves in this context. In our case, it was through the embedded reflexivity of the *action learning cycle* that the new program manager was provoked to question the merits of the systems that were in place to assist or govern the young workers. Shifting the failures of the program from the perceived inadequacies of the participants, to the structures that were put in place to support them, created the conditions for the development of a new training model.

In the absence of strategic interventions, the social and cultural forms of marginalisation would have continued to restrain hope, nurture resentment and reproduce failure. Where the starting point is systemic or generational marginalisation, on the grounds of culture, class or ethnicity, where failure is, in a range of discursive spaces, normalised, the challenge of transformation is at its greatest. Within this context, assisting Indigenous young people from marginalised and disadvantaged backgrounds, to develop skills and aptitudes for active labour market engagement is complex work. Here, interventions need to go beyond the rhetoric of altruism to invoke true paradigmatic change in ways that are respectful, tolerant and culturally inclusive. *Getting real* about tackling entrenched disadvantage requires more than hope and goodwill, it demands a deep organisational, cultural and structural commitment to valuing difference and diversity. For this to be successful it should be done with participants, not for them!

References

Australian Bureau of Statistics (ABS). 2010. *Work: Aboriginal and Torres Strait Islander Peoples, Measures of Australia's Progress,* 1370.0, Australian Social Trends, Australian Bureau of Statistics. Available from: http://www.abs.gov.au/.

Australian Bureau of Statistics (ABS). 2011. *Education and Indigenous Wellbeing,* 4102.0 Australian Social Trends, Australian Bureau of Statistics. Available from: http://www.abs.gov.au/.

Atkinson, J. 2002. *Trauma Trails: Recreating Song Lines.* Melbourne, Spinifex Press.

Black, R. 2010. 'Promise or practice?: Student participation in low socioeconomic communities'. In, *Youth Studies Australia,* 29(2): 9–16.

Braidotti, R. 2013. *The Posthuman.* Cambridge, Polity Press.

Campbell, P., P. Kelly & L. Harrison (2011) *Social Enterprises: Challenges and Opportunities,* Working Papers Series 2, No. 19. Geelong, Alfred Deakin Research Institute, Deakin University.

Campbell, P., P. Kelly & L. Harrison 2012. *The problem of Aboriginal marginalisation: Education, labour markets and social and emotional well-being,* Working Papers Series 2, No. 31. Geelong, Alfred Deakin Research Institute, Deakin University.

Fredericks, B. & D. Legge 2011. *Revitalizing Health for All: International Indigenous Representative Group Learning from the Experience of Comprehensive Primary Health Care in Aboriginal Australia—A Commentary on Three Project Reports.* Melbourne, The Lowitja Institute.

Gonin, M., M. Besharov & W. Smith 2012. 'Managing Social-Business Tensions: A Review and Research Agenda for Social Enterprises'. In, *NYU Stern Conference on Social Entrepreneurship,* November 2012. http://www3.unil.ch/wpmu/ess-vd/files/2013/05/Managing_Social_Business_Tensions_NYU_submission.pdf.

Harms, L., J. Middleton, J. Whyte, I. Anderson, A. Clarke, J. Sloan, M. Hagel & M. Smith 2011. 'Social work with Aboriginal clients: Perspectives on educational preparation and practice'. In, *Australian Social Work,* 64(2),156–168.

Harrison, L., G. Shacklock, J. Angwin & A. Kamp 2004 '"At school I am just like everyone else": Teenage pregnancy, schooling and educational outcomes', Paper prepared for the *Learning from the Margins Conference,* July 2004, Melbourne. Published on-line by the Quality Learning Research Priority Area, Deakin University, Geelong. Paper accessed via http://www.deakin.edu.au/education/quality_learning.

Harrison, L. & G. Shacklock 2007 'At school I am just like everybody else: Teenage pregnancy, schooling and educational outcomes'. In, J. McLeod & A. Allard (Eds.), *Learning from the margins: Inclusion/exclusion and 'at risk' young women.* London, Routledge.

Henderson, S., Holland, J., McGrellis., Sharpe, S. & Thomson, R. 2007. *Inventing Adulthoods: a biographical approach to youth transitions.* London, Sage.

Kelly, D. 2000. Pregnant with Meaning: Teen Mothers and the Politics of Inclusive Schooling. New York: Peter Lang.

Lewin, K. 1946. 'Action research and minority problems'. In, *Journal of Social Issues,* 2(4): 34–46.

Mission Australia. 2012. *Mission Australia Victoria Report.* Mission Australia.

McLachlan, R., G. Gilfillan & J. Gordon 2013. *Deep and persistent disadvantage in Australia.* In, Productivity Commission Staff Working Paper, Canberra.

Memmott, P. & R. Horsman 1991. *A changing culture: The Lardil Aborigines of Mornington Island.* Wentworth Falls, Social Science Press.

Palmer, D. 2003. 'Youth Work, Aboriginal Young People and Ambivalence'. In, *Youth Studies Australia,* 22(4): 11–18.

Paulsen, N. & A. McDonald 2010. 'Doing social enterprise: a reflection and view from the field'. In, *Third Sector Review,* 16(2): 109–126.

Pearson, N. 1996. An Australian history for us all. *Address at the Chancellor's Club Dinner.* University of Western Sydney.

Pearson, N. 2011. Constitutional Reform crucial to Indigenous wellbeing. *The Weekend Australian.* December 24–25, p.20.

Sandri, R. 2016. 'From the other side: reflections of an Indigenous researcher on Western research'. In, M. Kumar & S. Pattanayak (Eds) *Positioning Research: Shifting Paradigms, Interdisciplinarity and Indigeneity.* New Delhi, Sage.

Vinson, T. 2007. *Dropping off the Edge: The Distribution of Disadvantage in Australia.* Melbourne.

CHAPTER 9

Dreams of Ordinariness: The "missing middle" of Youth Aspirations in Sardinia

Giuliana Mandich

1   Introduction

In this chapter I discuss some of the empirical results of a research project on young people's imagined futures in Sardinia (Italy) in the frame of the questions proposed by the *Politics of outrage and hope* conference in Melbourne in 2015. The purpose of the research project – the "iFuture" project – was to explore young Sardinian's *capacity to aspire* (Appadurai, 2004) in a regional environment that, in the context of contemporary European wide concerns with youth unemployment and the consequences of sovereign debt crises and austerity programs, offers a very limited range of opportunities both in the labour market, and in the educational system. According to Appadurai the capacity to aspire goes beyond the most immediate, visible inventory of wants and wishes that individuals express. This capacity has to be found in the production of "justifications, narratives, metaphors, and pathways through which bundles of goods and services are actually tied to wider social scenes and contexts, and to still more abstract norms and beliefs" (Appadurai, 2004, 68).

In this sense our project's focus was not on the detection of young people's biographical projects or aspirations, but on the uncovering of a much broader set of cultural resources they use to project themselves into the future. We considered asking young people to write an essay about an imagined future life to be an appropriate research tool that required an imaginative effort on the part of the students, and which provided them a wider possibility to imagine, to navigate the field of the future. The students were asked to write an essay imagining what life they were living at the age of 90, and to tell how their future (in the past) would be. This particular methodology is inspired by the UK based research project "Living and Working in Sheppey" (Lyon & Crow 2012), which presents participants with a very similar question[1].

---

[1] This latter study is a follow up of a first strand, which was conducted in 1978, with aims shaped by the research interests of that time. There now exist several others research projects using

In the context of our research project, 340 essays were collected from 18 year-old students in two Sardinian cities. Most of the essays (290) were collected in Cagliari, the main city of Sardinia, on the Southern coast. A smaller sample of 50 were collected in Nuoro, a city in the mountainous internal area of the island.[2]

The analysis of the young people's imagined biographies was, from the beginning, provocative and fascinating. The interpretation of the essays became not simply an experiment or exercise within larger research on youth aspirations, but its main task. Each of the essays is a small stand-alone story. Sometimes funny, other times a bit sad. In some cases short, in other cases more elaborate. But most of the times, largely optimistic, very lively and touching in different ways. The analysis of the essays allowed us to grasp beyond the apparent varieties of the stories, a set of very important common elements characterising young people's exercise of imagination, including, the use of mobility as a common device to imagine some kind of successful future (Cuzzocrea et al. 2016), and the emergence of the medical profession as one of the strongly imagined careers, especially for middle class students.

In this chapter I will focus on two more themes from our data: in the first place the apparent ordinariness of the imagined biographies; and, in the second instance, the *rearward gaze*, instead of the *forward gaze of the deployed imagination*. The essential outline of the majority of imagined biographies is very simple: getting a job, getting married and having children. It is possible to say that these young people imagine that they will have a life just like the ones that their parents had. To gain a deeper look into the narratives I will focus on an element of the stories that expresses more strongly the ordinary and almost nostalgic character of these young people's imagination; young people's imagining of *being retired*.

Both the ordinariness of the stories and their nostalgic character appears to be somehow in contradiction with both the imaginative purpose of the essay ("imagining" often means opening up and going forward), and with the "imaginaries" of the researchers in the research group. So, in reading the essays, in being confronted with the apparent "ordinariness" and "nostalgia" of young

---

this technique with young people (Elliott 2010; Lyon & Crow 2012; Heggli et al. 2013), although participant's ages may vary. To our knowledge, though, this method has not been applied so far in Italy.

2 The gender ratio was 215 female (approx. 63%) and 125 male (approx. 36%). This unequal balance was due to the fact that some of the chosen schools are predominantly female. The schools involved were classical lyceum, usually chosen by middle class students oriented to continue further with university studies, and from technical schools. A very small number of essays were collected in more vocational oriented schools. In Italy there is a very strong correlation between the type of school and social class.

people's imagination, we tried to position ourselves in relation to our personal expectations, we tried to explore our "disappointment," and to question ourselves about what imagination is, and the relationship between imagination and the ordinary.

This chapter positions the ordinariness of the narratives collected within two main theoretical and conceptual frames that outline quite powerfully the problems we encountered in the research within the more general questions of a "politics of hope." The first frame centres around the so-called "missing middle" debate, which has recently gained some centrality in youth studies (Roberts 2011; Woodman 2011, 2013). This debate endorses the idea that paying attention to the "ordinary" in young people's lives enables researchers to uncover new and more complex dimensions of youth. The second frame is that of "the exploration of the imagination" suggested by Latimer and Skeggs (2011). That is to say, the question of how to "keep open and critical," and how to try to "pause ahead" of "making judgments that are almost too ready to hand" (Latimer and Skeggs 2011, 395). I suggest that the arguments developed in the two debates are mutually reinforcing and can be a fruitful ground for the analysis of young people's imagined futures.

2 Essays about Imagined Futures

As it is clear from the introduction, we considered the essay form a very interesting and productive way of collecting narratives about the future because the character of the essay genre opens young people and researchers to the uses of imagination. The task that we proposed to the students was:

> Imagine you are 90. Looking back at your life until that point, tell what happened to you. There is no need to invent something unlikely to happen. Simply tell the story of your life, how according to you it could have unfolded. Clearly, you cannot know what is going to happen to you, but you could try and describe how things could go if things go how you think or you wish. Try and tell the whole of your life from the moment in which you finish school. Write as long as you think is needed.

As with other kind of narratives, our essays are stories that are chronological, meaningful and produced for a specific audience (Elliott 2005). In our case, these narratives have two more characteristics that are specific: they are narratives about the future and as such, they have to do not only with young people's experience but also with their anticipatory capacities; and they are explicitly fictive texts.

To grasp the complexity of these narratives we had to use a very wide analytical strategy. All essays were thematically coded through NVivo. We used the software to give order to the vast amount of data and the richness that emerged in the stories, and to create a simplified picture. In our analysis we were looking for word frequencies (Elliot 2005), and for a set of dimensions characterizing projectivity – such as reach, breath, and clarity (Mische 2009, 2014).

As a research team we held a series of sessions of what we called "collective hermeneutics," guided by the awareness of at least three different elements that were influencing how the stories were told. In the first place, the connection to available genres, tropes and plots (Maynes 2008). In our case, the "essay at school" genre informed the way the narratives of an imagined life have been constructed. At the same time, a strong influence of new media (Facebook and SMS), TV fiction and popular movies was also evident (Cuzzorea et al. forthcoming). In the second instance, we always tell a story to someone, that is to say, we must take into account who the presumed audience of a narrative is (Elliot 2005; Maynes et al. 2008). In the case of our essays, we can pinpoint two different audiences: student's peers, and the researchers who invited young people to write the essays. We know, from a collective encounter aimed at the discussion of the first research results, that the students who wrote the essays were proud to be the focus of sociological research and to have their voices heard. We also know from the same encounter that the essays have been the object of many discussions between the students. To complicate the picture we take into account our own expectations both due to our experience (what we might have written at age 18), and the theoretical and analytical elements that we were using to frame our research.

We also had to take seriously the fictional nature of these texts. All fictional texts bring together factually existing and imagined things (Beckert, 2016; Iser, 1993). In the case of this kind of narrative – where imagination and fiction are always present when narratives of the future are concerned (Beckert 2016) – we quickly saw the impossibility of using clear-cut concepts such as "realistic vs non-realistic," or "dream-like vs project-like," to classify these stories. For example, the young people were often referring to different kinds of reality. The narratives often use "media reality," including the plots of TV fiction, movies or talent shows, to describe how they imagine their life in the future. Media discourses are real in the sense that they are already there. They are not the product of individual imagination. They are part of the set of symbolic resources people can use to transcend and reframe ordinary social life. Media and migration are, according to Appadurai (1992), the forces allowing imagination to be deployed in contemporary societies.

At the same time, in the essays Sardinian young people wrote, reference to reality is lacking in details. There is no idea most of the time of how to get to where they imagine their lives to be, very often there is no link between education and work, no precise idea of professional careers or employability paths.

When it comes to reality, there was little of what Ann Mische (2009) calls *clarity*: the degree of detail and accuracy with which the future is imagined. Also the dimension of *volition* was very weak, that is to say, the relation of motion or influence that the actor holds about the impending future. Very often there was a passive, receptive stance toward an approaching future over which we have little control.

If we look, finally, at the actual achievements young people imagine realizing in their narratives (getting married, having children, getting a house, having a job, and enjoying retirement) these are plausible, even possible, but not the probable outcomes, given the future education, work and housing scenarios that characterize many aspects of contemporary Italian society.

3 Young Sardinian's Utopias: Or Being Happy in Retirement

This peculiar character of "unrealistic realism," as we could call it, comes out very strongly in the ways in which the phase of retirement is depicted in these imagined biographies. We imagined that young people must know that one of the most discussed issues in contemporary Italian society is the collapse of the Italian pension fund system. With a few exceptions there is no trace in these narratives of the public debate pointing to the fact that getting retirement funds will be quite difficult for these generations of young people. On the contrary, many young people see retirement as the happiest period of their imagined biography.

The exact word "retirement" is present in many essays (90 essays), and it is described in a very detailed way as a positive experience, as an important turning point in these young people's imagined biography. On the one hand, this data can be explained, as Mische (2009, 2014) would emphasize, by the fact that people develop greater clarity about possible futures that are modelled around them. The data suggests that grandparents are, for young people in their 18th year, as important, possibly even more important than their parents are, from an emotional and everyday life support point of view. Indeed, grandparents' characters are described with great animation in these narratives:

> I remember the amazing Sundays spent at my grandmother's house. Poor thing she was 98 hard earning in the world … [sic], because in those well

> remembered Sunday dinners all the family was reunited, my brother and my sister in law with the two children, my wonderful nephews I loved as my children, my parents and all the happy family. I miss so much those days. I miss so much my grandmother, I understand her so well now that I am her age! (DelF68[3]).

We must also acknowledge that the element the narrative form suggested by the assignment – starting "from the end" – has certainly influenced the centrality of the "retirement phase of life" in the telling of these imagined biographies. While we acknowledge this the positive value, the expressive force given to that part of the essay, and the set of meanings accompanying the imagination of retirement, is strongly evident. It comes into imagined biographies as a positive experience.

Young people find in retirement not only a rhetorical device able to meet the requirements of the assignment but a meaningful turning point able to give shape to biographical narratives. For some students it plays a role, which is similar to the one that mobility plays in many narratives, as a sort of "magical device" (Isabella and Mandich 2014) that makes future agency possible. Mobility is clearly a powerful fictionalizing expedient, and, at the same time, it refers to different realities (stories of family migration) and to media reality (movies, TV fictions) (Cuzzocrea et al. 2016). In a similar way telling the imagined future through the lens of retirement allows young people to say: *At the end I made it*. Indeed, the term *enjoy* (the Italian term is *godere*) is quite often used to describe life after retirement and often associated with adverbs such as *finally* or *at last* to express a strong sense of relief mixed with satisfaction.

> After fifty years of hard work I finally retired and I could enjoy peace and remember old times (BucM28).
> At 67 I retired and finally I could enjoy my family (BucM29).
> Once retired I started to enjoy my time: theatre, evenings with girlfriends and grandsons (DelF28).
> And now I can enjoy being retired (DelM23).
> And at 65–70, after a life of being a worker, a husband and above all a father, if possible even earlier, I would like to retire so to live 100% my family life and take many holiday trips and visit a lot of unknown places, even if I travelled a lot while working (Nu_Lin_M13).

---

3   The acronym indicates the school attended by the student, the gender and a serial number to identify the narrative.

Last shot: I receive from the medical association the award for my retirement benefits and this is the occasion for some thoughts. I can say I am very satisfied with my life and all the choices I made to live happily and in peace with myself, and realize my values. After retirement, my life took a very quiet and well-off turn. If I could go back in time, I wouldn't shift a day, even if I regret most of all the strength, the calm and the carefreeness of my youth (DetM52).

Retirement is also the occasion to travel again. Moreover, it gives the opportunity to resume old hobbies and passions that working life had impeded, in a way it gives the possibility to be young again:

> Now that we retired me and my husband we travel a lot (DelF14).
> I finally could rest when I got retired, at 65, I spent the rest of my days taking care of the animals I always loved and of the house (DelF44).
> At 75 my wife and I we decided to buy a boat. Being retired we used to spend a lot of time in the boat (Del M69).
> At 60 I retired. If someone would have told me at school I would have laughed at it as a joke. I still kept my passion for the music, this is what helped me when I was a teenager and in my difficult times: so I carried on, also being retired, to play nice songs with my guitar (DetM27).

The range of detail these young people are able to express through their narratives of retirement is significant: for instance the age of retirement is 65 years old according to the majority of students. The age of retirement is also the age in which the intergenerational bond explicitly appears as a link with the generations of grandparents, and at the same time, it allows these students to define the kind of relationship they imagine with their offspring:

> At 65 I got retired and I handed my professional activity to my daughter Nicole who decided to follow my steps (DelF36).
> Finally 65 arrived. I asked for my retirement benefits and my request has been granted after few months. From that day I decided to leave my firm to my children and enjoy the most the last years of my life with my dear wife very quietly (MarM17).

The strength that these narratives of retirement have in imagined biographies is due to multiple influences, and assumes in these young people's imagined life, different and important meanings. Even if these young people live in a sort of "bubble of time" they "feel" and in a way anticipate (through their parent's experience) social acceleration (Rosa 2013), and dream of retirement as a sort of decelerated phase of life. In opposition to the positivity and peacefulness of retirement, work life (adult life) is foreseen as a very difficult and hard experience. Being retired, on the contrary, means *having time*. One of the students writes how she used (as she actually does in her present reality) look forward to retirement:

> During retirement I had plenty of free time for me and my grandsons. When I was young, about 16, I used to think that being retired would have been the greatest achievement, I looked forward to it because I thought I could have spent my day in no hurry, I would have a lot of time available to me (DelF38).

Narratives on retirement have all the strength of a strongly desired future, which is not only collectively constructed, but culturally shared. In Appadurai's (1992) words, we can talk of "communities of sentiment" as groups of people imagining and feeling together, using the same expressions, having in mind the same images, when they talk about retirement or about mobility in the future biography.

It can also be interesting to underline that the narratives of retirement are more elaborate, more detailed, and more emotionally significant in the essays of the students from technical schools. As I have already suggested there is a very strong correlation between the type of school and social class in the Italian context (Triventi 2014). The students from technical and vocational schools are more likely to come from family backgrounds characterised by low income and low education. These young people have a stronger sense that the reality of their life and future is going to be very difficult. One of the strategies they use to make up a feel-good story in the future is to stress retirement as a positive phase of life. The appeal of the (imagined) past – of the securities of well-organized "fordist society," which they "should" know is not going to be there when they grow old (and in Sardinia in a way was never there) – is strong for these young people. Hope, is for them, a sort of nostalgia for old times. Hope is not forward looking but backward looking.

4   Missing the Middle and Closing the Imagination Down: Young Sardinians, Utopias and the "ordinary"

The metaphor of a "missing middle" (Cairns et al. 2014) in youth research is increasingly being used in contemporary debates about young people (Roberts

2011; MacDonald 2011; Woodman 2011, 2013; Cairns 2014). In general, we can say that the "missing middle" perspective questions an apparent tendency in youth studies to emphasise "extraordinary experience" over the "ordinary." A missing middle comes into view when qualitatively interesting matters (*extraordinary*), are highlighted in research and policy at the expense of less spectacular but quantitatively more significant matters (*ordinary*). Through focusing on the fringes rather than the centre:

> we lose the opportunity to observe 'young people or the youth phase per se' and 'broader processes of social change and, as such, to answer questions of wider relevance for sociology'.
> MACDONALD 2011, 428

The debate has underlined several different "missing middles" that youth sociology should attend to (Woodman 2013). Sometimes the stress is on the empirical focus, and at other times on methodology (Cairns 2014). In this project we targeted something very similar to what the youth studies literature would call a "missing middle" from the empirical point of view: "normal" or "typical" young Sardinians attending the second to last year of secondary school; no school "dropouts" with difficult situations; and no "exceptional" young people already engaged in political or cultural activities in the public sphere. What is interesting in a debate on young people and the "politics of hope," is that these "ordinary" young people imagine "ordinary" futures. Finding a job. Getting married. Having a couple of children. The apparent "ordinariness" of these narratives cannot be easily dismissed as unimportant.

This "ordinariness" certainly clashes with the definition that imagination is usually given, both in public discourse, and in sociological analysis. Imagination and the ordinary are, indeed, often viewed as oppositional terms in the same way that "dreams" (that share with imagination an openness to the future) seem to be opposed to "projects" (as closed temporal orientations) (Leccardi 2005). These student's narratives, their imagined lives, are not forward looking and do not apparently show the open character that an imaginative tale of the future is supposed to have. From the perspective of a "politics of hope" these narratives do not look "explorative" or "imaginative." As such it may seem they do not help us to identify and explore the challenges and opportunities, the possibilities and limitations that young people think they will encounter in the future.

For this reason, discovering the imagined futures of these young women and young men was at the same time fascinating, although somehow deceiving. During the collective discussions of the essays, it emerged very strongly that every member in the research group was expecting something that could not be found in these narratives. On the one side we might have hoped, implicitly, if not explicitly, for more presence of political awareness due to the economic crisis, or some dystopian climate-change narratives, or technological utopias. On the other hand, in ways similar to many European institutions (Olsson et al. 2011), we might have expected these students to be "innovative," to face the future's challenges with original and unexpected projects, new jobs, new ways of life, new models of family. As a consequence, the possibilities for giving these exercises of imagination a meaning requires us to develop a more thoughtful reflection on imagination, to bear in mind at the same time the openness of imagination, and the possibility that imagination is fostered and shaped by cultural resources in society. On the first point it is important to keep in mind Latimer and Skeggs' (2011, 395) suggestion that:

> imagination can be understood not just as topic and resource, but as a space to be found in between discursive and material events and practices, that is potentially transformative ... as a force, that transforms the present by opening up a different past and a different future.

Latimer and Skeggs (2011) further argue that imagination and the future are deeply intertwined through the open character of the present: "The future is not present, but there is an opening onto it; and because there is a future, a context is always open. What we call opening of the context is another name for what is still to come" (Derrida & Ferraris 2001, 19–20, cited in Latimer & Skeggs 2011, 393). As Appadurai (1992) argues, the transformative character of imagination needs to be contextualised within the cultural field. He suggests that having broken out of the special expressive space of art, myth and ritual, imagination has now become a part of the quotidian mental work of ordinary people in many societies that are heavily influenced by media and migrations.

How do we account for these dreams of ordinariness? Do we contribute to *closing the imagination down* (Latimer & Skeggs 2011), dichotomising young people's reactions to uncertainty into either protest or exit, resistance or compliance? Certainly these young people's way of imagining their future has to be taken into account and cannot simply be dismissed as a shrinking of life projects in the private sphere. Hopes cannot be put aside as childish and petty expectations, or as unrealistic optimism.

If we compare this study with the existing literature on young people's hopes for the future (Threadgold 2012) we can say that our students also seem to separate the long term future of society from the anticipation of their future lives. In ways that are different from previous research material the future these young people imagine is not a short-term future, a future they are able to plan, they are asked to travel forward seventy years into the future. In addition, they are asked to start from the end and to move backwards in time. So, the horizon of a planning trajectory is subverted. However, the futures constructed here are usually very private futures. There is little, or no trace of society. These young people only very occasionally describe the social, economic and climate conditions in which their imagined lives will take place (Cuzzocrea et al. forthcoming). Moreover, the society of the future does not change. In the essays there is little, if any, description of possible/impossible alternative societies. It is, in a way, a sort of two track thinking that has been seen as a strategy for managing the anxiety that young people associate with the long term future (Threadgold 2012), or as a way of managing frustration with the inability to create meaningful change.

At least in the Italian case, the uncertainties relating to the short-term future are possibly stronger than fears for the long-term future of society. Young people in Italian society are not only socially marginalized but also subjected to very strong "symbolic violence" (Bourdieu & Wacquant 1992). On the one side, they are told that there is no future for them, no jobs, and no pension funds. On the other, young men are regularly accused of being "mummy's boys," or a spoiled and selfish generation without autonomy or drive.

What these young people need, possibly, is to find a mechanism of re-enchantment, counterbalancing the fears of uncertainty (Cook 2015) which are much more alarming for them than the distant climate change dystopias. This is why, I suggest, that what is usually called "unrealistic optimism," shares (in our case) some of the characteristics of utopian thinking. These narratives express hope, and a very strong "desire for a better way of being or of living" (Levitas 2013, 52). These hopes and desires resemble what Brown de Graaf and Hillen (2015) define as "hope as want," as a general desire for a positive future. And as Desroche (1979, 23) maintains utopia and hope are strongly related: "Are not utopia and hope, in particular, twin sisters? In utopia there is the hope of a different society. In hope there is the utopia of a different world. In both of them there is the strategy of alterity." In our essays the most powerful of these mechanisms, these hopes and desires, is mobility, but retirement also shares a similar character. The stronger difference is the protension toward the past that the tale of retirement contains.

This way of looking hopefully into the future has a second important meaning that can be better understood if we go back to Appadurai. The future,

Appadurai suggests (2013, 287), is not just a technical or a neutral space, but is shot through with "affect and with sensations," is a collective process and a human capacity. People do have different access to future-making practices and the "capacity to aspire" demands and promotes recognition. Appadurai (2013, 289–290) is particularly concerned with the fact that through such "navigational capacity [...] poor people can effectively change the 'terms of recognition' within which they are generally trapped."

5   Conclusion

A "capacity to aspire" seems to be a very important element for young people today. The construction of imagined futures is, in the first place, a sort of stage for the projection of the self. So imagining a positive future is for those young people a demand for recognition of a space in society, a space that is maybe different from the one the adult society tends to imagine for them. A space that is not of "innovation" or "creativity" but is a sort of "re-enchantment of the ordinary." Imagination is more generally an important part of what Appadurai defines as capacity to aspire, a move to find a new ethics of possibility. In Appadurai's (2013, 295) words, an ethics of possibility amounts to "those ways of thinking, feeling and acting that increase the horizons of hope, that expand the field of the imagination." Therefore, the capacity to transcend and reconfigure everyday life, to configure "communities of sentiment" (groups of people that imagine and feel things together) is a crucial resource, particularly for young people. These imagined futures can be seen as shared utopias, as openings into a future that is usually described in public discourse as very difficult and uncertain. From this perspective, imagining retirement against all odds can be regarded as a form of resistance, at the symbolic level, to the bleak futures prevailing in European, Italian and Sardinian economic and political discourse. For many Sardinian young people these imaginings constitute, to a large degree, what a "politics of hope" might look and feel like.

References

Appadurai, Arjun. 1992. *Modernity at Large*. Minneapolis: University of Minnesota Press.
Appadurai, Arjun. 2004. "The Capacity to aspire. Culture and the Terms of Recognition." In *Cultural and Public Action*, edited by Vijayendra Rao and Michael Walton, pp. 59–84. Stanford: Stanford University Press.

Appadurai, Arjun. 2013. *The Future As Cultural Fact: Essays on the Global Condition.* London: Verso.

Beckert, Jens. 2016. *Futures. Fictional expectation and capitalist dynamic*, Cambridge, Massachussets, Harvard University Press.

Bourdieu, Pierre and L. Wacquant. 1992. *An Invitation to a Reflexive Sociology.* Chicago: University of Chicago Press.

Brown, Patrick, Sabine de Graaf ·and Marij Hillen. 2015 "The Inherent Tensions and Ambiguities of Hope: Towards a Post-Formal Analysis of Experiences of Advanced-Cancer Patients" *Health* 19(2): 207–25.

Cairns 2014 "I Wouldn't Stay Here: Economic Crisis and Youth Mobility in Ireland" *International Migration.* 52 (3): 236–249.

Cairns, David, Katarzyna Growiec and Nuno de Almeida Alves. 2014. "Another 'Missing Middle'? The marginalised majority of tertiary-educated youth in Portugal during the economic crisis." *Journal of Youth Studies.* 17 (8): 1046–1060.

Cook, Julia. 2015. "Young adults' hopes for the long-term future: from re-enchantment with technology to faith in humanity," *Journal of Youth Studies* 19 (4): 517–532.

Cuzzocrea, Valentina and G. Mandich 2016 "Students' narratives of the future: Imagined mobilities as forms of youth agency?" *Journal of Youth Studies.* 19 (4): 552–567.

Cuzzocrea, Valentina and Simona Isabella, forthcoming, *Narrare il Futuro*, Carocci, Roma.

Derrida, Jacques and Ferraris, Maurizio. (2001). *A Taste for the Secret*, Polity Press, Cambridge.

Desroche, Henry. 1979. *The Sociology of Hope.* London: Routledge.

Elliott, Jane. 2005. *Using Narratives in Social research. Qualitative and quantitative approaches.* London: Sage.

Elliott, Jane. 2010. "Imagining a Gendered Future: Children's Essays from the National Child Development Study in 1969." *Sociology* 44(6): 1073–1090.

Heggli, Gry et al. 2013 "Fearing the future? Young people envisioning their working lives in the Czech Republic, Norway and Tunisia," *Journal of Youth Studies.* 16 (7): 916–931.

Isabella, Simona G. Mandich. 2014. "Connecting to the future: the role of spatial mobilities in young people's imagined biographies", *Perspectives on Youth*, 2:51–62.

Iser, Wolfang. 1993. *The fictive and the Imaginary*, Baltimore: JHU Press.

Latimer, Joanna and Beverley Skeggs. 2011. "The politics of imagination: keeping open and critical" *The Sociological Review*, 59 (3): 393–410.

Leccardi, Carmen. 2005. "Facing uncertainty: temporality and biographies in the new century." *Young* 13 (2): 123–146.

Levitas, Ruth. 2013. *Utopia as a method. The imaginary reconstruction of society*, London, Palgrave Macmillan.

Lyon, Dawn, and Graham Crow. 2012. "The challenges and opportunities of re-studying community on Sheppey: young people's imagined futures." *Sociological Review* 60(3): 498–517.

Maynes, Mary Jo, Jennifer L. Pierce, Berbara Laslett. 2008. *Telling Stories: The Use of Personal Narratives in the Social Sciences and History*, Ithaca and London: Cornell University Press.

MacDonald, R. 2011. "Youth transitions, unemployment and underemployment Plus ça change, plus c'est la même chose?" Journal of Sociology. 47(4): 427–444.

Mische, Ann. 2009 "Projects and Possibilities: Researching Futures in Action," *Sociological Forum*. 24 (3): 694–704.

Mische, Ann. 2014. "Measuring futures in action: projective grammars in the Rio + 20 debates" *Theory and Society*. 43 (3): 437–464.

Olsson, U., K. Petersson and J.B. Krejsler 2011. "'Youth' Making Us Fit: on Europe as operator of political technologies." *European Educational Research Journal*. 10 (1): 1–10.

Rosa, Hartmund. 2013. *Social Acceleration: A New Theory of Modernity*, New York, Columbia University Press.

Roberts, Steven. 2011. "Beyond 'NEET' and 'tidy' pathways: considering the 'missing middle' of youth transition studies." *Journal of Youth Studies*. 14 (1): 21–39.

Threadgold, Steve. 2012. "I reckon my life will be easy, but my kids will be buggered': ambivalence in young people's positive perceptions of individual futures and their visions of environmental collapse." *Journal of Youth Studies* 15(1): 17–32.

Triventi, Moris. 2014. "Educational inequalities by social background: A review of the literature on the Italian case." Scuola Democratica. 2: 321–342.

Woodman, Dan. 2013. "Researching 'Ordinary' Young People in a Changing World: The Sociology of Generations and the 'Missing Middle' in Youth Research." *Sociological Research Online* 18(1).

Woodman, Dan. 2011. "Young People and the Future: Multiple Temporal Orientations Shaped in Interaction with Significant Others." *Young* 19 (2): 111–128.

CHAPTER 10

Beyond Hope and Outrage: Conceptualizing and Harnessing Adversity Capital in Young People

Lucas Walsh

1   Introduction

Young people's worlds are characterized by fluidity, exclusion, uncertainty and change. These are evident in the political, economic and cultural dimensions of their lives, which can be exacerbated by austerity measures and other forms of policy seeking to promote neoliberal perspectives. A good example of this, which had the potential to reverberate across the lives of young people, emerged during a short-lived government whose policy vision arguably represented a new chapter of neoliberalism in Australia.

This discussion focuses on a political moment and source of outrage in response to Tony Abbott's leadership of the Liberal National Party (LNP) coalition government (2013–2015). This brief conservative government signalled a lurch in Australian politics farther to the right and pushed the boundaries of austerity government. It reflected a form of neoliberalism that was questionable even by the LNP's own senior ministry (Hartcher and Massola, 2015). In this chapter I briefly provide three examples of how the neoliberal language of that government fostered forms of economic, political and cultural exclusion. Specific proposals and inactions are identified that directly and inadvertently sought to lock out ways of belonging and participating in contemporary society, promoting a lack of security and an erosion of trust.

The discussion then develops a conceptual framework for equipping young people with the skills and competencies to navigate conditions exacerbated by neoliberalism. Building on previous work (Walsh 2016, 2017) it develops the concept of adversity capital as both a way of understanding, and as a basis to respond to, certain challenges confronting young people today. It includes a brief overview of renewed international interest in developing certain "soft skills," competencies and literacies in young people to navigate uncertainty, exclusion and precarity. These "skills" include problem solving, communication, digital literacy and other employability skills, as well as cultural competencies and political literacy. This chapter further develops and positions the concept in the areas of work, political participation and culture.

While adversity capital seeks to enable young people to be more adaptive, flexible and resilient, the development of these skills as part of adversity capital could be seen to reflect a shift towards reinforcing the neoliberal "entrepreneurial self," in which subjectivity is characterized by responsibility and individual self-management (Kelly 2013). To address this potential limitation, the following discussion critically locates the theoretical concept of adversity capital in a moral economy of youth. This dimension of adversity capital also offers a basis for resistance. Written from the perspective of an educator, this conceptual approach is about equipping young people to navigate and challenge dominant neoliberal views.

2   Locked Up, Locked Down and Locked Out

> "We don't support, as a Government and as a Coalition, further lock-ups of our forests."
>
> Former Prime Minister TONY ABBOTT, 4 March 2014 (ABC 2014a)

When speaking at a timber industry dinner in early 2014, former Prime Minister Tony Abbott proposed repealing part of Tasmania's Wilderness World Heritage Area to prevent "lock-ups" of forests through preservation from commercial exploitation. He suggested that Australia had enough public national parks: "We have quite enough locked-up forests already. In fact… we have too much locked-up forest." Heritage land preserved for environmental conservation and public enjoyment was characterised as an unused, locked-up commercial asset.

Though that proposal failed (ABC 2014b), the language he used provides some insight into how a contemporary neoliberal government views key domains of public interest and governance. Upon election in 2013, the new federal government announced that Australia was "open for business". A corollary of this was a neoliberal ideological assault on the Australian public. The language used here reflected a wider narrative that emerged throughout many of the Abbott government's various proposals, according to which people, public property and ways of life were seen to be inimical or irrelevant to neoliberal logics of the free market. Proposals including the deregulation of higher education; changes to law related to racial vilification; the espousal of certain attitudes to a housing market that is hostile to young people, all bear the hallmarks of a view according to which people and ways of living are locked up and/or locked out. Three examples illustrate this narrative.

3   Example 1: Locked Out of Security, Higher Education and Home

> "The starting point for a first home buyer is to get a good job that pays good money."
>
> Former Treasurer, JOE HOCKEY, 8 June 2015 (CLARKE and BENNETT 2015)

Following a controversial budget speech during which he proclaimed an end to the age of entitlement, the then treasurer, Joe Hockey, mooted changing superannuation regulations to allow first home buyers to dip into their future self-funded pension to enter the housing market (Hockey 2014, Hutchens 2015). This was in response to growing concern about housing affordability in Australia's capital cities. Housing unaffordability has become a recurrent concern amongst young people (AYAC 2010, Australia Institute 2013) who feel that they are locked out of the housing market. This is not an unreasonable point of view. Where the average home loan was 23 per cent of the average disposable household income in 1988, by 2015 the proportion had swelled to 134 per cent (RBA, cited in FYA 2016, 6).

As quoted above, another response from Hockey to those locked out of the housing market was to get a "good job." Young people throughout the world are increasingly locked out of secure, stable work, and in some instances, any form of employment (Walsh 2016). In the wake of the Global Financial Crisis (GFC), the number of young people looking for work increased globally. According to one estimate, the figure ballooned to nearly 73 million by the end of 2014 (ILO 2015). Much of the work that is available is characterized by casualization and precarity. Howie and Campbell write that "Young people who had hoped that their emergence into adulthood could be modelled upon the experiences of their parents were confronted with ambiguous futures and fewer options for employment or a career" (2016, 906). As Kahn et al. (2012, 5) suggest, the downturn in the global economy diminished job opportunities, especially for young people: "Consequently, young people today enter a world of unparalleled uncertainty…with the most marginalized and vulnerable facing the greatest threat."

In Australia – a country that did not experience the economic downturn as severely as other countries following the GFC – teenagers face steadily declining opportunities for secure fulltime work, while those with post-school qualifications such as degrees appear to be attaining secure, fulltime work later in life. By 2013, it was reported that the number of young people seeking fulltime work had reached the highest rate in 15 years at 27.3 per cent (McGrath 2013). Casual work is high, with 20 per cent of all casual workers being aged 15–19 (ACTU 2012). Some of this is by choice, but levels of underemployment suggest that many young people want to work more. Of those in the workforce, nearly 30 per cent of young Australians are unemployed or underemployed (Skujins and Lim 2015). Those seeking pathways such as higher education face additional challenges.

The Abbott government also sought to deregulate higher education, ostensibly to unlock new university funding sources through the marketization of the sector. It was argued that this policy could force up the price of tertiary study for some students (Universities Australia 2014). Former Education Minister Christopher Pyne's proposals for fee deregulation sought to effectively shift a burden of debt onto young people seeking university study and their families to be paid off later, amounting to a potential second mortgage for young people upon entering work. Implied in this proposal was a "study now, pay later" logic. Those who could not afford the debt would be locked out of access to university study.[1]

But even for those who could afford the possible rise in fees, the promise of desirable work at the end of study is challenged. Fulltime employment outcomes for university graduates in the period of four months after they graduate declined from a peak of 84.4 per cent in 2008 to 65.2 per cent in 2014. Similarly, there was a decrease in the fulltime employment outcomes of Certificate III[2] or higher graduates, falling from 69.6 per cent in 2006 to 57.6 per cent in 2014 (Skujins and Lim 2015, 18). The labour market, and demand for certain skills and qualifications, is changing.

Technology is transforming the labour force through automation and increasing demands for digital literacy, with estimations that over half of the workforce as a whole will need the skills to "use, configure and or build digital systems in the next 2–3 years" (FYA 2015). A combination of technological change, global competition for jobs, and explosive growth in university educated

---

1 It should be noted that the previous Labor government removed around $2 billion in funding from the tertiary sector, affirming the pervasive nature of neoliberalism. It is by no means exclusive to one political party.
2 Certificate III is a vocational qualification to potentially enable individuals to progress from entry level positions to skilled work.

workers has, as Brown, Lauder and Ashton (2011) powerfully argue, severed the "opportunity bargain" according to which efforts to attain qualifications will lead to desirable, secure work.

Workforce uncertainty and insecurity has eroded some young people's ability to plan for the future, leading to a deferral of life choices like buying a home and starting a family. The unpredictability of working life can negatively affect social relations because of an inability to plan for even simple family gatherings (Woodman 2012).

The burden of navigating uncertainty is placed on individuals. The steady erosion of social (and educational) safety nets, combined with this market-driven fluidity, has resulted in a generation that have to accept that it is their individual (and their family's) responsibility to invest in education and to navigate the seas of workforce insecurity (Wyn and Cuervo 2014), even though the "opportunity bargain" might not be realized.

4   Example 2: Locked Out of Democracy

> "I want to say that we have made a good start, that the adults are back in charge and that strong, stable, methodical and purposeful government is once more the rule in our national capital."
>
> Former Prime Minister TONY ABBOTT (news.com.au 2013)

It was telling that student protests against Australian government funding cuts and other changes to higher education were met with derision and disdain (Berents 2014). One student protest briefly interrupted a popular Australia panel show involving former Education Minister Christopher Pyne. The act of outrage by unfurling a protest banner on television was labelled by the show's host Tony Jones as "unruly" and that it "is not what democracy is all about and those students should understand that" (ABC 2014c). And yet peaceful protest is arguably a healthy expression of democracy. Outrage is compounded by this contempt.

Perhaps this is why many young people see politicians as remote and party politics to be unappealing. Research into young people's attitudes to politics over the last two decades has shown frustration with governments' efforts to engage with youth that have been seen by young people as tokenistic, old, closed, controlled and irrelevant (Collin 2008). Many young people feel excluded from policy-making and comments like Abbott's take on a deeper meaning. One study into influences on voting behaviour found that "career politicians" make it difficult for young people to differentiate political parties from their members, and possibly due to this, that party identification among Australian youth is low (Edwards, Saha, and Print 2007). Importantly, however, the authors of this study suggest that this does not mean young people are apathetic, but rather that they do not consider political parties as representative of issues that impact upon them (Saha, Print, and Edwards 2011). One 2014 poll of young people found a turning away from democracy because it "is not working because there is no real difference between the policies of the major parties", and that "democracy only serves the interests of a few and not the majority" (Oliver 2014). The same poll conducted again in 2015 found only a minority (49 per cent) of 18–29 year-old Australians expressing a preference for democracy, with a quarter (26 per cent) saying "it doesn't matter what kind of government we have". While these figures are an improvement on results from 2014, there was an increase in those who said "in some circumstances, a non-democratic government can be preferable" (23 per cent) (Oliver 2015).

The distance between political representatives and young people is by no means confined to the LNP and extends to parties in general. Barriers to young people heighten this distance when they do seek to have their voices heard. Along with the disdain for youth protest held by the adult gaze, attitudes to youth protest need to be understood alongside efforts to curtail the right to protest. In the southern Australian state of Victoria, for example, the right to protest was outlawed when the Legislative Council of Victoria passed the Summary Offence Act 2013. Police were granted the power to "move on" groups of people at their will, including those involved in peaceful protests and pickets. Refusal to comply could result in fines, exclusion orders, or being locked up in prison.

Other channels for expression, debate and protest, such as "ethical consumption" through consumer boycotts, have also been threatened. In 2013, Senator Richard Colbeck mooted the possibility that the government might ban consumer and environmental activists from launching secondary boycotts. Rather than directly target a company, a secondary boycott targets consumers and those the company relies upon, such as its suppliers. In 2011, for example, activist group GetUp threatened to boycott grocery companies who opposed the carbon tax introduced by the previous government to mitigate environmentally harmful emissions (news.com.au 2011). Commentators from both the left and right condemned Senator Colbeck, with one from the latter suggesting that such boycotts are "a completely legitimate way to express political views" (Berg 2013). The Abbott government favoured some forms of expression over others.

5 Example 3: A Right to Bigotry

> "People do have a right to be bigots. In a free country people do have rights to say things that other people find offensive or insulting or bigoted."
>
> Former Attorney-General GEORGE BRANDIS (Griffiths 2014)

The former Abbott government evoked freedom of expression in selective ways. In March 2014, former Attorney-General, George Brandis, announced plans to repeal Section 18C of the Racial Vilification Act. Ostensibly the changes included measures to outlaw racial vilification "while at the same time removing provisions which unreasonably limit freedom of speech" (SBS 2014). One of the motivations to repeal the act stemmed from the successful prosecution of prominent conservative media figure Andrew Bolt in 2011. Bolt "was found to have broken the law over two articles he wrote in 2009 about light-skinned people who identify as Aboriginal" (Griffiths 2014). His commentary, which suggested that some light-skinned people identified as Aboriginal for personal gain, was deemed by a Federal Court judge to have been of possible offence to members of the Aboriginal community (ABC 2011). Bolt decried the decision as "a terrible day for free speech in this country". Brandis proposed the amendment to ensure that apparent curtailments of free speech like Bolt's "can never happen in Australia again" (Griffiths 2014).

Neoliberal efforts like this to detach issues of racism from the rule of law are not new. In the US, as I shall discuss in further detail below, Angela Davis (2012) has highlighted the colour-blindedness of neoliberalism, and the evocation of the rule of law and free speech as assuming primacy over matters of race. The explicit claim of "a right to bigotry" sent a problematic message to young people. As one young student, Nicholas Jones (2014), pointed out at the time:

> As a young Australian it is deeply concerning to me to hear a senior politician of a major political party defend bigotry. The legacy of bigotry throughout history is damaging. If our leaders today are promoting it, then it is likely that the current issues of classism, racism, violence and sexism in Australia will not be solved in the near future. To me, a white male, Australian-born, Anglo, English-speaking, middle-class heterosexual, this is a frightening prospect. What does it mean for people with a less privileged status in Australia?

Brandis' attempt to evoke freedom of speech in this way has particular salience in light of recent data showing high levels of racism experienced by young people in Australia, expressed through beliefs, prejudices or behaviours/ practices and can be "based on race, ethnicity, culture or religion" (Paradies et al. 2009, 7). A large proportion of young Australians routinely experience exclusion through racism, often expressed in terms of a particular group or individual not belonging (Priest et al. 2014, 6). Arguably, Brandis was privileging one right – the free speech of a white male commentator – over the right of others to belong and feel safe in so doing.

6 Framing a Response: Adversity Capital

Adversity capital is a means of responding to the complex challenges of neoliberalism described above. Derived from the practical, lived experiences of young people and how they navigate adversity, it is "a form of capital that can be productive of other forms of capital upon which young people can critically confront and navigate precarity and potentially build a better life" (Walsh 2016, 90). Pavlidis (2009, 11) first defined adversity capital as "a resource that people can use to transform adverse life experiences into an asset". But its use here differs from Pavlidis in that resilience is potentially strengthened through the development of these skills, competencies and literacies. It situates these skills and competencies in wider social, political, economic and cultural contexts as something that can be developed in preventative ways within the social ecologies of schools and other community, educational and workplace settings. This includes the array of influences, values, discourses and practices that constitute the moral economies of young people.

Where I have argued previously for a need to develop these skills, competencies and literacies in relation to shifting job markets (Walsh 2016), I now wish to widen this scope to political and cultural life. Adversity capital includes the capacity to critically navigate different economic, political and cultural contexts, including capabilities such as social intelligence, emotional resilience (Roberts 2009), problem solving, oracy (IYF 2013), critical thinking, technological literacy, amongst others (Partnership for 21st Century Skills 2009). Critical and political literacies include capabilities to critique prevailing ideologies, dominant views and injustice and participate in making change. Global and cross-cultural competencies can enhance the capacity to understand and "move across cultures" (Zhao 2009, 173) by offering up for scrutiny "our sense of our own identities, core values, and cultural practices" (Hannon et al. 2011, 4). An overlapping term, cultural literacy, "refers to an individual's world view, ways to interact with people, character, personal ethics, values and style" (Hui and Cheung 2015, 553). These skills, competencies and literacies are linked to the cohesion of communities (Kahn et al. 2012). These collectively form a part of adversity capital, enabling young people to become more adaptive and resilient when facing hardship, exclusion, insecurity and change.

It also might be argued that adversity capital is necessary for the guerrilla self described by Campbell and Howie in this book. Elsewhere, they

> identified three forms that guerrilla selfhood might take – entrepreneurial forms, where guerrilla selfhood can emerge at the interstices of ordinary business models; forms that make use of waste where situations and spaces once thought to be worthless or of low value are reimagined in economically and socially productive ways; and organisational forms where business and prosperity are imagined in other ways that value social progress and cooperation over profiteering and competition.
> HOWIE and CAMPBELL 2016, 917

This same approach is evident in other research of young social entrepreneurs (Walsh and Black 2018) that I have conducted with Rosalyn Black, who find themselves working at the interstices and intersections of business, government and the not-for-sector. Amongst other things, they seek the knowledge and tools to navigate the neoliberal terrain, of which adversity capital is arguably a part. Many also experience a distance from political representatives and see social enterprise as a vehicle to make social change. Like Campbell and Howie's young interviewees significantly impacted by the GFC described in this book, these social entrepreneurs also have hope. Whether these young people can work within and beyond their subjective construction as neoliberal entrepreneurial selves – who must carry the mantle of individual responsibility and self-management – remains to be seen. In uncertain and precarious times, they must live "everyday, one moment at a time".

The notion of adversity capital presented in this discussion may be problematic. For example, the need to better develop these skills, competencies and literacies – though valuable – may also be seen to reaffirm conditions of precarity by positioning young people within deregulated markets and dominant forms of power as permanent subjects of the "flexible" demands of economic capital and power. When viewed in isolation, the development of these skills, competencies and literacies only represents one facet of adversity capital. That is, without a deeper moral economy underpinning their development, it could be inferred that they reflect an acceptance and entrenchment of the volatility and fluidity of contemporary life described by Bauman (2000, 2013). They could arguably be developed to service the individualized precarity and forms of governance brought about by neoliberalism.

Where neoliberal policy espouses "an outmoded notion of resilience that decontextualises it from cultural contexts, social structures and political processes" (Bottrell 2013), the development of adversity capital seeks to develop young people as critical agents in everyday life. This move beyond an individualized notion of resilience reflects a recognition by sociologists such as Rose (2014) of "the polyvalence of resilient strategies" available to resist neoliberalism and its apparently totalising prevalence. It acknowledges that "whether a young person, parent or community endures, copes or thrives is dependent on the resources of the community that are accessible and culturally meaningful" (Bottrell 2013). Communities remain durable sources of resilient strategies.

The political and moral economy underpinning this concept is based on a notion of resilience that is located not in the individualized competencies, resources and dispositions to bounce back from adversity, but within a wider social ecology (Rose 2014; Ungar 2013). Here, the social and physical ecologies that surround young people, such as peers, family and teachers are important. This notion of resilience locates young people within vital social support networks and peers which can play an important role in developing resilience.

Adversity capital incorporates a moral economy of youth that challenges the assumptions, values and impacts of neoliberalism on economic, political and cultural life. The theoretical frame here draws from Sayer's (2007, 261) concept of moral economy that seeks to reinvigorate questions of "morality to everyday life and the experience of well-being and ill-being without reducing it to a matter of individual subjectivity or social convention, as tends to happen in sociology and economics". This critical moral economy "turns questions of economic behaviour back into questions of validity, by asking not only what happens but on the basis of what kinds of legitimation, and it assesses those legitimations" (Sayer 2007, 268). For example, adversity capital opens up the possibility for critiquing what Davis (2012, 169) refers to as "the neoliberalist discourse of 'color-blindness' and the assertion that equality can only be achieved when the law, as well as individual subjects, become blind to race". Where neoliberalism places value in the market above all things, and treats racism as an aberration, there is scope to not only understand the historical and cultural constructs of neoliberalism, but also to interrogate the ways that it erodes trust and community and "fails to apprehend the material and ideological work that race continues to do" (Davis 2012, 169). Adversity capital can also be harnessed to navigate and question the nature of labour markets and the erosion of their rights within them.

Schools and other informal and non-formal contexts of teaching and learning become important contexts in which adversity capital can be harnessed and developed. From an educational perspective, this involves the use of forms of pedagogy as:

> a critical practice [which] should provide the classroom conditions that provide the knowledge, skills, and culture of questioning necessary for students to engage in critical dialogue with the past, question authority (whether sacred or secular) and its effects, struggle with ongoing relations of power, and prepare themselves for what it means to be critical, active citizens in the interrelated local, national, and global public spheres.
> GIROUX and GIROUX 2006, 28

This educational response starts by acknowledging the nature of the contemporary labour market, legal and social norms, forms of exclusion and political power, and their inherent challenges and limitations, but also questions the moral economies fostered by neoliberalism and their pervasive "normality." Critical literacy through lived experience is a vital skill here, which when used in combination with others can be a powerful source of agency. Following Friere (2001), critical literacy continues to be a means through which one can, for example, "ask questions about their conditions and argue for their rights" (Comber 2015, 363), including navigating the complex navigation of rights to expression and belonging inflamed by Brandis above.

7 Conclusion

This chapter has argued for renewed interest in the development of certain skills, competencies and literacies as a means for young people to navigate some of the challenges of contemporary society. By some current measures, more work needs to be done within education institutions. Official estimates, for example, suggest low levels of technological competency amongst many students. Official data suggests that digital competence amongst Year 10 students decreased from 65 per cent meeting or exceeding the (minimum level) proficient standard in 2011, to 52 per cent in 2014 (ACARA 2015, 32). To take another example, efforts to improve political literacy through the national curriculum have made modest gains. Recent measures of civics and citizenship literacy captured through the National Assessment Plan (NAP-CC) assessments suggest that it has improved but remains low. 44 per cent of Australian Year 10 students attained a proficient standard in the civics and citizenship assessment in 2013, in contrast to 39 per cent in 2010 (Skujins and Lim 2015, 16).

But the development of skills, competencies and literacies as a part of adversity capital only represents one educational response to the many challenges confronting young people in contemporary society. Responses to racism, for example, are complex and not reducible to the competencies outlined in this paper.

The outrage arising from the political moment of the Abbott government arose from this particularly punitive manifestation of neoliberalism – one that persisted with his successor, Malcolm Turnbull. But there is potentially a source of hope arising from this moment. As writer George Megalongenis (2016, 12) notes, "the Abbott–Turnbull government … set for itself what it thought would be a simple test of competence – balancing the budget – and failed in the most spectacular way". This failure extended beyond its expansion of Australia's government deficit. All of the policy proposals outlined in this chapter failed to become law under the Abbott government, whose leadership imploded with Abbott's removal as Prime Minister by his own party in 2015. Other exclusionary policies persist, such as the brutal offshore detainment of refugees, a policy that was a continuation of measures implemented by the previous Labor government, and one that seeks to lock out the most vulnerable.

But there is hope here as these other failures suggest that the boundaries of neoliberalism may have limits. Megalogenis (2016,12) suggests that:

> the people keep sending the main parties back to the centre because Australia is one of the few countries that have not been broken by capitalism's 21st-century crisis. We may not handle the next shock as well as the last, but while our national political temperament remains moderate there is still hope that Australia can make something of this moment.

Globally, the worlds inhabited by young people are characterized by growing uncertainty, fluidity and change. These conditions seem pervasive and young people must navigate them on a daily basis. Educators must deal with these real and imagined worlds on a daily basis. This chapter has attempted to lay out an argument for how to equip young people with the knowledge, skills and dispositions to learn and adapt to the challenges of contemporary society, but perhaps more importantly, to develop new ways of critiquing neoliberalism and formulate alternatives; that is, to make something of this moment. One small part of the response to the changing nature of the economy and society includes the more explicit development of skills, competencies and literacies, embedded within the framework of adversity capital. But adversity capital represents only part of a response to politics of outrage, and must be located within the context of broader structural forces related to that which binds (social capital), and that which divides people (policy and individualisation). It also relies, to some extent, on a language of possibility (hope).

References

ABC. 2011. *Bolt breached discrimination act, judge rules.* http://www.abc.net.au/news/2011-09-28/bolt-found-guilty-of-breaching-discrimination-act/3025918 Accessed 20 June 2016.

ABC. 2014a. *Tony Abbott says too much Tasmanian forest 'locked up', forms new council to support timber industry.* http://www.abc.net.au/news/2014-03-05/abbott-timber-industry-dinner-forestry-council-forest-locked-up/5299046 Accessed 15 June 2016.

ABC. 2014b. *UNESCO rejects Coalition's bid to delist Tasmanian World Heritage forest.*: http://www.abc.net.au/news/2014-06-24/unesco-rejects-bid-to-delist-world-heritage-forest/5538946 Accessed 16 June 2016.

ABC. 2014c. *Protesters target Education Minister Christopher Pyne on set of ABC's Q&A program.* Retireved 20 June 2015 at: http://www.abc.net.au/news/2014-05-05/q-and-a-protesters-target-pyne/5432200 Accessed 20 June 2015.

ACARA. 2015. *National Assessment Program – ICT Literacy Years 6 and 10 Report 2014.* http://www.nap.edu.au/verve/_resources/D15_8761__NAP-ICT_2014_Public_Report_Final.pdf.

ACTU. 2012. *Lives on Hold. Unlocking the Potential of Australia's Workforce. The Report of the Independent Inquiry into Insecure Work in Australia.* Melbourne: Australian Council of Trade Unions.

The Australia Institute. 2013. *Youth value 'trust' but undecided on federal election.* https://www.tai.org.au/file.php?file=/media_releases/MR%20youth%20survey%20June%202013.pdf.

AYAC. 2010. "Where are you going with that? Maximising Young People's Impact on Organisational and Public Policy." https://www.thelibrarybook.net/pdf-where-are-you-going-with-that-maximising-young-people-s-impact-on-organisational-public-policy.html Accessed 14 June 2016.

Bauman, Z. 2000. *Liquid Modernity.* Cambridge: Polity Press.

Bauman, Z. 2013. *The Individualized Society.* Cambridge: Polity Press.

Berents, H. 2014. *Slackers or delinquents? No, just politically engaged youth.* https://theconversation.com/slackers-or-delinquents-no-just-politically-engaged-youth-27218 Accessed 20 June 2014.

Berg, C. 2013. *Freedom of speech means freedom to boycott.* http://www.abc.net.au/news/2013-09-04/berg-freedom-of-speech-means-freedom-to-boycott/4977410 Accessed 20 June 2016.

Bottrell, D. 2013. "Responsibilised Resilience? Reworking Neoliberal Social Policy Texts." In *M/C Journal of Media and Culture, 16*(5) October. http://journal.media-culture.org.au/index.php/mcjournal/article/viewArticle/708 Accessed 25 May 2015.

Brown, P., H. Lauder, and D. Ashton 2011. *The Global Auction: The Broken Promises of Education, Jobs, and Incomes.* New York: Oxford University Press.

Clarke, M., and J. Bennett 2015. *'Get a good job': Joe Hockey accused of insensitivity over advice to first-home buyers.* http://www.abc.net.au/news/2015-06-09/joe-hockey-accused-of-insensitivity-over-sydney-house-prices/6532630 Accessed 15 June 2016.

Collin, P. 2008. *Young People Imagining a New Democracy: Literature Review.* Whitlam Institute.

Comber, B. 2015. "Critical Literacy and Social Justice." In *Journal of Adolescent and Adult Literacy 58*, 362–367.

Davis, A. 2012. *The Meaning of Freedom and Other Difficult Dialogues.* San Francisco: City Lights Books.

Edwards, K., L. Saha, and M. Print 2007. "Report 4: Youth, Political Parties, and the Intention to Vote." *Australian Electoral Commission.* http://www.aec.gov.au/About_AEC/Publications/youth_study/youth_study_4/index.htm Accessed 14 March 2016.

FYA. 2015. *New Work Order.* Melbourne: The Foundation for Young Australians. http://www.fya.org.au/wp-content/uploads/2015/08/The-New-Work-Order-infographic-1-overview1.png Accessed 15 June 2016.

FYA. 2016. *Renewing Australia's Promise. Report Card 2016. Foundation for Young Australians (FYA).* http://www.fya.org.au/wp-content/uploads/2016/06/RenewingAusPromise_ReportCard_finalwebappend.pdf Accessed 15 June 2016.

Friere, P. 2001. *Politics of the Oppressed.* London: Bloomsbury.

Giroux, H.A., and S.S. Giroux 2006. "Challenging Neoliberalism's New World Order: The Promise of Critical Pedagogy." In *Cultural Studies Critical Methodologies;* 6; 21–32.

Griffiths, E. 2014. *George Brandis defends 'right to be a bigot' amid Government plan to amend Racial Discrimination Act.* http://www.abc.net.au/news/2014-03-24/brandis-defends-right-to-be-a-bigot/5341552 Accessed 15 June 2016.

Hannon, V., A. Patton, and J. Temperley 2011. "Developing an Innovation Ecosystem for Education." *Cisco White Paper, December 2011.* http://www.cisco.com/web/strategy/docs/education/ecosystem_for_edu.pdf Accessed 2 June 2014.

Hartcher, P., and J. Massola 2015. *Cabinet revolt over Tony Abbott and Peter Dutton plan to strip Australians of citizenship.* http://www.smh.com.au/federal-politics/political-news/cabinet-revolt-over-tony-abbott-and-peter-dutton-plan-to-strip-australians-of-citizenship-20150526-gh9q8y.html#ixzz4BilQ3MBL Accessed 16 June 2016.

Hockey, J. 2014. "Joe Hockey: We are a nation of lifters, not leaners." In *The Australian Financial Review, 14 May 2014.* http://www.afr.com/news/policy/tax/joe-hockey-we-are-a-nation-of-lifters-not-leaners-20140513-ituma.

Howie, L. and P. Campbell 2016. "Guerrilla selfhood: imagining young people's entrepreneurial futures," *Journal of Youth Studies*, 19:7, 906–920, DOI: 10.1080/13676261.2015.1123236.

Hui, S.K.F., and H.Y. Cheung 2015. "Cultural literacy and student engagement: The case of technical and vocational education and training (TVET) in Hong Kong." In *Journal of Further and Higher Education 39*, 553–578.

Hutchens, G. 2015. *Joe Hockey raises prospect of first home buyers using super to enter property market.* http://www.smh.com.au/federal-politics/political-news/joe-hockey-raises-prospect-of-first-home-buyers-using-super-to-enter-property-market-20150306-13xe3l.html#ixzz4BitvWBgL Accessed 16 June.

ILO. 2015. *World Employment and Social Outlook Trends 2015*. Geneva: International Labour Office. http://www.ilo.org/wcmsp5/groups/public/---dgreports/---dcomm/---publ/documents/publication/wcms_337070.pdf.

IYF. 2013. *Getting Youth in the Door: Defining Soft Skills Requirements for Entry-level Service Sector Jobs.* http://library.iyfnet.org/library/getting-youth-door-defining-soft-skills-requirements-entry-level-service-sector-jobs Accessed 1 May 2015.

Jones, N. 2014. *George Brandis' 2014 Section 18C Racial Discrimination Act speech.* Post in response to question: "What did you think of George Brandis' comments? Did you agree or disagree with the issues raised regarding people's 'right to be bigots' in a democratic society?" https://museumvictoria.com.au/immigrationmuseum/discoverycentre/identity/people-like-them/the-white-picket-fence/george-brandis-speech/.

Kahn, L., McNeil, B., Patrick, R., Sellick, V., Thompson, K., and Walsh, L. 2012. Developing skills for life and work: Accelerating social and emotional learning across South Australia. https://youngfoundation.org/wp-content/uploads/2012/10/Developing-skills-for-life-and-work-Accelerating-social-and-emotional-learning-across-South-Australia-February-2012.pdf.

Kelly, P. 2013. *The Self as Enterprise: Foucault and the Spirit of 21st Century Capitalism.* Surrey: Gower Publishing.

McGrath, P. 2013. *Australian unemployment rate climbs to 5.7 per cent.* http://www.abc.net.au/news/2013-07-11/unemployment-figures-for-june/4813876.

Megalogenis, G. 2016. "Back to the Centre." In *The Monthly, June*, 11–12.

News.com.au. 2011. *Get Up threatens boycott of grocery companies who oppose carbon tax.* http://www.news.com.au/finance/get-up-threatens-mass-boycott-of-grocery-companies-over-carbon-tax/story-e6frfm1i-1226090264041 Accessed 20 June 2016.

News.com.au. (2013). *Abbott promises respectful new parliament.* http://www.news.com.au/national/breaking-news/abbott-promises-respectful-new-parliament/story-e6frfku9-1226756393880 Accessed 16 June 2016.

Oliver, A. 2014. *The Lowy Institute Poll 2014.* http://www.lowyinstitute.org/files/final_2015_lowy_institute_poll.pdf Accessed 15 June 2015.

Oliver, A. 2015. *The Lowy Institute Poll 2015.* http://www.lowyinstitute.org/files/final_2015_lowy_institute_poll.pdf Accessed 15 June 2015.

Paradies, Y., L. Chandrakumar, N. Klocker, M. Frere, K. Webster, and M. Burrell 2009. *Building on our strengths: a framework to reduce race-based discrimination and support diversity in Victoria. Full Report.* Melbourne: Victorian Health Promotion Foundation.

Partnership for 21st Century Skills. 2009. *P21 Framework Definitions.* Washington, DC: P21. http://www.p21.org/storage/documents/ P21_Framework_Definitions.pdf Accessed 25 May 2015.

Pavlidis, A. 2009. "The Diverse Logics of Risk: Young People's Negotiations of the Risk Society." In *The Future of Sociology*, edited by S. Lockie, D. Bissell, A. Greig, M. Hynes, D. Marsh, L. Saha, J. Sikora, and D. Woodman The Australian National University, Canberra, 1–4 December 2009. Canberra: TASA.

Priest, N., A. Ferdinand, R. Perry, Y. Paradies, and M. Kelaher 2014. *Mental health impacts of racism and attitudes to diversity in Victorian schools: A Summary of Survey Findings.* Melbourne: VicHealth. http://www.deakin.edu.au/__data/assets/pdf_file/0005/229469/Mental-Health-Impacts-summay-report.pdf Accessed 23 July 2014.

Roberts, Y. 2009. *Grit: The Skills for Success and How They Are Grown.* London: The Young Foundation.

Rose, N. 2014. From Risk to Resilience: Responsible Citizens for Uncertain Times. Public Lecture, 28 August, Ian Potter Auditorium, Kenneth Myer Building, Royal Parade, Parkville, Australia.

Saha, L., M. Print, and K. Edwards 2011. "Youth Electoral Study Report 1: Enrolment and Voting." *Australian Electoral Commission.* http://www.aec.gov.au/About_AEC/publications/youth_study/youth_study_1/page04.htm Accessed 16 June 2015.

Sayer, A. 2007. *Moral Economy as Critique. New Political Economy.* 12(2), 261–270, DOI: 10.1080/13563460701303008.

SBS. 2014. *Factbox: Racial vilification laws in Australia.* SBS 2 April 2014. http://www.sbs.com.au/news/article/2014/03/27/factbox-racial-vilification-laws-australia Accessed 15 June 2016.

Skujins, P., and P. Lim 2015. *Unlimited Potential.* Melbourne: The Foundation for Young Australians.

Ungar, M. 2013. Introduction to the Volume, in *The Social Ecology of Resilience: A Handbook of Theory and Practice,* edited by M. New York Ungar, London: Springer, 1–12.

Universities Australia. 2014. *The impact of changes to HELP design on students.* 4 June 2014. https://www.universitiesaustralia.edu.au/ArticleDocuments/662/The%20Impact%20of%20Changes%20to%20HELP%20Design%20on%20Students.pdf.aspx Accessed 20 June 2016.

Walsh, L. 2016. *Educating Generation Next: Young People, Teachers and Schooling in Transition*. Hampshire: Palgrave Macmillan.

Walsh, L. 2017. "Treading water? The roles and possibilities of adversity capital in preparing young people for precarity." In *Neo-liberalism and Austerity: The Moral Economies of Young People's Health and Wellbeing*, edited by P. Kelly, and J. Pike Hampshire: Palgrave Macmillan.

Walsh, L., and R. Black (2018) *Rethinking Youth Citizenship After the Age of Entitlement*. London: Bloomsbury Academic.

Woodman, D. 2012. "Life out of Synch: How New Patterns of Further Education and the Rise of Precarious Employment Are Reshaping Young People's Relationships." In *Sociology, 46 (6), December*, 1074–90.

Wyn, J., and H Cuervo 2014. *Pain Now, Rewards Later? Young Lives Cannot Be Relived*. https://theconversation.com/pain-now-rewards-later-young-lives-cannot-be-relived-27376.

Zhao, Y. 2009. *Catching Up or Leading the Way: American Education in the Age of Globalization*. Alexandria, VA: Association for Supervision and Curriculum Development.

CHAPTER 11

The Youth Bulge: Remaking Precarity in Times of Illegitimacy

Emma E. Rowe

1   Introduction

In 2011, dubbed the 'year of protests', it was difficult to ignore the sense of growing social unrest, from the Arab Spring to the Chilean Winter, Occupy Wall Street and Occupy Together. Due to a high proportion of youthful participation within the Arab Spring, the movements were linked to the 'youth bulge' (Adams and Winthrop 2011, Austin 2011). Protests, riots, self-immolation, hunger strikes and civil unrest seemed to be spreading like wildfire across the globe, as the Occupy Movement took to semi-permanent occupations of urban space, frequently in central financial districts. The protests were hot on the heels of the 2007/2008 Global Financial Crisis. Certainly, there are distinctions to be made across the campaigning sites, although shared narratives emerged. Whilst the Arab Spring and Occupy Together were concerned with corporate greed, and the remaking of democracy, many protests turned to focus on social welfare and education. The Chilean Student Movement proclaimed the 'urgent need to recover education as a universal democratic, social and human right' (Confederación Nacional de Estudiantes de Chile (CONFECH) 2011).

In this chapter I explore states of precarity in times of illegitimacy, in relation to cultural and social movements for education. Precarity is a political, social and cultural endeavour as young people mobilise to 'invent new ... forms of labour organization' (Neilson and Rossiter 2008, 57). I explore the horizontal or collaborative methods of democratic participation and how this may speak to the reimagining of education within the 'technocapitalist' global landscape (Suarez-Villa 2012, 2000). At the heart of precarity for the young person is a hopeful expression of a new order; and whilst previous generations may cast doom and gloom predictions, I would argue these are not necessarily shared, and rather, challenges to education, democracy and government are expressions of reinvention and hope—a necessary ingredient for any generation.

The concept of the 'youth bulge', which refers to a higher proportion of young people within a population, was popularized in the media following

September 11 and grew in the wake of the Arab Spring or Arab Awakening[1] (Huntington 2001, Zakaria 2011, 2001). Before I discuss the youth bulge further, in relation to the Arab Awakening, I will first endeavour to position the discussion within critical perspectives of youth sociology (Furstenberg 2000, Bessant 2014, Patel Stevens et al. 2007).

2   Youth Sociology and Critical Perspectives

Do the global cultural uprisings in 2011 and beyond represent *generational rebellions* and the mobilization of youth-oriented social change? Furthermore, do these social uprisings suggest that young people are living within a unique and *critical* moment of illegitimacy?

Indeed, it is difficult it ignore the importance of digitalization for these social movements and the 'technoscape' (Appadurai 1990) in which these movements emerged. There are clearly tensions surrounding rapid and globalizing modernity, and as brought forth by the Arab Awakening, a clash between secularity and religion; modernity and traditionalism; poverty and the elites. Intellectuals such as Henry Giroux have argued that free-market capitalism has posited young people and adolescents within a new era of hostile economic conditions. Unencumbered stratums of totalitarianism under the façade of democracy, have risen to unprecedented heights, argues Giroux (2013). The 'war against youth' is also a 'war against democracy' utilizing 'special force and intensity against young people' (16). This 'special force' is perhaps most strikingly played out within the battlefield of schools and education, a theme I subsequently explore within this chapter.

Throughout history, young people have frequently been located in precarious states of legitimacy. This is evident in times of conflict but also times of cultural and social transition. During the industrialization era—and continued and perpetuated today in many parts of the world via the rationalities of consumerism—hundreds of thousands of children are regarded as cheap labour (Fisher 2011). During both World Wars, the vast majority of conscripted soldiers were young men and boys, and a large proportion did not return alive. Young people have often been at the centre of political campaigns or utilized as political weapons. The 'Hitler Youth' recruited children (from ages 10 to 18) to prepare boys for military service and girls for motherhood. Through these

---

[1] I refer to the Arab Spring subsequently as the 'Arab awakening'. I explain this further in the conclusion (Susser 2012).

events, we see how young people may be regarded as vulnerable to the machinations of political, social and cultural change.

Concern for youth is a generational concern, a 'practice that has a long history' (Bessant 2014, 82), in which young people are simultaneously located as deficient and idealized; at-risk or marginalized; dually in need of surveillance *and* protection. This is illuminated throughout the literature (e.g., Hall 1904). In the 1950s in post-war United States, Paul Goodman (1956) famously wrote *Growing up Absurd: Problems of Youth in the Organized System*, arguing that schooling—amongst other forms of social control—is damaging to young people's sense of autonomy and self-sufficiency. Goodman maintained that in times of severe adversity for youth, precarious forms of employment, growing poverty and wealth gaps, young men (sic) needed to resist and recapture their own claim to legitimacy and self-governance. With similar tones, Neil Postman wrote *The Disappearance of Childhood* (1982) contending that technology (in addition to the women's liberation movement) contributes to the continuous decline and contraction of childhood, and has been the case ever since the invention of the telegraph in the 1800s.

Given this history it becomes problematic to frame the recent protests and actions as occurring in a new/singular time and moment of illegitimacy. Although the time in which these protests have unfolded has its own particularities, it may be more feasible to contend that young people are located within a *continuum* of illegitimacy. With the intensification of formal schooling and the emphasis on school completion dramatically increasing (see, Connell et al. 1982, Campbell and Proctor 2014), this has resulted in a long and protracted transition to adulthood. In rendering the current social and economic milieu as a unique time or moment of illegitimacy, it is thus important to avoid idealized views of the past (such as Donald Trump's nostalgic slogans). Certainly, whilst no means complete or fulfilled, global organizations are attempting to 'protect' childhood in more recent centuries. *The Conventions on the Right of the Child* (UNICEF) was first introduced in 1989—the same year that hundreds of university students were massacred in Tiananmen Square as they protested and starved themselves in their pursuit for a more democratic society.

Furthermore, adopting a comparative perspective and evoking the category of 'young person' is not without its difficulties and constraints, as a social construct frequently framed within essentialist paradigms of age (Bessant 2014, Patel Stevens et al. 2007). Bessant (2014) asks, 'what does the idea of generation mean, and how can that idea best be used?' (7). The construct of 'youth' or 'young person' belies a sense of the in-between and incompletion, dually in need of surveillance and protection. This points to the continuum of illegitimacy, well captured by a simple paradox:

> Advanced industrial societies create adolescence and early adulthood as life stages in ways that inevitably render them problematic. In one way or another, much of the social science research on adolescence has been dominated by this cultural contradiction.
>
> FURSTENBERG 2000, 897

The paradox of surveillance versus protection, and the construction of the 'adolescent', is a useful frame to problematize the youth bulge—as a social and cultural construct centred around the 'risky' aspect of young people. The youth bulge may be useful for emphasizing disenfranchised youth who are immobilized within the transition from education to work.

3 The Youth Bulge

The youth bulge refers to a disproportionate percentage of young people within the population, typically males between the age of fifteen to twenty-four, in developing economies (Zakaria 2001, Roche 2014, LaGraffe 2012, Huntington 2001). Albeit, the precise age slightly differs within the literature. Across Northern Africa and the Middle East, there is a higher proportion of young people in comparison to countries such as Australia, the United States and Britain. For example, Egypt is experiencing a significant youth bulge, with fifty per cent of the population under the age of twenty-four (see Figure 11.1),[2] alongside high levels of unemployment amongst formally uneducated and educated young people. In these countries, the concept of the youth bulge is utilized to explain social unrest in the form of political violence, terrorism or conflict (Urdal 2007, Austin 2011, Roche 2014). As Urdal (2007) writes, 'young males are the main protagonists of criminal as well as political violence' and that empirical data points 'to a clear statistical relationship between youth bulges and an increased risk of both internal armed conflict, terrorism, and riots' (90, 91).

The notion of the youth bulge was popularized following September 11, when it was alleged that the majority of hijackers were young males between

---

[2] Saudi Arabia has a similar youth bulge with 46% of the population under the age of 25. The youth bulges are also attributed to significant population increases. Since 1901, Egypt has increased from approximately 10 million people to nearly 90 million people in 2015. This is a higher population growth rate (1.5–2% approximately) in comparison to developed economies in the OECD. For example, United States population growth rate is 0.78 or Australia 1.07% (see, Piketty 2014). Other developing economies have experienced a similar surge, including Nigeria, Pakistan.

the ages of twenty to twenty-four from Saudi Arabia[3] (U.S. Government 2004). Huntington (2001) argued that the 'key factor' in this act of terror was the demographic factor – 'generally speaking, the people who go out and kill other people are males between the ages of 16 and 30'. This is reiterated by Zakaria in another journalistic piece published in October 2001:

> A huge influx of restless young men in any country is bad news. When accompanied by even small economic and social change, it usually produces a new politics of protest. In the past, societies in these circumstances have fallen prey to a search for revolutionary solutions. (France went through a youth bulge just before the French Revolution, as did Iran before its 1979 revolution.) In the case of the Arab world, this revolution has taken the form of an Islamic resurgence.
> ZAKARIA 2001

In this paradigm, youth are risky—particularly males—and in need of intervention, surveillance and control. Young people are 'posited no longer as *at risk* but as *the risk* to democratic public life' (Giroux 2010, 52, italics in original). Whilst violent action is correlated with young people, so too is the more positive characterization of non-violent action and forms of protest. This is drawn out further by Howie and Campbell (2016) in their theorizing of the '*guerrilla self*' and methods of resistance in post-GFC United States, and Castells (2012) in his exploration of revolutionary movements across Egypt, Spain and Tunisia.

Non-violent resistance came to the fore during the Arab Awakening, another social movement linked with the youth bulge (LaGraffe 2012). Certainly, the countries involved in the non-violent and pro-democratic uprisings of the Arab Awakening across the Middle East and Northern Africa—including Tunisia, Egypt, Libya and Yemen—each retain a higher population of young people, in comparison to developed economies. I endeavour to illuminate this point further in the following graph (see Figure 11.1). Considering the data,[4] it is

---

3 The Final Report of the National Commission following 9/11 (see U.S. Government 2004) alleges that fourteen out of the nineteen hijackers were allegedly males aged between twenty to twenty-five, and predominantly from Saudi Arabia. According to this report, the hijackers were young, with the remaining four under the age of thirty. Only one hijacker was allegedly aged over 30 (a pilot, age 32).
4 The graph draws on data sourced from the Centre for Intelligence Agency Website, and triangulated with the literature (Yifu Lin 2012, Urdal 2007, LaGraffe 2012, Dhillon 2008, Zakaria 2011, 2001). The data that relates to the youth bulge and levels of unemployment represents the year 2016. This data is limited in capturing the demographics in 2011, the time of the Arab

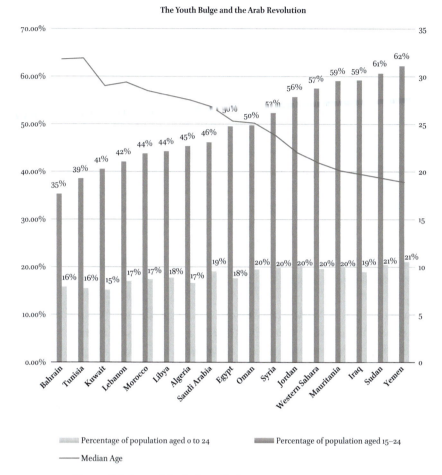

FIGURE 11.1 The youth bulge and the Arab revolution.
SOURCE: AUTHOR

feasible to argue that the countries involved with the Arab Awakening contain a younger polity:

Young people were clearly pivotal and instrumental in the cultural uprisings of the Arab Spring. For many western commentators this was marked out via the instrumentality and traction of social media in terms of collective organization and resistance. The BBC asserted that the Arab Spring was

Spring. Arguably it is useful in providing a snapshot of the high proportion of young people and levels of unemployment, which is further addressed elsewhere (Yifu Lin 2012, Urdal 2007, LaGraffe 2012, Dhillon 2008, Zakaria 2011, 2001).

a movement born on Facebook (BBC News 2011b), and rather than picking up weapons—like revolutions from the past—these movements organized online, utilizing *'technologies of resistance'* (Milberry 2014, 53, emphasis in original). Although, this 'clean' and westernised image of the uprisings largely ignores the violence perpetuated on the protestors (see, Abul-Magd 2012).

In addition to retaining this higher proportion of young people, these emerging economies struggle with high levels of youth unemployment and a lack of meaningful employment opportunities (as do many developed economies also), ranging from 37.6% in Tunisia, to 34.4% in Egypt (OECD 2016b). Whilst many of these countries invest relatively high proportions of their GDP into education, the lowly status of teachers, significant gender gaps, and lack of high-quality, low-cost education has contributed to high levels of illiteracy. The Arab Awakening was partially driven by young people 'stuck' and immobilized within the transition from education to employment, a life-stage invariably utilized to mark the transition from adolescence to adulthood.

In the same year as the Arab Awakening and the Occupy Movement, across the globe and receiving relatively little mainstream press attention, the Chilean Student Movement swelled and struggled in their bid for improved access to low-cost education. Whilst there are clearly nuances and distinctions between the social movements, there is a shared demand for equity, opportunity and improved transparency of governance, as brought forth by a younger generation in their mobilization of critical pedagogical spaces.

4   The Chilean Winter

The Chilean Student Movement was first initiated in 2006 when secondary students took to the streets, marching in black and white attire (referred to as the 'Penguin Revolution'). In their collective rallies through the streets, and long-term occupations of school buildings, students called for bus concessions for travel to school and increased government funding for secondary school education. University students later joined these protests in relation to the inaccessibility of higher education. In 2011 the movement hit a boiling point, dubbed by the mainstream press as the 'Chilean Winter' (gesturing to the Arab Spring).

The students protested against the disproportionate cost of education, calling for an end to profit-making in education. Students have consistently maintained their commitment to non-violent protest, although a young boy was reportedly shot and killed by the police during the 2011 national strike day (The Internationalist 2011, BBC News 2011a). Students are calling for free and quality education, often using imaginative means and consistently relying on social media to both distribute and build their movement. For '1800 consecutive hours', through day and night, the students ran an unending relay race around the presidential palace to 'symbolise the 18 billion Chilean pesos necessary to finance 1 year of free higher education' (Stromquist and Sanyal 2013, 167). The students employ non-violent protests involving: large-scale kiss ins (extended kissing between couples) to demonstrate their 'passion for education'; a mass-performance entitled 'mass suicide by education' in which students performed death; or collective choreographed dances where students dressed as zombies and danced to Michael Jackson's *Thriller*. This dance was used to illustrate 'death by debt' in reference to their imminent education debt (Barrionuevo 2011, Stromquist and Sanyal 2013, The Internationalist 2011, Taylor 2011, Bellei, Cabalin, and Orellana 2014).

The excessive education debt that faces young people forecloses the possibility of higher education to the broad majority. Chile is a largely privatized education system, following the Pinochet rule through the 1980s (Hsieh and Urquiola 2006, Harvey 2005). In comparison to other OECD countries, Chile retains a far higher proportion of students who attend private schools, with a percentage of students who attend public schools well below the OECD average (82%). Only 37% of the Chilean population attend public schools (otherwise known as municipal schools), with the remainder enrolled at private institutions (OECD 2013b). However, this is further obfuscated by the 'derivatives' of public schools, such as for-profit and non-profit charter schools, which are government-funded yet exclusive and often difficult for the broad majority to access. Chile records high-levels of student segregation within their schooling system as based on socio-economic status, in comparison to other OECD countries (Rambla, Valiente, and Frías 2011). This is illuminated by the Chilean Student Movement, who write on their website:

> Education in Chile is going through an acute crisis. We have a discriminatory system that perpetuates inequality through segregation and exclusion [and] operates from the schools to universities undermining democratic coexistence. There is an urgent need to recover education as a universal social and human right … This right must be guaranteed … and be based upon a new National System of Public Education, one that is to be Free, Democratic, and of High Quality, organized and financed by the state. (Confederación nacional de estudiantes de chile (CONFECH) 2011, capitalized in original) [Chile Student Movement Union].

Long-term and sustained social movements for education across OECD countries, including the Chilean Student Movement, demonstrate the fractured scope of education in the post-Fordist context. A lack of access to quality low-cost education exacerbates societal inequalities. The restructuring of public schooling contributes to higher levels of segregation and structural disadvantage, across the lines of socio-economic status, gender and race (Wells, Slayton, and Scott 2002, Roda 2015).

As the public school is increasingly reoriented in the logic of the market, the social movements potentially illuminate education as a structural mechanism reinforcing institutionalized precarity. Fisher (2011) describes schools as facing a 'crisis of legitimisation' in which the 'logic of privatization has diminished the role of schools as vital public spheres' (382). She writes:

> Fast-forward to the current moment and this theatre of absurdity has taken on entirely new proportions in the lives of all children and youth, but particularly those who are poor and/or minority ... thanks to the emergence and intensification of neoliberalism since the 1970s.
> FISHER 2011, 380

As a social, economic and cultural institution that principally serves young people, low-cost and high-quality education theoretically enables and empowers more vulnerable individuals to advance and improve upon their economic and labour conditions. Education as an accessible and authorizing social institution can potentially interrupt and destabilize pre-determined classifications around employment and income.

5 Disassembling Public Education

Public schools are historically understood as 'non-market' or located outside the purview of the market. Since the 1980s, and across OECD countries, the public school (also understood as the state, municipal or 'common' school) has experienced a series of fundamental policy shifts, emphasizing autonomy, decentralization and competition vis-à-vis the rationalities of free-market economics (Picower 2013, Hursh 2015, Whitty, Power, and Halpin 1998). Precarious policy conditions engender consistent pressure

> ...in rearticulating the public school in alignment with the market, producing tensions in serving the more historical conceptualizations of public schooling, coupled with contemporary profit-driven concerns.

> Conflict points are visible in global social movements and social activism around public education.
>
> ROWE 2017, 1

The dismantling of the traditional public school is strikingly played out via the numerous 'derivatives' of public schooling. The list of public schooling 'derivatives' is incredibly extensive and broad. Charter schools in the U.S., mini schools in Canada, private voucher schools in Chile, free schools and academies in England, the *friskolor* in Sweden, self-managing schools and Independent public schools in Australia, partnership schools in New Zealand (Yoon 2011, Lubienski 2001, Lubienski, Lee, and Gordon 2013, Whitty and Power 2000, Arreman and Holm 2011). Whilst there are differences between each model, public school derivatives share a commitment to autonomy and decentralization, a separation from the traditional public school, although they continue to receive government funding.

Traditional public schools are reoriented within the logic of the market as private capital to be consumed and acquired. This is a type of *rebranding* or refashioning of the traditional public school within the post-Fordist economy—differentiated and specialized for the individualized consumer (Harvey 2008, Amin 1994). Although the rebranding of public schooling may be endeavouring to move away from 'factory models' of schooling, creating differentiated schools for the differentiated consumer, schooling across OECD countries simultaneously and paradoxically grows more homogenous and standardized. For many countries, particularly Australia, there is heightened segregation of the student cohort (Windle 2015). Gorur (2014) argues that standardization by stealth is a means of measurement, in order to render education as simplified, evidence-based, quantifiable and entirely calculable.

The dismantling of the public school is structured and enabled via government policies, and largely financed and directed by the private, corporate sector. This is the global education business which has been valued by corporate bodies such as Apple, Intel and the World Bank as a trillion dollar industry (Verger, Lubienski, and Steiner-Khamsi 2016a). These authors write:

> We are seeing the emergence of the idea of education as a sector for investment and profit making, where organizations, practices and networks engaged in these endeavours take on an increasingly global scale ... Now we are witnessing the emergence of whole trade associations dedicated to optimizing opportunities for investors looking to capitalize on the education sector.
>
> VERGER, LUBIENSKI, and STEINER-KHAMSI 2016a, 3

The global education business (Ball 2012) or the global education industry (GEI) is dominated by private and transnational entities, such as The Bill and Melinda Gates Foundation, Pearson Affordable Learning Fund and Teach for All. These private bodies are incredibly influential in reshaping and redirecting educational policy—from the administration and design of standardized testing, to the professionalization and working conditions for teachers, to how schools are structured and funded (Hursh 2015, Ravitch 2011, Verger, Lubienski, and Steiner-Khamsi 2016b). In the United States, tax concessions and rebates are granted to encourage private corporations to convert existing public schools to charter schools (Lipman 2013). This is only one example of the policy machinations that aim to increase financial revenue and profit-making from education, whilst simultaneously claiming to work towards greater quality, equity and low-cost education. The generational uprisings of the Arab Awakening and the Chilean Student Movement indicate the temerity—or possibly the weakness—of these claims.

The generational uprisings of the Arab Awakening and the Chilean Winter are symptomatic of widening inequality, the fracturing of social services and the commodification of education. They also point to the crisis of representative democracy.

6   Representative Democracy and Technocapitalism

A growing proportion of young people are locked out of meaningful employment, access to affordable and high-quality education, house ownership or stable housing (OECD 2016a, 2013a). Economists argue that inequality is rising, and whilst living standards have largely improved in developed economies, the gap between the rich and the poor is greater than the post-war years (Atkinson 2015). Wealth is increasingly concentrated. Piketty (2014) contends that forces of convergence and forces of divergence are wider and stronger in the contemporary economy, than ever before. It is not only that the rich are growing richer, and the poor are growing poorer, but that economic growth is stagnant or declining for large proportions of the population. The OECD (2015) reports:

> In recent decades, as much as 40% of the population at the lower end of the distribution has benefited little from economic growth in many countries. In some cases, low earners have even seen their incomes fall in real terms … Just as with the rise of the 1%, the decline of the 40% raises social and political questions. When such a large group in the population

gains so little from economic growth, the social fabric frays and trust in institutions is weakened. (20, 21)

Widening inequality is hindering the democratic process, to such an extent that representative democracy is largely an illusion. As reflected in the social movements of 2011, the demands for improved social services and political legitimacy reflect a broader polity call for meaningful, authentic democracy. As put forth by the Occupy Movement, there is a demand for elected individuals to more closely represent the biddings of the polity. There is an increasing belief that representation stands for the wealthy minority, rather than the broader majority (e.g. we are the 99%). Suarez-Villa (2012) argues that we have entered into a new era of capitalism defined by the rise of corporate power and corporate control. This era maintains a lesser reliance on physical labour, depending more on 'intangible resources' (9) such as creativity and technological innovation. He writes:

> Technocapitalism's global reach depends on a new ethos of corporate control over technology and science, and on the unfettered expansion of corporate power, with consequences for humanity, life and nature that are all too often irreversible (8).

The rise of corporate power, but also the relationship between business and government, is clearly relevant within the context of the 2007/2008 Global Financial Crisis and the social movements that followed closely after. The interconnectedness of these events is mapped out by Castells (2012). The question becomes whether 'fast capitalism' (Castells 2012) and 'fast accumulation' (Suarez-Villa 2012) is contributing to a rapid decline of social democratic welfare measures, and public trust in social institutions. McWilliams and Bonet (2016) write,

> Scholars have argued that in the post-industrial moment, precarity has become 'unexceptional' as the social institutions of the welfare state that once guarded against the ruthless vagaries of capitalism have eroded and left the majority of the world's population exposed to free market caprice.
> CROSS, 2010; NEILSON & ROSSITER, 2008

With the growth of capitalism, there is little protection for social institutions—such as public schools—from the 'ruthless vagaries' of the market. Precariousness is thus a 'capitalist norm' (Mitropoulou 2011) constructing volatile economic and labour conditions. Smyth (2016) builds on these assertions:

> My proposition is: what if precarity were not so much an aberration or dysfunction of the fordist (or even post-fordist) system of work, but rather as people like Mitropoulos (2011) and Neilson and Rossiter (2008) argue, an inevitability of capitalism? ... What would such a reading mean for the lives of young people caught up in being displaced by capitalism? (130, 131).

The new era of capitalism, as corporate controlled democracy, disenfranchises young people via diminished, or perhaps less meaningful, participatory and representative democracy, and the capacity to influence political decisions. This was recently made evident via the Brexit vote, with young people disproportionally voting to remain in the European Union (Moore 2016).

The current state of education offers little hope for many young people, in that it guarantees generational debt, due to the excessive and rising costs of education. However, it is necessary to issue these arguments with caveats. In thinking about the displacement of young people, it may be more accurate to capture this as a structural, institutional and systemic war on *disadvantaged youth*—Indigenous youth in Australia; African-American youth in the United States; and, youth living in poverty and hardship. Whether one experiences disadvantage largely depends on sociological categories around race, gender and socio-economic status. In countries such as Tunisia, Egypt or Libya, females remain under-represented in formal education, and over-represented in unemployment and measures of illiteracy.

7   Conclusion

In this chapter, I have explored the notion of precarity in times of illegitimacy, as framed by social movements such as the Arab Awakening and the Chilean Winter. I sought to position the discussion within a critical sociology of youth and the concept of the 'youth bulge' to examine how social and cultural uprisings may represent generational rebellions and resistance. The call for accessible and high-quality education is a prescient demand that is routinely and consistently threaded through social movements and cultural uprisings, across OECD countries (see, Rowe 2017). As I have argued in this chapter, the corporatization of education has contributed to higher education debts, segregation and insurmountable gaps for a proportion of the population.

It is important to acknowledge that comparing the uprisings across the Middle East, with the Chilean Winter and Occupy Together, may function as an act of essentializing. There is a need to recognize political and cultural differences across the geo-political sites (Susser 2012). Indeed, the naming of the Arab

Spring as a 'spring' points to the dominant western lens. Susser (2012) explains that the 'Arab Spring' was a term primarily adopted by western commentators, although activists 'cast it as a "revolution" (*thawra*)' or an 'Arab awakening' (Susser 2012, 30, 34). The term 'spring' connotes the Prague Spring and the 'Spring of Nations' in Europe—national secularist uprisings that fought for liberal and democratic government. Although there were factions of the Arab Uprising fighting for secularist governance, Susser (2012) argues that the Arab revolution was far more complex than this westernised imaginary, and it

> ...is a striking case of "false universalism," due to its remoteness from reality and a flawed vision reflective of the inability, or unwillingness, to recognize the cultural difference of "the other". The deep undercurrents of Middle East political culture differ from those of the liberal/secular Western world (30).

In a journalistic piece, Fareed Zakaria (2001) writes about the conflicted nature of modernity in the Middle East—the 'clash of civilizations'—as the global West meets the Middle East. America 'thinks of modernity as all good' (Zakaria 2001). The hegemony of modernity and globalization is imposed upon myriad religious and cultural settings, positioned in tension with religious and social traditions. Modernity is imagined and provoked as progressive, neutral and intellectually superior (Rasmussen 2015).

The widespread use of social media sites and technology within the Arab awakening, in particular, signalled the global rise of modernity for certain commentators (e.g. Sakbani 2011). It is clear that young people effectively harnessed the transformative potential of social media during the Arab awakening, the Occupy Movement and the Chilean Winter. In holding up smart phones during rallies, organizing protests or capturing violent encounters and posting the images online, tools of technology built momentum but also enabled broad distribution and transparency. In this way, the movements were democratized and accessible for a wider audience. This is a collaborative (horizontal) means to gather, negotiate and generate alternative visions, hopes and ideas for society. Marina Sitrin (2012) writes about *horizontalidad*, horizontality, and horizontalism,

> *Horizontalidad* is a social relationship that implies, as its name suggests, a flat plane upon which to communicate. *Horizontalidad* necessarily implies the use of direct democracy and the striving for consensus, processes in which attempts are made so that everyone is heard and new relationships are created. *Horizontalidad* is a new way of relating, based in affective politics and against all the implications of 'isms'. It is a dynamic

social relationship. It is not an ideology or political program that must be met so as to create a new society or new idea. It is a break with these sorts of vertical ways of organizing and relating, and a break that is an opening.
SITRIN 2012

The notion of 'horizontalidad' further pushes back against critiques of the social movements in lacking specific demands, and criticisms that the movements were ineffective in producing desired change (see, Kitchen 2012, Lawson 2012, van de Sande 2013). For some protestors, the social movements elicited physicality, dialogue and collectivism—such as Judith Butler's claim of 'we the people' (Butler 2012). Thereby, *horizontalidad* or *horizontalism* is emulative of prefigurative politics—subversive, disruptive and open-ended. It is experimental and 'actualised in the here and now' (van de Sande 2013, 230), rather than institutionalized, vertical and objectified.

So too, technology can be transformative for opening up *critical pedagogical spaces* as problem-posing, dialogic and collaborative (Freire 2012). By utilizing social media, young people are able to create and control spaces not necessarily subjected to adult surveillance and vertical power structures. An example of this is during the Occupy and the Spanish Indignados movement. Both movements posted online to organize face-to-face collaborations (referred to as 'IRL' or 'F2F', meaning In Real Life and Face to Face) (Castells 2012, Sitrin 2012). The face-to-face collaborations and events routinely involved long and drawn out debates around democracy and the constitution of democracy. For the Occupy Movement, these events were understood as General Assemblies, and utilized detailed processes around how to select speakers (ensuring broad participation) and multiple hand gestures to enable constant interaction between the speaker and the crowd. Boler et al. (2014) discuss the General Assemblies during the Occupy Movement,

> To participate in any of the assemblies taking place throughout the United States, and in many places around the globe, means to stand or sit in a circle, with a handful of facilitators, and speak and listen in turn, usually with general guidelines and principles of unity, and then together attempt to reach consensus ... [This is] something like direct, real, or participatory democracy ... (444).

This is a highly valuable educative process in which young (and old) people are exchanging their ideas, negotiating and articulating their values, hopes and ambitions. This is the expression of hope amidst the context of outrage. In this exchange, young people are articulating their expression of the future—the political, social and cultural future—and engaged in provocative exchanges and articulations to reimagine the status quo. These spaces offer innovative and new visions of how to imagine education and educational spaces as critical, cooperative and democratic.

References

Abul-Magd, Zeinab. 2012. 'Occupying Tahrir Square: the myths and the realities of the Egyption revolution'. *The South Atlantic Quarterly* 111:565–572.

Adams, A., and R. Winthrop. 2011. 'The Role of Education in the Arab World Revolutions'. http://www.brookings.edu/research/opinions/2011/06/10-arab-world-education-winthrop.

Amin, Ash, ed. 1994. *Post-Fordism: a reader, Studies in urban and social change*. Oxford; Cambridge, Mass: Blackwell.

Appadurai, A. 1990. 'Disjuncture and Difference in the Global Cultural Economy'. *Theory, Culture & Society* 7 (2):295–310. doi: 10.1177/026327690007002017.

Arreman, Inger Erixon, and Ann-Sofie Holm. 2011. 'Privatisation of public education? The emergence of independent upper secondary schools in Sweden'. *Journal of Education Policy* 26 (2):225–243. doi: 10.1080/02680939.2010.502701.

Atkinson, A.B. 2015. *Inequality: what can be done?* Cambridge and London: Harvard University Press.

Austin, Leila. 2011. 'The Politics of Youth Bulge: From Islamic Activism to Democratic Reform in the Middle East and North Africa'. *SAIS Review* (2):81.

Ball, S.J. 2012. *Global education inc.: new policy networks and the neo-liberal imaginary*. Abingdon, Oxon; New York: Routledge.

Barrionuevo, A. 2011. 'With Kiss-Ins and Dances, Young Chileans Push for Reform'. Arthur Ochs Sulzberger Jr., Last Modified 4th August. http://www.nytimes.com/2011/08/05/world/americas/05chile.html?_r=0.

BBC News. 2011a. 'Chilean president seeks answers on protest death'. accessed September 3rd. http://www.bbc.com/news/world-latin-america-14705127.

BBC News. 2011b. 'How Facebook Changed the World: The Arab Spring'. http://www.bbc.co.uk/programmes/b014grsr.

Bellei, Cristián, Cristian Cabalin, and Víctor Orellana. 2014. 'The 2011 Chilean student movement against neoliberal educational policies'. *Studies in Higher Education* 39 (3):426–440. doi: 10.1080/03075079.2014.896179.

Bessant, J. 2014. *Democracy Bytes: new media, new politics and generational change*. Houndmills, Basingstoke, Hampshire: Palgrave Macmillan.

Butler, Judith. 2012. 'Bodies in public'. In *Occupy!, scenes from occupied America*, edited by Carla Blumenkranz, Keith Gessen, Mark Greif, Sarah Leonard and Sarah Resnick. New York: Verso.

Campbell, C., and H. Proctor. 2014. *A History of Australian Schooling*. Crows Nest, NSW: Allen & Unwin.

Castells, M. 2012. *Networks of Outrage and Hope: social movements in the internet age*. Cambridge, UK; Malden, USA: Polity Press.

Confederación Nacional de Estudiantes de Chile (CONFECH). 2011. 'Demandas [National Confederation of Chilean Students]'. accessed August 2nd. http://fech.cl/.

Connell, R., D. Ashenden, S. Kessler, and G. Dowsett. 1982. *Making the Difference: Schools, Families, and Social Division*. Sydney: Allen & Unwin.

Cross, J. 2010. Neoliberalism as unexceptional: Economic zones and the everyday precariousness of working life in South India. *Critique of Anthropology, 30*, 355–373. doi: 10.1177/0308275X10372467

Dhillon, N. 2008. 'Middle East Youth Bulge: Challenge or Opportunity?'. Brookings Institute, accessed July 15th. https://www.brookings.edu/on-the-record/middle-east-youth-bulge-challenge-or-opportunity/.

Fisher, J. 2011. '"The Walking Wounded": Youth, Public Education, and the Turn to Precarious Pedagogy'. *Review of Education, Pedagogy, and Cultural Studies* 33 (5):379–432. doi: 10.1080/10714413.2011.620858.

Freire, Paulo. 2012. *Pedagogy of the oppressed*. Translated by Myra Bergman Ramos. New York: The Continuum International Publishing Group Ltd.

Furstenberg, Frank F. 2000. 'The Sociology of Adolescence and Youth in the 1990s: A Critical Commentary'. *Journal of Marriage & Family* 62 (4):896–910.

Giroux, H.A. 2010. *Politics After Hope: Obama and the Crisis of Youth, Race, and Democracy*. Boulder, CO: Paradigm Publishers.

Giroux, H.A. 2013. *America's education deficit and the war on youth*. New York: Monthly Review Press.

Goodman, P. 1956. *Growing up Absurd: Problems of Youth in the Organized System*. New York, NY: Random House.

Gorur, Radhika. 2014. 'Towards a Sociology of Measurement in Education Policy'. *European Educational Research Journal* 13 (1):58.

Hall, G.S. 1904. *Adolescence: Its Psychology and Its Relations to Physiology, Anthropology, Sociology, Sex, Crime, Religion and Education*. New York: D. Appleton.

Harvey, D. 2005. *A Brief History of Neoliberalism*. Oxford and New York: Oxford University Press.

Harvey, David. 2008. 'Flexible Accumulation Through Urbanization: Reflections on 'Post-Modernism' in the American City'. In *Post-Fordism: A Reader*, edited by A. Amin, 361–386. Oxford & Cambridge: Blackwell Publishers Ltd.

Howie, Luke, and Perri Campbell. 2016. 'Guerrilla selfhood: imagining young people's entrepreneurial futures'. *Journal of Youth Studies* 19 (7):906.

Hsieh, Chang-Tai, and Miguel Urquiola. 2006. 'The effects of generalized school choice on achievement and stratification: Evidence from Chile's voucher program'. *Journal of Public Economics* 90 (8–9):1477–1503.

Huntington, S.P. 2001. 'So, Are Civilizations at War? [An Interview with Samuel Huntington]'. accessed March 8th. https://www.theguardian.com/world/2001/oct/21/afghanistan.religion2.

Hursh, D.W. 2015. *The End of Public Schools: The Corporate Reform Agenda to Privatize Education*. New York & London: Routledge.

Kitchen, Nicholas. 2012. 'Executive summary'. In *After the Arab spring: power change in the Middle East?*, edited by Nicholas Kitchen. London: London School of Economics.

LaGraffe, D. 2012. 'The Youth Bulge in Egypt: An Intersection of Demographics, Security, and the Arab Spring'. *Journal of Strategic Security* (2):64.

Lawson, George. 2012. 'The Arab uprisings: revolution or protests?' In *After the Arab spring: power change in the Middle East?*, edited by Nicholas Kitchen. London: London School of Economics.

Lipman, P. 2013. 'Economic crisis, accountability, and the state's coercive assault on public education in the USA'. *Journal of Education Policy* 28 (5):557–573. doi: 10.1080/02680939.2012.758816.

Lubienski, C. 2001. 'Redefining "Public" Education: Charter Schools, Common Schools, and the Rhetoric of Reform'. *Teachers College Record* 103 (4):634–666.

Lubienski, C., J. Lee, and L. Gordon. 2013. 'Self-managing schools and access for disadvantaged students: Organizational behaviour and school admissions'. *New Zealand Journal of Educational Studies* 48 (1):82–98.

McWilliams, J. A., and Bonet, S.W. 2016. Continuums of precarity: refugee youth transitions in American high schools. *International Journal of Lifelong Education,* 35 (2): 153–170. doi: 10.1080/02601370.2016.1164468.

Milberry, K. 2014. '(Re)making the Internet: Free Software and the Social Factory Hack'. In *DIY Citizenship: Critical Making and Social Media*, edited by M. Ratto and M. Boler, 53–64. Cambridge Massachusetts: The MIT Press.

Mitropoulos, A. 2011. 'From Precariousness to Risk Management and beyond'. accessed July 5th. http://eipcp.net/transversal/0811/mitropoulos/en.

Moore, P. 2016. 'How Britain Voted'. You Gov UK, accessed July 5th. https://yougov.co.uk/news/2016/06/27/how-britain-voted/.

Neilson, Brett, and Ned Rossiter. 2008. 'Precarity as a Political Concept, or, Fordism as Exception'. *Theory, Culture & Society* 25 (7–8):51–72. doi: 10.1177/0263276408097796.

OECD. 2013a. The OECD Action Plan for Youth: giving youth a better start in the labour market. Paris, France: OECD.

OECD. 2013b. PISA 2012 Results: What Makes Schools Successful? Resources, Policies and Practices. Paris, France: OECD.

OECD. 2015. *In It Together: Why Less Inequality Benefits All*. Paris: OECD.
OECD. 2016a. *Investing in Youth: Australia*. Paris, France: OECD Publishing.
OECD. 2016b. 'OECD Employment Outlook 2016'. OECD Publishing. http://www.keepeek.com/Digital-Asset-Management/oecd/employment/oecd-employment-outlook-2016_empl_outlook-2016-en#.V7KOFph97cs#page8.
Patel Stevens, L., L. Hunter, D. Pendergast, V. Carrington, N. Nahr, C. Kapitzke, and J. Mitchell. 2007. 'Reconceptualising the possible narratives of adolescence'. *Australian Educational Researcher* 34 (2):107–127.
Picower, Bree. 2013. 'Education should be free! Occupy the DOE!: teacher activists involved in the Occupy Wall Street movement'. *Critical Studies in Education* 54 (1):44–56. doi: 10.1080/17508487.2013.739569.
Piketty, T. 2014. *Capital in the Twenty-First Century*. Translated by Arthur Goldhammer. Cambridge and London: Harvard University Press.
Postman, N. 1982. *The Disappearance of Childhood*. New York, NY: Delacourte Press.
Rambla, Xavier, Óscar Valiente, and Carla Frías. 2011. 'The politics of school choice in two countries with large private-dependent sectors (Spain and Chile): family strategies, collective action and lobbying'. *Journal of Education Policy* 26 (3):431–447.
Rasmussen, M.L. 2015. *Progressive Sexuality Education: The Conceits of Secularism*. New York and London: Routledge.
Ravitch, D. 2011. *The Death and Life of the Great American School System: How Testing and Choice Are Undermining Education*. New York: Basic Books.
Roche, S. 2014. *Domesticating Youth: Youth Bulges and their Socio-political Implications in Tajikistan*: Berghahn Books.
Roda, A. 2015. *Inequality in Gifted and Talented Programs: Parental Choices about Status, School Opportunity, and Second-Generation Segregation*. New York: Palgrave Macmillan US.
Rowe, E.E. 2017. *Middle-class school choice in urban spaces: the economics of public schooling and globalized education reform*. New York & Milton Park: Routledge.
Sakbani, Michael. 2011. 'The revolutions of the Arab Spring: are democracy, development and modernity at the gates?' *Contemporary Arab Affairs* 4 (2):127–147. doi: 10.1080/17550912.2011.575106.
Sitrin, M. 2012. 'Horizontalism and Territory'. accessed 1/2/2017. http://www.possible-futures.org/2012/01/09/horizontalism-and-territory/#sthash.PnbwolBC.dpuf.
Smyth, J. 2016. 'Puncturing notions of precarity through critical educational research on young lives in Australia: towards a critical ethnography of youth'. *Ethnography and Education* 11 (2):129–141. doi: 10.1080/17457823.2015.1040429.
Stromquist, Nelly P., and Anita Sanyal. 2013. 'Student resistance to neoliberalism in Chile'. *International Studies in Sociology of Education* 23 (2):152–178.

Suarez-Villa, L. 2000. *Invention and the Rise of Technocapitalism*: Rowman & Littlefield Publishers.

Suarez-Villa, L. 2012. *Globalization and technocapitalism: the political economy of corporate power and technological domination*. Ashgate: Farnham, England; Burlington, VT. Book.

Susser, A. 2012. 'Tradition and Modernity in the "Arab Spring"'. *Strategic Assessment* 15 (1).

Taylor, A. 2011. 'Student Protests in Chile'. The Atlantic Monthly Group, accessed January 8th. http://www.theatlantic.com/photo/2011/08/student-protests-in-chile/100125/.

The Internationalist. 2011. 'The new battle of Chile for free, quality public education'. *The Internationalist*, September 1. http://www.internationalist.org/newbattleofchile1109.html.

U.S. Government. 2004. 'The 9/11 Commission Report: Final Report of the National Commission on Terrorist Attacks Upon the United States'. https://www.gpo.gov/fdsys/pkg/GPO-911REPORT/pdf/GPO-911REPORT.pdf.

Urdal, H. 2007. 'The Demographics of Political Violence: Youth Bulges, Insecurity, and Conflict'. In *Too Poor for Peace?: Global Poverty, Conflict, and Security in the 21st Century*, edited by L. Brainard and D. Chollet, 90–100. Washington: Brookings Institution Press.

van de Sande, M. 2013. 'The Prefigurative Politics of Tahrir Square-An Alternative Perspective on the 2011 Revolutions'. *Res Publica* 19 (3):223–239. doi: 10.1007/s11158-013-9215-9.

Verger, A., C. Lubienski, and G. Steiner-Khamsi. 2016a. 'The Emergence and Structuring of the Global Education Industry: Towards an analytical framework'. In *World Yearbook of Education 2016: The Global Education Industry*, edited by A. Verger, C. Lubienski and G. Steiner-Khamsi, 3–24. New York and London: Routledge.

Verger, A., C. Lubienski, and G. Steiner-Khamsi, eds. 2016b. *World Yearbook of Education 2016: The Global Education Industry*. New York and London: Taylor & Francis.

Wells, Amy Stuart, Julie Slayton, and Janelle Scott. 2002. 'Defining Democracy in the Neoliberal Age: Charter School Reform and Educational Consumption'. *American Educational Research Journal* 39 (2):337–361. doi: 10.3102/00028312039002337.

Whitty, Geoff, and Sally Power. 2000. 'Marketization and privatization in mass education systems'. *International Journal of Educational Development* 20:93–107. doi: 10.1016/S0738-0593(99)00061-9.

Whitty, G., S. Power, and D. Halpin. 1998. *Devolution and choice in education: the school, the state, and the market*. Melbourne: Open University Press.

Windle, J. 2015. *Making Sense of School Choice: Politics, Policies, and Practice under Conditions of Cultural Diversity*. New York: Palgrave Macmillan.

Yifu Lin, J. 2012. 'Youth Bulge: A Demographic Dividend or a Demographic Bomb in Developing Countries?', accessed March 5th. http://blogs.worldbank.org/developmenttalk/youth-bulge-a-demographic-dividend-or-a-demographic-bomb-in-developing-countries.

Yoon, E. 2011. 'Mini schools: the new global city communities of Vancouver'. *Discourse: Studies in the Cultural Politics of Education* 32 (2):253–268.

Zakaria, F. 2001. 'The Politics of Rage: Why Do They Hate Us?', accessed March 5th. http://www.newsweek.com/politics-rage-why-do-they-hate-us-154345.

Zakaria, F. 2011. 'Why There's No Turning Back in the Middle East'. http://content.time.com/time/magazine/article/0,9171,2050032,00.html.

PART 3

Cultures of Democracy and the Politics of Belonging

CHAPTER 12

The Moral Emotions of Youthful Politics and Anti-Politics

Kerry Montero and Judith Bessant

1   Introduction

'Defiantly weak and irritatingly empty-handed': a young man used these words to describe his reaction to events in Greece following the loss by the 'left-wing' ruling party Syriza of its parliamentary majority in August 2015 (Maragkidou 2015). His frustration, disillusionment, hopelessness and betrayal reflect the sentiments of many young people often described as politically apathetic and disengaged. At least that is the view of many working within conventional political and social science traditions which see politics as rationally determined behaviour that occurs within institutions or bureaucracies and government generally (Leftwich 2004; Heywood 2013, 17). Often working alongside this institutionalist approach is a behaviourist tradition that privileges 'scientific knowledge' and associated quantitative techniques which promotes the study of voting patterns, the behaviour of legislators, politicians and lobbyists. And while proponents of a 'neo institutionalism' emerged in the 1980s, extending their inquiry to provide sociological insight into those institutions, it remained faithful to the older tenets of that tradition (Meyer and Richard 1983). For an action to be recognized as political within these conventional traditions it had to be motivated by an impetus expressed in rational political language and uttered through legitimate recognized institutional means (Akram 2014, 382).

We argue this approach is problematic because it provides an overly narrow conceptualisation of politics (Pykett 2007). It is an account that omits a rich repertoire of motivations and activities expressed by the young people we interviewed and surveyed in our research project, material we use to inform this chapter. Moreover, it is an account that omits the critical role of new media and how that enables young people themselves to engage directly rather than through more traditional institutional means.

In short, the problematic this chapter addresses is that mainstream political and social science and common sense understandings of politics privilege electoral politics (For those offering alternatives to this approach see Mouffe 2005a and b; Loader, & Mercea, 2012, Manning and Holmes 2014; Mizen 2015; Mahler et al. 2014; Sauter, M. 2014; Manning, (ed) 2015, Bruter et al. 2016, Bessant et al., 2017, Pickard and Bessant 2017,). As critics point out, the mainstream understandings of politics relies on empirical and positivist research methods that encourage those with behaviourist inclinations and assume participants are autonomous, self-interested 'individuals' who act in rational ways to maximize their utility (Print et al. 2004; Bauerlein 2009). It is a tradition that articulates conventional rules of engagement, values and consensus over dissensus and privileges rational deliberation (Habermas 1984, 1996; Bohmann 1996; Benhabib 1996; Olson 2006). All this gives credence to a formalistic approach to political discourse and practice that understands 'behaviour' as rational action. Any human action that fails to fit this classification or the general ethos outlined by this approach is excluded from the category of political (Wenman 2013). It is a conceptualization of politics that is limiting because it excludes a full range of motives and actions that are deeply political (Bessant 2017: 204–221, Vromen 2017, Harris 2007).

2 Our Position

We argue against the conventional and popular view that a 'crisis of democracy' can be explained by young people's political disengagement (Skocpol 2003). It is a problematic claim because it relies on a view of politics that fails to recognize the changes taking place within the field of politics courtesy of new media and specifically the political actions of many young people. We draw on our recent research to demonstrate that young people are not disinterested in politics. In doing so we add to a growing body of literature that makes the same argument.

We also join others to argue that politics has never been shaped by norms of rationality or public opinion formed by rational debate oriented to consensus as set out in the Habermasian notion of the bourgeois public sphere (Kellner 1999; Manning and Holmes 2014; Bruter et al. 2016). Some take this critique further, pointing to the cognitivist biases contained within efforts that are reliant on rationality to understand human action (Keane 1995). Moreover, political action conventionally understood as instrumental goal-oriented rational action encourages us to ignore the contingency of politics and its disorderly, variable, and unexpected qualities, including the role of confusion, misguided conduct, accidents, deliberate deception, denial, ignorance and malice (Cohen 2000; McGoey 2014). We often believe things that aren't true when acknowledging scientific or others truths are too difficult, when they are inconvenient or too painful to recognize, and create our own truths when relying on common-sense that is inaccurate. For as Gross and McGoey (2015) argue, 'ignorance' always shadows and obscures our knowledge. In this way, as they argue, common-sense often undermines truth because knowledge is frequently valued more due to its social capital, (e.g. its capacity to improve particular interests) and less for its truth content. When common-sense protects the status quo, it is more often accepted than scientific or any other form of truth. All this also has the effect of ignoring the ways emotions variously expressed inform political action (Barbalet 1998; Manning and Holmes 2014; Bruter et al. 2016). In short, the focus on rationality ignores the role of 'non-rational' activities; it ignores emotions, ethics, play, irrational actions and creativity that so often inform political action.

In what follows, we explore the idea that young people's political actions are informed by powerful moral emotions such as hope, disillusionment, anger, pride and a sense of outrage. In so doing we underscore Critchley's insight that social movements like Spain's the *indignados* and the global occupy movement can be understood as responses to 'situational injustice', a release of 'ethical energy' brought forth through political actions (Critchley 2007). With this in mind we consider young people's political expressions of resistance, sense of indignation, and hope that reflect complex (and sometimes seemingly contradictory) feelings and positions.

3   The Study

To write this chapter, we drew on our research conducted in 2015 that inquired into the life worlds of young people between the ages of 15 and 30. Participants were invited through direct contact and through referrals ('snowballing'). They came from a range of political perspectives and from a diversity of geographic locations – e.g. young farmers' organisations, young Liberal (conservative political) party, conservative nationalist, refugee advocacy groups. All those interviewed directly were Australian based and most were from Victoria. With RMIT University Human Research Ethics approval we carried out eight face-to-face individual interviews and one focus group with twelve participants. They represented an even mix of male and female, and included members of formal politics like the Young Liberals and Young Labor and the Socialist Party, as well as others who did not identify as affiliated with any formal political organisation. We asked how they described and understood their motivations for what they did and did not do. We asked about their political engagement, how they described their own and other people's politics, and how they see themselves politically (their subjectivities, practice, identity). We also accessed a range of political views through youth sites[1] using social media groups and other online forums. Added to this were surveys of secondary source material in which the views of young people of various political persuasions were expressed which expanded our capacity for insight into relevant human situations and social spaces.[2]

We used an interpretivist approach in analysing the material which detailed how they experienced their own social context, and how and why they engaged in various actions. When interpreting this material we asked specifically what role, if any, did ethics or moral emotions play in what they thought and did, and whether new forms of political action were emerging (Critchley 2007; Mouffe 2005a; della Porta 2013).

This raises the question: *what are moral emotions*? By moral emotions we refer to a range of moral feelings that most people experience on a daily basis. They include guilt, righteous anger, patriotism and pride (e.g. in one's appearance, accomplishments, in others). They can move us to act to seek respect and honour for our country, people, land or family. They are emotions that can serve as an imperative to act, intended for example to protect the honour of family or territory from ridicule or other harms, or to seek revenge or payback, and as a way of settlement or balancing the moral books (Singer 1981; Katz 1988).

We use the insights offered by the young people who were part of this project to make a case that while their experiences, motives and actions do not always fit conventional accounts of politics, they were political. We draw on their accounts to support the now burgeoning literature which contests claims that young people are apolitical and disengaged and demonstrate the various ways they take politics seriously (Bruter et al. 2016; Manning 2015; Manning and Holmes 2014; Soler-i-Martí 2015; Coe et al. 2016; O'Toole and Gale 2010; Bessant 2014). We also extend this to argue that many young people's political action is informed by powerful moral and political emotions that energise actions directed towards changing institutional arrangements, challenging the status quo and particular power relations.

---

1 E.g. youtube videos and other postings on sites of activists like eg Friendly Jordie https://www.youtube.com/user/friendlyjordies and Fregmonto Stokes (https://www.youtube.com/watch?v=gHB1PkD1-_Y).
2 E.g. The EU's MYPLACE http://www.fp7-myplace.eu, Reclaim Australia https://www.youtube.com/watch?v=Wf47dZwW7Ls Eureka Youth League https://www.facebook.com/search/top/?q=eureka%20youth%20league, Friends of the Earth https://www.facebook.com/FoEAustralia/etc.

4 Moral Emotions as Imperatives for Political Action

While some political action is clearly instrumental and may be described as rational action, the proposition that politics may be expressive in character and connected to moral emotions also needs to be taken seriously. And while recognition of the role of ethico-political motivational energy in informing human action is not new, it is often ignored or not considered a legitimate form of participation within conventional social science and popular framings of politics (Manning 2012, 1–17; Mizen 2015, 167–182; Bessant 2016, 1–16).

In accounting for what constitutes politics we relied on the actors' own interpretative capacities to make sense of their own actions and to appreciate or interpret the intentions of others. In saying this we acknowledge that human actions are not political until they are interpreted or defined as such by those involved and by observers. This also includes reference to what people see as the 'objective' signs of politics (like polling booths, parliament house, flag waving, mass marches) as well as phenomenological insights offered into lived experiences of participants (e.g. reports of their political reasoning and emotions).x

It's an issue that also relates to the 'politics of recognition' and how identity, and political identity in this case, is shaped by a recognition from others or by the absence of it. As Charles Taylor argues the absence and misrecognition of identity can cause people to suffer harm, or 'real distortion', if those around them 'mirror back ... confining or demeaning or contemptible' images. Such non-recognition or misrecognition of ones identity can inflict damage and can be oppressive. The trick is to resist adopting such images and thereby avoid self-depreciation and purge oneself of the imposition of 'destructive identities or self hatred'. (Taylor 1994: 24–25) Thus, while some observers deny the actions of young people are political when young people see it as such, or indeed when observers deny the very idea that young people are capable of political action, that is regrettable, but it does not entirely matter. We say this because if young people themselves recognise their action as political, recognise themselves as political actors and consciously resist assuming or internalising those damaging messages then there are opportunities for change. Such responses with time and in with a continued commitment to the political agendas serve to demonstrate how they are political and in doing so contest those narrowly defined categories of political from which they were excluded. The young people in our project described their experiences of politics and their identities variously as those of 'ordinary' citizens, as disaffected outsiders, as disengaged from formal politics, and as active political agents. And while some spoke of structural issues (such as high levels of employment, poverty, education debt) when referring to politics, that was not given as the reason or 'cause' for their action. Rather, the reasons for their actions were their feelings about being unemployed or underemployed now and about facing job insecurity throughout their lives. They expressed anger at the fact that on graduation many searched in vain for jobs, and of having to take on unpaid internships with the slim promise they might secure a job. Those with tertiary credentials felt angry about the fact that many of their friends who didn't get a degree have very little hope of a future with a job and income on which they can support a family.

They expressed feelings of resentment about being exploited and underpaid, saying how unfair it was. This differs from conventional accounts of political action that identify structural explanations (unemployment, socio-economic factors) as the determining 'force' that leads to action such as civil unrest and demonstrations on the streets. What we report is that it is ethico-political energy and moral emotions that moved the young people to action.

They reported feeling anger, despondency and being deeply 'pissed off', (a colloquialism for feeling deeply annoyed) about having studied and worked hard, as they had been encouraged to do, about going into debt to pay fees, about being given promises and expectations of a decent job, and a home of their own that they saw as unattainable. We heard accounts of disenchantment, of being treated unfairly, about injustice and even rage. These moral emotions galvanized many to engage politically on individual and collective bases. Indeed the foremost reasons given for their political engagement (and disengagement) were disgust, rage, a sense of wrong doing, shame and need to protect important 'things' like their future, the environment, and identity.

Given the space limitations of this chapter, the moral emotions we focus on here revolve around three areas. The first relates to a powerful ethico-political feeling: a sense of altruism, loyalty or commitment to a common good. Sometimes this was associated with spurs to action such as protection and retaliation – e.g. defending self, family or friends from verbal, sexual or physical abuse, or revenge for perceived injury. The second area related to disillusionment, disgust and a sense of betrayal by established political actors. The third related to feelings about certain incidents or situations that incited anger, outrage and hope and which often led to an 'exit politics' or withdrawal from conventional fields of politics and-or engagement in new forms of politics. In the final section of the chapter we give consideration to the 'exit voice' and responses to decline in politics (Hirschman 1970).

We now turn to the task of providing accounts of those three domains and how they led to young people's political action.

(i) Altruism, Loyalty and Commitments to a Common Good

Our findings provide evidence that allows us to challenge conventional accounts of young people's withdrawal from politics – commonly expressed in descriptions of young people as selfish, 'Me Gen' with a deficiency in civic or political knowledge, a deeply exaggerated sense of entitlement and depending on the specific generational nomenclature, they are materialistic, greedy, unmotivated, politically disengaged, high risk media junkies and so forth (Twenge 2014; Stoerger 2009).

Indeed this portrayal was an issue some young people found offensive and contested themselves.

One young woman we interviewed, who did not identify with a political party, rejected the labels of apathetic or 'disengaged youth':

> Young people are constantly told their voices are irrelevant. That they are vapid and uninterested and that their votes won't count or make an effective difference. So they have become involved in a way that they see is tangible to them.
> ISABEL 18, individual interview

For Blanche (21, Young Labor) the motivation for her involvement in formal politics was her desire to affect political change to 'avenge the social disparities that exist'. She also recognised that other young people are uninterested and disillusioned with parliamentary politics and choose different forms of action. This she explained was evident in her own family: 'Whereas my brother, who, is 3 years younger, has gone down the path of just being really passionate about, um, anti-racism, and about human rights, in terms of marriage equality and, or, worker's rights in terms of equal pay', she continued:

> I would say there are a lot of issues that young people do see as ... and whether or not they are the biggest thing in the world, or the biggest problem faced in the world, a lot of them, do see it as inherent to their identity, or to their life. So, people are still getting like outraged, and um, you know wanting to see change in things.

Jason (20), a member of Young Labor, referred to altruistic feelings that moved him to join a political party:

> ...I actually remember the day that I decided ... I thought, where can I make an effective change? What can I do, like, how can I help someone...

According to Angus (19, Young Labor) other young people also want to 'make the world a better place' but take different paths away from formal politics:

> I have a lot of friends ... they're politically involved but they just don't see being a member of a party the best way to make change, they're involved in AYCC or whatever, all these different other sort of groups

Whether engaged in traditional political action or 'alternative' forms of political activity young people articulated a sense of political involvement oriented towards 'doing what is right', which was also an important aspect of their self-identity. As Mitch (22) explained: politics is 'that altruistic aspect, or end goal, of political involvement ... for a lot of people, if you like [that gives] – a sense of purpose'.

Those involved in more traditional political forms of organisation also often voiced disillusionment and frustration with their party leadership because they were not committed to pursuing what they saw as issues critical for the common good:

> ...we can't just pinpoint only a few key issues to get upset over, because ... what about the other issues. But ... you know we have a lot of sleepless nights, we spend a lot of time being really really upset with what our leaders might be doing, or what we are being asked to vote for at times, or we might be there at a conference and might be grappling with these issues and trying to convince people in our party to be supporting a position that we have. And then you think, well if I were to spit the dummy right now, to cut up my membership and put it in the bin and walk away, well then what do I, do I go and join GetUp! or go to a rally?
> ARABELLA 20, Young Labor

In recognising that many young people choose to participate in non-parliamentary political action, and or/reject and withdraw from conventional politics, one young member of the Labor party (Mitch) reflected on his party's failure to act humanely around issues pertaining to refugees and immigration. He explained certain strategic sacrifices needed to be made on issues that caused discomfort. For Mitch, it was the growing discomfort many young people felt about refugee and other policies of mainstream political parties that made them feel those organisations didn't act ethically and caused young people to deliberately condemn political parties with refugee policy platforms they found to be morally objectionable:

> ...the growing level of disengagement from mainstream politics and mainstream parties, people seem less, really willing to accept ... they're angry with everything. There's a tendency to throw the baby out with the bathwater. A lot of the people for example quit the party over the asylum seeker policy ... because people are increasingly less willing to compromise.
> MITCH 22

(ii)   *Disgust, Disillusionment, Betrayal and Exiting*

Among many of our participants was a pervasive tone of disillusionment, disgust and disappointment at the failing of their elders. Interviewees spoke of ethical and moral emotional responses to certain actions and inactions of political and policy experts and power elites. Reactions were particularly strong in respect to dishonesty on the part of many politicians. They spoke of the ways politicians blatantly break promises, lie and cheat. Beyond the 'outright dishonesty', interviewees described politicians as largely inept and unable do their job properly. There was a distinct lack of trust in the capacity of their elders to provide honest and effective leadership in the face of the complex challenges. As 19 year-old Anna said:

> World leaders, if you could see yourselves now from the eyes of a nine-year old, a lot of you would be sorely disappointed. Do you know what it's like to be a young person now and have absolutely no faith in adults to plan a safe future?

Many spoke not only of their own disillusionment, but that of their peers. According to 22 year-old Justin, many of his friends '...are of the view that all politicians are liars and can't be trusted. They also think that "the system" is broken.' Nicole (24) described this in terms of distrust: 'I remain pessimistic about politics for this reason, seeing it as a way in which people are controlled instead of a tool that frees society through conversation'. Amber (19) described politicians as self regarding, failing to make society more equitable. They abuse their power and use access to public funds for their own gain. One '...example would be politicians paying for personal services or holidays claiming it's for work therefore using taxpayers' money.'

In the eyes of some interviewees, that sense of disenchantment connected to their experience of being deliberately excluded from mainstream political processes:

> ...young people have become disillusioned by traditional mainstream political discourse that effectively works to isolate them from discussion,

hence finding it increasingly difficult to have faith in one political party or system. Or even to become politically active in the traditional sense.

ISABEL 18

Likewise for one 24 year old Greek man, disenchantment and disappointment with political leaders had a debilitating effect, yet in spite of this he was able to express his 'defiance'. As Stergios (24) explains to journalist Melpomeni Maragkidou:

> Two years ago it was frustration, now it's this feeling of inability to change the world ... 2013 was the last time I had the mental stamina to fight. I have no more fight left. I live my life feeling defiantly weak and irritatingly empty-handed.
>
> MARAGKIDOU 2015

Nicole (24) made a related point: 'The problem with politics is that it isn't egalitarian, and so we've seen those most powerful in society (corporations and others) hold influence over modern politics in Western societies'. Many young people used a distinctly ethical vocabulary to explain what they saw: the political elite 'don't care'; politicians are greedy, irresponsible, and even criminal. They expressed *disappointment* about the failure of politicians to address important social, environmental and moral issues, feeling that the politicians make things worse. For 19 year old Amber the government and people in power should not abuse the trust and responsibility they have.

As these interviewees saw it, the problem is not with young people, but with political elites who are disinterested and disengaging from young people and their interests. It is they who have unfairly and unjustly abandoned 'us', rather than the other way around. This is the moral and emotional betrayal.

(iii)   *Anger, Outrage and Hope*

Many spoke of how a sense of injustice and outrage over various wrong doings moved them to act. This took two forms: disengagement and non-conventional political action. A sense of betrayal and abandonment by politicians made many feel 'their future was pawned' (Blanche, 22). As Blanche explained in her account of education policies, decisions to increase student fees and the burden of student debt:

> ...as university students it would have an impact on us, whether that's in our current degrees or because you know, they are always saying well it

won't come in to affect for people at uni now, it will come into effect in 2 years ... or whatever they say as an excuse.

You know, it might be that we want to go on to do further study, or that we have siblings that will go on to do further study, like that's the direct connection, but there is also the broader connection of just empathy, knowing what it is like, struggling to pay the fees as it is, and knowing that you are going to have this huge HECS debt as it is, and to think that it'll be that much bigger. And it connects with other issues as well, like, wanting to buy a house, like, in our lifetime. I don't think, for a lot of us, that will ever be possible, to buy a house when we have such a huge HECS debt. Which could be even bigger. So, like, it does come down to the selfish reasons, it'll affect me, it'll affect someone I know, it's even broader than that.

5 The Politics of Exit

One response we heard described deliberate and well considered decisions to withdraw from mainstream politics. They were decisions to reject mainstream politics articulated in the language of ethical-moral emotions that motivated action. As Hirschman (1970) argued, there are a number of ways people can respond to disappointment. They can leave or remain and provide critiques from 'inside'. In our case exiting took two forms which sometimes segued into each other. It meant withdrawing from mainstream politics completely out of disgust, despair and a sense it was rotten which meant not voting or having any engagement with any form of politics. It also meant encouraging others to do so.

We can report along with other researchers (Hirschman 1970, Farthing 2010) that such an exit is also often accompanied by political engagement in 'alternative' forms of politics which the young critics considered more worthwhile and effective. In this way while mainstream politics may be free of 'brave critics' and allowed to rot, it is the case that new forms of political actions are emerging with the capacity to challenge more traditional political elites and in this way, revive and augment the life of our political culture.

In this way decisions to withdraw from mainstream politics can be interpreted as a deliberate well considered decision (Farthing 2010, 181–195). It was not an action (or inaction) caused by apathy, laziness or selfishness. As people like 22 year-old Sophia explained, it was the wrong-doings of political elites that caused distrust and young people's to seek alternative social action: 'they say to me, you know, "What's the point of voting? We're not going to make any change anyway, all politicians are the same"; you know everyone is just into career politics'.

Confronted by a 'lack of integrity' by political and financial leaders, many complained that contemporary politics was ethically void. The politicians and other leaders elite don't 'care', are greedy, irresponsible, criminal, are just concerned with their own advancement and interests. As Panagiotis (22), observed with regard to the Greek elections: 'I believe that elections just recycle the people in power while our misery levels kind of stay the same' (Maragkidou 2015).

Many in our study reported how their feelings of resentment and betrayal catalysed them to act politically, but in ways that avoided conventional electoral politics. Their disappointment, disillusionment and anger fuelled an 'ethical energy' that galvanised their commitment to 'be' political. For 'Alice' (24) it was the government's treatment of refugees, their lack of compassion and their cruelty that incensed her and moved her to action. For fifteen year-old Tim it was the politics of denial enacted by too many politicians around climate change that enraged him and his friends: 'I'm very concerned (and sometimes quite outraged) about the climate change humans are creating and the serious threat it poses to the ability of life to live on earth'. Emily's (23) empathy with those experiencing hardship is what disappointed her. She blamed policy decisions to divest her community of employment opportunities for her disappointment. She felt a connection with those who lost their livelihood, a sense of solidarity and a desire to protect 'her' community. As she explained: 'for us losing the car industry is a huge loss, a lot of us will work or live in suburbs where we are seeing the economic impact of that, on people's lives' (Emily 23). A sense of injustice and what they saw as an inability by too many political elites to empathise with others ran deep and fuelled a sense of unfairness. For some their exit or withdrawal meant not voting, not renewing their membership with political parties, retreating and refusing to have anything to do with 'mainstream politics'. These were acts of political resistance and disobedience. The voice of such protest also manifested in 'other' actions aimed at 'try[ing] to fix things' but for some like Panagiotis it meant abstaining:

> There are a lot of reasons why I didn't vote on Sunday, but the main reason is that I am opposed to the logic behind it. There is a widespread aversion to the political system and you can see it in the huge numbers of non-voters. When someone doesn't even bother getting up to vote—that indicates they find the gesture meaningless.
> PANAGIOTIS 22, in MARAGKIDOU, 2015

For others it meant alternative action aimed at 'remedying things'. As Takuya and Moeko explained:

> I joined the anti-war group for teenagers because for the first time something was happening politically that I thought would have an impact on my life
>
> TAKUYA 16

> We all have the right to make our individual voices heard, to come together and share our ideas ... that's why we're here in front of parliament just about every night.
>
> MOEKO 20

6   Conclusion

The role of moral emotions and their influence on our political judgments and actions are missing from conventional accounts of politics. Amongst other things, in some quarters that has produced a rather skewed understanding of young people's political engagement. Many political actions engaged in by young people are not recognised as such because they do not fit conventional accounts of politics. We found that some young people disengaged from formal politics for reasons to do with moral emotions: out of disgust, a sense of betrayal and due to the belief that the ideas of too many leaders were untenable and their actions based on interests that were not for the common good. We note too that moral judgements and emotions were also central to those who remained committed to mainstream politics.

We reported that moral emotions like disappointment, righteous anger, and frustration segued into actions that went someway towards politically enriching action Critchley (2007). Like Critchley (2007), Ranciere (2010) and Mouffe (2005b), we argued that ethico-political emotions are as essential to a healthy democratic culture and public sphere as the more traditionally valued attributes like rationality and deliberation.

We suggest that the willingness by those involved in this project to talk about politic and critique, it is itself, evidence of an interest in politics. We also observed well developed capacities to reflect on the dominant practices (habitus) that operate in the field of politics, as well as a good knowledge of how capital (power) was distributed in that domain. There was an acute awareness by young people of the fact that they are excluded from the public sphere or at best marginalised with little hope of accumulating the cultural capital needed to successfully compete politically in ways they considered desirable. Indeed for many, but not all, they simply did not want to play *that* game. The decision to withdraw from conventional politics was not a whim or an act of selfishness on the part of those who spoke about it. Rather it was a political act, based on a well considered decision.

Many of the young people we spoke to and whose actions we observed expressed a sense of freedom and confidence about their own capacity to imagine institutional arrangements that differ to what currently exists. The decision to withdraw partially or completely from the political culture they inherited and to orient their lives in the different directions seemed to create a sense of freedom that came with an ability to recognise and challenge the nostrums of established wisdom and orders of thought. It was a rejection that provided a sense of hope and confident expectation about the future. The critiques and the shift to non-conventional politics for those who chose that option were not rejections of politics. They were accompanied by their ideas about how transformation could occur through politics, a transformation to a future in which they were participants in the struggle.

Young people in our project were politically engaged and deeply concerned about a range of political issues. They often expressed their political views using the language of moral emotions. The project highlighted the readiness of too many social scientists to ignore and deny this political engagement (Gross and McGoey 2015).

References

Akram, Sadiya. 2014. 'Recognising the 2011 United Kingdom Riots as Political Protest', *British Journal of Criminology* 54: 375–92.

Barbalet, Jack. 1998. *Emotion, Social Theory and Social Structure.* Cambridge: Cambridge University Press.

Bauerlein, Mark. 2009. *The dumbest generation: How the digital age stupefies young Americans and jeopardizes our future.* New York: Penguin.

Benhabib, Seyla. 1996. *The Reluctant Modernism of Hannah Arendt.* London: Sage.

Bessant, Judith. 2014. *Democracy Bytes: New Media and New Politics and Generational Change,* UK: Palgrave Macmillan.

Bessant, Judith. 2016. 'New Politics and Satire: The Euro Financial Crisis and the One-Finger Salute', *Information, Communication & Society,* July: pp. 1–16.

Bessant, Judith. 2017, Digital Humour, Gag Laws and the Liberal Security State, in Rachel Baarda., and Rocci Luppicini., (eds), *Digital Media Integration for Participatory Democracy,* IGI Global publishers, pp. 204–221.

Bessant, Judith, Rys Farthing and Rob Watts, 2017, *The Precarious Generation: A Political Economy of Young People*. London and New York: Routledge.

Bohmann, James. 1996. *Public Deliberation; Pluralism, Complexity and Democracy*. Cambridge: MIT Press.

Bruter, Michael, Shakuntala Banaji, Sarah Harrison, Bart Cammaerts, Nicholas Anstead, and Byrt Whitwell. 2016. *Youth Participation in Democratic Life. Stories of Hope and Disillusion*. UK:Palgrave Macmillan.

Coe, Anna-Britt, Maria Wiklund, Margaretha Uttjek and Lennart Nygren. 2016. 'Youth politics as multiple processes: how teenagers construct political action in Sweden', *Journal of Youth Studies*, 19:10: 1321–1337.

Cohen, Stanley. 2000. *States of Denial: Knowing About Atrocities and Suffering*. Boston: Polity Press.

Critchley, Simon. 2007. *Infinitely demanding: Ethics of commitment, political of resistance*. London: Verso Books.

Della Porta, Donatella. 2013. *Can Democracy be Saved? Participation and social Movements*. Cambridge: Polity Press.

Farthing, Rys. (2010). 'The politics of youthful anti-politics: representing the 'issue' of youth participation in politics'. Journal of Youth Studies: 13:2: 181–195.

Gross, Matthias and Linsey McGoey (eds.). 2015. *Routledge International Handbook of Ignorance Studies*. London: Routledge.

Habermas, Jürgen, 1996. *Between Facts and Norms: Contributions to a Discourse Theory of Law and Democracy*, Cambridge MA: MIT Press.

Habermas, Jürgen. 1984. *The Theory of Communicative action: Reason and the rationalisation of the Life World*, Vol. 1. Boston: Beacon Press.

Harris, Anita, 2007, *Next wave cultures: feminism, subcultures, activism*, Routledge, NY.

Heywood, Andrew. 2013. *Politics* (4th ed.). London: Palgrave Macmillan.

Hirschman, Albert O. 1970. *Exit, Voice, and Loyalty: Responsibility to Decline in Firms, Organisations and States*. Cambridge, MA: Havard University Press.

Katz, Jack. 1988. *Seductions of Crime: Moral and Sensual Attractions in Doing Evil*. New York: Basic Books.

Keane, John. 1995. 'Structural Transformations of the Public Sphere'. *Communications Review*. 1, (1): 1–22.

Kellner, Douglas. 1999. 'Habermas, the Public Sphere, and Democracy: A Critical Intervention'. Retrieved from https://pages.gseis.ucla.edu/faculty/kellner/papers/habermas.htm.

Leftwich, Adrian. 2004. *What is Politics? The Activity and its study* Cambridge: Polity.

Loader, Brian, and Dan Mercea. (Eds.). 2012, *Social media and democracy: Innovations in participatory politics*. New York, NY: Routledge.

Mahler, Vincent A., David K. Jesuit and Poitr R. Paradowski. 2014. 'Electoral Turnout and State Redistribution: A Cross-National Study of Fourteen Developed Countries'. *Political Research Quarterly* 67(2): pp. 361–373.

Manning, Nathan. 2012. *'I mainly look at things on an issue by issue basis': Reflexivity and phronesis in young people's political engagements*. Journal of Youth Studies: pp. 1–17.

Manning, Nathan (ed.). 2015. *Political (dis)engagement: The changing nature of the political*. Bristol: The Policy Press.

Manning, Nathan and Mary Holmes. 2014. 'Political Emotions: A Role for Feelings of Affinity in Citizen's (Dis) Engagements with Electoral Politics?' *Sociology* 48 (4): 698–714.

Maragkidou, Melpomeni. 2015. 'Greek Millennials Are Sick of Politics', *Vice,* September 23, 2015. Accessed October 25th 2015. http://www.vice.com/en_au/read/millennial-greek-apathy-876.

McGoey, Linsey. 2014. *An introduction to the Sociology of ignorance: Essays on the limits of Knowing*. Oxon: Routledge.

Meyer, John W. and W. Richard Scott. 1983. *Organizational Environments: Ritual and Rationality*. Beverly Hills, CA: Sage.

Mizen, Phil. 2015. 'The madness that is the world: young activists' emotional reasoning and their participation in a local Occupy movement'. *The Sociological Review*, 63: 167–182.

Mouffe, Chantal. 2005a. *The Return of the Political*. London: Verso.

Mouffe, Chantal. 2005b. *On the Political*. London: Routledge.

O'Toole, Therese, and Richard Gale. 2010. 'Contemporary grammars of political action among ethnic minority young activists', *Ethnic and Racial Studies*, 33:1, 126–143.

Olson, Kevin. 2006. *Reflexive Democracy: Political Equality and the Welfare State,* Cambridge MA: MIT Press.

Pickard, S. and Bessant, J. (2017). *Young People Re-Generating Politics in Times of Crises*, Palgrave Macmillan.

Print, Murray, Lawrence J. Saha and Kathy Edwards. 2004. *Youth electoral study Report 2: Youth Political Engagement and Voting*, Sydney: Australian Electoral Commission.

Pykett, Jessica. 2007. 'Making Citizens Governable? The Crick Report as Governmental Technology'. *Journal of Education Policy*. 22.3: 301–319.

Rancière, Jacques. 2010. *Dissensus: On politics and aesthetics*. London: Continuum.

Sauter, Molly. 2014, The Coming Swarm: DDOS Actions, Hacktivism, and Civil Disobedience on the Internet. London: Bloomsbury.

Singer, Peter. 1981. *The Expanding Circle: Ethics, Evolution, and Moral Progress*, Princeton: Princeton University Press.

Skocpol, Theda. 2003. *Diminished Democracy: From Membership to Management in American Civic Life*. Norman, OK: University of Oklahoma Press.

Soler-i-Martí, Roger. 2015. 'Youth political involvement update: measuring the role of cause-oriented political interest in young people's activism'. *Journal of Youth Studies*, 18:3: 396–416.

Stoerger, Sharon. 2009. 'The Digital melting Pot: Bridging the digital native-digital immigrant divide'. *First Mind*, 14: 7 July. http://firstmonday.org/ojs/index.php/fm/article/view/2474/2243

Taylor, Charles. 1994. The politics of recognition. In *Multiculturalism and the politics of recognition*, ed. Amy Gutmann, 25–73. Princeton: Princeton University Press.

Twenge, J. 2014. *Generation Me - Revised and Updated: Why Today's Young Americans Are More Confident, Assertive, Entitled--and More Miserable Than Ever Before*, New York: Atria.

Vromen, Ariadne. 2017. *Digital Citizenship and Political Engagement: The Challenge from Online Campaigning and Advocacy Organisations*. London: Palgrave Macmillan.

Wenman, Mark. 2013. *Agonistic democracy; Constituent Power in the Era of Globalisation*. Cambridge: Cambridge University Press.

CHAPTER 13

Young Muslims and Everyday Political Practice: A DIY Citizenship Approach

Anita Harris and Joshua Roose

1   Introduction

This chapter considers what a 'DIY citizenship' approach can offer to analyses of the everyday political practices of first and second generation youth of Muslim migrant communities who are outside both radical and mainstream politics. We argue that the experiences of these youth raise interesting questions about political practice and citizenship for both youth studies and migration studies in the context of changing opportunities for youth engagement and expression, and generational shifts in the multicultural politics of representation. Youth citizenship studies has seen a move towards a broader conceptual framework that considers how activities such as cultural production and consumption, personal and local networking, and work on the self-function for young people as forms of political participation. Further, in super-diverse, multicultural countries such as Australia, we also see shifts away from a traditional focus on ethnic community representation and claim-making to efforts to understand how the multiplicity and fluidity of cultures enable less categorical forms of political identification and expression, especially for younger people. However, it is only recently that these frameworks have been applied to the circumstances of young Muslims of migrant background in non-Muslim majority countries. In this chapter we outline how a DIY citizenship approach relates to migrant background Muslim youth who are frequently regulated for appropriate forms of both youth and ethnic participation. We consider how it has been taken up amongst scholars researching Muslim youth in different contexts, and suggest how it might be developed for future use.

Muslim youth of migrant background in non-Muslim majority countries occupy a difficult position as political actors. Young Muslims today, who constitute the '9/11 generation' (Roose 2016), are subject to intense scrutiny of their political identities and activities and the over-determination of their 'Muslimness'. While all Muslim migrant groups have been targeted for attention, since events such as the London 7/7 bombings and the rise of ISIS, it is young Muslims and especially the second generation children of immigrants who have become 'particular objects of public anxiety in relation to their civic and political participation' (O'Toole & Gale 2009, 2). The bulk of the research on this group is concerned with marginalisation, social exclusion/inclusion and especially radicalisation. Government-commissioned research alone indicates significant interest in both monitoring young Muslims' political behaviour and integrating them into formal, mainstream forms of political activity. For example, successive Australian governments have initiated a range of programmes and projects to investigate and remedy young Muslims' assumed civics deficit. This includes a series of Muslim Youth Summits, many youth-focused strategies, plans and policies regarding social cohesion, civic values and security, and at least five reports into young Muslims' civic and political engagement, including research into their volunteering behaviour (Madkhul 2007), young Muslim women's participation (McCue 2008), young Muslim men's participation (CIRCA 2010), another on Muslim youth and political participation in general (Al-Momani et al. 2010) and a fifth on sources of their political and theological views (Jakubowicz et al. 2012).

These reports and the initiatives they have spawned tend to focus on mainstream forms of political participation. For example, while Al-Momani et al. (2010, 12) define participation broadly as 'behaviours directed toward influencing the public scene' the report concentrates quite narrowly on voting, standing for office, joining an action group, supporting a campaign, or contacting a member of Parliament or the media. We suggest that an over-attention to conventional indicators of participation not only perpetuates the 'civics deficit' thesis and legitimates regulation, however seriously limits the ways we can understand young Muslims' political practices today. This is particularly pertinent given that the research on which many of these reports, programs and policies are based ascertains that alternative practices and places for politics are highly relevant to young Muslims. For example, online spaces; arts, subcultural and youth-initiated activities, and peer social networks were found to be especially important to young Muslims' political expression and mobilisation in all these reports, but these are considered marginal to 'real' or more conventional forms of political participation and are sidelined in the discussion. We suggest that it is important to take these practices seriously, and moreover that it is fruitful to situate them in a new participation landscape that reduces both opportunities for and desirability of conventional political engagement along with enabling (and even demanding) a form of 'DIY citizenship' to emerge, especially for youth.

Within youth citizenship studies there have been efforts to understand how conditions of globalisation, risk, insecurity and especially individualisation have transformed the nature of political identities and activities (Bauman

2001, Beck & Beck-Gernsheim 2001). As Bennett (2012, 22) argues, 'The interesting difference in today's participation landscape is that widespread social fragmentation has produced individuation as the modal social condition in postindustrial democracies, particularly among younger generations'. Different theorists have variously described this individuated political subjectivity amongst youth as a new biography of citizenship characterised by 'dynamic identities, open, weak-tie relationships and more fluid, short-lived commitments in informal permeable institutions and associations' (Vinken 2005, 155); or as a form of 'self-actualising' citizenship (Bennett 2003, 3), meaning citizenship paths that are defined through individually expressive personal action frames and transient, issue-based engagements (Bennett 2012, 20). Bang (2004,18) characterises these new kinds of political actors as 'everyday makers', meaning those who are less engaged with the state and other formal sites of traditional citizenship activity and more focused on creating local networks and enacting change in ways that are 'individualistic, more project oriented, more 'on' and 'off' and 'hit' and 'run' ... more pleasure oriented and more fun-seeking'.

A personalised form of pre-figurative politics may play a role in this citizenship activity, that is, efforts to model a better future in the present by 'being the change you want', with a particular focus on how to perform within everyday space and through the body (Jeffrey & Dyson 2016). In this framework, political action is not about change 'as a horizon event but as the cumulative precipitate of action in the present' (Jeffrey & Dyson 2016). Such fluid, unstructured, localised, immediate and personally relevant forms of political participation are particularly evident amongst young people (Fahmy 2006, Vromen & Collin 2010, Harris, Wyn & Younes 2010). Some research suggests that this kind of everyday, ad hoc engagement is especially important to marginalised youth, as they may struggle to have their voices heard in more formal political spaces (Smith et al. 2005, Roker 2008, O'Toole & Gale 2009), and may not identify with traditional, hierarchical, association-based politics organised around fixed identities such as ethnic community groups, which tend to be dominated by an older generation. Tabar et al. (2003, 278) argue that such ethnic community groups require state sanction and valorisation to maintain their funding and sustainability, resulting in their co-option to political agendas and disconnection from younger generations who are infrequently legitimised as community representatives capable of liaising effectively with the state.

In our own work (Harris & Roose 2014) we have used the term 'DIY citizenship' to describe this turn to a new citizenship biography and have argued that while this approach has only recently received attention in scholarship on Muslim youth participation, it warrants greater uptake. In our research, involving in depth peer interviews with 80 young Muslim Australians in Melbourne and Brisbane,[1] we have found that cultural production and consumption, engagement in personal networks and local projects, and politico-religious work on the self as an ethical citizen in the present are three important forms of participation for those who are outside both radical and mainstream politics but still seeking to 'influence the public scene' (Al-Momani et al. 2010, 12) through their everyday practices. For example, a majority of our research participants felt that it was through social and non-mainstream media and creative culture that young people could best have their voices heard on issues, and two thirds had themselves expressed their views in these ways. Such activities included blogs, online forums, rap, dance, independent radio, and fashion design. Informal social networks and engagement in local issues were also very important forms of their participatory practice. A large majority talked regularly to others about social and political issues, thereby operationalizing their 'citizen communication networks' (Yeung et al. 2012, 77). A significant majority were also engaged in locally focused practices such as volunteering (for example, at schools and hospitals) and getting involved in local causes (for example, community projects), indicating how communicative networks translated into action for civic improvement and change.

There was also evidence that many forged a sense of civic and political responsibility through religion and especially that they strove to embody piety (McDonald 2008; Johns et al. 2015) in their everyday lives in order to enact an ethical way of being in the world. They indicated that individual efforts to work on the self as an ethical citizen were entrenched in Islam as a 'way of life', so their own everyday lives were always inflected by moral and political reflection and guidance for action. In this sense, Islam functioned as a positive civic enabler sparking individuals' ethical responsibility to others, their participation in action for social justice, and facilitating practices of engagement that are consistent with the new youth citizenship biography which emphasises 'self-organization, individuality, self-confrontation' (Vinken 2007, 53). Many explained that they had created their own personal pathways towards an individualised, ethical, civic-oriented Islam that was not simply handed down from parents or teachers. Some were critical of religious and ethnic group leaders and institutions when they were perceived to prefer youth to be passive and unquestioning recipients of their religious and cultural knowledge and instead saw themselves as 'everyday makers' of politico-religious subjectivities.

This research, and the theoretical framework of 'DIY citizenship', has since been acknowledged, adopted, adapted and extended in subsequent work on

---

1   For a discussion of the methodology, see Vassadis, Karimshah, Harris and Youssef (2015).

young Muslims' political and civic engagement. In the next section of this chapter we consider how these ideas have been utilised and modified and what this suggests about their possibilities, limitations and some future directions in theorising participatory practice for this cohort. Several scholars have drawn on our article, which first appeared in the *Journal of Youth Studies* (online 2013, published 2014), with uptake from Australia to the United Kingdom, the Netherlands, Italy, Russia and Singapore. Whilst some of these constitute cursory references forming part of a broader review of literature, others have engaged more deeply with the concept, revealing important insights into both where the concept has been utilised and how it has been understood and applied. Five scholars (or teams) in particular have encouraged us to re-evaluate how we have wielded the concept and to consider how to best draw out its potential. Two fundamental issues emerge out of their use of our work: the relationship between DIY citizenship and what has been described as 'cultural citizenship', and the benefits and disadvantages of incorporating the non-formal into an appraisal of young Muslims' civic and political activities.

2   Clarifying the Relationship between Cultural Citizenship and DIY Citizenship

In his 2016 monograph *Globalized Muslim Youth in the Asia Pacific*, Kamaludeen Mohamed Nasir uses the concept of DIY citizenship amongst young Muslims as a synonym for 'cultural citizenship'. His is a sociological study of Muslim youth cultures in Singapore and Sydney, comparing experiences amongst young Muslims in the two cities. One chapter focuses on 'youth resistance' through cultural consumption. Nasir considers that consumption choices enabled young Muslims in Sydney to project a 'bicultural stance', something he refers to as cultural citizenship, 'which has also been described as a form of "do-it-yourself" citizenship' (Nasir 2015, 168). Nasir interprets both DIY and cultural citizenship here as concerned with assertion of cultural identity; that is, these young people actively claim a hybrid and simultaneously local and global Muslim identity through creative consumption and production, for example, through the design, promotion, sale and display of Muslim youth culture products such as street wear. His work prompts us to consider the relationship of 'DIY citizenship' to 'cultural citizenship'. Are they basically correlates or do they differ markedly in their form and function and why is it important to differentiate between the two?

The concept of cultural citizenship has been particularly influential in cultural anthropology (Ong et al. 1996, Rosaldo 1997), sociology and cultural studies. In its broadest sense, it denotes recognition of difference (often of ethnic background, but also sexual identity, religious affiliation and so on) and the right to expression of this difference without discrimination. Castles and Davidson (2000, 126) note that under conditions of globalisation and increasing ethnocultural diversity, cultural rights, including maintenance of minority languages, cultures, customs and lifestyles, as well as the right to intercultural and international communication, are an essential part of citizenship. From a sociological perspective, work by Pakulski (1997) and Turner (2001) has been particularly influential. In the first edition of the key journal *Citizenship Studies*, Pakulski outlines how cultural citizenship could be analysed as,

> ...a new set of citizenship claims that involve the right to unhindered and legitimate representation and propagation of identities and lifestyles through the information systems and in public fora (1997, 80).

He considers further that,

> ...full cultural citizenship is seen primarily not as a matter of legal, political and socioeconomic location, but as a matter of symbolic representation, cultural-status recognition and cultural promotion' (Ibid).

Turner notes that the cultural underpinnings of citizenship have been neglected aspects of contemporary studies of citizenship (2001, 11). He defines cultural citizenship as 'cultural empowerment, namely the capacity to participate effectively, creatively and successfully within a national culture' (Ibid). To this extent, cultural citizenship may be understood as relational (to a dominant national culture), and as empowerment through the expression of diverse identities in the public sphere. In extensions in the field of cultural studies, cultural citizenship has tended to be related to creative production and consumption of culture in everyday life, especially entertainment, leisure and media (Burgess et al. 2006). In particular, ICTs and new media are seen to enable decentralised opportunities for participatory culture and produce new forms of creative collective civic and political practice.

Recent studies of young people of migrant background, and especially young Muslims in the West, have drawn on both of these concepts of cultural citizenship to capture the links between recognition of cultural identities, multiple belongings and young people's efforts for participation that take more 'cultural', creative, everyday or informal forms. For example, Maira (2009, 89) discusses how school, peer networks, media, popular culture and workplaces are all everyday sites where young Muslims in the US express and practice key forms of cultural citizenship such as belonging in the city, cultural consumption and subcultural affiliations. How then does this fit with the concept of DIY citizenship and in particular, the concept as applied in our study of the everyday, self-actualising civic practices of Young Muslims of immigrant background in the West? Are the concepts readily interchangeable and is DIY citizenship thus little more than a new label for an old phenomenon?

To some extent the theoretical origins of DIY citizenship certainly draw upon earlier conceptions of cultural citizenship due to a focus on rights to cultural difference, yet there are significant developments that make the concept distinct. We note in our article that the 'DIY citizen' thesis has taken hold in many domains of youth citizenship studies. The term is intended to 'highlight the diversity of ways citizenship is enacted and performed' (Ratto & Boler 2014, 1) from the overtly political to those acting in unconventional domains and denotes 'those making it up as they go along' (ibid, 2). This has particular significance in multicultural societies, where ethnic difference, and cultural citizenship as acknowledgement of the legitimacy of this difference, is governed through state recognition of representative groups, usually controlled by older first generation male migrants. These groups effectively bid for state resources and political influence and are situated in static institutional structures. Numerous studies, including Nasir's (2015, 20) have established that ethnicity has less significance for practicing young Muslims (Mandaville 2002, Roose 2016), as do the political institutions and civic associations governed and controlled by first generation migrants. Thus, in contrast to these conventional notions of cultural citizenship, as deployed in multicultural contexts, DIY citizenship instead denotes how young people use everyday cultural commodities (Maira 2009, 156) or forms (such as sports, arts, media, youth subcultures) to make informal and creative claims of belonging, recognition and participation given their exclusion from or disenchantment with traditional civic and political ethnic associations.

Some scholars who have taken up our concept use it to specifically explore young Muslims' alternative use of online public spheres to consider how such acts of citizenship play out in collective networked publics as facilitated by new media. For example, in her chapter titled 'Faith, Space and Negotiated Subjectivities: Young Muslims in Suburban Australia', Chloe Patton draws on her ethnographic work amongst young Muslims in Melbourne to explore how they conceptualise and enact their position within both the local and wider national imaginary and situates our work within the context of her exploration of young Muslim participation in 'alternative online public spheres' (2016, 18). Patton draws attention to our finding that 60% of participants actively participate in online media forums and considers how young Muslims now have a 'direct and immediate means of questioning the authority of those who speak on their behalf' (Ibid). It is in what Patton terms 'alternative online public spheres' that those without a political voice can both have their say and organise. Patton argues that youth online activism to boycott *Iftar* dinners[2] organised by the Australian Federal Police and supported by Muslim community group leaders (even after the introduction of new anti-terrorism laws) is one such example of the possibility for young Muslims to circumvent traditional political representation. She notes that this activity in new publics suggests a need to move beyond conceptual frameworks of Muslim youth citizenship founded in 'cultural identity' toward better understandings of the emergence of new political subjectivities that operate beyond community elites (Patton 2016, 19).

In a similar vein, Amelia Johns explores our work in the context of young Muslims online and 'acts of citizenship in socially networked spaces' (2014, 71). Johns situates our work amongst a broader body of literature that is developing an evolving understanding of what constitutes civic participation, bringing attention to 'new styles of self-presentation' and 'everyday cultures arising from internet and social media use' (2014, 72). For Johns, our more fluid definition of civic engagement as activities oriented towards the 'common good' and the concept of DIY citizenship stand in productive contrast to older models of civic participation (2014, 73) and contribute to a better understanding of the potential for new media technology to,

> ...open up positive spaces of interaction between Muslim and non-Muslim citizens and global publics, thus countering the marginalisation of Muslim voices and perspectives in western, national public spheres (2014, 79).

Johns considers that this has implications for policy-makers, requiring them to move beyond traditional notions of active citizenship and reconsider how they define civic and political engagement to include a range of culture, religious and popular resources used by young Muslims. She also notes the importance of conceptual approaches that can interrogate new performances of Muslim youth identity in networked spaces that integrate religious and civic aspirations and explore how and why Muslim youth forge new transnational communicative networks rather than engage with either the political institutions of the nation-state or local ethnic civic associations (Johns 2014, 80).

These scholars find value in the concept of DIY citizenship as something more than cultural citizenship. The DIY approach bridges and extends both a

---

2 An *Iftar* dinner is a celebratory meal to break the Ramadan fast.

conceptualisation of ethnic/cultural rights and participatory practice through consumption and production of everyday culture and media. In our research, young Muslim men and women of immigrant background acted at the everyday level, drawing upon their faith for both inspiration and guidance in shaping their creative actions as citizens, but not positioning themselves categorically as representatives of a 'culture' demanding its rights. The fluidity and dynamism of their projects of self-expression and self-determination has warranted the application of a concept that moves beyond traditional bounded notions of community, culture and the politics of representation that predominate in the governance of multicultural societies, including more rigid notions of cultural citizenship. At the same time, we also deepen the more 'cultural studies' interpretation of cultural citizenship as involving everyday creative practices of participation and new kinds of network building by considering what this means for a cohort who cannot easily shake free of an imposed, stigmatised 'groupness' even while older and more inflexible models of group representation and rights-claiming may not work for them. Through the DIY citizenship approach we try to capture the creative ways young Muslims of migrant background construct themselves in everyday ways as political subjects while managing their simultaneous interpellation as an undifferentiated cohort of culturally suspect citizens).

3 DIY Citizenship as 'Casting too wide a net'

In *Muslim Citizenship in Liberal Democracies: Civic and Political Participation in the West*, Mario Peucker draws on research in Australia and Germany and seeks to explore whether there is 'a Muslim quality' to the citizenship of Muslims in the West (2016, 2) and how and why Muslims participate in civil society. In many respects, Peucker's work finds common ground with the broader project in which our article was situated (titled *The Civic Lives of Young Muslims: Active citizenship, community belonging and social inclusion*). However, Peucker seeks to distinguish his work by focussing on more formal mechanisms of political and civic activism. He states that,

> ...notwithstanding that such interactions [informal civic networking building in everyday space including work and neighbourhoods] are important subjects of research and meaningful contextual factors in active citizenship, they are of an entirely different quality than people's commitment and deliberate decision to become politically and civically active (2016, 24).

Peucker cites Bellamy (2010) in warning against,

> ...casting the net of citizenship studies too wide' and to assert that 'citizenship is different... to other kinds of social relationship, such as being a parent, a friend, a neighbour, a colleague or a customer (2016, 24).

The question that arises then is what constitutes the space and the practice of the political or the civic in everyday life? And, how should this be regarded in the contemporary social context, especially against more formal political engagement through established mechanisms and institutions and for marginalised populations?

To some extent, this is an old and unproductive bifurcation in youth citizenship studies, as though analysis of citizenship acts must focus on either formal public spheres and conventional modes of engagement on the one hand, or realms and practices of the informal, incidental and intimate on the other. However, there is much evidence that the two inform each other, especially in the lives of marginalised youth who may seek several overlapping opportunities and pathways for social change and political participation (see for example Roker 2008). As we have noted earlier, over-attention to conventional indicators of participation not only perpetuates the 'civics deficit' thesis and legitimates regulation, but seriously limits the ways we can understand young Muslims' political practices today. For those lacking the necessary resources to participate in more formal forms of political activism, including those that are most commonly noted and valued by the 'formalists', such as Muslim community groups and local councils (Peucker 2016), everyday spaces constitute valuable opportunities to enact (an often Islam inflected) citizenship, be it through contributing to a work social committee or commenting online. Indeed, it has become a truism that some of the most significant recent revolutions across the Islamic world were fermented and sparked through the use of social media by those left out of more formal political associations (see Castells 2012).

We would also argue that being an ethical neighbour, friend or colleague (which are sometimes the only relationships through which young people have the capacity to act and be heard), can be the foundation of citizenship when these relationships work deliberatively and through vibrant exchange toward public ethics of responsibility, respect and social justice. This argument has gained purchase amongst those who have used our approach to understand links between the more individualised practices that the 'DIY' concept captures and more formal or collectively sustained citizenship work that more traditional citizenship studies scholarship recognises. For example, writing from a Social Psychology perspective on the topic of 'offline and online civic engagement intentions between Italian and migrant youth', Elvira Cicognani et. al. use our work to consider the extent to which the perceived effectiveness of more personal past civic engagement and experiences shapes the likelihood of future engagement in more formal and ongoing political and civic activism both offline and online. This group of scholars reads our work in the context of the challenges faced by young Italians of immigrant background and 'active attempts to develop individualised strategies and standards of behaviour and engagement' (2016, 285). In contrast to Peucker, Cicognani et al. argue that,

> ...in part as a consequence of these processes, young Moroccans display a strong motivation for social and civic engagement within organised contexts, with the aim to produce social change and find a place for themselves within the host country (Ibid).

In this sense, individual 'identity work' to bridge cultural differences and to establish personal standards and strategies for ethical local relations enables immigrant youths to make substantive contributions as citizens in a more formal capacity.

In considering the value of a DIY versus 'formal' citizenship approach, it is important to recall our point that many of the formal spaces for community voice and political engagement are dominated by the first generation of migrant males competing for state resources. To only legitimise as 'citizenship' activities such as engagement in organisations assumes equal access to the necessary cultural and social capital to participate successfully and overlooks important power dynamics between first and second generations within Muslim communities. The concept of DIY citizenship in this case is less an attempt to cast everything as citizenship and more a way to bring to light the drivers behind young Muslims' efforts to 'do citizenship' in other spaces and through other modes in times of heightened regulation, individualisation, exclusion and disenchantment. Our work still adheres to some fundamental touchstones regarding definitions of civic and political practices, in particular, Vromen's (2003, 82–3) conceptualisation of participation as 'acts that can occur, either individually or collectively, that are intrinsically concerned with shaping the society that we want to live in'. However, rather than starting with normative and decontextualised assumptions about what these acts should consist of and where they should be performed, a DIY citizenship approach considers first what acts are possible, visible, scalable, and what are the particular conditions within which young Muslims' citizenship opportunities are produced, such that a turn to the individual and the cultural can be appropriately theorised rather than discounted out of hand as not 'real' citizenship.

Overall, the concept of DIY citizenship is intended to outline the vital significance of the everyday, particularly for youth at the margins and those alienated from formal mechanisms of political and civic engagement; both at the level of the state and civil society. This has important implications in the context of immense scrutiny of Muslim communities and in particular, young Muslims in Western contexts. It is increasingly recognised that government and agency efforts at engagement through formal mechanisms may be somewhat misplaced. They are premised on formal notions of participation and often result in engagement and reengagement with the same community figures and self-proclaimed leaders. This concept opens up new ground for research and approaches to participation, highlighting the eclectic blend of ways that young Muslims engage at the everyday level to shape the society they want.

By casting a light on under-researched and poorly understood forms of citizenship, the concept has explanatory potential, revealing that amongst young Muslims, for example, invisibility in formal activist and ethnic group politics should not be equated with a lack of interest in political and civic life or rejection of democracy. However, the effectiveness of any concept is only as good as its take up and how it is employed as an analytical tool. The uses of our work that we have noted here represent some of the more substantive recent engagements and show ways that this approach might be strengthened and where it may be applied most fruitfully. In responding to these uses and critiques, here we have sought to clarify the relationship between DIY citizenship and cultural citizenship, and outline the value of more relational and processual approaches to the spheres of informal and formal civic and political action. Our intention is that the concept of DIY citizenship can contribute to a paradigm shift in approaches to citizenship in both youth studies and migration studies, and can create a space for an alternate, less heated discourse about the civic and political place of Muslims in Western contexts.

References

Al-Momani, K., N. Dados, M. Maddox, and A. Wise. 2010. *Political Participation of Muslims in Australia*. Sydney, Macquarie University Centre for Research on Social Inclusion.

Bang, H. 2004. *Everyday Makers and Expert Citizens: Building Political Not Social Capital*. Australian National University, School of Social Sciences. Accessed August 2009. http://dspace-prod1.anu.edu.au/handle/1885/42117.

Bauman, Z. 2001. *Community: Seeking Safety in an Insecure World*. Cambridge, Polity.

Beck, U. & E. Beck-Gernsheim 2001, *Individualization*. London, Sage.

Bennett, W.L. 2012. 'The Personalization of Politics: Political Identity, Social Media and Changing Patterns of Participation'. In, *The ANNALS of the American Academy of Political and Social Science*, 644: 20–39.

Burgess, J.E., M. Foth, H.G. Klaebe 2006. 'Everyday Creativity as Civic Engagement: A Cultural Citizenship View of New Media.' In, *Communications Policy and Research Forum*. Sydney, September 25–26.

Castells, M. 2012. *Networks of Outrage and Hope: Social Movements in the Internet Age*. Cambridge, Polity Press.

Castles, S., A. Davidson 2000. *Citizenship and Migration: Globalization and the Politics of Belonging*. London, Macmillan Press.

Cicognani, E. Albanesi, C. Mazzoni, D. Prati, G. Zani, B. 'Explaining offline and online civic engagement intentions between Italisian and migrant youth'. In, *International Journal of Social Psychology*. Vol. 31, No. 2: 282–316.

CIRCA (Cultural and Indigenous Research Centre Australia). 2010. *Social and Civic Participation of Australian Muslim Men*. Sydney, Department of Immigration and Citizenship.

Fahmy, E. 2006. *Young citizens: Young People's Involvement in Politics and Decision making*. Bristol, Ashgate.

Harris, A. & J. Roose 2014 'DIY Citizenship Amongst Young Muslims: Experiences of the Ordinary'. In, *Journal of Youth Studies*, 17(5–6): 794–813.

Harris, A., J. Wyn, and S. Younes. 2010. 'Beyond apathetic or activist youth: 'Ordinary' young people and contemporary forms of participation'. In, *Young: Nordic Journal of Youth Studies* 18(1): 9–32.

Jakubowicz, A.H., J.H. Collins, & W.F. Chafic. 2012. 'Young Australian Muslims: Social Ecology and Cultural Capital'. In, *Muslims in the West and the Challenges of Belonging*, edited by F. Mansouri and V. Marotta, 34–59. Melbourne, Melbourne University Press.

Johns, A. 2014. 'Muslim young people online: "Acts of Citizenship" in socially networked spaces'. In, *Social Inclusion*, Vol. 2, No. 2: 71–82.

Johns, A., F. Mansouri, & M. Lobo. 2015. 'Religiosity, Citizenship and Belonging: the Everyday Experiences of Young Australian Muslims'. In, *Journal of Muslim Minority Affairs* 35(2): 171–190.

Jeffrey, C. and J. Dyson. 2016. 'Prefigurative Politics Through a North Indian Lens'. In, *Economy and Society*, 45 (1–2): 77–100.

Madkhul, D. 2007. *Supporting Volunteering Activities in Australian Muslim Communities, Particularly Youth: A Literature Review Building on the Findings from the National Survey of Australian Volunteers From Diverse Cultural and Linguistic Backgrounds*. Volunteering Australia.

Maira, S.M. 2009. *Youth, Citizenship and Empire After 9/11*, Durham, Duke University Press.

Mandaville, P. 2002. 'Muslim Youth in Europe' In Shireen T. Hunter (ed.) *Islam, Europe's Second Religion: The New Social, Cultural and Political Landscape*. Westport CT, Greenwood Press: 219–230.

McCue, H. 2008. *The civil and social participation of Australian Muslim women in Australian community life*. Department of Immigration and Citizenship: AGPS.

McDonald, K. 2008. 'Globalization, Civil Imagination and Islamic Movements'. In, *Muslim Modernities. Expressions of the Civil Imagination*, edited by A.B. Sujoo, 183–206. London, I.B. Taurus.

Nasir, Kamaludeen Mohamed. 2015. *Globalized Muslim Youth in the Asia Pacific: Popular Culture in Sydney and Singapore*. Palgrave Macmillan.

Ong, A., Dominguez, V.D. Friedman, J. Schiller, N.G. Stolcke, V. Wu, D.Y.H. Ying, H. 1996. 'Cultural Citizenship as Subject-Making: Immigrants Negotiate Racial and Cultural Boundaries in the United States'. In, *Current Anthropology*, Vol. 37, No. 5: 373–762.

O'Toole, T. & R. Gale. 2009. 'Contemporary Grammars of Political Action among Ethnic Minority Young Activists'. In, *Ethnic and Racial Studies*, 33 (1): 126–143.

Pakulski, J. 1997. 'Cultural Citizenship'. In, *Citizenship Studies*, Vol. 1, No. 1: 73–86.

Patton, C. 2016. 'Faith, Space and Negotiated Subjectivities: Young Muslims in Suburban Australia'. In Claire Dwyer and Nancy Worth (eds.) *Identities and Subjectivities*. London, Springer: 193–214.

Peucker, M. 2016. *Muslim Citizenship in Liberal Democracies: Civic and Political Participation in the West*. London, Palgrave.

Ratto, M., M. Boler 2014. 'Introduction'. In Ratto Matt and Megan Boler (eds). *DIY Citizenship: Critical Making and Social Media*: 23–29.

Roker, D. 2008. 'Young Women and Social Action in the United Kingdom'. In, *Next Wave Cultures: Feminism, Activism, Subcultures*, edited by A. Harris. New York, Routledge: 149–170.

Roose, J.M. 2016. *Political Islam and Masculinity: Muslim Men in Australia*. New York, Palgrave Macmillan.

Rosaldo, R. 1997. 'Cultural Citizenship, Inequality and Multiculturalism'. In, William V. Flores and Ria Benmayor (eds.) *Latino Cultural Citizenship: Claiming Identity, Space and rights*. Boston, Beacon Press: 27–38.

Smith, N., R. Lister, S. Middleton & L. Cox. 2005. 'Young People as Real Citizens: Towards an Inclusionary Understanding of Citizenship'. In, *Journal of Youth Studies* 8 (4): 425–444.

Tabar, P., G. Noble, S. Poynting 2003. 'The rise and falter of the field of ethnic politics in Australia: the case of the Lebanese community leadership'. In, *Journal of Intercultural Studies* Vol. 23, No. 3: 267–287.

Turner, B.S. 2001. 'Outline of a General Theory of Cultural Citizenship'. In, Nick Stevenson (ed.) *Culture and Citizenship*: 11–33.

Vassadis, A., A. Karimshah, A. Harris, & Y. Youssef 2015. 'Peer Research with Young Muslims and the Politics of Knowledge Production'. In, *Qualitative Research Journal*, 15(3): 268–281.

Vinken, H. 2005. 'Young People's Civic Engagement: The Need for New Perspectives'. In, *Contemporary Youth Research: Local Expressions and Global Connections*, edited by H. Helve and G. Holm. Aldershot, Ashgate: 147–158.

Vinken, H. 2007. 'Changing Life Courses, Citizenship and New Media: The Impact of Reflexive Biographisation'. In, *Young Citizens and New Media*, edited by P. Dahlgren. New York, Routledge: 41–57.

Vromen, A. 2003. 'People Try to Put Us Down... Participatory Citizenship of Generation X'. In, *Australian Journal of Political Science* 38 (1): 79–99.

Vromen, A. and P. Collin. 2010. 'Everyday Youth Participation? Contrasting Views from Australian Policymakers and Young People'. In, *Young: Nordic Journal of Youth Research* 18 (1): 97–112.

Yeung, P., A. Passmore & T. Packer 2012. 'Examining Citizenship Participation in Young Australian Adults: a structural equation analysis'. *Journal of Youth Studies* 15 (1): 73–98.

CHAPTER 14

Young Indonesians and WikiDPR: Between Apathy and Engagement

Michael Hatherell

1   Introduction

This chapter explores a compelling case study of youth political engagement from Indonesia. Despite a sense of apathy and disappointment that is increasingly characterising political discourse, a young group of citizens have found a unique way to engage with one of the country's most unpopular political institutions. WikiDPR are an activist organisation staffed by young people, who use a combination of social media and youthful energy to engage with members of the national parliament (the *Dewan Perwakilan Rakyat* – DPR).

The emergence of WikiDPR takes place at an interesting time in the history of Indonesian political reform. It has been 18 years since the beginning of the reform era known locally as *reformasi*, and there are divergent assessments regarding the trajectory of reform (Mietzner & Aspinall 2010, 1–2). Observers have long noted the significant successes achieved by *reformasi* in Indonesia – the opening up of the political arena, the freedom now experienced by the press, and a series of democratically elected Presidents, governors, mayors and parliaments (Tornquist 2013, 43–44). At the same time, some observers have identified and critiqued the deep oligarchic political roots that have continued to flourish even after democratisation (Hadiz & Robison 2013). There is also a growing perception that whatever momentum the reform movement possessed has now been lost, with continuing corruption, violence against minority groups and creeping authoritarian tendencies seemingly threatening the achievements of *reformasi* (Dick & Mulholland 2016, 45). Some of these trends led to a deterioration in the Freedom House ranking for Indonesia (FreedomHouse, 2016), but, more importantly, are impacting the mood of public discourse within in Indonesia.

Within the context of this supposed stagnation of reform in Indonesia, the concern that young citizens are disengaged has increasingly been raised. Comparatively poor voter turnout in 2009 spurred a number of campaigns leading up to the 2014 election where young people were encouraged not to *Golput* – an Indonesian term used to describe absenteeism or the act of lodging an invalid ballot. While youth were an important support base for the successful presidential campaign of Joko Widodo (better known as Jokowi), a narrative had begun to emerge that presented young people as part of the 'problem' with Indonesian politics, due to their purported apathetic attitude. Political parties, politicians, civil society groups and religious organisations began to actively urge young Indonesians to use their vote to shape the future of their country. Young converts to this agenda set up petitions to encourage their compatriots to take part in the election. Of course, the narrative that young citizens are apathetic or unengaged in politics because of their voting habits is not unique to Indonesia. But research has also pointed to the need to consider broader forms of political participation - in the context of Western democracies, for instance, Martin (2012, 138) has argued that 'electoral forms of activity and engagement are becoming less popular among the young while non-electoral forms of engagement seem to be becoming more popular'.

Against this backdrop, the case of WikiDPR is insightful. In the context of Indonesian politics, it is important to ask why an organisation like this emerged, and why this group of young people are so actively engaging in politics. The members of WikiDPR may represent a tiny minority of Indonesian youth, but they can provide important lessons about the factors that drive diverse forms of political engagement. Indeed, this case study invites researchers to look beyond national voting data to uncover the diverse role played by young people in civic and political life. This is an important avenue for research in Indonesia, but within the context of this volume, common trends in the experience and civic engagement of young people across borders are also significant.

2 Researching WikiDPR

WikiDPR is a not for profit organisation established in 2014. According to its founder, Hayati Indah Putri, the impulse for creating the organisation was the lack of information available to the public about the work of parliamentarians (Hatherell 2015). Indonesia's parliament does not operate a publically available Hansard, meaning that it is difficult for citizens to access what is discussed in parliament, or to even know whether their local representatives are attending sessions. WikiDPR has sought to correct this gap by using social media (particularly twitter) to report on activities and discussions within the parliament. A central twitter account is supported by several subsidiary twitter accounts where volunteers live tweet the progress of sessions, statements of parliamentarians and upload images of committee attendance. WikiDPR also operate a website (wikidpr.org) where data about each individual politician is compiled from their activities and statements in parliament. In addition to these core activities, WikiDPR also collate news stories on their website and provide other content, such as interviews with members of parliament on youtube. The organisation is also active in collecting other forms of data, such as parliamentary session attendance rates for different political parties.

What is perhaps most impressive about WikiDPR is that it is run entirely by volunteers. Most of these volunteers are young undergradate students at universities around Jakarta, who learn about WikiDPR through friends or university networks. In order to provide constant social media updates, WikiDPR volunteers sit patiently for hours and record vast amounts of detail from parliamentary sessions. Often these sessions are heavy on technical detail, and last for extended periods of time. It is not unusual for parliamentarians, who are paid to attend these sessions, to fall asleep – a luxury not available to the WikiDPR volunteers!

Given their dedication to their volunteer work in the context of a society where young people are often described as politically apathetic, it is important to ask why WikiDPR members have decided to volunteer for such an organisation. In order to address this question, this study invited WikiDPR members to participate in a qualitative survey. The survey was conducted online in the national language of Indonesia, Bahasa Indonesia. The age of participants was the only piece of personal information collected, in order to protect the identity of participants and to encourage unmediated responses. Participants were reached through a link to the survey, which was distributed via organisers within WikiDPR. In total, 27 volunteers took part in the study. The total numbers of volunteers within WikiDPR at any one time is somewhat fluid due to ongoing recruitment, but this number represents approximately one third of the active volunteer cohort at the time the research was conducted. Those who completed the informed consent and agreed to participate in the research were presented with eight questions or prompts, with space to write as little or as much as they wanted. While names and gender were not recorded, pseudonyms have been included below to link content from single participants and for stylistic purposes. The gender of the pseudonyms used may not reflect the gender of the participant.

3   The State of Politics and Democracy in Indonesia

In attempting to understand emotional responses like apathy, despair or even hope, it is important to understand the role of worldview and perspective in shaping the attitudes of young people. In Indonesia, a society with a tumultuous 71 year history of independence, this endeavour is especially important. For older Indonesians, the period of authoritarian rule prior to 1998 provides some point of comparison, but for younger Indonesians, successive democratically elected governments have formed their only lived reality. While young Indonesians live in a more transparent and connected Indonesia, domestic frustrations, such as ongoing corruption scandals, are openly discussed and shared face-to-face as well as on social media. At the same time, internet enabled smartphones and increased opportunities for international travel enable Indonesian youths to construct a richer view of the political and social context of other nations. Some aspects of Indonesia's present political reality are no doubt context specific, but as other chapters in this book suggest, the lived experiences of young people in different societies share some common traits.

This study began by exploring the perspective of WikiDPR volunteers regarding politics and democracy. Participants were asked to discuss their perspective regarding the current state of politics in Indonesia, before being asked their views on democracy as a system of government and its suitability for Indonesia. These questions sought to identify the perspective of these young Indonesians on the political world around them, in order to better understand why they have chosen to engage in this world. Like the other questions within the survey, these questions were open-ended, and allowed participants to write as little or as much as they preferred. The open-ended nature of the research also meant that responses to other questions sometimes strayed into discussing worldview.

It was clear that many of the young Indonesians surveyed were concerned about the state of politics in their country. Quite often this concern was based on the view that politics had simply become a tool for pursuing power, rather than furthering the interests of the community. Ruli, for instance, argued that:

> Our political system is very concerning because politics is often a tool for achieving power. In the end it is the community that becomes the victim and the current political conditions are due to the bureaucrats who seem to be too busy scrambling for the seats of power.

Similarly, Ani argued that Indonesia's current political system was 'badly damaged because the political elite rarely have a concern for the Indonesian nation and only prioritise themselves and money'.

The major concern for these young Indonesians was not, it seemed, about the system itself, but rather the individual politicians and bureaucrats who operated it. These political operatives were often labelled as corrupt, self-interested or immoral. For Rini, Indonesian politics is filled by 'people who are lacking ethics, who can't become a good example, who have questionable work ethic'. Similarly, Imam argued that at this time Indonesian politics was experiencing 'moral degradation'. The majority of responses focused on the moral behaviour of politicians, bureaucrats and parties. In this way the responses in this study connected to a wider theme in social discourse within Indonesia which frames Indonesia's contemporary political problems as the result of a 'moral crisis' rather than a failure of systems, institutional design or as a stage in development. This notion has a long history in Indonesia – Herb Feith (1962, 223), for instance, noted the discussions of moral crisis in Indonesia as far back as the 1950s.

Despite this pessimism, some participants also saw reasons for optimism. Sari, for instance, argued that:

> ...it is still as it has been, but there is starting to be a change. We are starting to see the emergence of figures who care about this nation and give a glimmer of hope...

For Roro, optimism about Indonesian politics was connected to the involvement of the community:

> we are on the way to democracy as it should be, hopefully. Although there is still a lot that needs to be improved and that requires the input of the community as a whole.

The notion that Indonesian politics were still undergoing change appeared in several responses. For Yudi there had been a 'lot of change, both positive and negative', while for Wati the political system was already 'quite good, because it had started to become transparent'.

With this mix of concern and hope about the state of Indonesian politics, it was interesting to observe the response of these young Indonesians to the idea of democracy itself. Participants responded in greater detail to this question, and a wide variety of answers were provided. These responses demonstrated a diversity of perspectives regarding what democracy actually is, as well as different views regarding the weaknesses of democratic politics in Indonesia.

For a number of participants, democracy was seen as a positive framework for Indonesia's political system, albeit with some caveats. As Putri reflected:

> actually it's good because it invites all of the community to contribute directly in government, but it is best that this system of democracy is

complimented with responses or feedback that flow in two directions so we are not just left with apathy in regards to each other's opinions.

Similarly, Imam argued that:

> democracy can become a good political system in this country if the culture of corruption, collusion and nepotism is removed, the anti-corruption efforts are carried out, everything that still has strong roots that injure democracy has to be removed so that democracy can become mature in Indonesia and Indonesia can see improvement.

According to these views and others within the research, it is not the concept or institutions of democracy itself that are at fault, but rather the practical problems which still impact the culture and practice of democracy in Indonesia. 'I think it is good', stated Fahmi in response to this question, 'it is just the reality which has been carried out that is not fit. If it is done well it will be a good political system'. This view was also shared by Lani, who argued that:

> At their heart all political systems are good. They have a good aim. All this time we have been blaming and continuously changing the system alone without realising…why isn't it the actors within that political system who are corrected, because the system cannot change itself. The deviation is not in the system but in those who carry out the system. No political system will lead to good results if the ones who run the system are not as good as the original values or goals of the system.

A number of responses also appeared to connect values and norms related to democracy. Ideas about power, and the relationship between holders of power, emerged. Nina, for instance, responded:

> Yes, because power is held by the people [in a democracy]. Although in practice there is not much which works in line with that principle of democracy.

Other participants were interested in connecting with 'Indonesian' values, particularly values tied to *Pancasila*. *Pancasila* is a set of principles established during the 20th century as a basis for the Indonesian state. This guiding ideology was a key component of the discursive and institutional structure of the Suharto regime, but has retained much of its influence during the reform era. Yudi, for instance, connected with this concept in stating that:

> For me, democracy in the political world is very important. Democracy is very suitable to be implemented in Indonesia and infused with the values of *Pancasila*. But it has to be observed that, a quality democracy is a democracy which is accountable. Prepared to act, prepared to be responsible.

A number of participants held less favourable views of democracy, either as a political system or as practiced in the current context. As one of the key themes in this book attests, apathy regarding the state of politics in liberal democratic states is not unusual for young people in many different socio-political contexts around the world. It should also be noted that public opinion surveys in Indonesia have found that the majority of young Indonesians tend to see democracy as the most preferable form of government – and in slightly higher numbers than young Australians (Lowy Institute 2014). Yet within this research, there were specific concerns about democracy that rested upon assumptions about the nature of Indonesian society, culture or the current stage of political development. Ani, for instance, argued that:

> Indonesia as a nation is not yet ready to use democracy like the system used in America because our political education is still lacking so we need guidance…I prefer the use of guided democracy like in the time of Sukarno which is more suitable for Indonesia.

Similarly, Yeni argued that:

> in my opinion democracy is not the best system. What is suitable is Pancasila because the source is the values of the Indonesian nation. Democracy in Indonesia can't be as open as in the West because Indonesia needs firmness in the running of its political system.

The need for more 'authoritarian' sources of power within Indonesian politics was echoed by several respondents – Ismail for instance argued that:

> Yes [democracy is suitable for Indonesia], but for a couple of reasons also an authoritarian approach to governance. Because not everyone who governs is bad and not all parts of the community in Indonesia are good.

This observation echoes arguments that have been made throughout Indonesia's history – though it should be noted that these claims have always been contested.

Ideas about democracy and authoritarianism were also reflected by some participants with reference to perceived weaknesses in Indonesian society itself. The Indonesian term *kebablasan* (going too far) was used by several respondents to suggest that Indonesian society was not ready for democracy without strong leadership. Siti, for instance, argued that:

> Maybe Indonesia needs leaders who are a little dictatorial. Democracy is indeed good, but Indonesian society tends to go too far or be excessive, and it results in the emergence of unnecessary commotion.

Rini also noted that:

> …our democracy is too excessive. When everyone is too free to have an opinion and express themselves, harmful actions become unclear. The public doesn't know what is true or false…quality democracy should have strong control so that the process of democracy is directed.

These comments clearly echo some historical concerns in Indonesian social and political discourse regarding the desirability of political stability and leadership.

Overall, participants demonstrated a range of views on the existing political context in Indonesia. While there was generally a negative assessment of the state of politics, some participants saw room for optimism. The assessment of democracy was decidedly mixed, with some participants seeing the current form of democracy as suitable for Indonesia, while others sought to balance or integrate democratic principles with other political notions such as *Pancasila* and even authoritarianism.

4   The Role and Representation of Young People

In this study, participants were also invited to reflect on the representation of young people and the role of young people in Indonesia's political system. These questions sought to further establish some of the contextual factors that informed these young Indonesian's views of the world around them. The role of young people in politics is particularly interesting in Indonesia, where youths have played an important role during several important historical moments. During the critical months of the *reformasi* movement in 1998, for instance, young university students played a pivotal role in bringing about the resignation of President Suharto through continuous street protests. Young people were also a key driving factor in the nationalist movement that would eventually lead to an independent Indonesia in the 1940s, as Suryadinata (1978, 113) identifies:

> It is clear that the pre-war youth movement in Indonesia not only constituted a vital component of Indonesian nationalism but on many occasions became the actual vanguard of the nationalist struggle. It was the secular youth movement which created and first popularized the Indonesian "national symbols" – the name of the country and the people ("Indonesia" and "bangsa Indonesia"), the Indonesian language, the Red-White Flag, and what was to become the Indonesian national anthem.

Even today, the historically important *Sumpah Pemuda* (youth pledge) taken by young nationalists in 1928 has become a national day and is widely celebrated by young and old Indonesians alike (Foulcher 2000, 377).

Within this study, participants were asked to discuss the views of their friends or the people around them in their life regarding politics. A number of pejorative adjectives were used in response to this question, but the most common were *'apatis'* (apathetic) and *'tidak peduli'* (don't care). In many cases this sense of apathy was connected to the idea that the political process does not lead to real change. Fahmi, for instance, stated that:

> …they consider politics as something negative. They really don't care because in their opinion politics in Indonesia doesn't influence change in relation to the nation.

Ruli similarly argued that 'most of them don't want to care because in their opinion caring about politics won't change their life'. Nina argued that:

> … most of my friends or the people in the environment around me don't care about politics. They consider politics to be mind-numbing.

Some participants attributed apathetic attitudes to other sources. For Lani, the media were part of the problem:

> Most of them tend to be apathetic because of the image that is created by the mass media and they don't want to put in too much effort to find out what is really going on.

For Putri, the system itself made young people look apathetic:

> Actually the generation of young people now really cares about politics in Indonesia, but because the discourse surrounding the delivery of aspirations is not sufficient, they end up looking apathetic.

Some participants like Uda saw an opportunity for change:

> They still don't care very much, because they think that there is no influence for their everyday life, but I'm certain that if I keep employing my approach of providing information about political problems, bit by bit they will understand just how important knowledge about politics is.

When asked about the role of young people within politics and their potential to bring about change, participants responded with overwhelming positivity. This idealism contrasted strongly with the characterisations of the political system, and pointed towards the justification for becoming politically active. Siti, for instance, argued that:

> ... of course the young generation is very influential because the young generation are currently enthusiastic and idealistic in terms of creating a better political system.

Rini similarly contended that:

> ... young people are agents of change, young people who get involved in large scale movements can change the history of politics in Indonesia. One important point is that young people should be active because of objective reasons, not because they are influenced by political interests.

These views were shared by a number of other participants, including Ruli:

> The young generation is a huge influence in Indonesia's political system, because it will be the young people who will build Indonesia. Like Sukarno said: 'give me 10 youths and I will change the world'.

While some participants thought that young people faced challenges in becoming a powerful political force, there was general agreement that young people were an important source of change. Yeni summed up this feeling well, stating that:

> The younger generation is so important because they can provide a re-generation of politics in Indonesia's system of government. Youths can change the political map of Indonesia if they can find a common vision for a better Indonesia.

These perspectives suggest a connection between today's youth in Indonesia and popular notions of the role that young Indonesians have played during significant moments in Indonesia's history. Importantly, these notions are not based simply on youth participation in voting, but instead on broader civic engagement. Hence while much contemporary discourse focuses on the supposed apathy of youth, and some participants identified this apathy in their own environment, there are clearly potential competing narratives.

5   Why Engage in WikiDPR?

As we have seen, WikiDPR volunteers surveyed here generally acknowledge the problems facing Indonesian politics, but see the potential for young people to participate in change. The study sought to understand the key motivations for these young people choosing to join WikiDPR and engage directly with the political system. To do this, the study asked participants firstly whether they have been active in politics previously, before asking them to reflect on their reasons for joining WikiDPR as well as what they hoped their involvement would achieve.

The majority of participants noted that they had not been involved in politics before joining WikiDPR. Sari, for instance, noted that:

> … beforehand I was never active…I only knew politics from the media on television and even that was not something I often followed.

Further, Maya reported, '…never, the most involved I have been was voting in the presidential election (2004)'. There were a couple of exceptions, with one member stating their involvement in politics on a university campus, while a couple of other members had been involved in activist organisations previously. For most, however, WikiDPR was their first experience of political activism.

For some participants curiosity was part of their rationale for joining WikiDPR. Ari claimed that he was '…interested because the activities within WikiDPR could allow me to see and witness directly the political process'. Joko stated that there was '…a feeling of curiosity with the actual work of the DPR, the work that the community and the media were saying was so bad.' Susi explained that:

> I like the political world but I don't understand politics. WikiDPR gives me access to learn and see politics in reality and directly from the political operatives.

Uda had similar motivations, hoping to:

> ... know directly the work of the respected members who say that they represent the community, I had no sense of internal satisfaction even when I can see them on tv, because much of what is presented in the media is already sanitised.

These responses and others point to a shared interest in comparing the image of politics and politicians common in the media and public discourse with the reality. Enclosed within this desire was a sense of hope that the reality might be more positive – or at least more varied – than depicted.

For others, the reason for joining WikiDPR had more to do with a sense of duty or hope to change something about Indonesia's political system. Ruli stated that she joined WikiDPR:

> ... because what I read in the profile of WikiDPR, is that their mission is to connect the community with their representatives, and I'm interested in taking part in that.

Putri said that "I was interested because there is not yet a community of young people who can enter directly into the area of politics", while Bambang explained that it was his:

> ... initiative as a young person who cares about the work of the DPR, and thus wanted to know more about the extent of credibility possessed by the DPR members.

When participants were asked about what they hoped to achieve with the organisation, the result was a mixture of desire to develop personally from the experience, and of hope regarding shaping the future direction of Indonesia. Ari, for instance, argued that he wanted to:

> ... add to my awareness about the world of politics, participate in overseeing government, and be able to judge political events on more than just the reporting of the media.

Joko wanted to:

> ... participate in opening up the awareness of the public about the performance of the DPR, the work of the people's representatives that are elected by the community. And I also want to add to my own awareness about the issues that are now being discussed by the DPR that relate to my studies.

Some participants also spoke about the opportunity to make connections, to network, to make friends and to add to their experience.

A number of responses emphasised the desire to make a difference by being active in WikiDPR. These participants largely echoed the stated aims of WikiDPR itself, but with their own points of emphases. Dhani, for instance, wanted to '...give information clearly and independently to the community, without being edited by the considerations of group interests' while Uda hoped that through his engagement with WikiDPR:

> ... the community can truly know about the members who represent them...there are members of the DPR who perform well but this is not heard, so that later when the election is held, the community can be sure of which people are suitable to represent the community of Indonesia.

Ismail observed that:

> ... there are an increasing number joining WikiDPR. Increasing numbers of young people that are aware that to advance we need to not just act but to do something. That is the same as being quiet and not doing anything. It is a waste.

Wisnu had a more specific aim for her participation:

> I hope that the political world in Indonesia can be more open for the press, because whatever happens, the media has an important role in the reporting of politics in Indonesia.

Ari simply states that, apart from other personal interests, 'WikiDPR has become my way of contributing as a young person'.

For participants in WikiDPR and this research, it was clear that there were a number of reasons for becoming politically active. The participants were generally not active before joining WikiDPR, and saw the potential for both personal growth and contribution to the community. Clearly WikiDPR's volunteers do not participate out of an entirely benevolent desire to do social good, as clearly there are also self-interested reasons for joining the group. In the competitive Indonesian job market, volunteering is one way of developing useful networks and experience. Yet self-interest and contributing to society are not necessarily mutually exclusive. For many participants, the development of one's own civic engagement stood as an example and beginning point for other young people to follow.

6   Conclusion

This chapter in itself makes no claims about the broader engagement of young people in Indonesia, or the way Indonesia's youth as a whole see politics. The aim of this study was to explore one prominent case of youth political engagement, and try to understand the sources of hope and enthusiasm driving the participants. The experiences of hope and activism presented in this study contrast in some ways with other research presented in this collection, but there are some common themes.

Importantly, the young people included in this study were not unrealistic about their political context. Through the research it was clear that these young people generally possessed a quite sober understanding of the nature of politics in Indonesia and had divergent opinions about the appropriateness of democracy as a political system, and the change that they thought needed to take place.

Yet their response to their political context is important. Volunteering with WikiDPR is a choice to engage directly with the existing political system, and specifically with the unpopular national parliament. This form of activism could be contrasted with other responses, including abstaining from voting or protesting. While narratives surrounding young people in Indonesia have typically focused on apathy, this chapter, although presenting findings from a small group of young people, provides some counterbalance to established narratives about young people. WikiDPR is an example of an inventive and thoughtful application of time and energy by young Indonesians, aimed at addressing deficits within the Indonesian political context. The views of volunteers themselves largely demonstrate their belief that young people can still make a difference within Indonesia's political system, and that joining an organisation like WikiDPR is one way of achieving this.

While it is important to understand that this is a small piece of the puzzle in a country as large as Indonesia, the findings presented here suggest that we may find other cases that challenge established ideas regarding the political roles and behaviours of young people. National voting rates are only one measure of these trends: we need to also look at the involvement of young people in local politics, in neighbourhood and religious organisations, in social movements, and indeed in digitally focused initiatives like WikiDPR. Just as Martin (2012) has noted that young people in western democracies are choosing to be active in new and innovative ways, the same is likely to be true in Indonesia. Grasping this tapestry of civic and political engagement will provide a more nuanced and complete picture of the role of young Indonesians in their society, and given they will inherit the political system in the future, this is an important endeavour.

References

Feith, H. 1962. *The Decline of Constitutional Democracy in Indonesia*. Ithaca, New York: Cornell University Press.

Foulcher, K. 2000. "Sumpah Pemuda: the Making and Meaning of a Symbol of Indonesian Nationhood". In, *Asian Studies Review 24 (3)*: 377–410.

FreedomHouse. 2016. *Freedom House Report on Indonesia*. https://freedomhouse.org/country/indonesia. Accessed 24 July 2016.

Hadiz, V. and R. Richard 2013. "The Political Economy of Oligarchy and the Reorganization of Power in Indonesia", In, *Indonesia, 96*: 35–57.

Hatherell, M. 2015. "Engaging Young Indonesians in Politics and the Case of Wikidpr." In, *Inside Indonesia*. http://www.insideindonesia.org/engaging-young-indonesians-in-politics-and-the-case-of-wikidpr. Accessed 20 August 2016.

Lowy Institute. 2014. *Lowy Institute Poll 2014*. http://www.lowyinstitute.org/publications/lowy-institute-poll-2014. Accessed 10 August 2016.

Martin, A.J. 2012. *Young People and Politics: Political Engagement in the Anglo-American Democracies*. London; New York: Routledge.

Mietzner, M. and E. Aspinall. 2010. "An Overview." in *Problems of Democratisation in Indonesia: Elections, Institutions and Society*, edited by Marcus Mietzner and Ed Aspinall. Singapore: ISEAS.

Suryadinata, L. 1978. "Indonesian Nationalism and the Pre-war Youth Movement: A Reexamination." In, *Journal of Southeast Asian Studies 9: (1)*: 99–114.

Törnquist, O. 2013. *Assessing Dynamics of Democratisation: Transformative Politics, New Institutions, and the Case of Indonesia*. Basingstoke: Palgrave Macmillan.

WikiDPR. 2016. *WikiDPR Website*. www.wikidpr.org. Accessed June 13 2016.

CHAPTER 15

Strategic Space for Progressive Alternatives: Syriza and Democracy in Greece

John Bourdouvalis

1   Introduction

On the 25th of January 2015 the radical left political party Syriza won the Greek elections. Syriza's election victory was the first time a party of the radical Left had taken office since World War Two (Ovenden, 2015: xv). It was elected on a platform of bargaining against the neoliberal austerity that had been imposed by previous governments under the strict instructions of the governing body Troika[1] (Gindin and Panitch, 2015). Austerity in the European Union (EU) has made the economic crisis more severe and has contributed to the many social mobilisations demanding a genuine democracy (Pitty, 2014, 125). Syriza's election victory initially seemed to provide a nascent strategic opening for mobilising further support against neoliberal austerity politics in Europe. The then incoming Prime Minister, Alexis Tsipras (2015a), described the victory as a historic opportunity to reverse destructive austerity policies and gradually build towards a more democratically inclusive society. However, framing the tension in the Eurozone as a question of financial crisis management is a one-dimensional interpretation of a more entrenched problem. Such a framing implies that the problems of neoliberalism are situated at a regulatory or policy level and can be overcome with prudential economic management (Konings and Panitch, 2009, 67). Such interpretations rely on technocratic, top-down prescriptions that negate the involvement of young people and other alienated cleavages of society, to contribute viable alternatives.

Syriza's politics is reflective of ongoing youth revolts against neoliberal austerity, and the failure of the established political class to represent the interests of disaffected and alienated young people. Prior to the economic crisis of 2008, Syriza's focus of actively appealing to youth movements was part of a shift away from the language of 'radical left renewal' (connected to the

---

1   Troika refers to the three institutional bodies, the European Commission, the European Central Bank and the International Monetary Fund, which have been responsible for the imposition and surveillance of all three economic adjustment programs in Greece since 2010.

Euro-communist tradition), towards a 'radical politics' that sought to express the demands of social movements against neoliberalism (Katsambekis, 2015, 153). The movement has a youth wing called 'Syriza Youth' that displays a greater degree of radicalism and advocates for issues that are often deemed unpopular in Greek society, including: human rights matters, immigration advocacy and LGBT rights (Spourdalakis, 2015). Importantly, Syriza Youth treats the notion of 'youth' as an autonomous category driven by specific objectives for the abolition of exploitative social relations, which are guided by practices of collective organisation and social mobilisation (Youth of Syriza 2016). The class perspective of these objectives centre on social transformation and the rights of young people who have been pushed into the 'grey zone of unemployment and precariousness' by economic crisis (Syriza, 2013). This chapter will examine the politics of Syriza, the autonomous youth wing of the party, and the expectations young Greek people have for Syriza to affect change. First, this chapter will discuss the rise of Syriza as a heterogeneous coalition of movements that sought to articulate a renewed left-wing politics through closer engagement with Greek civil society. Second, it will focus on the important role of youth activism in the struggle against deficiencies of the Greek political system and neoliberalism. Third, the chapter will provide an analysis of the domestic and transnational challenges faced by the Syriza government. Finally, I shift the focus to the future of Syriza and the function of youth activism and social movements in overcoming the weaknesses of democracy.

2   The Rise of Syriza

Syriza is best described as a self-contradictory and internally antagonistic coalition of left thought and practice (Gourgouris, 2015). Syriza evolved as a hybrid entity that operates both within social movements and representative politics and has been highly active in Greek social struggles over the past fifteen years (Budgen and Kouvelakis, 2015). Throughout its evolution and development Syriza has relied on social movements and was driven by networks of protest that cut across class lines to include gender and sexuality activism, student activism, alter-globalisation activists, and various other kinds of social advocacy groups (Gourgouris, 2015). Stathis Kouvelakis (2015), who was a prominent member of the party's influential Left Platform and member of the Central Committee, defines Syriza as a hybrid entity that constitutes a synthesis of the Greek communist movement and other forms of radicalism that emerged gradually from the decomposition of the Greek Left since the early 1990s. Formally, the party emerged in 2004 as a coalition of several groups of the parliamentary and extra-parliamentary Left (Katsambekis, 2015, 153). It built on the experience of labour, feminist, youth and anti-racism movements, as well as movements resisting the commodification of social goods (Laskos and Tsakalotos, 2014, 77; Tsakatika and Eleftheriou, 2013, 89). Rather than impose a theoretical dogmatism on social movements through ready-made emancipatory politics, there has been a tendency in the party to connect with civil society in a more proactive and generative manner (Spourdalakis, 2014: 358). This more fluid approach to political mobilisation demonstrates the need to ensure that programmatic solutions at the level of representative politics are connected to concrete social dynamics (Spourdalakis, 2014). Appealing to the struggles of young people was part of a broader strategy of building a multi-tendency movement of which the youth could provide an important source of synergy and creativity in popular struggles (Syriza, n.d.). Syriza Youth is more than an organisation wedded to youth identity and youth struggles. It focusses on the role of young people in contributing to debates about nationalism, sexism, class, social welfare, unemployment, immigrant rights and, in the context of current economic circumstances, resistance to neoliberal austerity.

Syriza's gradual restructuring into a more conventional political party is the result of a strategic decision made by leader Alexis Tsipras prior to the May 2012 elections to build towards a broad coalition of the Left and contest state power (Spourdalakis, 2014, 359). According to Tsipras (2015a) part of Syriza's strength was that it provided a better understanding of the crisis and the need to challenge austerity at the European level, but also to support grassroots initiatives and social solidarity networks. These grassroots initiatives and networks envisioned alternative societies and provided the language for change. Indeed, Syriza Youth (n.d) views the participation of young people in these projects as part of the process of transformation necessary exit the crisis in favour of working people. Therefore, Syriza was not about claiming the political ground vacated by the centre-Left or continuing along a traditional social democratic route (Tsipras, 2015a). Rather, the goal of uniting the political Left was driven by an agenda that spoke to the transformation of society based on socialism and democracy of which young people had a part in contributing to (Tsipras, 2015a). Forming such new social alliances was necessary in order to compete for state power against a well-funded and deeply entrenched political elite. In this context, youth movements and resistance to education reforms were also seen as offering an alternative political discourse. Within the party youth elements were progressively subsumed by a broader discourse that attempted to articulate the struggle of the 'people' against austerity in general (Stavrakakis and Katsambekis, 2014, 127). By placing itself close to social movements Syriza has been able to benefit from engagement with social forums, civil rights and immigrant groups, and environmental movements without doing damage to the autonomy of these social formations (Spourdalakis, 2014, 358).

Syriza was able to provide an accurate understanding of the economic crisis and turn itself into a viable alternative in a way that no other fringe political formations have been able to (Iglesias, 2015, 17). However, Syriza's rise was not self-generated (Stavrakakis and Katsambekis, 2014, 126). It benefited greatly from the political space left behind by the collapse of electoral support for the major political parties, most notably that of the formerly powerful Pasok (Laskos and Tsakalotos, 2014, 10; Spourdalakis, 2014, 357). Significantly, sustained mobilisations during the years of austerity, sometimes measuring up to 20% of the population, helped propel Syriza from a fringe party to the doors of government (Watkins, 2016, 8). Other estimates suggest that at one point or another, up to one third of the population has participated in anti-austerity protests (Tekin and Tekin, 2015, 133). The party has been able to attract disaffected voters across the entire political spectrum, but the movements in the squares of Athens by the self-styled *Aganaktismenoi* (The Indignant Citizens Movement) played a key role creating a political space that Syriza was able to exploit from 2012 onwards. The heterogeneity of the *Aganaktismenoi* was evident in the complexity of mass demonstrations, which included neighbourhood committees and open citizen assemblies where participants were not organised by political parties or trade unions (Psimitis 2011, 195). During the June 2012 elections young people voted heavily for Syriza in the hope that it would be able to challenge the conditions that had been imposed by the Troika (Sitrin and Azzellini, 2014, 72). There was a sense that a Left government, unhindered by the machinations of the Greek clientalist state, would lead to less state oppression (Sitrin and Azzellini, 2014, 109).

This optimism was tempered by a concern that a Left government would lead to the instrumentalisation and de-mobilisation of social movements (Sitrin and Azzellini, 2014, 109). Syriza emerged as the only political party that was actively supporting the novel forms of social mobilisation and horizontal political organisation that emerged in 2011 (Katsambekis, 2015, 156). The accumulated knowledge and skills of young people, wasted by the consequences of the financial crisis and forced to look abroad for a future, are an important source of energy for change. Therefore, Syriza and the Left in Greece require a strong youth organisation capable of articulating the different elements of youth identity that speaks to a hopeful future (Syriza 2013). This is consistent with what Syriza deputy, Yiannis Dragasakis, refers to as a political process of movement building, which aims to act as a lynchpin between the party's presence both within and outside public institutions (Spourdalakis, 2014: 358–59). In contrast, the Communist Party (KKE) was openly critical of the movements in the squares because they saw them as a non-political force that could not be sublimated by a vanguard position (Katsambekis, 2015, 156). The KKE claimed that the *Aganaktismenoi* did not represent a danger to the establishment as their demands simply entailed the rejection of the government and austerity rather than an alternative to capitalism (Prentoulis and Thomassen, 2014, 213).

What was happening, however, was the displacement and de-alignment of politics as usual. The organisation and mobilisation of participants inside and outside the framework of elections challenged the idea that the focal point of politics is representative democracy (Tormey, 2015, 25). The occupation of the squares did not represent an organised Left mobilisation but it did encompass a general hostility to all political parties (Ovenden, 2015, 55). Inspired by similar experiences in Tahir Square and Puerta del Sol, the movements in the squares of Athens represented a break with traditional forms of protest and focused on the creation of open ongoing assemblies not dominated by political parties or unions (Sitrin and Azzellini, 2014, 69).

Given Syriza framed its political strategies around active involvement in social movements there is the danger that shifts in political discourse, and a more unitary organisational structure, may do damage to the multitude of social forces it seeks to represent and incorporate into a social majority. Challenging the duopoly of Greek democracy, which has essentially been a rotation of power between New Democracy (ND) and Pasok since 1974, required an active shift to the terrain of the state (Katsambekis, 2015, 152). The convergence of ND and Pasok towards what Tariq Ali (2015) refers to as the 'Extreme Centre' was part of the reason why the two main political parties were able to govern as a coalition between 2011 and 2015 under discursive banners such as a 'government of national salvation' (Katsambekis, 2015, 156). Other political formations were either unwilling to recognise the legitimacy of the street mobilisations or were actively hostile to them. Also, there was the realisation that expecting the culpable, post-democratic elite to provide credible solutions to a severe sovereign debt crisis was misguided (Douzinas, 2013, 39). This social and political environment generated questions within the social imaginary about what alternatives might look like, what social forces will drive them, and how they will be coordinated to challenge conditions of precarity and austerity.

3   The Role of Youth Activism since 2008

Greek youth activism developed throughout the alter-globalisation and anarchist movements of the early 2000s. These movements involved a constant and strong appeal to the 'youth' and its struggles and allowed Syriza to strengthen its presence amongst students (Budgen and Kouvelakis, 2015; Katsambekis, 2015, 153). Party members were encouraged to participate in various social movements in a manner that respected their autonomous social dynamics (Katsambekis, 2015, 154). This strategy was intended to act as a process of learning that would allow members to gain valuable experience whilst bringing the party closer to civil society (Katsambekis, 2015, 154). Another important development was Syriza's support of the Student Protests in 2006–2007 against privatisation of the education sector and the Youth Riots of 2008. These movements became constant themes in Syriza's public discourse and enabled the Greek people to identify with the general concerns that have been expressed by numerous anti-globalisation protests since the turn of the century (Katsambekis, 2015, 153). People were concerned with the ongoing integration of Greek society into the EU, which facilitated neoliberal restructuring enhancing the importance of Greek industrialists and bankers (Petropoulou, 2010, 218). In the face of these changes youth activism involved an opposition to the ongoing precarisation of work and the commodification of social and educational life (Standing, 2011). The notion of the Precariat as a social category denoting a position of perennial insecurity in the process of the reproduction of capitalism was clearly at play in pre-crisis Greece (Standing, 2011; Della Porta, 2015).

The 2008 Youth Riots represented a condensation of frustration and the disillusionment of Greek youth with the political establishment characterised by corruption, nepotism and clientelism (Memos, 2010, 214). These riots were a massive leaderless insurrection that involved a cross section of students and labour carrying out rallies, marches and occupations (Douzinas, 2014, 84; Memos, 2010, 210). The riots signified an important moment of rupture and lead to the awakening of a generation condemned by the Left and Right as apolitical, ill-informed and apathetic (Douzinas, 2013, 139). The riots themselves were sparked by the murder of fifteen-year-old Alexandros Grigoropoulos, who was shot by a member of the police Special Guard unit after they had an altercation with a number of youths in the anarchist Athenian neighbourhood of Exarcheia. Historically, Exarcheia has been a sight of radical and intellectual activism, with the most significant event being the 1974 student occupation of the Athens Polytechnic University in protest against the then military Junta. The degree of mobilisation was considered unique in Greek history and expressed a deep anti-systemic sentiment prevalent in segments of the youth (Sotiris, 2010, 203). The Youth Riots taught people how to communicate and organise against police and state repression, and led to the politicization of young people (Douzinas, 2013, 143). The youth mobilisation spread nationally and included high school and university strikes, students targeting police stations as well as the brief occupation of municipal buildings, television and radio stations (Sotiris, 2010, 203). In effect, the movement targeted various nodes of power, both public and private, that were perceived as contributing to diminishing social opportunities for Greek youth.

Even before the onset of the crisis in 2009, Greek youth unemployment stood at 22.3% for 15–24 year olds, whereas the EU average during the same time stood at 16.7% (Sotiris, 2011, 204). The high unemployment growth rates during the mid-90s to 2007, were largely driven by a credit-fuelled expansion in banking, construction and consumption, and coincided with the ongoing deterioration of employment prospects for young people (Sotiris, 2010, 203). During this time, better qualifications did not necessarily translate into better employment prospects, which undermined the Third Way notion that investment in human capital would enable people to exploit the opportunities of a dynamic globalising economy (Sotiris, 2010, 204; Cerny, 1999, 455). In 2014 youth unemployment stood at 51.1% and the number of young people either unemployed or not in education or training sat at 28.3% (OECD, 2015; OECD, 2016). This means that nearly one third of the Greek population aged between 15 and 30 are currently idle, or rely on threadbare welfare or alternative forms of assistance, such as the solidarity networks or family. Donatella Della Porta (2015, 4) explains how the social precariat includes the young and the unemployed or underemployed who must make do with limited social protection under conditions of extreme austerity. The common denominator for Greek youth, despite differences in social status, educational and vocational paths, is a unity in the deterioration of employment prospects and the general precarisation of social life (Sotiris, 2010, 204).

Syriza's ability to identify with the concerns of youthful social movements, activists and protesters provided the means to connect the party's objectives with the emerging social climate. However, the transition from protest party to one capable of governing, involved a transformation of political and social discourse that may yet threaten the singularity of the social cleavages that provide its point of difference. For example, Syriza began to articulate its discourse in terms of an active appeal to the 'people' as the effects of austerity and social unrest reached across all strata of Greek society. This meant that an active appeal to youth was abandoned in favour of political language that was framed in terms of the anti-austerity 'people' versus the pro-memorandum 'establishment' (Katsambekis, 2015, 155). Framing political discourse in this way is not in-itself incompatible with an active appeal to youth movements. Nevertheless, shifting to a populist expression of indignation subsumed youth voices, among others, into a generalised resistance against neoliberal austerity.

However, this does not necessarily diminish the validity of Syriza's broad strategic objectives. Christos Laskos and Euclid Tsakalotos (2013, 14) claim that Syriza's pre-crisis objectives were to mobilise large sections of society in order sustain a gradual transformation of the state that would entail an alternative to neoliberalism and a different kind of economy. The need for deep reform of the Greek state, to rid it of the vestiges of corruption and party hegemony, forms the key imperative for turning the state into a tool for social justice (Douzinas, 2013, 37). Whilst movements play a role in articulating alternative forms of social organisation and challenging the power of capital, social movements must organise and develop a collective discourse that can be institutionalised in new forms of democratic practice (Prentoulis and Thomassen, 2014, 216). By acting in the interest of various social movements (student, feminist and ecological) in a coordinated manner, Syriza (2013) attempted to represent popular democratic demands at the institutional level. Admittedly, these challenges go beyond the parameters of youth politics. However, the role of youth activism in Greece, and the politics of Syriza Youth itself, connects to broader societal concerns regarding neoliberalism, and more recently, the consequences of austerity. The challenge is how to unite struggles without doing violence to their singularity, and find chains of equivalence that establish relations between different forms of resistance.

4 An Opportunity for an Alternative?

Syriza's election victory came with a sense of euphoria and hope that had been absent in much of Greek society since the onset of the economic crisis in 2009. It created unprecedented expectation and hope in a population that had been severely wearied by the external imposition of austerity with the full complicity of the Greek political elite (Gourgouris, 2015; Douzinas, 2015). It emerged as the most advanced political opposition to the Brussels-Berlin-Frankfurt European capitalist axis, but was severely limited in exercising its democratic mandate (Kouvelakis, 2016, 45). Therefore, the problem Syriza faces is altering an internal institutional framework under conditions of external institutional assault in a state that is, for all intents and purposes, bankrupt – and has been since 2010 (Gourgouris, 2015). The key question that remains is how can social forces be formed and organised to circumvent the external and internal limitations that will continue to neuter any radical proposals Syriza may put forward? If Syriza adopts the conventional discourses and practices of a governing party, and moves too far away from its strategy of active involvement alongside social movements, it is highly likely that it will deprive itself of any genuine progressive impetus.

Emerging as the hegemonic agent in representative politics capable of channelling the demands of recent Greek social movements, Syriza situated itself in three fronts of political negotiation (Prentoulis and Thomassen, 2014, 228). The first being between the Greek political elite and the Troika; second, within the various organisations and coalitions that constitutes Syriza; and third with the demands of other groups and social movements (Prentoulis and Thomassen, 2014, 228). This division of political fronts is indicative of Syriza's nature as a heterogonous, pluralistic and multi-levelled coalition open to public displays of internal dissent (Gourgouris, 2015). However, the trajectory from a euphoric election victory in January, to failed negotiations with European creditors, and then finally to the acceptance of a whole new program of neoliberal restructuring, via a third bailout arrangement, has prompted significant debate and divisions within the Greek Left. So much so that the party's autonomous youth organ and senior members of the Left Platform have split from Syriza proper (Syriza Youth, 2015; Budgen and Lapavitsas, 2015; Kouvelakis, 2015). This has prompted renewed debates regarding the limits of reformism, and also strategies to re-mobilise grassroots movements, re-energise labour and organise young people and the unemployed, mainly outside the formal channels of the state and representative politics (Vgontzas, 2015).

Those critical of Syriza's submission to the EU and its unwillingness to consider exiting the Euro have characterised the situation as a humiliating back down, especially after the resounding July 5th referendum victory that rejected continuing with austerity policies (Anderson, 2015; Kouvelakis, 2016; Budgen and Lapavitsas, 2015). In a recent publication in the *New Left Review*, former Syriza member Stathis Kouvelakis (2016:, 45) argues that this was the predictable outcome of the party's contradictory strategy of attempting to reject austerity whilst staying in the Eurozone. There is considerable merit to such judgements, especially when you consider that by February 2015 Syriza had backed down on more than 70% of its anti-austerity objectives, which were outlined in the party's 2014 Thessaloniki Programme (Kouvelakis, 2016: 54). More tempered, and sympathetic appraisals focus on the challenges of long term capacity building and the gradual integration of social movements and social solidarity networks into a transformed and democratised state (Gourgouris, 2015; Spourdalakis, 2015; Gindin and Panitch, 2015). Indeed this is an area that two prominent Syriza members, Christos Laskos and Euclid Tsakalotos (2014, 18), state that more could be done to transform experiments in the social economy into viable alternatives. In this respect they argue that challenging capitalist hegemony and meeting the devaluation of politics head on would require the Left to demonstrate that it does things differently to the elite (Laskos and Tsakalotos, 2014, 18).

Greece's limited access to capital markets meant that Syriza's efforts to negotiate with its EU partners put it in a position of weakness. Without a threat or at least a plan to leave the Eurozone it was somewhat expected that Syriza would eventually have to choose between its anti-austerity platform and staying within the Euro. This doesn't absolve Syriza from clear tactical mistakes, but it does point the absence of youth voices, among many others, when it comes to negotiations between the EU and member states. Nevertheless, Stathis Gourgouris' (2015) discussion of radical democracy and the problem of left governmentality in Greece claims that consigning the Syriza phenomenon as a co-opted and defeated force is thinking too much too quickly. It fails to recognise that once in government Syriza was responsible for all of Greece not just to some part, or faction of the party (Gourgouris, 2015). The focus should be on identifying the social bases of resistance that may serve as strategic nodal points capable of channelling long term pressure on the current balance of political forces.

Greek youth, many of whom are bilingual, highly educated and have seen their opportunities diminished by severe economic depression, are a key component in providing the energy for a progressive recovery of Greek society. Indeed, the election victory in January 2015 did not reduce the need for social mobilisations but rather created new contexts in which more of them were required. Kevin Ovenden (2015, 15) states that there was a realisation amongst trade unions, social movements and activists that the period of social mobilisation had not ended with Syriza's election victory. The social forces that had undermined the Greek political establishment, and had opened new spaces for democratic practices on the streets of Athens, would be crucial to any long-term struggle against the EU's neoliberal policies. In lieu of this Costas Douzinas (2014) makes a rather prescient observation about 'Left' theory and practice, and the allure of neat theories that purportedly explain complex social events. He contends that the 'Left' does not need another brilliant theory or 'ideal' party but the ability to learn from the popular mobilisations that broke out without leaders and common ideologies (Douzinas, 2014, 83). Following the government's capitulation to its creditors, outgoing members of Syriza Youth (2015) stated: 'The youth, working classes, women, immigrants and refugees, the LGBTQI community are potentially the "yeast" of truly revolutionary social majority'. Therefore, questions of strategy must encompass continual efforts to mobilise socially active cleavages of society in order to avoid a new wave of instrumentalisation by political elites at both the national and European level.

5   The Future of Syriza

A broader question is how does Syriza fit into, and respond to the current crisis of democracy in Europe? The problems of the Eurozone reach beyond economics and touch on matters of democratic efficacy and credibility. The general discontent with the trajectory of global capitalism seems to also encompass a systemic failure of representative democracy (Tekin and Tekin, 2015: 129). As expressed by Pitty (2014, 125), '[t]he economic crisis in Europe is also a political crisis, and principally a crisis of democracy'. Whilst the crisis cut across all cleavages of Greek society, the affect it has had on young people is telling. First, and most obviously, the absurd levels of youth unemployment has led to a lost generation. Over 400,000 Greeks, in a population of just over 11 million, have emigrated since 2008, most of which have been educated young people escaping economic hardship (DW, 2016). Second, the droves of young, qualified and ambitious people emigrating to build a future abroad not only repeats the journeys of past generations but also deprives Greece of the very people best capable of leading the recovery. Instead, the imposition of austerity on the troubled Eurozone state has brought to the surface class politics, riots and political instability (Blyth, 2013, 299). At the time of writing Syriza retreated from its anti-austerity position, and has accepted the conditions of a Third Memorandum, albeit with a vague strategy of attempting to undermine austerity from within the confines of the program (Kouvelakis, 2016, 57). Despite this, it still offers an effective point of reference to analyse the challenges that progressive political movements face in articulating alternative democratic practices in unfavourable political and economic conditions.

The challenge, in a post-Marxian sense, is to identify the conditions and limitations of the emergence of collective action against the types of subordination and inequality perpetrated by the politics of neoliberal austerity in Greece and Europe (Laclau and Mouffe, 1985, 153). By accepting the complexity and social heterogeneity of recent social mobilisations across Europe we are able to better appreciate the way in which these formations may contribute to novel forms of democratic practice outside the formal channels of political participation. Namely, this means letting the movements speak for themselves, rather than imposing a theoretical or analytical dogmatism on them. The mass movements in the squares in places like Athens and Madrid often rejected the parties of the traditional Left and unions, which suggests a more sophisticated and contested understanding of democracy was being articulated in these spaces (Prentoulis and Thomassen, 2014, 213).

It is under the guise of austerity that the concrete practices of neoliberalism are laid bare. This includes the dismantling of social infrastructure and the privatisation of public goods for the purpose of exposing them to free market logics (Brown, 2015, 201). Therefore, Colin Crouch (2013, 8) is correct when he contends that neoliberalism is actually about enhancing the power of corporations and wealthy individuals, rather than the effective functioning of markets. These are the social and economic conditions that have provided the political space for Syriza to attempt a radical alternative for Greece's economic and social recovery.

However, as Syriza's experience has proven, a strong democratic mandate loosely representative of progressive social mobilisation with a vibrant and organised youth presence is not sufficient to challenge the balance of political forces in the EU. The subsequent fragmentation of Syriza, after the July 5th referendum, which involved the resignation of key members at both the senior and youth level, is a reminder of the challenges faced by progressive social forces. Overall, Syriza's success will depend on it being able to harness the aspirations and disappointments of a dissonant youth to channel broad social coalitions necessary to renew the democratic practices of Greek society.

6 Conclusion

Radicalism is best measured by results and not by purity of ideas, especially when resisting from a position of weakness (Iglesias, 2015, 12–13). Unnecessary fixations with theoretically consistent alternatives lead to a focus on small differences between progressive forces (Douzinas, 2013, 82). Given the history of Left government, riddled as it is with partial victories and numerous defeats, Syriza's focus should be the institutional relays that connect representative democracy with social movements (Gourgouris, 2015). Whilst laws and decrees are necessary for social transformation, they are insufficient without collective organisation (Tsipras, 2015d). In this regard, the role of young people should be to contribute to the organisation of social movements that oppose those defending the status quo (Tsipras, 2015d). The fragmentation of Syriza, at both the senior and youth levels, following its acceptance of a new wave of austerity measures suggests a rather significant re-organisation of the Greek Left is taking place. The disappointment of the Youth of Syriza, especially given the role that young people played in organising the No campaign for the July 5th referendum indicates that Syriza's support among social movements may likely diminish as more austerity is applied. Given that the options for challenging austerity remain limited, it is crucial that Syriza remain committed to bolstering its presence in civil society. Its capacity to operate as a party in representative politics and as a social movement serves as a means to leverage what little power the Greek state has, and also to provide a channel for young people to reclaim a future that they have been deprived of. For all the debates regarding strategy and programmatic solutions the most crucial resource that Syriza requires is time to strengthen the linkages between a renewal of democratic practice and the forms of social resistance that underpin it.

References

Ali, T. 2015. *The Extreme Centre: A Warning*. London: Verso.

Anderson, P. 2015. "The Greek Debacle." In, *Jacobin*, https://www.jacobinmag.com/2015/07/tspiras-syriza-euro-perry-anderson/ Accessed 15 July 2016.

Blyth, M. 2013. *Austerity: The History of a Dangerous Idea*. Oxford: Oxford University Press.

Brown, W. 2015. *Undoing the demos: neoliberalism's stealth revolution*. New York: Zone Books.

Budgen, S. and S. Kouvelakis 2015. "Greece: Phase One." In, *Jacobin*. https://www.jacobinmag.com/2015/01/phase-one/ Accessed 12 September 2015.

Budgen, S. and C. Lapavitsas 2015. "Awaken the European Left." In, *Jacobin*, https://www.jacobinmag.com/?s=Costas+Lapavitsas Accessed 21 July 2016.

Cerny, P. 1999. "Globalization and the Changing Logic of Collective Action." In, *International Political Economy*, edited by J Frieden and D Lake. Abingdon: Taylor and Francis.

Crouch, C. 2013. *Making Capitalism Fit for Society*. Cambridge: Policy Press.

Della Porta, D. 2015. *Social Movements in Times of Austerity: Bringing Capitalism Back Into Protest Analysis*. Cambridge: Polity.

Douzinas, C. 2015 "Syriza: the Greek spring." In, *openDemocracy*. https://www.opendemocracy.net/can-europe-make-it/costas-douzinas/syriza-greek-spring Accessed 27 July 2016.

Douzinas, C. 2013. *"Philosophy and Resistance in the Crisis: Greece and the Future of Europe."* Cambridge: Polity Press.

Douzinas, C. 2014. "Notes Towards an Analytics of Resistance." In, *New Formations*. Issue 83: 79–98. Accessed 15 July 2016.

DW, 2016. "Greece Central Bank reports 'brain drain' of 427,000 young, educated Greeks since 2008." http://www.dw.com/en/greece-central-bank-reports-brain-drain-of-427000-young-educated-greeks-since-2008/a-19373527 Accessed 11 May 2018.

Gourgouris, S. 2015. "The Syriza problem: radical democracy and left governmentality in Greece." In, *openDemocracy*. https://www.opendemocracy.net/can-europe-make-it/stathis-gourgouris/syriza-problem-radical-democracy-and-left-governmentality-in-g Accessed 13 October 2015.

Iglesias, P. 2015. *Politics in a Time of Crisis: Podemos and the Future of Democracy in Europe*. London: Verso Books.

Katsambekis, G. 2015. "The Rise of the Greek Radical Left: Notes on Syriza's Discourse and Strategy." In, *Linea Sur 9. 152–161*. https://www.academia.edu/15178672/The_Rise_of_the_Greek_Radical_Left_to_Power_Notes_on_Syriza_s_Discourse_and_Strategy?auto=download Accessed 3 November 2015.

Kouvelakis, S. 2016. "Syriza's Rise and Fall." In, *New Left Review, Issue 97: 45–70*. Accessed 25 June 2016.

Kouvelakis, S. 2015. "After Syriza." In, *Jacobin*. https://www.jacobinmag.com/2015/08/greece-grexit-popular-unity-syriza/ Accessed 21 July 2016.

Laclau, E. and C. Mouffe 1985. *Hegemony and Socialist Strategy: Towards a Radical Democratic Politics*. London: Verso.

Laskos, C. and E. Tsakalotos 2014. "Out of the mirror arguments from the Greek left." In, *Soundings, Issue 57. 8–22*. Accessed 2 August 2015.

Memos, C. 2010. "Neoliberalism, Identification Process and the Dialectics of Crisis." In, *International Journal of Urban and Regional Research, vol 34. no 1: 210–216*. DOI:10.1111/j.1468-2427.2010.00950.x Accessed 28 October 2016.

OECD. 2015. "Employment Outlook 2015." http://www.oecd.org/greece/Employment-Outlook-Greece-EN.pdf Accessed 25 July 2016.

OECD. 2016. "Youth not in employment, education or training." DOI: 10.1787/72d1033a-en Accessed 30 August 2016.

Ovenden, K. 2015. *Syriza: Inside the Labyrinth*. London: Pluto Press.

Panitch, L. and M. Konings 2009. "Myths of Neoliberal Deregulation." In, *New Left Review. vol 57: 67–83*. http://newleftreview.org/II/57/leo-panitch-martijn-konings-myths-of-neoliberal-deregulation Accessed 9 December 2015.

Panitch, L. 2015. "A Different Kind of State." In, *Jacobin*. https://www.jacobinmag.com/2015/02/syriza-interview-leo-panitch-solidarity/ Accessed 15 October 2015.

Panitch, L and S. Gindin 2015. "The Syriza Dilemma." *Jacobin*. https://www.jacobinmag.com/2015/07/tsipras-debt-germany-troika-memorandum/ Accessed 3 October 2015.

Petropoulou, C. 2010. "From December Youth Uprising to the Rebirth of Social Movements: A Space-Time Approach." In, *International Journal of Urban and Regional Research. Vol 43. Issue 1: 217–224*. DOI: 10.1111/j.1468-2427.2010.00951.x. Accessed 21 July 2016.

Pitty, R. 2014. "Disintegrating European Austerity in Greece and Germany", In *Democracy and Crisis: Democratising Governance in the Twenty-First Century*, edited by B Isakhan and S Slaughter. New York: Palgrave Macmillan, 125–148.

Prentoulis, M. and L. Thomassen. 2014. "Autonomy and Hegemony in the Squares: The 2011 Protests in Greece and Spain." In, *Radical Democracy and Collective Movements Today: The Biopolitics of the Multitude versus the Hegemony of the People*, edited by Alexandros Kioupkiolis and G. Katsambekis. Surrey: Ashgate.

Psimitis, M. 2011. "The Protest Cycle of Spring 2010 in Greece." In, *Social Movement Studies. Vol 10. No 2: 191–197*. DOI: 10.1080/14742837.2011.562365 Accessed 15 July 2015.

Sitrin, Marina and D. Azzellini 2014. *They Can't Represent Us: Reinventing Democracy from Greece to Occupy*. London: Verso Books.

Sotiris, P. 2010. "Rebels with a Cause: The December 2008 Greek Youth Movement as the Condensation of Deeper Social and Political Contradictions." In, *International Journal of Urban and Regional Research, vol 34: Issue 1: 203–209.* DOI:10.1111/j.1468-2427.2010.00949.x Accessed 5 September 2015.

Spourdalakis, M. 2014. "The Miraculous Rise of the "SYRIZA Phenomenon", *International Critical Thought.*" vol 4. no 3: 354–366.

Spourdalakis, M. 2015. "To Fight Another Day." In, *Jacobin.* https://www.jacobinmag.com/2015/09/syriza-election-greece-memorandum-austerity-popular-unity-tsipras/ Accessed 15 November 2015.

Standing, G. 2011. *The Precariat: The Dangerous New Class.* London: Bloomsbury Academic.

Stavrakakis, Y. and G. Katsambekis 2014. "Left-wing populism in the European periphery: the case of SYRIZA." *Journal of Political Ideologies.* vol 19. no 2: 119–142. DOI: 10.1080/13569317.2014.909266.

Syriza Youth Central Committee Members. 2015. "Why We Broke with Syriza." In, *Jacobin,* https://www.jacobinmag.com/2015/09/tsipras-greece-snap-elections-syriza-youth/ Accessed 25 November 2015.

Syriza. 2013. "The political resolution of the 1st Congress of Syriza", *Left GR,* 8th May 2013, https://left.gr/news/political-resolution-1st-congress-syriza.

Tekin, B. and R. Tekin 2015. "Political Economy of European Mobilisation". In, *Waves of Social Movement Mobilizations in the Twenty-First Century: Challenges to the Neo-Liberal World Order and Democracy,* edited by Konak N, Nahide and Donmez, Rasim O. Lanham: Lexington Books.

Tormey, S. 2015. *The end of representative politics.* Cambridge: Polity Press.

Tsakatika, M. and C. Elefteriou 2013. "The Radical Left's Turn towards Civil Society in Greece: One Strategy, Two Paths." In, *South European Society and Politics. vol 18. no 1: 81–99.* DOI: 10.1080/13608746.2012.757455 Accessed 16 July 2016.

Tsipras, A. 2015a. "A Historic Opportunity." In, *Jacobin.* https://www.jacobinmag.com/2015/01/alexis-tsipras-interview-syriza/ Accessed 20 August 2015.

Tsipras, A. 2015b. "An End to the Blackmail." In *Jacobin.* https://www.jacobinmag.com/2015/06/tsipras-speech-referendum-bailout-troika/ Accessed 3 September 2015.

Tsipras, A. 2015c. "Behind the Compromise." In, *Jacobin.* https://www.jacobinmag.com/2015/08/greece-memorandum-austerity-coup-tsipras-syriza-interview/ Accessed 20 September 2015.

Tsipras, A. 2015d. "Speech of Alexis Tsipras at the Youth of Syriza Conference." *Syriza Youth,* 2nd December 2015 http://international.neolaiasyriza.gr/speech-of-alexis-tsipras-at-the-youth-of-syriza-conference/.

Vgontzas, N. 2015. "Beyond Reform vs Rupture." In, *Jacobin*, https://www.jacobinmag.com/2015/09/tsipras-greece-eurozone-election-austerity/ Accessed 20 November 2015.

Watkins, S. 2016. "Oppositions." In, *New Left Review, issue 98: 5–30*. https://newleftreview.org/II/98/susan-watkins-oppositions Accessed 2 May 2016.

Youth of Syriza. n.d. *About US* http://international.neolaiasyriza.gr/ Accessed 23 July 2016.

CHAPTER 16

The Socio-Demographic and Political Contexts and Legacies of the Arab Spring

Ken Roberts

1   Introduction

The 'Arab Spring' has not led to the outcomes that were envisaged in 2011 by the 'international community' (in practice the USA and its Western allies). The term 'Arab Spring' was invented by this international community. It has never been widely used in the countries where the events occurred. In addition to naming the events, in 2011 the international community decided that the events had been instigated by young people who were frustrated when facing the limited life chances that their countries offered and who were pro-democracy, looking Westward for an alternative future. The European Union (EU) was an active player in this 'framing' of the Arab Spring (Hyvonen, 2014). As the protests spread from country to country, and as regimes fell in Tunisia then Egypt, it became possible to anticipate or at least hope that democracy would spread and take root throughout the region.

We now know that the outcomes have differed from country to country. Tunisia in 2016 is more democratic but less secure for foreigners than in 2011. In Egypt the 'reforms' have turned full circle with a government backed by the military once again in control. In other countries the protests died down or were suppressed with only modest or no constitutional reforms. In Libya and Syria civil wars are ongoing. Islamic State (IS) has become another militant Islamist hub with which supporters in any country can identify. Six years on, we now have evidence that enables us to eliminate some postulated causes, to focus on those that remain credible, and thereby better understand why the outcomes up to now have varied so remarkably. This involves separating relatively enduring contexts from more recent pre-2011 developments, and unpredictable (as regards timing) sequences of events, adding the histories and current states of party political mobilisation and organisation in the relevant

---

* This chapter has been prepared within the research project FP7-SSH-2013-2 SAHWA: empowering the young generation; towards a new social contract in South and East Mediterranean countries.

countries, into which the motivations and worldviews of key actors in 2011 must be inserted. The following passages interrogate whether the uprisings can be understood as generation wars, signalling the formation of new political generations (see Mannheim, 1928–1952), and also whether the grievances that sparked the protests included impediments experienced by young people in their transitions from education to employment, and housing and family life stage transitions.

2 Contexts

I begin by examining more or less enduring contexts, starting with the 'demographic surge', the expansion in the size of youth cohorts in the years preceding 2011, followed by trends in young people's situations in 2011 in relation to education-to-work, and family and housing life stage transitions. No one claims that any one of these features of youth's condition in 2011 was *the* cause of the protests that erupted. However, in the spate of quick-fire analysis that accompanied and followed the events of 2011, it was claimed that, in combination, the conditions had produced a 'shared generational experience' (Murphy, 2012) thereby creating a 'new sociological generation' (Desrues, 2012). Shared grievances were said to have united different factions of young people in a 'movement of movements' (Singerman, 2013). The initial slogans of the protestors in Egypt were 'Bread, Freedom, Social Justice and Human Dignity' (Fahmy, 2012). In Egypt, and possibly elsewhere, the incumbent regime is said to have lost middle class support by adopting neo-liberal policies which undermined middle class jobs, standards of living and lifestyles while creating a new class of regime-linked tycoon capitalists (Kandil, 2012). These are among the claims that the following passages interrogate.

2.1 *The Demographic Surge*

The so-called demographic surge has been favoured by many commentators as at least contributing to the Arab Spring of 2011. A youth survey of 15–29 year olds by Egypt's Population Council in 1998 had noted the increasing size of cohorts in the child age groups. This report noted that the swollen child cohorts would become swollen youth and young adult cohorts during the early-21st century which, the report argued, could be a demographic gift or disaster depending on whether jobs and housing were available. By the time of a second Egypt youth survey in 2009 the swollen cohorts had indeed become young people and young adults (Population Council, 2011). There has been exactly the same trend across the whole of North Africa and the Middle-East. The region

TABLE 16.1 Fertility rates by country (in percentages)

Year	Algeria Total fertility rate (births per woman)	Morocco Total fertility rate (births per woman)	Tunisia Total fertility rate (births per woman)	Egypt Total fertility rate (births per woman)
1990	4.7	4.0	3.6	4.4
2000	2.6	2.7	2.1	3.3
2009	2.3	2.3	2.1	2.8

SOURCE: THOLEN J. 2014.

is currently experiencing the same demographic transition as happened in first-wave industrial countries a century and more ago. Birth rates in North Africa have now declined (see Table 16.1).

Current cohorts of young adults are having fewer children than their own parents reared. This will create a demographic contraction in the child, then youth, then adult age groups, and the region will one day address the same ageing population demographic that exists today in economically advanced countries. However, the countries all currently have population pyramids with the numbers in each age group declining progressively from age 25 onwards.

Could this surge have triggered the Arab Spring? It was part of the context, but can it have been even a contributor? There are two grounds for doubt. First, all the countries have experienced steep and steady population growth for over 50 years. For example, Algeria's population has tripled since independence in 1962 (Hammouda, 2010). Second, the progressive contraction in the size of age groups above age 25 is not due solely to higher infant and child mortality rates in the over 25 year old cohorts. Outward migration has also contributed. The outflow is continuing, so the countries are likely to retain population pyramids even alongside declining fertility rates.

2.2 Labour Markets and Education

The demographic surge was predicted to turn into a social and economic disaster unless the young people could be offered opportunities to progress to full adulthood, meaning that they needed routes towards then into adult jobs and access to independent housing.

General unemployment rates across North Africa were not particularly high in the years preceding or at the time of the Arab Spring (see Table 16.2). In Algeria and Morocco unemployment had been falling throughout the 1990s and 2000s,

TABLE 16.2 Unemployment rates (in percentages)

Unemployment rates	Algeria	Morocco	Tunisia	Egypt
1991–1995	24	18	16 (1996–2000)	10
2006–2009	10	10	14	9
2012	11	9	17	13

SOURCE: THOLEN J. 2014.

TABLE 16.3 Youth unemployment rates (in percentages)

Unemployment rates (15–24 year olds)	Algeria (2011)	Morocco (2012)	Tunisia (2011)	Egypt (2010)
Males	19	18	N/A	15
Females	38	19	N/A	54
Total	28	19	42	25

SOURCE: THOLEN J. 2014.

and in 2012 the rates were between 9 percent and 17 percent in all four countries in Table 16.4. Youth unemployment rates were consistently higher: between 19 percent and 28 percent in Algeria, Egypt and Morocco but as high as 42 percent in Tunisia (Table 16.3). Youth unemployment was much higher among females than males in Algeria and Egypt but not in Morocco, and no gender breakdown is available in the data for Tunisia. The latter country apart, in 2011–2012 youth unemployment rates were much higher across the Mediterranean in southern Europe.

However, there are two features of labour markets in North Africa and the Middle-East that depress the unemployment rates when these are measured in internationally standardised ways, as in Labour Force Surveys. First, there are low rates of labour market participation in all the countries, especially among women (see Tables 16.4 and 16.5). North Africa and the Middle-East have lower rates of youth labour force participation than any other world regions (Roudi, 2011). Second, significant proportions of employment are in non-waged (usually

TABLE 16.4 Labour force participation rates (in percentages)

Labour force participation rates (15+)	Algeria	Morocco	Tunisia	Egypt
1991–1995	51	53	48	50
2006–2009	58	52	48	48

SOURCE: THOLEN J. 2014.

TABLE 16.5 Female labour force participation rates (in percentages)

Labour force participation rates (15+)	Algeria	Morocco	Tunisia	Egypt
1991–1995	25	25	23	26
2006–2009	30	26	27	24

SOURCE: THOLEN J. 2014.

family) employment and informal jobs (without a contract) which may or may not pay a regular wage. Egypt's 2009 youth survey provides a classification of types of youth employment that matches realities in the region more closely than international classifications (see Table 16.6). The most common types of employment for 15–29 year old males in 2009 were informal jobs with private employers that paid a regular wage (44 percent) and similar jobs without a regular wage (25 percent). For females, with much lower rates of labour market participation, the most common types of employment were with the government or a public enterprise (38 percent) and informal jobs paying a regular wage in the private sector (32 percent).

Throughout North Africa and the Middle-East, as in the rest of the global South, there has been considerable youth migration from rural areas into cities (see Hansen, 2008) where the newcomers have overwhelmed the supply of formal jobs and official housing. Hence the sprawl of unplanned and unregulated housing tracts on city peripheries. In a similar way, the excess of labour in cities has led to the spread of informal employment, which may be as well-paid and as regularly paid as official employment. That said, informal employment is inherently precarious. Employees have no legal protection and do not

TABLE 16.6 Types of employment: 15–29 year olds in Egypt, 2009

Types of Employment	Males	Females
Government	8	35
Public enterprise	2	3
Formal private regular wage	8	12
Informal private regular wage	44	32
Irregular wage	25	8
Unpaid family worker	9	7
Self-employed/employer	4	4

SOURCE: POPULATION COUNCIL, 2011; THOLEN J. 2014.

accumulate state welfare entitlements. As we have seen, in Egypt in 2009 most employed young males were in informal jobs.

Another trend has been steady growth in educational enrolments at all levels. Completion of elementary/primary education is now virtually universal across North Africa among males and females. Enrolments in secondary and higher education have also risen, again, equally strongly among males and females. In Algeria around 25 percent of males and 36 percent of young women now enrol in tertiary education (Hammounda, 2010). Honwana (2013) estimates that over a half of young Tunisians were enrolling in higher education by 2011. In Egypt in 2009 around a quarter of all males and slightly fewer females aged 15–29 had completed, were progressing through, or heading towards higher education (Population Council, 2011). Unlike in North America and most European countries, in North Africa there are higher than average rates of unemployment among young people who complete academic secondary education without continuing into Higher Education, and also among those who do progress through higher education. In Morocco a National Association of Unemployed Graduates was formed in the early-1990s and its protests became a familiar feature of the cityscape in Rabat, the country's capital city. The protestors' demand was for the government to create the public sector graduate jobs that the unemployed young people felt they had earned (Boggaert and Emparador, 2011). In the years preceding 2011 Tunisia had the highest youth unemployment rate in North Africa and also the region's highest participation rate in higher education. Boughzala (2013) argues that Tunisia's graduates prefer to wait for secure, decently paid government jobs rather than enter the informal private sector where jobs are far easier to obtain.

Secondary and higher education are probably effective in raising young people's aspirations and sense of entitlement. As noted above, university graduates are unlikely to be satisfied with non-waged family work or, indeed, any informal employment. They will expect careers in management and the professions. Honwana's (2013) research in Tunisia identified the highly educated unemployed and under-employed as the main source of the cyber-activists and street demonstrators in the events that set the Arab Spring in motion in January 2011. However, these inferences from ethnographic fieldwork have yet to be confirmed in representative samples of young people in Tunisia. Gallup Poll data collected in Egypt during March-April 2011 found that only 20 percent of those who had been demonstrating had received over 15 years of education, which means that higher education graduates were far from the majority among the protestors (Brym et al., 2014). The idea that Egypt's protestors were mainly from the educated middle class appears to have been media constructed, with much input from the country's intellectuals (Mellor, 2014).

2.3   Housing and Family Transitions

Throughout North Africa and the Middle-East (as in many other parts of the world) marriage is considered essential in order to achieve full adulthood. Typical ages of marriage have been rising and now differ considerably from country to country. In Morocco the mean ages for first marriages in 2009 were 31 for men and 26 for women (Boudarbat and Ajbilou, 2009). In Egypt in 2009 the most common ages of first marriages were 20–26 for men and 16–20 for women (Population Council, 2011). Young women in the region typically marry older men.

Ideally, in all the countries, marrying couples move into their own homes, but an alternative is to start married life with the husband's family. Very few young men (just seven percent in Egypt in 2009) said that they would accept living with in-laws. Young women in Egypt were more accepting, but only 54 percent said that this arrangement would be acceptable (Population Council, 2011). In 2009 the dwellings in which Egypt's 15–29 year olds were living typically contained more persons than rooms. Young men were often unable to marry because they did not have jobs that supplied incomes that would enable them to support independent households, or there was no suitable accommodation in their parents' homes, or their intended brides found this arrangement unacceptable. For young women, the shortage was of marriageable men of a similar age to themselves. Singerman (2007) argues that the cost of weddings (clothing, gifts and celebrations) is another reason why marriages are delayed. She calculates that in Egypt the typical total cost of a wedding has risen to around eleven times the average household's annual spending per capita.

The combination of blocked progress from education to (acceptable) adult employment and transitions to independent households is said to mean that throughout the region the youth life stage is often followed by an indefinitely prolonged 'waithood' rather than adulthood (Dhillon and Yousef, 2009). However, 'waithood' is also a common life stage in Mediterranean Europe where it has continued to be customary for young people to remain in their parents' homes and delay marriage until their late-20s or even 30s, and this has been the context in which southern Europe's 20-somethings are unlikely to be offered permanent jobs and adult salaries (most do not need them) (see Cavalli, 1997; Galland, 1995; Golsch, 2003). The 'bottom line' is surely that in the years preceding 2011, in 2011 itself, and subsequently up to now, the region's youth have seemingly been able to secure livelihoods which have enabled them to make family and housing transitions. Fifty-five percent of the demonstrators in Egypt were married (Brym et al., 2014).

3 Actors' Motivations

Here we move on to the political motivations and goals of the protestors, and how and why the Arab Spring was able to spread so rapidly from country to country. Contexts alone are never a sufficient explanation of people's behaviour. Their own 'definitions of the situation' and their own agency must always be foregrounded. The mass protests were not about jobs or housing. Certainly the region's young people wanted more and better jobs and housing. They were also pro-democracy at least in principle (see ASDA'A Burson-Marsteller, 2009). However, these were not the main reasons why the young people took to the streets. The demonstrators were 'angry' and 'anti'. Specifically, the protestors were united in being anti-government. There was anger over police brutality, political and economic corruption, extremes of inequality, and governments' embrace of neo-liberal policies at least in the sense of withdrawal from funding basic services – housing, health care, education and pensions (see, for example, Fahmy, 2012). The demonstrators wanted to change their countries' ruling regimes, or force the regimes to change their policies and methods. A little more than 10 percent of Egypt's population aged over 14 took to the streets in 2011, but they had the support of another 70 percent (Brym et al., 2014). There was anger and outrage at the luxurious lifestyles at home and the wealth being stored abroad by the countries' inter-connected political and business elites. There was anger at the brutal oppression of any dissent and at the abuse of power by police and other public officials. These grievances are aptly illustrated by the event in Tunisia that sparked the protests of 2011 (see below).

It was the Western media that decided that the North African mobilisations were pro-democracy. Western governments aligned tentatively with the protestors, though all the regimes had been valued partners of Western governments up to 2011. Surveys of Egypt's population in the 2000s had shown that popular support for democracy was at best ambivalent. According to 79 percent of a representative sample that was questioned, democracy was 'very important', but when asked which party they were most likely to support in an election 73 percent chose the party of President Mubarak (Sika, 2012). There were no signs in Egypt of any significant differences in values or political orientations between age groups (Rizzo et al., 2014). The events of 2011 do not appear to have signalled the birth of a new political generation. The protestors wanted change, but the desire for change was neither new in 2011 nor age-specific. The Arab Spring would not have spread in the absence of 'events' that were unpredictable, at least as regards timing.

4   Events

4.1   *The Spark*

On December 17 2010 in Sidi Bouzid, a small town in Tunisia, Mohamed Bouazizi, a 26 year old street vendor, poured paint thinner over his left arm and set it alight when a policewoman instructed him to cease trading because he did not have a licence, or his licence was confiscated for some alleged infringement. There are different versions of what actually happened on December 17th. Was the policewoman hoping for a bribe? Was this an attempted suicide? We shall never know but we know for certain that Bouazizi died on January 4th 2011, which sparked protests in Tunis where the crowds of protestors refused to disperse despite facing gunfire and suffering fatalities.

4.2   *Amplification*

Protests had been recurrent across North Africa throughout the 1990s and 2000s, but had always been dispersed using whatever force was necessary, as had happened to anti-regime mobilisations in Eastern Europe before 1989. In Tunis the security forces declined to use the necessary force. Protestors were seen to be standing their ground. This was sufficient to encourage protestors to gather in Cairo's Tahrir Square. Then Tunisia's President Ben Ali fled the country and obtained refuge in Saudi Arabia. Ben Ali was hoping to return before long, but following his exit from Tunis Egypt's military hierarchy decided that

President Mubarak was dispensable. The floodgates were then open for protests across the remainder of North Africa (except Algeria) and the rest of the Middle-East.

4.3 *Spreading the Flames: Old and New Media*

Some commentators have highlighted the role of mobile phones and social media in drawing the crowds of protestors across the region (see Cole, 2014; Shahine, 2011). A similar phenomenon has been identified in England's city riots in 2011, and in the rapid spread of the *Indignados* protests in Spain, and the subsequent Occupy movement (all in 2011). However, the 1981 riots in England and the 1989 revolutions in Eastern Europe were unaided by new media. Robert Brym and his colleagues (2014) have used Gallup Poll data to show that using social media did increase the likelihood of the users becoming street demonstrators, but this was far less important than political grievances, existing, non-virtual, social network connections and structural availability. Demonstrators with smartphones could upload images to YouTube from where they were picked up by older media. Al-Jazeera was probably crucial in creating a public space for protestors' voices (Noueihed and Warren, 2013). That said, the mobilisations would very likely have occurred in the absence of any new media.

A more plausible explanation of all the contagions in 2011 is the apparent success of the first protests. It was the apparent success of the protests in Tunis and Cairo that unleashed the Arab Spring across North Africa and throughout the Middle East. Likewise in 1989, the installation of a non-communist government in Poland following the June 4th election demonstrated that change was possible, and before long citizens were mobilising in the German Democratic Republic, in Czechoslovakia, then in the East Balkans, and then in the West Balkans (see Roberts, 2012).

The new media were probably most influential in North Africa prior to 2011 in assisting the formation of networks of civil society associations. For example, in Egypt the *Egyptian Movement for Change* (popularly known as *Kefaya*) was created in 2004 to combat President Mubarak's bid for a further term in office and the grooming of his son as successor. The 'information age generation' was by then forming a series of protest groups. The most influential in Egypt was probably the *April 6 Movement*, which was launched by four young people on Facebook in 2008 in support of a planned strike by textile workers (Fahmy, 2012). There was a similar upsurge of extra-institutional political activity in Tunisia (Chomiak, 2011). These developments, combined with multi-channel satellite television, were probably especially crucial in facilitating private horizontal communications, in further eroding the regimes' previous control of flows of information and ideas (Hafez, 2013), and in enabling 'movements of movements' to coalesce rapidly in 2011 (Singerman, 2013). However, to repeat, and as Chomiak (2011) has also noted, there were similar developments, unaided by any new media, throughout Eastern Europe in the decades preceding 1989.

5   Legacies

5.1   *Politics and Government*

The immediate outcomes of the events of 2011 differed from country to country, as might have been expected given that the countries differed from one another at the beginning of the year, not least in the character of their political systems. As Skalli (2013) argues, if we are to fully understand what happened in 2011 we need to disaggregate the countries. During 2011 there were regime changes in Egypt, Libya (with assistance from NATO forces) Tunisia, and also in Yemen. None of the changes of regime can be described as revolutionary. None led to economic or social transformations. Elsewhere, as in Morocco, the regimes survived having conceded modest reforms, dispersed the protestors, or just waited until the protestors dwindled, except in Libya (see Vandevalle, 2012) and Syria where the initial confrontations led to civil wars. Western donors who had been supporting civil society and pro-democracy groups found their resources being sucked into local socio-political dynamics (Staeheli and Nagel, 2012). The flows of ideas and practices across transnational protest networks (Porta and Mattoni, 2014) suffered the same fate. Egypt underwent double regime change. Elections in 2011–2012 made the Freedom and Justice Party, the political arm of the Moslem Brotherhood, the largest party in the parliament and created a Moslem Brotherhood president, Mohamed Morsi. The parliament was subsequently dissolved by the judiciary and the president and his government were deposed in a military coup in 2013 (see Osman, 2013). The unity of 'the people' during the protests at the beginning of 2011 was short-lived. People whose ideal polity would be a Western-type democracy can simultaneously believe that, at present, an authoritarian ruler is best for their own countries. Shahine (2011) argues that in Egypt, by 2011, 'stability' meant 'no prospects' and 'no progress' rather than 'security', but evaluations appear to have changed (see below) since the Arab Spring developed into civil wars in Libya and Syria.

Western-type democracies need to be built, which usually takes decades, and the context must be favourable. Over 50 years ago Seymour Martin Lipset (1960), the American political sociologist, argued that Western-type democracies would work satisfactorily only if defeated parties found rule by their opponents acceptable. Democracy itself was supposed to foster this outcome because all parties that sought power would be obliged to position themselves on a common middle ground. Maybe this would be the outcome if democracy was given a long-run in North Africa and the Middle-East but this is unlikely to happen in most of the countries. Even Tunisia's currently functioning democracy may prove fragile. Surveys in 2009 found that no more than half of respondents across North Africa and the Middle-East (41 per cent in Egypt) supported freedom of speech, assembly and religion (Brym et al., 2014).

The region's countries are split into imperfectly coinciding divisions between the rural and the urban, the traditional and the modern, and the religious and the secular. We can illustrate these divisions from the results of the 2009 youth survey of 15–29 year olds in Egypt. Fifty-five percent of males and 70 percent of females said that they prayed more than once a day. Ninety percent of 25–29 year old females, 85 percent of 18–24 year olds and 79 percent of 15–17 year olds had been circumcised. This practice has been illegal in Egypt since 2007 but it still happens. Seventy percent of males and 58 percent of females argued that female circumcision was 'necessary'. Seventy-one percent of the males and 49 percent of females said that a sister should always obey her brother, even a younger brother (Population Council, 2011). These views and practices are anathema to many modern Egyptians.

Modern youth in North Africa and the Middle-East may idealise Western-type democracy but realise that their best protection against Islamic rule in the short-term is a secular, non-democratic authoritarian ruler. Perhaps regime change (where this happened in 2011 or 2012) has led to progress, meaning not democratisation but in terms of the protestors' own aims: less expropriation of resources by political and business elites, less corruption within state agencies, and less repression of all dissent in some countries (Morocco and Tunisia, but not Egypt or Algeria). In all the countries the events of 2011 accelerated the replacement of older with younger cohorts of political leaders, but this has been traditional politics throughout Africa (Muna et al., 2014).

Parties that compete for power in stable democracies cannot be formed instantly. Such parties will not arise from pre-existing divisions and interest groups. This leads to political fragmentation. Successful parties need to build blocs of support and thereby organise their societies (see Leon et al., 2015). This means appealing to and speaking for a variety of groups. Tugal (2015) explains how this has been achieved over many decades in Turkey whereas Egypt's Moslem Brotherhood simply claimed to represent all Muslims then found that this was not the case. In Tunisia the necessary blocs may have been built successfully before and following 2011 by Ennahda (the moderate Islamic party that led the government from 2011–2014), and its successor in power, the secular Nidaa Tounes. Rule led by either of these parties has proved acceptable to the other. Neither party is acceptable to the country's militant Islamists. Also, political activity, even voting in Tunisia's 2014 election, was dominated by the university educated (Berman and Nugent, 2015). Neither of the major parties has been able to mobilise the country's less educated majority who populate the country's poorer regions.

5.2 *Young People's Views*

It is possible to generalise about how young people's attitudes have been affected by the events of 2011 and their aftermath. Since 2008 the ASDA'A Burson-Marsteller Arab Youth Surveys have monitored changes in the attitudes of 18–24 year olds across North Africa and the Middle East. In 2009 young people's priority was to live in a democratic country, and the desire for democracy strengthened during the Arab Spring. Then by 2012 and 2013 fair pay and home ownership had become the top priorities and civil unrest had joined lack of democracy as a lesser concern. In 2014 civil unrest was a greater concern than lack of democracy. Then by 2015 there had been a decline to just 15 percent in the proportion of Arab youth who believed that lack of democracy was the greatest problem facing their countries. Their main concerns were unemployment (81 percent) and the growing influence of IS (73 percent). Possibly the main legacy of 2011 has been the creation of this additional umbrella organisation with bases in Syria and Iraq, and also in Libya, the countries in which civil wars are ongoing. That said, in 2015 57 percent of Arab youth felt that their own countries were headed in the right direction (ASDA'A Burson-Marsteller, 2009, 2011, 2012, 2013, 2014, 2015).

6 Conclusions

It is probably still too soon to offer a final summary of what was achieved by the Arab Spring. None of the countries has become a secure Western-type democracy. However, Morocco and Tunisia have arguably become more democratic (Perkins, 2014). Some powers have been transferred from the king to the parliament in Morocco. The composition of governments in Tunisia is now determined by the result of elections. It is only in these two countries (not in Algeria, Libya, Egypt or any Middle-East state) where new space has been created for citizens to express their views and mobilise. During a brief time window there was such space in Egypt, which was used most effectively by Islamic groups. Everywhere it was Islamic groups, which could use existing organisations, that were the first to be able to fill this space, but since then in Tunisia new secular political parties have been able to form. Given more time, this might have happened in Egypt, but the Moslem Brotherhood's opponents appear to have preferred a quick return to power by a military backed regime. The regimes in Morocco and Tunisia appear to be less repressive. Maybe all the North African regimes, Libya excepted, are now less prone to syphon their countries' resources into private bank accounts, and public officials (including police) may have become less corrupt. Some police forces may have become less brutal. In other words, there have been mixed but generally positive outcomes in terms of the protestors' own objectives.

However, there has been no progress anywhere in improving young people's employment and housing prospects. The events of 2011 damaged all the countries' economies. Tourism was always a casualty having become an increasingly important source of jobs and foreign currency. It is still too early to give a final verdict on whether the events of 2011 were the start of longer-term changes, or just outbursts of protest which happen periodically in the histories of countries where little else changes in young people's or other citizens' circumstances. At present it looks highly unlikely that 2011 signalled the birth of a new political generation that will be a force for continuous change as its members become majorities of citizens and politicians. In this instance, it is not too soon to tell.

References

ASDA'A Burson-Marsteller. 2009. *Second Annual ASDA'A Burson-Marsteller Arab Youth Survey*. Dubai: ASDA'A Burson-Marsteller.

ASDA'A Burson-Marsteller. 2011. *Third Annual ASDA'A Burson-Marsteller Arab Youth Survey*. Dubai: ASDA'A Burson-Marsteller.

ASDA'A Burson-Marsteller. 2012. *After the Arab Spring: ASDA'A Burson-Marsteller Arab Youth Survey* 2012. Dubai: ASDA'A Burson-Marsteller.

ASDA'A Burson-Marsteller. 2013. *Our Best Days are Ahead of Us: ASDA'A Burson-Marsteller Arab Youth Survey 2013*. Dubai: ASDA'A Burson-Marsteller.

ASDA'A Burson-Marsteller. 2014. *ASDA'A Burson-Marsteller Arab Youth Survey 2014*. Dubai: ASDA'A Burson-Marsteller.

ASDA'A Burson-Marsteller. 2015, *Arab Youth Survey 2015*, Dubai: ASDA'A Burson-Marsteller.

Berman, C.E. and E.R. Nugent 2015. "Defining Political Choices: Tunisia's Second Democratic Elections From the Ground Up". In *Analysis Paper 38, Center for Middle East Policy*. Washington DC: Brookings Institution.

Boudarbat, B. and A. Ajbilou 2009, "Moroccan youth in an era of volatile growth, urbanization and poverty". In N. Dhillon and T. Yousef, *Generation in Waiting: The Unfulfilled Promise of Young People in the Middle East.* Washington DC: Brookings Institute Press, 166–188.

Boughzala, M. 2013. "Youth Employment and Economic Transition in Tunisia". In *Global Economy and Development Working Paper 57.* Washington DC: Brookings Institution.

Brym, R., M. Godbout, A. Hoffbauer, G. Menard and T.H. Zhang 2014. "Social media in the 2001 Egyptian uprising". In *British Journal of Sociology, 65,* 266–292.

Cavalli, A. 1997. "The delayed entry into adulthood: is it good or bad for society?" In *Jouvens em Mundanca,* Instituto de Ciencias Socias, edited by J.M. Pais and L Chisholm. Lisbon: University of Lisbon.

Chomiak, L. 2011. "The making of a revolution in Tunisia". In *Middle East Law and Governance, 3,* 68–83.

Cole, J. 2014. *The New Arabs: How the Millennial Generation is Changing the Middle East.* New York: Simon and Schuster.

Desrues, T. 2012. "Moroccan youth and the forming of a new generation: social change, collective action and political activism". In *Mediterranean Politics, 17,* 23–40.

Dhillon, N. and Yousef T. eds 2009. *Generation in Waiting: The Unfulfilled Promise of Young People in the Middle East.* Washington DC: Brookings Institute Press.

Fahmy, H. 2012. "An initial perspective on "The Winter of Discontent": the root causes of the Egyptian revolution". In *Social Research, 79,* 349–376.

Galland, O. 1995. "Introduction: what is youth?" In *Youth in Europe,* edited by A. Cavalli and O. Galland London: Pinter,1–6.

Golsch, K. 2003. "Employment flexibility in Spain and its impact on transitions to adulthood". In *Work, Employment and Society, 17,* 691–718.

Hafez, B.N. 2013. "New social movements and the Egyptian Spring: a comparative analysis between the April 6 Movement and the Revolutionary Socialists". In *Perspectives on Global Development and Technology, 12,* 98–113.

Hammouda, N-E. 2010. *Young, Educated and Unemployed: A Review of Algeria's Labour Market Reality.* Geneva: Bureau International du Travail.

Hansen, K.T. 2008. "Introduction: youth and the city". In *Youth and the City in the Global South,* edited by K.T. Hansen with A.L. Dalsgaard Bloomington: Indiana University Press, 3–23.

Honwana, A. 2013. *Youth and Revolution in Tunisia.* London: Zed Books.

Hyvonen, A-E. 2014. "From event to process: the EU and the Arab Spring". In *Spreading Protest: Social Movements in Times of Crisis,* edited by Porta D Della and Mattoni A. Colchester: ECPR Press, 91–116.

Kandil, H. 2012. "Why did the Egyptian middle class march to Tahrir Square?" In *Mediterranean Politics, 17,* 197–215.

Leon, C. de., M. Desai and C. Tugal 2015. "Introduction. Political articulation: the structured creativity of parties". In *Building Blocs: How Parties Organize Society*, edited by C. de. Leon, M. Desai and C. Tugal Stanford: Stanford University Press, 1–35.

Lipset, S.M. 1960. *Political Man*. New York: Doubleday.

Mannheim, K. 1928/1952. "The problem of generations". In *Essays on the Sociology of Knowledge*. London: Routledge.

Mellor, N. 2014. "Who represents the revolutionaries? Examples from the Egyptian Revolution 2011" In *Mediterranean Politics, 19*, 82–98.

Muna, W.K., A. Stanton and D.M. Mwau 2014. "Deconstructing intergenerational politics between 'Young Turks' and 'Old Guards' in Africa: an exploration of the perception of leadership and governance in Kenya". In *Journal of Youth Studies, 17*, 1378–1394.

Murphy, E.C. 2012. "Problematizing Arab youth: generational narratives of systemic failure". *Mediterranean Politics, 17*, 5–22.

Noueihed, L. and A. Warren 2013. *The Battle for the Arab Spring: Revolution, Counter-Revolution and the Making of a New Era*. New Haven: Yale University Press.

Osman, T. 2013. *Egypt on the Brink: From Nasser to the Muslim Brotherhood*. New Haven: Yale University Press.

Perkins, K. 2014. *A History of Modern Tunisia, Second Edition*. New York: Cambridge University Press.

Population Council. 1998. *Adolescence and Social Change in Egypt*. Cairo: Population Council.

Population Council. 2011. *Survey of Young People in Egypt*. Cairo: Population Council.

Porta, D. della and A. Mattoni 2014. "Patterns of diffusion and the transnational dimension of protests in the movements of the crisis: an introduction". In Spreading Protest: Social Movements in Times of Crisis, edited by D. della Porta and A. Mattoni Colchester: ECPR Press, 1–18.

Rizzo, H., A-H. Abdel-Latif and A. El-Moghazy 2014. "The road to revolution and Egyptian youth: findings from the Value Surveys". In *International Sociological Association World Congress*. Yokohama.

Roberts, K. 2012. "1989: so hard to remember and so easy to forget". In *1989 – Young People and Social Change After the Fall of the Berlin Wall*, edited by C. Leccardi, C. Feixa, S. Kovacheva, H. Reiter and T. Sekulic Strasbourg: Council of Europe.

Roudi, F. 2011. *Youth Population Employment in the Middle East and North Africa*. Washington DC: Population Reference Bureau.

Shahine, S.H. 2011. "Youth and the revolution in Egypt" In *Anthropology Today, 27*, 1–3.

Sika, N. 2012. "Youth political engagement in Egypt: from abstention to uprising". In *British Journal of Middle Eastern Studies, 39*, 181–199.

Singerman, D. 2007. "The Economic Imperatives of Marriage: Emerging Practices and Identities among Youth in the Middle East, Working Paper 6". In *The Middle East Youth Initiative*. Dubai: Wolfensohn Center for Development.

Singerman, D. 2013. "Youth, gender and dignity in the Egyptian uprising". In *Journal of Middle East Women's Studies, 9*, 1–27.

Skalli, L.H. 2013. "Youth, media and the politics of change in North Africa: negotiating identities, spaces and power". In *Middle East Journal of Culture and Communication, 6*, 5–14.

Staeheli, L. and C.R. Nagel 2012. "Whose awakening is it? Youth and the geopolitics of civic engagement in the "Arab Awakening"". In *European Urban and Regional Studies, 20*, 115–119.

Tholen, J. 2014. *Employment, Education and Social Inclusion: Algeria, Morocco, Tunisia, Egypt and Lebanon, SAHWA BP/01-2014*. Barcelona: CIDOB.

Tugal, C. 2015. "Religious politics, hegemony, and the market economy: parties in the making of Turkey's liberal-conservative bloc and Egypt's diffuse Islamization". In *Building Blocs: How Parties Organize Society*, edited by C. de. Leon, M. Desai and C. Tugal Stanford: Stanford University Press, 87–122.

Vandewalle, D. 2012. *A History of Modern Libya*. Cambridge: Cambridge University Press.

CHAPTER 17

Outrageous Disparities: Young Peoples' Perspectives on Wealth Inequality, Collectivity, and Hope in New York City

Madeline Fox and Brett Stoudt

1   Introduction

In the United States we are in an acute moment of outrage and polarization as epitomized by the contentious election of Donald Trump as the 45th president of the United States. In this moment, some, emboldened by Trump himself, are building and activating a white nationalist far-right. The Black Lives Matter movement has emerged as a deeply grassroots and wide-reaching social justice project that is resisting structural racism, racist policing, and making radical demands for deep accountability, reparations, racial justice. Meanwhile, there is a groundswell of low-wage and profoundly disrespected workers like teachers and fast-food workers who are taking action to demand dignity and improved working conditions. And, in the background – or rather – as the bedrock beneath much of this, wealth inequality is stark, increasing, and racialized. After several decades of living conditions produced by neoliberal public policies, tensions and discontent abound.

The question we explore in this chapter is: in the face of outrageous economic, social, and educational policies and grossly widening disparities, how might we notice, listen to, harness, and be in solidarity with the experiences and outrage of young people in relation to the injustices of wealth inequality? In order to do this, we will share, detail, and reflect on exploratory findings from a survey in New York City on youth interpretations of income inequality. Our findings shed light on young peoples' concerns for their communities, their active engagement in their communities, and their aspirations to contribute meaningfully now and in the future.

What does it mean to grow up in intensely neoliberal contexts like the U.S.? Youth in the United States are often characterized as overly peer-oriented, irresponsible, apathetic, and focused on self (Lesko, 2001). These characterizations of young people have been long-held, indeed since the construct of adolescence emerged as a salient demographic group (Lesko, 2001; Rakow, 1971). However, some recent research has investigated young peoples' experiences of neoliberalism showing that as neoliberalism has persisted over the past several decades, young people have experienced a rise in individualism and a decrease in collectivist and community values (Park et al., 2014). This is reflected in research and also cultural products like TV shows, music lyrics, increased materialism, and a dramatic surge in social media which profits from individual self-promotion. However, Heejung Park, Jean Twenge and Patricia Greenfield (2014) found that during times of economic hardship, like the Great Recession (also known as the Global Financial Crisis) that began in 2008, young people reported increasing levels of collectivism. And, Ben Kirshner (2009) found that young people in his study expressed an initial individualistic view – what he calls *atomism* – but that after participating in an organizing effort addressing educational issues that directly impacted them and increasing critical consciousness, young people's expression of *atomism* disappeared and their expression of what Kirshner calls 'collective agency' took hold.

We are interested in understanding – and building with – youth interpretations and analyses of disparities and inequality. In this chapter, we consider how young people make sense of wealth inequality, and how, where, and why there is outrage and hope. Fine and Ruglis (2009, 25) put forward a 'circuits and consequences of dispossession' analysis to explain the ways policies facilitate disadvantages that accumulate for those already disadvantaged, and simultaneously facilitate accumulation of various kinds of capital for those most advantaged. We saw evidence of this relationship and the complexity of young peoples' lives in the findings from the Polling for Justice (PFJ) survey that we conducted in collaboration with a multi-generational research team (Fine et al., 2010; Stoudt et al., 2012). In this chapter we share findings from the PFJ survey that asked young people for their explanations of wealth inequality. The survey responses were collected in 2008–2009 in New York City in the midst of the Great Recession. We reflect on what we can learn from the responses, how these findings have shaped our current program of research, and we call for further research on outrageous wealth inequality with, by, and for young people and us all.

2 Background: The Polling for Justice Study

In 2008, as the Great Recession was beginning, we launched a study in New York City that was aimed at taking the pulse of young people's every day experiences at the intersections of education, criminal justice, and public health policies. PFJ was profoundly committed to the idea that those most impacted by the research questions should be the leaders of inquiry, and so the project was designed as a youth-centered participatory action research project. As a participatory study, high school aged young people were in the lead and at the center as we formed the research question, and through design, data collection, analysis, and dissemination. The study was called Polling for Justice (PFJ) and it centered around a city-wide, youth-to-youth survey that we collected from over 1,000 young people between 2008 and 2009. The project was jointly conceived by Michelle Fine and the Public Science Project at the CUNY Graduate Center as well as the Urban Youth Collaborative and the Annenberg Center for School Reform. From the outset, the PFJ project embodied a collective community-university desire to investigate conditions for New York City youth.

The PFJ project included over 40 young people from across NYC, along with academics, community organizers, public health officials, and community lawyers who collectively drafted a city-wide survey for NYC youth on experiences with education, public health and criminal justice.[1] The survey was distributed by internet and hard copy via snowball and purposive sampling and the demographic breakdown of the 1,000+ survey respondents reflected the population of NYC public high school students. The survey focused on youth experiences at the intersections of policing, schooling, and public health. It was designed to gain insight into young peoples' every day lives across public policy sectors. The survey was quite comprehensive, including questions about young peoples' feelings about their teachers, access to health care, how youth reported handling feeling stressed, details about daily interactions with police, and young people's activisms and resistance.

Through PFJ findings we were able to probe the conditions under which young people experienced dispossession in a neoliberal context (Harvey 2004) and trace how negative experiences accumulated for particular populations of young people. The PFJ survey results highlight the ways that public policies have profound social and institutional consequences for young people. We found that youth of color, those living in poverty, youth who identify as LGBTQ, and youth who are immigrants experience the highest levels of policy betrayals in terms of education policy, health care, and in terms of increased rates of incarceration and surveillance. (To learn more about PFJ and these findings see: Fine et al., 2010; Stoudt et al., 2011; Fox & Fine, 2012 & 2013; Fox, 2015).

---

1 The Polling for Justice core research team was made up of Niara Calliste, Michelle Fine, Madeline Fox, Darius Francis, Candace Greene, Una Osato, Jaquana Pearson, Maybelline Santos, Jessica Wise, and Brett Stoudt and also included Erik McKenzie, Dominique Ramsey, Alisha Vierira, and Paige Taylor. The Polling for Justice project was made possible thanks to the Surdna Foundation, Overbrook Foundation, Hazen Foundation, Glass Foundation, Schott Foundation, the ADCO Foundation, Urban Youth Collaborative, the Public Science Project, and the Youth Studies Research Fund at the CUNY Graduate Center.

Overall, PFJ survey respondents reported having high educational aspirations, feeling hopeful about the future, and caring about working with other young people to improve their communities. For the most part, young people reported feeling good about their educational experiences. However, young people also registered their dissatisfaction with their schooling experiences, including feeling bored in school, feeling that too much class time was spent getting ready to pass high-stakes standardized tests, reporting overcrowded classrooms, and many students reported feeling pushed to leave school for one reason or another.

The PFJ data allowed us to detail how young peoples' lived experiences of public policies in a neoliberal context were uneven. The data also highlighted the outrageousness of normalized everyday experiences for some young people. For instance, in response to youth-generated survey items about everyday interactions with police (prompts like, 'In the last six months: I was helped by a police officer; I was given a summons/ticket; I was arrested; I was touched inappropriately by police?'), young people reported high levels of negative interactions with the police. Nearly half of the survey respondents (48.1%) reported negative contact with police in the previous six months. And of those 481 young people who had recent negative contact, nearly all of them reported a negative verbal experience (84%), almost half had a negative legal experience (47%), slightly more than a third reported a negative physical experience (34%), and a quarter had negative experiences that were sexual in nature (25%) (Stoudt et al., 2011).

The PFJ youth researchers and PFJ survey respondents were growing up with intimate, every day experiences with police in part because of key policy changes in NYC in the years prior to the survey. In 1998 NYC implemented a policy putting the police department in charge of security in all the public schools. The result is over 5000 police *inside* NYC schools, which is equivalent to the 5th largest police force in the United States (Mukherjee 2007, 4). Other factors that contributed to the aggressive policing of young people in NYC included the New York Police Department's practice of order maintenance policing, discriminatory stop and frisk practices, and strict sentencing laws for non-violence crimes. In the PFJ survey, youth from Central Brooklyn and the South Bronx reported the highest levels of interactions with police and youth identifying as LGBQ, males, and Black and Brown youth reported higher rates of negative interaction with police than their peers (Stoudt, Fine & Fox, 2011). The findings from the PFJ study on youth experiences of every day policing were in many ways our most powerful findings. Though aggressive, discriminatory policing was not such a surprise, the survey provided new evidence about the extent to which young people and particular populations, like LGBTQ young people of color, were being targeted. The findings informed social science, ongoing organizing efforts, and future research. However, the survey as a whole was intended to gather

OUTRAGEOUS DISPARITIES   293

The United states right now is very much like this picture. A few people have most of
the wealth in the country while a lot of people make do with what is left.

Credit: United For a Fair Economy

In fact, only 10% of the U.S. population owns 71% of all of American's wealth . . .
and on the other hand

the rest of the 90% of the population owns only 29% of all of American's wealth . ..

In other words, there is huge gap between the very few wealthy and the rest; particularly the poor.

FIGURE 17.1   PFJ survey question asking for explanation of wealth disparity
                 SOURCE: AUTHOR

data on a wide range of youth experiences, opinions, and ideas including youth experiences of and ideas about inequality and social justice (see Figure 17.1).

Within the PFJ survey there were a handful of open-ended questions where young people were invited to contribute their thoughts, ideas, experiences, and opinions through words and paragraphs. One set of open-ended questions asked young people to reflect on their experiences and perceptions of income inequality. It is this set of questions that we will explore in this chapter. In the survey, in order to ask about inequality, we first we provided basic information about wealth inequality and then invited survey participants to provide explanations. Using an infographic image from the Center for Popular Economics, we provided text and graphics to explain that 10% of the U.S. population owns 71% of U.S. wealth (See Figure 17.2).

We followed the information with the question: 'Help us understand what to make of this. Why are some so wealthy and some so poor?' In the next question, we provided more information about how inequality is racialized. We wrote: 'Some race and ethnic groups seem to have more wealth as a group than others. For example, look at the graph below. Only 8% of the White community is living in poverty while 25% of the Black community is living in poverty, and 22% of people of Hispanic origin are living in poverty.[2]' We followed this information with the question: 'Why do you think some racial and ethnic groups are more likely to be poor than others?' Finally, we asked, 'Is

---

2   Our open-ended survey sequence on inequality included three questions. For the sake of clarity, we chose to discuss the first and third questions in this chapter. We will address the second question on racial inequality in another article.

there anything that can or should be done about some groups being poorer or wealthier than others? Is there anything you have done about it?'

3 What We Found

PFJ sampled across two waves. For this analysis, we explored the first wave of 494 young people who answered the open-ended questions. We conducted an analysis in a grounded, iterative fashion. First, we used software to examine the frequency of words in a cursory way to get a feel for the types of phrases the youth used to answer the open ended question. Second, we determined what broad themes emerged *between* each person's responses and then determined what specific themes emerged *within* the broad themes. We read the open-ended responses – between and within – multiple times until themes were satisfactorily saturated. Third, based on the themes that arose organically, we created dichotomous variables (coded 0 and 1) so relationships could be explored between the open-ended responses and the rest of the PFJ survey data. We pulled out four representative quotes for each theme and all created variables were broken down by gender, race, sexual orientation and mother's educational status.[3]

What follows is an exploration of the PFJ open-ended questions in three parts. We first walk through the responses to the question: 'Why are some people so wealthy and others so poor?', we then explore the responses to the question: 'What can and should be done?', and finally, we share key insights from an analysis of the final question in the PFJ survey: 'What three questions do you think we should be asking other NYC teens?'

4 Why are Some People so Wealthy and Others so Poor?

Of the youth who attempted to explain the wealth gap, most had thoughts and ideas about why it existed. Only 18 youth (3.6%) stated they did not know. Though some reflected further:

> [4]To be honest I have no idea. I feel as though things should be fair like if you work hard you get what you deserve but then there are other people who don't even work hard and make a lot.

---

3 We used mother's educational status as an imperfect proxy for socio-economic status, as is practice with our public health colleagues in the U.S.

4 All excerpts from survey data in this paper are unedited, as the survey participants wrote them.

Most of the people who are wealthy are white, and the poor people are colored. I really don't know but that's what I see.

From our analysis, New York City youth used eleven broad themes to provide explanations for income inequality. These included: Government & Economy; Opportunity & Resources; Education; Jobs; Aptitude, Knowledge, & Characteristics; Hard Work & Determination, Decisions & Choices; Discrimination, Oppression & Historical Inequality; Family & Family Inheritance; Luck, Reproduction, & Determinism; Obstacles, Relationships, & Context (see Figure 17.2: Thematic Tree)

The most representative theme was 'Education' (24.3%) Youth explained that young people who work hard finish school and achieve wealth: 'Some

FIGURE 17.2 PFI survey explanations for inequality thematic tree
SOURCE: AUTHOR

people waste their lives by not finishing school, so the ones who are wealthy have the education while the others do not'. Other's pointed to racial disparities in education: 'I think the majority of the people that are wealthy are white and have higher education levels than every other race on average'. Others pointed out how a lack of education contributed to poverty:

> Most people are wealthy because of education. Those who are impoverished is due to the lack of education. Big companies or businesses do not want individuals who are not well educated because they know that their company will not get too far.

Twenty-three percent of the survey respondents referred to 'Hard Work & Determination' (23.1%) as an explanation for wealth inequality. Some young people described poor people not working hard enough: 'People became poor because they couldn't keep a job or just don't care to work and live off the government'. Others described people who are wealthy as having worked for it:

> Certain people are more willing to work harder than others therefore the outcome of the more hardworking person will be better. Wealthy people are rich because they were smart or hardworking compared to a lazy person he will be poor.

Others pointed to the negative attitudes or lack of motivation for people with low-incomes:

> I think some are poor because the kids don't care for themselves or anything they don't go to school. And some are rich because they care, they go to school and stay in school.

The third most frequently referred to explanation for wealth inequality was what we called 'Discrimination, Oppression & Historical Inequality' (22.5%). Some young people referred to wealth inequality as a technology of social control:

> People in the US are so self centered and closed minded but yet our community is very diverse and somewhat there should be a chance to everyone to become what they wanna be, but since 9.11 racism towards different types of people has became more of a problem throughout time,

more and more people disliking each other so since the government is very closed minded and maybe they fear that one day the minority will have control of this country.

Others explained: 'The world is prejudice and sexist'. And, other young people pointed directly to capitalism:

> Capitalism. It drives people to be greedy and makes them think that having and accumulating a lot of wealth is the main purpose in life. It forces people of color, immigrants and the poor to work and live in conditions that are not equitable to that of the wealthy white person. It has also put women, queer folks, people of color and anyone who is not white, male and wealthy in subordinate and ostracized positions.

While these findings are interesting in various ways, what stands out most from the analysis of youth explanations of wealth inequality is the diversity of responses. Some responses reflect a structural analysis, some reflect a neoliberal analysis, in some you can see reflections of dominant narratives that locate blame on individuals, and in others you can read complex and critical responses to current conditions. We see, importantly, that young people are holding multiple, sometimes contradictory, narratives as explanations for the gross disparities in their/our everyday lives. Within each of the themes we coded, one can note tensions between different explanations across the different responses and also sometimes even within. Indeed, across the sample, the majority of young people's responses (62.1%) held at least two explanations simultaneously. For instance, in the quotes above about education, one can read meritocratic analyses, but these are laced with analyses of white supremacy and/or capitalism. It is likely that if we'd surveyed adults the responses would have been as diverse, contradictory, and complex. However, as we reflect on the youth responses, we note the potential for building complex and liberatory analyses with young people through collaborative investigation, discussion, and political education. The closed-ended questions of the PFJ survey were designed to investigate youth lived experiences of public policy. We were interested in working with young people to research daily experiences of public policy because we understand that adolescent perspectives hold key insights and analyses. The responses to questions about inequality allowed our intergenerational research team to gain a glimpse into how the survey participants were making sense of the context in which their daily experiences were taking place.

5 Responses to the PFJ Survey Question *What Can and Should be Done?*

In the pfj survey, we asked about what should be done. Four hundred twenty-seven youth responded to the question 'Is there anything that can or should be done about some groups being poorer or wealthier than others?',
- 26% (110/427) believed nothing could or should be done beyond individualism; the onus is on the individual, hard work, and skill.
- 74% (317/427) believed that something can or should be done beyond individual meritocracy. Of those who believed this, 97% (307/317) gave specific solutions.
- 140 youth responded to the follow-up question 'Is there anything you have done about it?'.
- Forty-five percent (63/140) reported that they have done something about it. See Figures 17.3 and 17.4 for the themes that emerged.

The largest percentage of those who said 'yes', they'd done something about wealth inequality (43%, 27/63), identified personal achievement as their way of helping economic injustice. A few believed it was important to take it upon oneself to become critically informed about the past so as not to repeat it in the future. For instance, one young person responded:

> For me, I am doing everything I can to learn about my history and others as well as my own and passing it to my peers or whoever don't have a clue and want to learn. In order to progress in the future you have to know where you come from.

Many saw a formal education as the best thing they could do to help:

> I have not been able to do nothing but try to get the most education I can get and learn as much as I can. So at one point I can help my community by giving them some service back to it.

Several young people felt that taking responsibility for their lives, through jobs, was a way to ease the economic burden of their parent(s):

> I try to save money and help my parents take care of me by making healthy choices and getting small jobs to pay for the things I want and let them get the things I need.

Some explained that, being among the disadvantaged groups, the way they can help is to simply not become a statistic:

I'm going to college, I bet on it. No one can look at me and say, 'Oh, she's just another statistic, she's not smart. The young African American girls are easy and a threat to the world'. NO, I make a difference and that's what I plan on doing.

Most of the youth reported feeling a responsibility to give back:

I'm working now and I use it to help my parents in food and for my necessities like soap bar, pads, etc. ... I'm also almost done with high school and after college the money that I earn I will give it to my village back in Mexico and to my parents. Not going to spend it on phones, ipods, or go to movie theaters, buy "American clothes" etc. No I'm going togive my money to those who NEED it and I want to make others happy.

A similar sentiment is expressed by another respondent:

Well let me answer your second question first, I am trying to graduate high school and figure out what I want to do when I get to college depending on if I get to college!!! I want to do something that is going to set me up financially so my family won't have to worry about anything, and so I and my loved ones won't be a part of the stereotypes!

Of those who responded that they had done something about wealth inequality, 22% (14/63) reported that they give donations to charity (e.g. 'I empty out my drawers every month and give clothes and shoes to the Salvation Army and Planet Aid'). Others (21%, 13/63) explained that they offered informal, often relational help to people in their daily interactions for example among their friends:

I personally try to make sure all around me are doing well when I'm doing well. However, I also try to educate my peers to try and do for themselves instead of depending on others. I use the resources available to me,

or among homeless people they see on the streets:

What I do is provide food and money to those many unwealthy people that remain on the rains and on the streets of New York begging for money and/or food.

Twenty-one percent (13/63) of the youth who responded 'yes' to having done something about wealth inequality reported that they'd participated in collective organizing and political activities. A few volunteered for political campaigns, 'I campaign for Barak Obama, so he can change America'. Several took part in school programs, 'In my school I became apart of the student success center as a youth ambassador'. Others belonged to youth organizations that addressed a range of social justice issues. For example, one fought for minimum wage rights, 'My organization fights for the equal right so workers get paid minimum wage and above'. Another worked on immigration issues:

> Yes, I have joined DRUM which is a nonprofit organization who aims to make immigrants have rights. Social security must not be asked for college/university and working papers should be able to be obtained by students who don't have social security, like me. I am legal on a TN Visa but I'm not allowed to volunteer or work at most places because I don't have working papers because I don't have social security.

One young person described working on job and housing placements:

> I have worked with an organization advocating for other issues but spreading the word of job training and housing placements have been something that I have tried to do and helped others with.

And still another worked with drug laws:

> In high school, I worked with the NYCLU in educating people about the Rockefeller Drug Laws that affect African Americans more than they affect Caucasians.

This statistic should be read against young people's aspirations to do something about wealth inequality to gain a better picture of young people's interest in getting involved. While 55% reported that they have not done something about economic disparity, 68% (53/77) of them believed that something can or should be done about it. In fact, 26% (20/77) explained that they would like to do something about it in the future, 'I have done nothing about this but I hope to do something about it when I have the power to do something for these people'. Others have more specific plans,

> In the future, I wish to fund a shelter for kids who are abandoned and poor. It's been a lifelong goal I wish to start working on as soon as I graduate from college,

or,

> Well, I don't know but would love to help out. I always wanted to become a lawyer and open a place that takes in the homeless and the poor and helps them get on their feet.

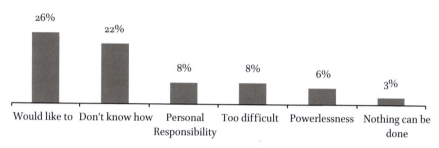

FIGURE 17.3   Themes that emerged from the question: Is there anything you have done about some groups being poorer or wealthier than others?
SOURCE: AUTHOR

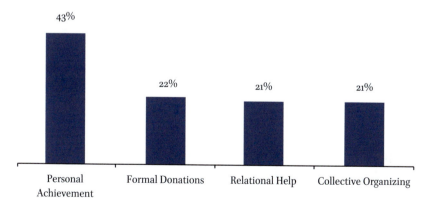

FIGURE 17.4   Themes that emerged from the question: Is there anything you have done about some groups being poorer or wealthier than others?
SOURCE: AUTHOR

Some of the youth (22%, 17/77) reported that they do not know how to help, 'I have not done anything. I don't know what I should do'. Others expressed skepticism, 'I have not done anything about this because I don't know if anything can be done'. Others (8% 6/77) felt like doing something about it was too difficult, particularly given their lack of resources. 'I can't do anything about it because I'm not wealthy', or that they are only one person,

> I really haven't done anything about it cause I believe one can only do so much. It is all about the society coming in together and doing it all as one.

Several (6% or 5/77) reported that they are too young to be taken seriously: 'I have not done anything about it, who is going to take advice from a 16+ year old'. Some (8% or 6/77) felt that the responsibility for fixing economic disparity was on those who were disadvantaged: 'Nah it's nothing I would do about that, if they chose to be poor that waz their choice', or that there is nothing to be done, because inequality is part of society (3% or 2/77), 'I have no done anything about it because not everyone can have money'.

What is of note, is that the data does not reveal a group of apathetic, uninterested young people. While the majority of survey respondents reported they have not yet done anything about economic disparity, almost half reported that they planned to or wanted to but did not know how to help. Others saw barriers getting in the way—like not having money, being only one person, or being young. One interpretation is that to consider action beyond personal achievement is a luxury, particularly for those most effected by neoliberal policies; however, many other young people report having found spaces, both relational and institutional, where they can contribute to lessening the economic disparity gap and make justice claims. Indeed, in a different section of the PFJ survey, 85.7% (415/484) of the participants agreed or strongly agreed with the statement, 'In general, young people like me can make a difference in society'. And, 45.2% of the youth reported that they belonged to youth organizations, many of which were oriented toward youth social justice activism.

6   What Three Questions Do You Think We Should be Asking Other New York City Teens?

In the PFJ survey, we ended the survey by giving the 1,000+ survey-takers an opportunity to be researchers with us: we invited each respondent to contribute three questions that they thought should be asked of NYC young people. Across the survey as a whole, survey participants generated over 2,000 questions. The young people offered a range of questions about sex, peer pressure, and drugs, and questions of their peers injustice, meritocracy, sense of self, harm and danger, and about care of others and community.

The youth-to-youth questions are an enormous collection of questions on a wide range of issues and experiences. However, in addition to considering the survey responses in aggregate, we took into account that each survey was completed by one person whose responses are of one piece. Thus, we looked at the three questions each respondent wrote as a set. As a way of resisting neoliberal forces that encourage even researchers to divide lives and only consider discrete parts, we sought out analytic approaches to take the whole into account, paradoxes and contradictions welcome. When analyzing the 'three questions' in this way, we considered the three questions each survey-taker asked to gain insight into that person. We found that each person's three questions often expressed a poignant set of concerns across a wide range of sectors, issues, and scales. Responses spanned disciplines, public policy sectors, macro and micro perspectives, and even differing political standpoints. One young person asked: 'Do you like your school lunch? Do you have any mentors in your community? Have you ever been sexually abused?' Another young person asked, 'What is it about your community you feel should be improved? How is the air pollution affecting other members of your community? Do you feel your school should have better resources or services to its students?' To give a sense of the scope, Figure 17.5, below, provides a selection of the three questions offered: each square contains three questions asked by one young person.

We find the diversity of responses, the breadth of critique, and the depth of personal concern contained in each 'Three Questions' stunning and complex. Each set of questions provides a sense of what it takes for young people to make sense who they are and contend with an unjust world while navigating who they are told they are. We consider the 'Three Questions' a call to action to allied adults, the academy, practitioners, and policy makers to find ways to consider teenage young people capable of contributing meaningfully through thought and action to their schools, neighborhoods, and the city. We note young peoples' desire for more time, space, and support to make sense of the contradictions we all swim in. We are reminded by the 'Three Questions' that even when building structural analyses with young people, we need to pay attention to individual experiences, relationships, and the interconnections. And, the 'Three Questions' are a push for further participatory research to investigate the ways young peoples' experiences make visible our reticulated, intersecting, and interdependent lives.

Post-it 1
If you were confronted by the police, do you think you deserved it?

What is your family's income?

What do you do in your free time?

Post-it 2
How are drugs helping you?

What is the main cause of your stress?

Can you remain abstinent until marriage?

Post-it 3
Have you ever been peer pressured?

Have you ever stopped going to school because you felt like it?

How many times did you not sleep this year?

Post-it 4
What are your views on drugs?

What are your views on sex between minors and adults?

Do you believe the police system is unjust?

Post-it 5
What are your view of LGBTQ teens of color?

Do you think racism exists in the Gay community?

Do you believe that the mainstream (white) LGBTQ community exploits the precedent of the Black civil rights movement?

Post-it 6
How do you feel in school?

What are the different types of family problems that you face?

How do relationships make you feel about yourself?

Post-it 7
What is it about your community you feel should be improved?

How is the air pollution affecting other residents in your community?

Do you feel your school should have better resources or services to its students?

Post-it 8
Have you ever been physically or sexually abused?

Is it worth living for you because of the problems you have?

Why do 'wealthier' people have to be so unfair in society?

Post-it 9
What are your plans for the future?

What do you wish to change in your school?

Do you think the Presidential election can change the United States? The World?

Post-it 10
Is your school helping with your college application?

How do you feel about the economic crises?

Do you think the 700 billion dollar bail out was effective?

Post-it 11
What/who has the biggest impact in your life?

On the average day, how do you feel about yourself (race, sex, etc)?

How well do you interact with people in your community?

Post-it 12
Do you like your school lunch?

Do you have any mentors in your community?

Have you ever been sexually abused?

FIGURE 17.5 A selection of PFJ responses to: What three questions do you think we should be asking NYC teens?
SOURCE: AUTHOR

7 Young People, Social Change, and Research: Swimming in a Neoliberal Soup

In order to achieve transformative structural change, we need to better understand young peoples' experiences with and attitudes towards the complex context of interconnected inequalities, policies, and practices organized by a neoliberal logic. PFJ was designed with young people to understand the extent and texture of youth outrage in order to generate viable strategies to engage structural change. The PFJ study results, for example – lead by young people and rooted in the complex lives of young people – revealed the intolerably aggressive and frequently brutal treatment of young people of color by police. These results spurred further research and fed ongoing organizing campaigns (Stoudt et al., 2015; 2011; Stoudt et al., 2016; Chmielewski et al., 2016). As we continue to pursue research for social justice with young people in the context of gross inequality, we seek ways to pry open dominant narratives, make space for counter-stories, produce complex analyses that can speak back to the hydra of neoliberalism (Picower & Mayorga, 2015). The survey data presented in this chapter provides attempts to do this and in the process, offer some insights and raise questions about the ways young people interpret inequality and engagement in society. We believe that participatory action research with young people about the lived experience of inequality and with room for reflection about the context of neoliberal inequality is necessary to fuel a collective sense of outrage and hope towards action.

References

Bakan, D. (1971). Adolescence in America: From idea to social fact. *Daedalus, 100*(4), 979–995.

Chmielewski, J., K. Belmonte, M. Fine & B. Stoudt 2016. 'Intersectional Inquiries with LGBTQ and Gender Nonconforming Youth of Color: Participatory Research on Discipline Disparities at the Race/Sexuality/Gender Nexus'. In, *Inequality in School Discipline*. US, Palgrave Macmillan: 171–188.

Fine, M. & J. Ruglis 2009. 'Circuits and Consequences of Dispossession: The Racialized Realignment of the Public Sphere for U.S. youth'. In, *Transforming Anthropology* 17(1): 20–33. doi:10.1111/j.1548-7466.2009.01037.x.

Fine, M., B. Stoudt, M. Fox & Maybelline Santos. 2010. 'The Uneven Distribution of Social Suffering: Documenting the Social Health Consequences of Neo-liberal Social Policy on Marginalized Youth'. In, *European Health Psychologist, 12*(September), 30–35.

Fox, M. 2015. 'Embodied Methodologies, Participation, and the Art of Research'. In, *Social and Personality Psychology Compass*. 9(7): 321–3332.

Fox, M., & M. Fine 2013. 'Accountable to Whom? A Critical Science Counter-Story About a City that Stopped Caring for its Young'. In, *Children & Society*, 27(4): 321–335. doi:10.1111/chso.12031.

Fox, M., & M. Fine 2012. 'Circulating Critical Research: Reflections on Performance and Moving Inquiry into Action'. In S. Steinberg & G. Cannella (Eds.), *Critical Qualitative Research Reader*. (Vol. 2, pp. 153–165). New York, N.Y, Peter Lang Publishing.

Harvey, D. 2004. *Understanding the New imperialism*. Accessed November 27, 2013 http://globetrotter.berkeley.edu/people4/Harvey/harvey-con4.html.

Heejung, P., J. Twenge & P. Greenfeld 2014. 'The Great Recession: Implications for Adolescent Values and Behavior'. In, *Social Psychological and Personality Science* 5(3): 310–318.

Kirshner, B. 2009. 'Power in Numbers: Youth organizing as a context for exploring civic identity'. In, *Journal of Research on Adolescence* 19(3): 414–440.

Lesko, N. (2001). *Act your age!: A cultural construction of adolescence*. New York, NY: Routledge.

Mukherjee, E. 2007. *Criminalizing the Classroom: The Over-Policing of New York City Schools*. New York, New York Civil Liberties Union and American Civil Liberties Union.

Park, H. Twenge, J. M. & Greenfield, P. M. 2014. *The great recession: Implications for adolescent values and behavior*. Social Psychological and Personality Science, 5(3): 310–318.

Pfeffer, F., S. Danziger & R. Schoeni 2013. 'Wealth Disparities Before and After the Great Recession'. In, *The ANNALS of the American Academy of Political and Social Science*. 650, No. 1: 98–123.

Picower, B. & E. Mayorga 2015. eds. *What's Race Got To Do With It?: How Current School Reform Policy Maintains Racial And Economic Inequality*. New York, Routledge.

Stoudt, B., C. Cahill, X. Darian, K. Belmonte, S. Djokovic, J. Lopez, A. Matles, A. Pimentel & M. Torre 2016. 'Participatory Action Research as Youth Activism'. In, *Contemporary Youth Activism: Advancing Social Justice in the United States*: 327. New York, NY: ABC-CLIO.

Stoudt, B., M. Fine & M. Fox 2011. 'Growing up Policed in the Age of Aggressive Policing Policies'. In, *New York Law School Law Review*, 56: 1331–1370.

Stoudt, B., M. Fox, & M. Fine 2012. 'Contesting Privilege with Critical Participatory Action Research'. *Journal of Social Issues*, 68(1): 178–193.

Stoudt, B.G., M.E. Torre, P. Bartley, F. Bracy, H. Caldwell, A. Downs, C. Greene, J. Haldipur, P. Hassan, E. Manoff, N. Sheppard & J. Yates 2015. Participatory action research and policy change. In, C. Durose & L. Richardson (Eds.), *Designing Public Policy for Co-production: Theory, Practice and Change:* pp. 125–137. Bristol, United Kingdom: Policy Press.

CHAPTER 18

2011 and World Revolutionary Moments: Mapping New Strategies and Alliances in Australian Youth Activism

Freg J Stokes

1 Introduction

One of the focuses of this collection is the 2011 'Year of the Protester' and its influence on youth engagement with politics. '2011' serves as a useful short hand for the subsequent surge of militancy which has arisen internationally, as seen in the fraught aftermath of the various movements and revolutions collectively dubbed the Arab Spring, the Occupy movement and Black Lives Matter campaigns in the US, the revolutions and student uprisings in Sub-Saharan Africa (for example, Burkina Faso and South Africa), and the general pushback against austerity in Europe. This chapter will explore how international events during and after 2011 have impacted on Australian activist methods, goals and viewpoints, particularly amongst young participants within the climate and refugee movements.

'Occupy Melbourne' and 'Occupy Sydney' were the most obvious short term manifestations of the 2011 protest wave in Australia. However, there have also been several instances of strategies associated with the 2011 protests, such as horizontal organization and direct action methods, being used successfully within the Australian climate and refugee movement in the years following 2011. The two most recent examples of this are the campaign against unconventional gas extraction in Victoria, which resulted in the state government's permanent ban on fracking and Coal Seam Gas extraction in August 2016; and the continued boycott and divestment campaign against companies associated with offshore detention, which has recently forced Wilson's Security to terminate its contract at Australia's off-shore refugee detention centre on the Pacific island of Nauru (Davey, 2016; Wiggins, 2016).

With these moments/movements in mind, this chapter focuses on two avenues of investigation: direct links between the local iterations of Occupy and the climate and refugee movements, and at a broader level, instances of affinity and cross-fertilization between the local climate and refugee movements and the international wave of post-2011 militancy. One key issue is to establish how the new cohort of young people involved in Australian social movements differ in their concerns, strategies, constraints and opportunities from those of previous generations. I will provide a historical context by looking at previous world revolutionary waves, utilizing World Systems theory and Italian Autonomist Marxist analyses of social struggle. In doing so I will employ the terminology of Immanuel Wallerstein, who frames the 2011 uprisings as a 'World Revolutionary Moment,' in order to assess its ongoing international aftermath and to compare it with previous such moments (Wallerstein, 2004, 2011a, 2012). I draw on David Graeber's contemporary take on both World Systems Theory and Italian Autonomist Marxist analysis, and complement the use of these theories with further reference to recent developments such as the emergence of intersectionality as a key framework in the study of social movements (Graeber, 2011, 2013; Fisher, Dow, & Ray, 2017). In semi-structured interviews with ten young Australian activists aged from 23 to 28, I discussed their participation in Occupy Melbourne, the Australian climate movement and refugee movements. I use these interviews, in conjunction with a world revolution framework, to analyse the direct and indirect effects of Occupy and the 2011 uprisings more broadly on the refugee and climate movements in Australia.

2   Historical Context

Wallerstein argues that the spread of capitalism and the creation of a global economic world system has been punctuated by a series of world revolutions, from 1789 through to today (Wallerstein, 2004). Each revolutionary moment, he proposes, then sparks a series of subsequent social transformations and demands for change. Each revolution has a different set of goals, for instance the 1917 wave was preoccupied with the redistribution of wealth and the overthrow of capital, while the 1968 wave included stronger feminist, environmentalist and anti-colonial currents. These revolutions are global because they frequently end up having as much influence in other parts of the world as in their country of origin. For instance, the creation of the Welfare state in Europe can be seen in part as a reaction by the political establishment to the threat of Communist revolution emanating from the Soviet Union (Graeber, 2013).

The tables below give a brief overview of the major 'World Revolutions' identified up until the present day. A glance at the '1789' revolutionary moment (see Table 18.1) reveals the complexity of these events and their international, dialectical nature. While '1789' has been chosen by Wallerstein and others as the emblematic year to represent this revolutionary moment, the process stretched well beyond the confines of any one year. As Walter Mignolo points out, the French Revolution was preceded by the 1775 rebellion of the British North American colonies, and the revolutionary wave was still playing out forty years later, with the independence wars in the Spanish American colonies (Mignolo, 2005). This is an important qualification, as decentering (or provincializing, as Chakrabarty would put it) the European experience of revolution allows us to analyse the interaction between these events and the ongoing process of colonization outside Europe (Chakrabarty, 2000). One element which distinguishes the 1968 and 2011 world revolutions from their predecessors at a global level (See Table 18.2) is the emergence of more thorough critiques of colonialism, from Césaire and Fanon onwards (Mignolo, 2005). An awareness and integration of these de-colonial critiques is essential to any analysis of the flow on effects of 2011 in a settler-colonial state such as Australia. It is critical to note here that the use of a particular year as a shorthand does not denote a simplistic causal relationship between the events of that year and all subsequent upheavals and emergent social movements in the following years. 1789, 1968 and 2011 signify a point of rupture and transformation in the general political ferment of their respective epochs.

The concept of world revolutions interacting with capitalist expansion aligns with theories emerging from the Italian Autonomist Marxist School, such as those of Mario Tronti, who proposed that capital should not be seen as the primary driver of history and economic development, as it is constantly having to improvise and transform in the face of resistance from labour (Tronti, 2006). In this way the neoliberal destruction of the welfare state can be reconceived as a response to the popular rebellions of the '60s and '70s. These rebellions had already denounced and discredited the bureaucratic stagnation and suffocating conformity of welfare state capitalism in the name of individual self-expression and sexual liberation (Shukaitis and Graeber, 2007). Neoliberal economic reforms integrated the call of the '68 protesters for greater individual freedom and women's demands to enter the workforce, but simultaneously cut back employment security and the social safety net (Fraser, 2013).

Anthropologist David Graeber, a participant in Occupy Wall Street, has argued that while 2011 can be placed in the historical lineage of World Revolutionary Moments, it is still too early to tell what the long term effects of this 'revolution' will be. He argues that if we look back at previous such events, including those of 1848 and 1968, the revolutionaries involved almost universally failed to seize power, yet their actions lead to dramatic long term transformations in their societies (Graeber, 2011). The push for universal suffrage and universal education did not meet with immediate success in 1848, but by the turn of the century they were accepted as basic rights across Europe

TABLE 18.1 World Revolutions, 1789–1917

Year of 'World Revolution'	Initial Spark	Ideologies/Goals	Long Term Outcomes	Establishment Reactions
1775/1789	From the American colonies to France and back again.	Republicanism, Jacobinism, Black Liberation	Representative democracy based on sovereignty of 'the people', consolidation of Bourgeois power, independence of nearly all the Americas followed by internal colonisation, abolition of slavery in Haiti and the former Spanish colonies	Monarchical Restoration, Concert of Europe
1848	Europe and the Americas	Liberalism, proto-socialism	Universal Education and Suffrage	Nationalist state formation
1917	Russia	Marxist-Leninism	Communist hegemony in Eurasia, contributing factor in the dissolution of European empires	Fascism, the New Deal, European Welfare States

SOURCE: AUTHOR

TABLE 18.2 World Revolutions, 1968–2011

Year of 'World Revolution'	Initial Spark	Ideologies/Goals	Long term outcomes	Establishment Reaction
1968	Started in both US and Soviet satellite states and spread globally	Third world liberation, women's liberation, environmentalism, revolt against bureaucracy	Modern Feminism, environmental reforms	Neoliberalism/Monetarism
1989	Started in Soviet satellite states, in parallel to democratisation in Latin America and South Africa	Civil liberties, social democracy	Further integration of these areas into the global market	Consolidation of neoliberalism and the Washington Consensus
2011	Started in US satellite states and spread globally	New wave of Feminist militancy, de-colonialism, climate justice, Trans and Queer activism, class struggle	Yet to be revealed	A shift away from neoliberal cosmopolitanism towards protectionist ethno-nationalism?

SOURCE: AUTHOR

and its settler-colonies. In 1968, Nixon won the US presidential election and De Gaulle's parliamentary allies were re-elected in France, but the most important long term result may be the emergence of feminism. In this analysis, revolutionary upheavals, while not always successful in their short term political objectives, play a critical role in sparking reforms that then take place over a longer time frame. It is with these qualifications in mind that we should view the current revolutionary wave.

The 2011 world revolutionary moment has seen a revival of discussions around inequality, decolonisation, feminism and class critique, filtered through online networks and social media, a digital context which distinguishes this wave of activism from the analogue revolution of 1968 (Castells 2012). The aftermath of 2011 continues to play out, varying in its impact and political repercussions from region to region. World revolutionary moments are often accompanied by horrendous short and medium term suffering, with numerous groups and ideologies competing to establish their legacy. It is primarily in West Asia and North Africa that revolutionaries were able to overthrow ruling government regimes. Outside of this region, with the arguable exception of Syriza in Greece, political parties with links to youth protest movements have not yet been able to take control of the state through the electoral process. In this sense, the 2011 world revolution is looking more like 1968 than 1917, for example. The resurgence of Black and Indigenous militancy in Anglosphere settler colonies (Idle No More in Canada, Black Lives Matter in the USA, Warriors of the Aboriginal Resistance in Australia) echoes the previous wave of Black civil rights and Indigenous land rights movements after 1968. In Herbert Ruffin's (2016) analysis, Black Lives Matter draws inspiration from the 1960s civil right/black power movement, 1980s black feminism, and Occupy Wall Street in 2011, and used social media outreach to avoid the charismatic male leader focused organisational structures of the earlier civil rights movement. The use of new technologies has facilitated the disruption of existing hierarchies, though maintaining these decentralised, egalitarian models of organisation has been more of a challenge, as seen in revolutions in the Arab world (Castells, 2012; Della Porta, 2014, Kucuk and Ozselcuk, 2016; Üstündağ, 2016, Yassin-Kassab and Al-Shami, 2016).

In Europe and the US, a key debate amongst participants in the youth dominated Occupy and Indignados protests has been whether to focus on electoral or non-electoral methods of social change. Some in the movement have argued that the pursuit of political office can be compatible with direct action methods such as occupations, strikes, blockades and other non-violent campaigns of civil disobedience. However, the anti-statist branch of the movement has questioned this position, instead advocating for a rejection of electoral politics, a position based on a variety of anarchist, communist and revolutionary principles (Chase-Dunn, 2013). Anarchist and autonomist concepts of mutual aid and direct democracy can be seen in initiatives as diverse as the Occupy Sandy relief effort in New York and the Skouries mine blockades in Greece (Maslin Nir, 2013; Klein 2014). On the electoral side of the spectrum, Bernie Sanders in the US, Jeremy Corbyn in the UK, Syriza in Greece and Podemos in Spain have all utilised the class based critiques of the 2011 protests, and have drawn in young activists from these movements into their campaigns, and appealed more broadly to a generation of younger voters disenchanted by a climate of economic malaise. Podemos in particular has attempted to appeal to young *indignados* participants while also reaching out to an older, working class base (Delclós, 2015).

However, the translation of this rebellious energy into representative politics has met with mixed results, with Syriza failing to escape German financial hegemony, and Podemos yet to break out of an ongoing deadlock following on from two inconclusive elections (Sotiris, 2016; Kennedy, 2016). The other side of this drift from the 'neoliberal centre' is the rise of the populist right in the form of Donald Trump, Brexit, and various anti-immigration parties in Europe. These campaigns are not always ideologically coherent, particularly in Trump's case, but the resurgence of the populist right indicates an establishment reaction to the twin crisis of democratic and economic legitimacy: the emergence of a dichotomy between neoliberal cosmopolitanism and protectionist ethno-nationalism that excludes other more progressive alternatives (Denvir, 2016).

Despite nominally being part of the 'Anglosphere,' Australia has not suffered as heavily from the 2007 GFC as the North Atlantic polities, with its economic and political fortunes seemingly more closely linked to the vagaries of the Chinese market than to events in Europe and North America (Priestley, 2010). The context of economic crisis which had proved such a fertile ground for uprisings in the Mediterranean and North America did not exist in Australia to anywhere near the same degree. Yet local Occupy protests were still planned and carried out. I will now examine the short and medium term effects of Australia's Occupy protests, and the post 2011 period of increased global youth militancy more generally, on Australian youth activism.

3   Occupy Melbourne

In order to understand links between the local iterations of Occupy and the climate and refugee movements, and at a broader level, instances of affinity and cross-fertilization between the local climate and refugee movements and the international wave of post 2011 militancy, I carried out interviews with participants of the Occupy movement, climate movement and refugee movement in

Australia. My key lines of questioning centred on the interviewees' experiences and analysis of these campaigns, and on their assessment of whether (and to what extent) these local actions had links to a broader world revolutionary moment. Information reported through the single interview process is by nature subjective and contextual (Mcleod, 2000), but this method also allows an in-depth discussion of themes raised by the theoretical framework (in this case world systems theory), and a testing of the practical applicability of that framework in a local context.

When it began, many activists looked on 'Occupy Melbourne' with a mixture of confusion and scepticism. Some interviewees believed that it was a somewhat artificial transplanting of an American concept onto Australian soil. The event was co-organised and attended by many non-activists, engaging a wider group of young people in politics. In his reflections on the event, participant James Muldoon identified several categories amongst the participants, including a 'neo-romantic' branch, a description of a diverse set of actors including cyber activists, libertarians and 'those championing a global festival culture' (Muldoon, 2012a: 46). Various participants described the early key promotional role held by inexperienced newcomers within this grouping as a double edged sword, with the lack of involvement from many existing activist organisations weakening Occupy's capacity for critical analysis.

The focus on political commonalities between metropolitan Australian youth and their counterparts in the US and Europe comes in part from Occupy Melbourne's internet origins. In a parallel to the analysis of Manuel Castells, interviewee Liz Patterson described the current militant wave as a consequence of the intersection between social media activism (as seen on Tumblr, Twitter and so on) with the critiques of material inequality arising after the 2008 financial crisis (Castells, 2012). But she also pointed out the blind spots inherent in this digital activism. In looking at purportedly global phenomena such as Occupy, there must be an awareness of how initially non-Western uprisings were distilled through a European, and more specifically an English language lens, before reaching Australia. An uprising sparked by the self-immolation of a street vendor in Tunisia in December 2010 spread via the Arab world to the Mediterranean (Spain and Greece), and only reached the US nine months later, yet the initial Australian promotional material focused on Occupy Wall Street as the central, instigating event (Benslama 2011).

Nevertheless, many first-time activists found Occupy Melbourne to be a galvanising experience, and one that opened up new intersectional frameworks of analysis for them. Beth Muldoon, (2012a) sister of James, had been politicised by her involvement in the May 15 movement while on exchange in Spain and was enthused by the possibility of testing out the principles of participatory democracy in a public space in Australia. Numerous other participants had also experienced the Mediterranean uprisings while on student exchanges, offering a counterpoint to the US focused, internet derived, conception of Occupy Melbourne. Beth Muldoon and others supported Occupy Melbourne's focus on material inequality, with the inclusion and provision of food for homeless people in the city centre being one practical outcome of this approach. She also argued that the creation of feminist and Indigenous working groups allowed new activists to gain access to existing networks and deepen their analysis. This corresponds with the development of intersectional analysis in overseas social movements over the last decade, particularly in the US, in which various modes of oppression (based on race, gender, class, sexuality, etc.) are recognised as an interconnecting system. While intersectionality builds on the insights of feminist and civil rights activism during the post'68 revolutionary wave, a new generation of young militants have engaged with the concept both online and in their communities and universities in recent years, facilitating its rapid spread as a central framework of analysis amongst millennial activists (Fisher, Dow, & Ray, 2017).

There was agreement from several interviewees that the material experience of police brutality and collective resistance on the day of the eviction from City Square radicalised many young, previously 'liberal' participants, encouraging them to develop a more critical understanding of state power and its uses. There was also a broad consensus among participants around the problems with Occupy Melbourne. The General Assemblies, while empowering to those involved, were difficult to coordinate and subject to being waylaid by small, organised sub-groups. Some of the initial organisers had links to the online Anonymous subculture, which had become famous for its distributed denial of service attacks on state and corporate websites, but had also developed a reputation for unreflexive misogyny. Despite attempts by feminist working groups to deal with this, Beth Muldoon stated in her interview that misogyny among some male 'occupiers' remained an issue throughout the encampments at City Square, Treasury Gardens and Flagstaff Gardens (Cox, 2012:18). While a significant number of participants in the Occupy and Indignados movements have become involved in electoral politics in North America and Europe, there has been no evidence of similar trends occurring in Australia on the same mass scale. Participants concurred that Occupy's focus on material inequality did not have the same electoral resonance in Australia's relatively affluent context as it did in New York, London and elsewhere. In contrast to the meagre electoral outcomes, the experience of direct democracy by young participants during Occupy Melbourne have had a more concrete effect, particularly for those working within the climate movement.

4 The Climate Movement

The Australian climate movement has a strong youth driven contingent, with young people playing key roles in organisations such as the Australian Youth Climate Coalition, as well as the Stop Adani campaign. The Victorian government's announcement of a permanent ban on onshore unconventional gas extraction is a significant victory for the state's climate movement, and one built on horizontalist, democratic methods of community mobilisation carried out by a coalition of predominantly young activists and older rural landowners. The campaign had begun with the odds stacked against it. In 2012 there was bipartisan political support for the Latrobe Valley and South Gippsland to be turned into a mining export hub 'on the scale of the Pilbara or the Hunter Valley,' with the Gillard government's Resources and Energy Minister Martin Ferguson and the Victoria's coalition government under Ted Baillieu both pushing for further brown coal and unconventional gas extraction (Morton, 2012). Extensive unconventional gas extraction was already under way in New South Wales and Queensland, with tenders being opened for exploration in Victoria. The rural communities under threat were in areas with high levels of support for the National Party and a distrust of urban 'greenies,' as some participants jokingly described themselves.

'Quit Coal' activist Dominic O'Dwyer outlined how during the process of Victoria's 'Coal and Gas Free Communities' campaign, a distinctive alliance was developed between urban, predominantly young activists and rural landowners.[1] O'Dwyer had been involved in Occupy Melbourne, and described it as a key moment in his politicisation. The experience of direct democracy during Occupy also proved to be an educational moment for the organisers of the 'Coal and Gas Free Communities' campaign. Horizontal organising and non-hierarchical consensus decision making lay at the heart of 'Coal and Gas Free Communities,' which involved tens of thousands of local community members (Quit Coal, 2016). Forums were set up across affected towns in rural Victoria, and nominally conservative communities engaged in participatory decision making to express their opposition to gas extraction not just in their own local areas, but across the state. Large group facilitation was used sparingly, with participants instead being separated quickly into smaller action groups, a decision in part informed by the difficulties encountered during the Assembly process in Occupy Melbourne.

The coordination of a united, clear message calling for a permanent ban from communities across the state proved to be critical in influencing the

---

[1] Interview with Dom O'Dwyer.

government's eventual decision. Occupations of fracking and other extraction sites across Victoria, coupled with vigils held outside state ministerial offices, maintained pressure on the government while it contemplated its decision. Four years after Federal Labor's Martin Ferguson and Nicola Roxon had deemed the climate movement to be a security threat in need of infiltration by ASIO and the Federal Police, Victorian Labor Premier Daniel Andrews explicitly referenced the 'Coal and Gas Free Communities' campaign in his government's decision, describing it as 'democracy at its best' (Hamilton, 2014; Lannen, 2016). He also declared that: 'Victorians have made it clear that they don't support fracking and that the health and environmental risks involved outweigh any potential benefits.' (Premier of Victoria, 2016).

During semi structured interviews I carried out with participants including Mr O'Dwyer, they reported conversations they had had with the state government, in which government representatives praised the campaign's high level of organisation and its ability to rapidly rebut critiques and claims made by the fossil fuel industry. Horizontal organising also defined The Leard State Forest occupation in New South Wales, the first blockade of a new coal mine in Australian history. While ultimately unsuccessful, it mobilised thousands of participants and gained mainstream media attention through the involvement of figures such as David Pocock, former captain of the Wallabies, the Australian men's Rugby Union team (Farrell, 2014). The mass scale of these campaigns in Australia can be seen as part of a broader international trend which Naomi Klein and others have described as 'Blockadia,' a shifting transnational archipelago of conflict wherever new extractive projects arise (Klein, 2014: 294). In recent years, and particularly since 2011, there has been an increasing shift to frame these campaigns around 'climate justice,' combining climate activism with a critique of global inequality and the dispossession of indigenous groups.

Seen through this lens, the focus of 'Coal and Gas Free Communities,' 'Lock the Gate' and other such campaigns on the property rights of rural landowners raises difficult questions around the settler-colonial legacy in Australia[2] If we follow Patrick Wolfe and assess invasion as 'a structure not an event,' then the organisation of predominantly white landowners against mining companies, for all its environmental merit, could be reduced to a conflict between two competing groups of beneficiaries from the colonial project (Wolfe, 2006).

In their interviews O'Dwyer and the other young participants described their concern about this issue, and the push for subsequent collaborations

---

2 Originating in Queensland, Lock the Gate is a national coalition of predominantly rural property owners, organised to oppose the encroachment of the mining and coal seam gas industries onto agricultural land and ecologically fragile areas.

between Aboriginal Traditional Owners and white farmers in New South Wales against mining projects. Opposition to the Shenhua Watermark Mine in Northwest New South Wales had opened a dialogue between the local Gomeroi people and farmers in the area, with the groups signing treaties together to formalise their alliance (Brown, 2015). In the US, the convergence of thousands of Standing Rock Sioux and other Native American protestors, together with non-indigenous allies, to blockade the Dakota Access Pipeline, offers another practical example of indigenous led direct action, and a potential source of inspiration for actors in Australia (McKibben, 2016). These developments again reflect the increasing debates around intersectionality by young participants in the climate justice and other social movements over the last decade. One participant in the refugee movement, when asked by the author why they'd chosen activism in that area rather than in the climate movement, described the latter as 'pretty white.' This participant, who identified as a person of colour, wished to remain anonymous, suggesting that making such observations within the Australian context remains an uncomfortable task that can leave non-white critics feeling vulnerable, even when taking into account the increasing awareness of intersectionality amongst young activists. While the Australian climate movement has made attempts to address this problem in recent years, it is the radical wing of the refugee movement where a more focused critique of racism in Australia has emerged.

5   The Refugee Movement

The announcements by both Broadspectrum and Wilson Security that they would not re-tender for work at the Nauru and Manus Island detention centres once their contracts finished in 2017 were brought about by pressure from boycott and divestment campaigns (Wiggins, 2016). Wilson's Melbourne and Sydney parking centres were blockaded by WACA (the Whistle-blowers and Citizens Alliance), while Broadspectrum had been targeted by a separate organisation, No Business in Abuse, in collaboration with Get Up (a progressive Australian lobby group). The tactics used by these groups have been applied to companies working in Australian detention centres over the last three years, with increasingly effective results.

In 2013 the consensus between the Labor and Liberal Parties on asylum seeker policy reached a new level of intensity with then Prime Minister Kevin Rudd's announcement of the PNG solution, with all asylum seekers coming by sea without a visa to be refused settlement in Australia. This event, swiftly followed by Prime Minister Tony Abbott's brief stumble across the national stage, proved to be a catalyst for the formation of a new organisation in Melbourne, Beyond Borders, which coordinated with an existing Sydney based collective, Crossborder Operational Matters, in devising new direct-action methods focused around the identification and targeted disruption of corporate supply chains (XBorder, 2016). While Beyond Borders has since disbanded, the tactics developed during this period have inspired subsequent waves of divestment action. One of the most recognised actions organised by these two groups was the artists' boycott of the Sydney Biennale in 2014, which led to the Biennale severing all links with Transfield (the previous name for Broadspectrum before a failed attempt at rebranding), the resignation of Biennale chairman Luca Belgiorno-Nettis, and the enragement of the coalition government. Then Communications Minister Malcolm Turnbull denounced the artists' 'vicious ingratitude,' while then Arts Minister George Brandis threatened to change arts funding policy to punish artists and festival organisers who 'unreasonably' refused corporate sponsorship (Swan, 2014; Jabour, 2014). The subsequent cuts to the Australia Council (in favour of a government controlled 'National Program for Excellence') were perceived by several of the participants interviewed as being linked to the Biennale Boycott. This then lead to further calls for direct action by artists to challenge the government's decision (Pledger, 2016), with various participants involved in the process of mobilising artists (many of whom were also in their 20s) to conduct a boycott.

At the time of the Boycott even some left leaning commentators questioned the wisdom of targeting companies profiting from detention rather than directly attacking the government (Razer, 2014). But this switch in focus was an intentional strategy by Beyond Borders. Liz Patterson, Max Kaiser and other members described a lack of faith in the group around the potential of parliamentary politics, with the ALP's shared immigration platform with the Coalition indicating that the true locus of political change lay elsewhere. Instead, the collective believed that direct action was in part a necessary way of imagining alternatives to the dead end of representative politics, where continuous rallies by an urban, liberal minority around the treatment of asylum seekers was met with indifference by the major parties. There was a consensus in Beyond Borders that appeals to public empathy could be reframed by detainment advocates themselves with 'compassionate' calls to prevent deaths at sea, and that an unambiguous call to close the camps needed to be made.

This approach was inspired by the resistance and protests of detained asylum seekers themselves, as well as the asylum seekers and refugees who had subsequently moved into the Australian community and formed RISE (Refugees Survivors and Ex-Detainees), which had been making similar demands for an immediate end to detention since 2009 (RISE, 2016a; Fernandez, 2016). The intellectual work of figures such as Angela Mitropolous and others in critiquing Australia's border security industry (as seen in the xborder website and collective), as well as earlier direct actions such as the Woomera breakout, were other key reference points (Mitropolous and Kiem, 2015). Investigations into supply chains and divestment strategies by members with links to the boycott, divestment and Sanctions (BDS) movement against Israel also underpinned the strategy. The level of frustration expressed by government ministers at these types of actions indicated the astuteness of moving on from an electoral focus. Since 2013, the major threats to the government's detention policy have come from outside the Australian electoral arena. Besides local divestment campaigns, pressure from international human rights organisations and the PNG Supreme Court's ruling that the Manus Island detention centre was illegal under the country's constitution have also had damaging effects on the share prices of Broadspectrum, G4S and other companies invested in detention (Davidson and Doherty, 2016; Wiggins, 2016).

The focus of these new Australian anti-detention organisations on supply chain boycotts and divestment parallels an international trend among activist organisations since 2011. In North America and Europe, similar strategies have been employed by the climate movement to target fossil fuel companies, and by Black Lives Matter affiliated organisations such as the Afrikan Black Coalition, which successfully forced the University of California to divest from private prisons in the US (Song, 2015). In part then, this is a case of an international practice being mobilised in Australia, though it's important to note that the shift away from electoral campaigning by groups like Beyond Borders also reflects specific local circumstances. Multiple participants stated that Australia's history of racism and xenophobia had led them to a pragmatic acceptance that a large section of the voting population would continue supporting mandatory detention, and that a direct targeting of capital was likely to achieve quicker results. This historical analysis also necessitates a de-colonial framing of anti-racism, as seen in the expressions of solidarity from RISE ex-detainees for Aboriginal protests organised in the wake of the Don Dale detention centre abuses (RISE, 2016b; Lawrence & Dua, 2005).

Direct links between anti-detention campaigns and Occupy also exist, with the Melbourne Street Medics, formed during Occupy Melbourne, playing a prominent and ongoing role in the popularisation of stopdep (stop deportation) actions. Overall, the detention divestment campaigns have shown that smart tactics can yield results even in unpromising political circumstances. The targeting of weak points in the detention industry, namely the ability of the corporations involved to maintain their profit margins and public image, has infuriated the government, limited its scope of action and made the maintenance of offshore detention centres increasingly difficult.

6 Conclusions

On a global scale the concept of world revolutions offers an explanatory framework for both previous moments of political upheaval, and the contemporary relationships and exchange of strategies between militant youth led movements across Europe, Africa, West Asia and the Americas since 2011.

The 2011 world revolutionary moment has technically only seen the overthrow of governments by youth led protest movements in a small number of countries (Tunisia, Egypt, Burkina Faso), but there has been a clear resurgence of social movement militancy throughout the years since, the full consequences of which will only be assessable in the coming decades. The revival of intersectional critiques discussing material inequality, feminism, climate justice and decolonisation show links with 1968, with these discussions facilitated by online networks that have allowed a rupture with some of the more hierarchical, male led organisational formations of earlier revolutionary moments.

In the Australian context, an analysis of the local iterations of Occupy, and the direct action focused wing of the climate and anti-detention movements, indicates that the international wave has had some local ripple effects. For instance, participants were able to take away specific organisational lessons (such as the difficulties of coordinating mass attempts at direct democracy) – elaborate the lessons and what they subsequently did and apply them to other projects like the 'Coal and Gas Free Communities' campaign. The post 2011 shift to electoral politics by radical youth led organisations seen in Europe and the US has not occurred in Australia. Instead a pragmatic acceptance of the ongoing racism underpinning Australian immigration politics, coupled with an astute assessment of the possibilities of boycott and divestment campaigns, has helped the anti-detention movement to put significant pressure on corporations associated with the government's offshore detention policy.

While they are beyond the scope of this investigation, other local examples of the new militancy worthy of further investigation include the emergence of youth-led Aboriginal organisations groups such as WAR (Warriors of the Aboriginal Resistance), which consciously seeks to revive the militant Aboriginal activism of the 1970s (DeWitt, 2015). As for Australia's more radical youth led climate and anti-detention organisations, their concerns and structures, in particular their experiments with democratic organising; their focus on intersectional justice; their attempts to grapple with historical violence and racism; and their focus on direct action and material objectives, all point to commonalities with youth driven movements and practices beyond Australia's shores, such as the global fossil fuels divestment campaign, the new groundswell of anti-racist and decolonial groups (Black Lives Matter, Idle No More) and groups that combine both indigenous sovereignty and environmental protection as objectives (the Standing Rock Sioux Dakota Pipeline protests, La Via Campesina). The long term prospect of climate disaster and the present brutality of Australia's immigration policies, combined with a drive to re-examine the colonial past and present, is inspiring a new generation of militancy in Australia, a distinctive swell within the greater global wave.

Acknowledgements

I would like to thank the activists who I interviewed for this chapter, including Liz Patterson, Beth Muldoon, Dominic O'Dwyer, Max Kaiser, and others who wished to remain anonymous.

References

Benslama, F. 2011. *Suddenly, Revolution! Tunisia to the Arab World: The Meaning of an Uprising*. Paris: Denoël.
Brown, E. 2015. "Aboriginal Group Says it is Fighting Coal Mine for its Heritage." In, *ABC*, http://www.abc.net.au/news/2015-02-26/aboriginal-group-fighting-coal-mine/6263304 Accessed September 18, 2016.
Castells, M. 2012. *Networks of Outrage and Hope: Social Movements in the Internet Age*. London: Polity Press.
Chakrabarty, D. 2000. *Provincializing Europe: Postcolonial Thought and Historical Differences*. New Jersey: Princeton University Press.
Chase-Dunn, C. 2013. "The World Revolution of 2011: Assembling a United Front of the New Global Left."In, paper presented August 10, 2013 at the Society for the Study of Social Problems session on, *Social Mobilizations and the Dialectic of Change*, organized by Lauren Langman, The Westin New York at Times Square. http://irows.ucr.edu/papers/irows82/irows82.htm Accessed August 20, 2016.
Cox, H. 2012. "For the Women of Occupy." In, *Occupy Reflects Journal*. Melbourne, 18–19.

Davey, M. 2016. "Victoria to Permanently Ban Fracking and Coal Seam Gas Exploration." In, *The Guardian,* https://www.theguardian.com/environment/2016/aug/30/victoria-to-permanently-ban-fracking-and-coal-seam-gas-exploration. Accessed September 1, 2016.

Davidson, H and B. Doherty. 2016. "Manus Island Detention Centre to Close, Papua New Guinea Prime Minister Says." In, *The Guardian.* https://www.theguardian.com/australia-news/2016/apr/27/manus-island-detention-centre-to-close-papua-new-guinea-prime-minister-says Accessed 28 July, 2016.

Delclós, Carlos. 2015. "No One Represents Us: On the Links between Podemos and the Indignados." In, *Novara Media,* http://novaramedia.com/2015/12/20/no-one-represents-us-on-the-links-between-podemos-and-the-indignados/ Accessed 1 November, 2016.

Della Porta, D. 2014. *Mobilising Democracy: Comparing 1989 and 2011.* Oxford: OUP.

Denvir, D. 2016. "Socialism or Barbarism: Only the Far Left Can Defeat the Rise of the Radical Right." In, *Salon.* http://www.salon.com/2016/06/28/socialism_or_barbarism_only_the_far_left_can_defeat_the_rise_of_the_radical_right/ Accessed August 1, 2016.

DeWitt, C. 2015. "We Interviewed Australia's Warriors of the Aboriginal Resistance." In, *Vice.* http://www.vice.com/read/interview-with-the-warriors-of-aboriginal-resistance Accessed August 7, 2016.

Farrell, P. 2014. "Wallaby David Pocock Arrested after Chaining Himself to Coal Digger." In, *The Guardian.* https://www.theguardian.com/environment/2014/nov/30/former-wallabies-captain-david-pocock-chain-digger-coal-protest Accessed August 18, 2016.

Fernandez, R. 2016. "Malcolm Turnbull's Kirribilli Fast: It Will Take More Than A Dinner to Keep Us Quiet." In, *New Matilda.* https://newmatilda.com/2016/06/20/it-will-take-more-than-a-dinner-to-keep-us-quiet/ Accessed August 16, 2016.

Fisher, D., D. Dow & R. Ray 2017, "Intersectionality takes it to the streets: Mobilizing across diverse interests for the Women's March." In, *Science Advances*, 3: 9, 1–8.

Fraser, N. 2013. *Fortunes of Feminism: From State-Managed Capitalism to Neoliberal Crisis.* London: Verso.

Graeber, D. 2011. "Situating Occupy." In, *Adbusters.* https://www.adbusters.org/article/situating-occupy/ Accessed August 5, 2016.

Graeber, D. 2013. "A Practical Utopian's Guide to the Coming Collapse." In, *The Baffler*, 22. http://thebaffler.com/salvos/a-practical-utopians-guide-to-the-coming-collapse Accessed August 15, 2016.

Graeber, D. & S. Shukaitis 2007. Introduction to *Constituent Imagination: Militant Investigations, Collective Theorization,* edited by D. Graeber, S. Shukaitis, & E. Biddle Edinburgh: AK Press, 11–37.

Hamilton, C. 2014. "Is spying on anti-coal activists just the tip of the iceberg?" In, *The Conversation*. https://theconversation.com/is-spying-on-anti-coal-activists-just-the-tip-of-the-iceberg-27570 Accessed August 20, 2016.

Jabour, B. 2014. "Arts Groups Refusing Tobacco Funding May Be Penalised." In, *The Guardian*. https://www.theguardian.com/world/2014/mar/14/arts-refusing-corporate-funding-face-penalties Accessed June 6, 2016.

Kennedy, P. 2016. "Once again a Spanish election saves the establishment and deals Podemos a blow." In, *The Conversation*. https://theconversation.com/once-again-a-spanish-election-saves-the-establishment-and-deals-podemos-a-blow-61465 Accessed August 27, 2016.

Klein, N. 2014. *This Changes Everything: Capitalism Vs. the Climate.* New York: Simon & Schuster.

Kucuk, B. & C. Ozselcuk 2016. "The Rojava experience: possibilities and challenges of building a democratic life." In, *South Atlantic Quarterly, 15:1*, 184-196.

Lannen, D. 2016. "Premier Daniel Andrews hails Victoria's Fracking Ban a Win for People Power." In, *The Geelong Advertiser*. http://www.geelongadvertiser.com.au/news/geelong/premier-daniel-andrews-hails-victorias-fracking-ban-a-win-for-people-power/news-story/dbe497c89937474db002d8abb47ae6ff.

Larwence, B. & E. Dua 2005. "Decolonizing Antiracism." In, *Social Justice, 32:4*, 120–142

Maslin Nir, S. 2013. "Storm Effort Causes a Rift in Occupy Movement." In, *The New York Times*. http://www.nytimes.com/2013/05/01/nyregion/occupy-movements-changing-focus-causes-rift.html?_r=0 Accessed August 24 2016.

McKibben, B. 2016. "A Pipeline Fight and America's Dark Past." In, *The New Yorker*. http://www.newyorker.com/news/daily-comment/a-pipeline-fight-and-americas-dark-past.

Mcleod, J. 2000. "Metaphors of the Self: Searching for young people's identity through. interviews." In, *Researching Youth*, edited by J. McLeod & K. Malone. Hobart: Australian Clearinghouse for Youth Studies, 45–58.

Mignolo, W. 2005. *The Idea of Latin America*. Oxford: Blackwell Publishing.

Mitropolous, A. & M. Kiem 2015. "Crossborder Operations." In, *The New Inquiry*. http://thenewinquiry.com/features/cross-border-operations/ Accessed September 4, 2016.

Morton, A. 2012. "Pilbara Plan for Victoria." In, *The Age*. http://www.theage.com.au/victoria/pilbara-plan-for-victoria-20120418-1x70x.html Accessed September 1 2016.

Muldoon, B. 2012a. "Power and Privilege at Occupy Melbourne." In, *Occupy Reflects Journal*. Melbourne.

Muldoon, J. 2012b. "A Socio-Political Analysis of Occupy Melbourne." In, *Occupy Reflects Journal*. Melbourne.

Pledger, D. 2016. "Brandis is Waging a Cultural War: Artists Must Take Direct Action." In, *The Conversation*. https://theconversation.com/brandis-is-waging-a-culture-war-artists-must-take-direct-action-42615 Accessed July 7, 2016.

Premier of Victoria. 2016. "Victoria Bans Fracking to Protect Farmers." http://www.premier.vic.gov.au/victoria-bans-fracking-to-protect-farmers/ Accessed September 4, 2016.

Priestley, M. 2010. "Australia, China and the Global Financial Crisis.'" *Parliament of Australia.* http://www.aph.gov.au/About_Parliament/Parliamentary_Departments/Parliamentary_Library/pubs/BriefingBook43p/australiachinagfc Accessed August 2, 2016.

Quit Coal. *Coal and Gas Free Communities.* https://quitcoal.org.au/coal-and-gas-free-communities/ Accessed September 3, 2016.

Razer, H. 2014. "Sydney Biennale: Artists Divide Over Dirty Money." In, *Daily Review.* http://dailyreview.com.au/sydney-biennale-artists-divide-over-dirty-money/ Accessed March 9, 2014.

RISE. "Who We Are." http://riserefugee.org/who-we-are/ Accessed September 1, 2016a.

RISE. "We Ex-Detainees and Survivors of Torture and Abuse at RISE, Support the Emergency Actions for the Children of Don Dale and all Prisons Rally Organised by First Nations Community Groups across Australia." http://riserefugee.org/we-ex-detainees-and-survivors-of-torture-and-abuse-at-rise-support-the-emergency-actions-for-the-children-of-don-dale-and-all-prisons-rally-organised-by-first-nations-community-groups-across-australi/ Accessed November 2, 2016b.

Ruffin, H. 2016. "Black Lives Matter: The Growth of a New Social Justice Movement." http://www.blackpast.org/perspectives/black-lives-matter-growth-new-social-justice-movement, accessed May 26, 2018.

Song, J. 2015. "UC system divests $30 million in prison holdings amid student pressure." In, *LA Times.* http://www.latimes.com/local/education/la-me-uc-divestment-prisons-20151226-story.html Accessed July 30, 2016.

Sotiris, P. 2016. "The Dream that Became a Nightmare." In, *Jacobin.* https://www.jacobinmag.com/2016/02/greece-syriza-alexis-tsipras-varoufakis-austerity-farmer-blockade-protests/ Accessed August 4, 2016.

Swan, J. 2014. "Malcolm Turnbull Denounces "Vicious Ingratitude" of Biennale Artists After Transfield Withdraws as Sponsor." In, *Sydney Morning Herald.* http://www.smh.com.au/federal-politics/political-news/malcolm-turnbull-denounces-vicious-ingratitude-of-biennale-artists-after-transfield-withdraws-as-sponsor-20140310-34ik6.html Accessed July 8, 2016.

Tronti, M. 2006 [1966]. *Operai e capitale*, Roma: Derive Approdi.

Üstündağ, N. 2016. "Self-Defense as a Revolutionary Practice in Rojava, or How to Unmake the State." In, *South Atlantic Quarterly*, 115:1, 197–210.

Wallerstein, I. 2004. *World-Systems Analysis.* Durham, NC: Duke University Press.

Wallerstein, I. 2011a. "Structural Crisis in the World System." In, *The Monthly Review*, 62. http://monthlyreview.org/2011/03/01/structural-crisis-in-the-world-system/ Accessed September 1 2016.

Wallerstein, I. 2011b [1974]. *The Modern World-System I: Capitalist Agriculture and the Origins of the European World-Economy in the Sixteenth Century*. Berkeley: University of California Press.

Wallerstein, I. 2012. *The World Left After 2011*. http://iwallerstein.com/world-left-2011/ Accessed 21 August 2016.

Wiggins, J. 2016. "Security Contractors Bow to Activist Pressure on Detention Centre." In, *Australian Financial Review*. http://www.afr.com/business/security-contractors-bow-to-activist-pressure-on-detention-centres-20160902-gr7kwr#ixzz4JLCrUaJJ Accessed September 5 2016.

Wolfe, P. 2006. *Journal of Genocide Research, 8(4)*, 387–409.

Xborder. *Crossborder Operational Matters*. https://xborderoperationalmatters.wordpress.com/ Accessed August 23, 2016.

Yassin-Kassab, R. & L. Al-Shami 2016. *Burning Country: Syrians in Revolution and War*. London: Pluto Press.

Index

ABC (Australian Broadcasting Corporation)   170, 173, 191
absenteeism   130, 148, 241
Abul-Magd, Z.   192
ACARA   170
action learning   142, 150, 152
active citizenship   123–132, 135, 179, 233
activism   64, 66, 67, 74, 116, 137, 195, 233–236, 251, 254, 257, 260–263, 302, 312–317
ACTU   172
Adam, B.   91, 93, 94
Adams, A. & Winthrop, R.   186
adversity capital   17, 170, 176–178, 180
    and soft skills   169
Agamben   83, 107
Ahmad, S.   99, 117
Akar, B.   128
Akram, S.   76, 209
Aldenmyr, S.   127
Alexander, M.   32, 33n
Ali, T.   260
Al-Momani, K.N Dados, N., Maddox, M. & Wise, A.   227, 229
Amadae, S.   78
Ambivalence   70, 107, 113, 116–117
Amin, A.   195
Amnå, E. & Ekman, J.   127
Anderson, L.   5
Anderson, P.   264
Andersson, E.   127
Anonymous   73–76, 81–83, 85–89, 315
Appadurai, A.   95, 96, 124, 126, 135, 155, 158, 164–167, 187
apparatus (*dispositif*)   29, 31, 39, 90, 107–109
Arab Spring (or Arab Awakening)   5, 64, 99, 186–189, 191–192, 196–199, 272–274, 278–282, 284–287, 307, 308
Arendt, H.   35, 36, 41
Arnot, M. & Swartz, S.   130
Aronowitz, S.   37, 38
Arreman, I. & Holm, A.   195
aspiration (aspirations, aspirational)   62, 70, 115, 117, 123, 125–126, 130–134, 142, 151, 153, 158, 166, 267, 278, 289, 300
assemblies   200, 259, 260, 315

asylum seekers   107, 111, 124, 217, 318–319
    anti-detention campaigns   320–321
Atkinson, A.   196
Austerity   61, 119, 123, 133, 169, 256–260, 262–264, 266–267, 307
Austin, L.   186, 189
Authoritarianism   28, 35–36, 40, 248
Autonomist Marxist School   308–309
AYAC.   171

Bakan, D.   289
Baker, A.   127
Balko, R.   33n
Ball, S.   196
Ball, S. J, & Olmedo, A.   95
Banaji, S.   127
Bang, H.   228
Barbalet, J.   211
Barrionuevo, A.   193
Bartlett, J.   47
Bauerlein, M.   77, 210
Bauman, Z.   30, 63, 74, 86, 107, 110–113, 116, 117, 177, 227, 237
    and liquid life   63, 71
    and wasted lives   107, 110, 111
Beadle, S.   135
Beck, U.   7, 113
Beck, U. & Beck-Gersheim, E.   228
Becker, G.   76
Beckert, J.   158
Bellei, C, Cabalin, C. and Orellana, V.   193
Belonging   8, 10, 11, 64, 83, 123–124, 134–135, 169, 176, 179, 231–234
Benhabib, S.   76, 210
Benjamin, A.   40
Bennett, W.L.   228
Benslama, F.   314
Berg, C.   174
Berlant, L.   15, 48, 58, 117, 135
Berman, C.E. & Nugent, E.R.   284
Bessant, J.   77, 187, 188, 210, 212, 213
Bessant, J. & Montero, K.   63
Bidisha   123
Biehl, J.   29
Black Lives Matter   61, 64, 66, 307, 312, 320, 322

Black, R. 132
Black, R, Gray, E. Leahy, D. 128
Blenker, Y. 53, 56, 58
Blyth, M. 266
Bohmann, J. 76, 210
Bottrell, D. 178
Boudarbat, B. & Aibilou, A. 278
Boudreau, J.A, Liguori, M. & Séguin-Manegre, M. 127
Boughzala, M. 277
Bourdieu, P. 45, 49, 50, 53
  and critical reflexivity 52
  and *habitus* 50–52
  and field 51
  and Wacquant, L. 165
Bradford, S. & Cullen, F. 126
Braidotti, R. 5, 7, 70, 141
Brannen, J, & Nilsen, A. 92
Brown, E. 318
Brown, P, de Graaf, S. & Hillen, M. 165
Brown, P., Lauder, H. & Ashton, D. 46, 48, 49, 53, 179
Brown, W. 64, 266
Bruter, M., Banaji, S., Harrison, S., Cammaerts, B. Anstead, N. & Whitwell, B. 210–212
Bryant, J. & Ellard, J. 131
Brym, R., Godbout, M., A. Hoffbauer, A., Menard, G. & Zhang, T. H. 278, 279, 281, 283
Budgen, S. & Kouvelakis, S. 257, 261
Budgen, S. & Lapavitsas, C. 264
Burgess, J, Foth, M. & Klaebe, H.G. 231
Butler, J. 6, 200
Butler, J. & Athanasiou, A. 63–65

Cairns, D. 163
Cairns, D, Growiec, K. & de Almeida Alves, N. 162
Calacal, C. 32
Cammaerts, B., Bruter, M., Banaji, S., Harrison, S. & Anstead, N. 124, 127
Campbell, C. & Proctor, H. 188
Campbell, P. 5
Campbell, P, Kelly, P. & Harrison, L. 140, 141
Capital 44, 48, 50–51, 55, 93, 97, 100–101, 128, 135, 181, 195, 211, 221, 236, 262–263, 290, 320
  diversity 170, 176–178, 180
  Information 98
  Identity 99

Capitalism 106–107, 110–113, 117, 125, 187, 197–198, 260–261, 266, 297, 308
  Casino 28, 30, 34–37, 39–40
Carabelli, G, & Lyon, D. 91, 93, 98, 99
Castells, M. 2, 4–6, 78, 190, 197, 200, 235, 312, 314
Castles, S & Davidson, A. 231
Cavalli, A. 279
Cerny, P. 262
Chakrabarty, D. 209
Chase-Dunn, C. 328
Chilean Student Movement 187, 192–194, 196
choice 41–45, 62–63, 70, 76, 106–107, 111–113, 115–117, 161, 172–173, 230, 254, 295, 298, 302
  mythic dimensions of 107, 112
  the illusion of 105–107, 112, 115–117
Chomiak, L. 281, 282
Cicognani, E., Albanesi, C., Mazzoni, D., Prati, G. & Zani, B. 236
citizenship 28, 30, 34, 123–132, 134–135, 179, 227–237
  cultural 229–234, 236, 237
  DIY and young Muslims 226–230, 232–237
Clarke, M. & Bennett, J. 171
Clegg, S. 93
climate action movements 126, 220, 307, 308, 311, 316, 318, 320–322
Coe, A., Wiklund, M. Uttjek, M. & Nygren, L. 212
Coffey, J, & Farrugia, D. 92
Cole, J. 281
Coleman, G. 73, 74
Collin, P. 5, 77, 173
Comber, B. 179
communicative action 74, 80–82, 229
Connell, R. 49
Connell, R., Ashenden, D., Kessler, S. & Dowsett, G. 188
consensus 28, 78, 80, 83–85, 199, 200, 210, 311, 315–319
Cook, J. 165
Cooper, C. 123, 125
Côté, J. 94–97, 99, 101
Council of Europe 125, 126, 133
Cox, H. 315
creative culture 229–232, 234

INDEX

Critchley, S.   79, 84, 106, 211, 212, 221
Cross J.   197
Crouch, C.   266
Crowley, J.   11
cruel optimism   15, 16, 117, 135
Cuervo, H.   126
Cultures of Democracy   9
Cuzzocrea, V. & Mandich, G   156, 160
Cuzzocrea, V. & Isabella, S.   158, 165

Dahlberg, L.   78, 80
Danziger, K.   75
Davey, M.   307
Davis, A.   175, 178
Davidson, H. & Doherty, B.   320
DeGraw, D.   33
Delclós, C.   313
deliberative democracy   76, 79, 84
Della Porta, D.   212, 261, 262, 312
Denvir, D.   313
Derrida, J.   41, 164
Desroche, H.   165
Desrues, T.   273
DeWitt, C.   321
Dhillon, N.   190n, 191n
Dhillon, N. & Yousef, T.   279
digital disruption   46, 94–95, 102, 312
direct action   83, 308, 312, 318–322
dispossession   64–65, 70, 290, 291, 317
Douzinas, C.   260, 261, 265, 267
Down, B.   127
Dunleavy, P.   76

Eagleton, T.   115, 116
Easton, D.   75
Education
    Democratic   34, 37–38, 40, 45, 48–49, 55, 57, 96, 125, 186, 193, 201
    Higher Education   28–29, 34, 37–39, 49, 99, 101, 109, 170, 173, 193, 198, 277–278, 296
    Vocational   48, 99, 156n, 162, 172n, 262
    for profit   27, 110, 192–196
Edwards, K.   127
Edwards, K, Saha, L. & Print, M   174
Elliott, J.   157
entrepreneurial self   61, 63, 70, 98, 102, 115, 177
ethical citizenship   244, 235, 236
ethos of survival and responsibilisation   61, 65, 70

European Commission   125, 126
European Union (EU)   126, 198, 256, 272

Facebook   78, 82, 98, 158, 192, 212n, 281
Fahmy, E.   228, 273, 279, 281
Farrell, P.   217
Farrugia, D.   98
Farrugia, D. & Watson, J.   135
Farthing, R.   77
Feith, H.   245
Feminism   106, 311–312, 321
Fernandez, R.   319
Figures   61
    and the guerrilla self   60–63, 65, 69
    the hacker   90, 97–102
    immigrant, asylum seeker and refugee   111
Fine, M.   291
Fine, M. & Ruglis, J.   290
Fine, M., B. Stoudt, M. Fox & M. Santos.   290
Fisher, D, Dow, D. & Ray R.   308, 315
Fisher, J.   187, 194
Fitzpatrick, M.   29
Flores, R.   66
Flyvberg, B.   128
Foucault, M.   63, 97, 108–109, 115, 116, 164
    and power   113, 114
    care of the self   65
    dispositif   108, 112
    ethics   6, 107
    governmentality   12, 94, 107, 114, 265
    practice of freedom   39, 107, 114–115
Foulcher, K.   249
4chan,   73–76, 81, 82, 85
Fox, M. & Fine, M.   291
France, A, & Threadgold, S.   95, 100
Fraser, N.   78, 209
Fredericks, B. & Legge, D.   149
freedomhouse.org.   241
Freud, S.   105, 107, 112
Friedman, M. & Friedman, R.   113
Fuchs, C.   46, 74
Furedi, F.   77
Furlong, A. & Cartmel, F.   77
Furlong, A, Woodman, D. & Wyn J.   91
Furstenberg, F.   187, 189
Free market   28, 37, 113, 170, 187, 194, 197, 266
FYA (Foundation for Young Australians)   171, 172

Galland, O. 179
Gaonkar, D. P. 9, 10
Gardiner, L. 50
GetUp 174, 216
Ghonim, W. 5
Gimmler, A. 79
Gindin, S. & Panitch, L. 256, 264
Girouz, H. 49, 110, 132, 187, 190
Giroux, H. & Giroux, S. 179
Global Financial Crisis (GFC) 49, 60, 67, 100, 109, 123, 171, 187, 290
   the Great Recession 109, 290
globalisation 110, 111, 124, 199, 227, 231, 257, 260, 261
Golsch, K. 279
Gonin, M, Besharov, M. & Smith, W. 141
Goodman, P. 188
Google Play Music. 69
Gordon, H. & Taft, J. 77, 127
Gorur, R. 195
Gould-Wartofsky, M. A. 5, 60
Gourgouris, S. 257, 263–265, 267
Governance 28, 31–36, 91, 170, 177, 188, 192, 199, 234, 247
governmentality (*See* Foucault, M.)
Graeber, D. 308, 309
Gray, J. 105–107, 112, 113, 116
Greenwald, G. 311n
Griffiths, E. 175
Gross, M. & McGoey, L. 211, 222
Guerrilla Self (*See* figures)

Habermas, J. 74, 76–83, 85
Hacking 91, 97
Hadiz, V. & Richard, R. 242
Hafez, B.N. 281
Hall, S. 37
Hall, S. & Back, L. 37
Hall, S, Massey, D. & Rustin, M. 29
Hamilton, C. 217
Hammouda, N-E. 274
Hannon, V, Patton, A. & Temperley, J. 176
Hansen, K.T. 276
Haraway, D. 61
Harris, A. 210
Harris, A. & Roose, J. 127, 228
Harris, A., Wyn, J. & Younes, S. 77, 127

Harrison, L., Shacklock, G., Angwin, J. & Kamp, A. 149
Harrison, L. & Kelly, P. 135
Harrison, L. & Shacklock, G. 149
Hartcher, P. & Massola, J. 169
Harvey, D. 193, 195, 291
Hatherall, M. 242
Hayek, F.A. 113
Hedges, C. 36
Heejung P, Twenge, J. & Greenfeld, P. 290
Henderson, S., Holland, J., McGrellis, S., Sharpe, S. & Thomson, R. 142
Henn, M., Weinstein, M. & Hodgkinson, S. 77
Herwig, J. 73
Heywood, A. 210
Hilton, M., McKay, J., Crowson, N. & Mouhot, J-F. 77
Hirschman, A. 214, 219
Hobart, C. & Sendek, H. 69
Hockey, J. 171
Honwana, A. 12, 277, 279
Hope
   as an anticipatory virtue 117
   and ambivalence 70
   a discourse of 107
   and hopelessness 68, 70, 209
   as prophylactic 130, 131
   without optimism 115
horizontalidad 199–200
horizontal organisation 259, 316, 317
Hounshell, B. 5
Howie, L. & Campbell, P. 3, 5, 60, 61, 62, 65, 68, 171, 177, 190
Hsieh, C. & Urquiola, M. 193
Hughes, S. 3, 4
Hui, S. & Cheung, H. 176
Huntington, S.P. 1, 187, 189, 190
Hursh, D.W. 194, 196
Hutchens, G. 171
Hyvonen, A-E. 272

ILO (International Labour Organization) 50, 171
imagined futures 9, 70, 143, 157–159, 163–166
income inequality 33, 196, 289, 293–296
individualism 63, 70, 85, 106, 290

INDEX

Internet   73–79, 82–83, 233, 244, 291, 314–315
    Of Things   45
Isabella, S. & Mandich, G.   160
Iser, W.   158
Isin, E.   124, 127, 128
ISIS (Islamic State)   28, 61, 73, 85, 226
IYF (International Youth Foundation)   176

Jabour, B.   319
Jakubowicz, A.H, Collins, J.H. &
    Chafic, W. F.   227
Jamie's Kitchen (*See Working in Jamie's Kitchen*)
Jeffrey, C. & Dyson, J.   228
Johns, A.   233
Johns, A, Mansouri, F. & Lobo, M.   229
Jordan, T.   97, 98
Jones, N.   175
Juris, J.S. & Pleyers, G.H.   127

Kandil, H.   273
Karatzogianni, A., Nguyen, D. &
    Serafinelli, E.   79
Katsambekis, G.   257–262
Katz, J.   212
Keane, J.   210
Kehily, M.J & Nayak, A.   94, 99, 100, 102
Kellner, D.   7, 8, 210
Kelly, D.   149
Kelly, P.   63, 91, 93, 99, 100, 102, 107, 109, 110,
    114, 125, 128, 134, 170
Kelly, P. & Harrison, L.   111
Kelly, P. & Pike, J   107
Kennedy, P.   313
Kennelly, J.   127
Kennelly, J. & Dillabough, J.A.   126
Kimberlee, R. H.   77
Kirshner, B   290
Kitchen, N.   200
Klein, N.   313, 317
Kouvelakis, S.   257, 261, 263, 264, 282
Konings, M. & Panitch, P.   256
Kucuk, B. & Ozselcuk, C.   312
Kurzweil, R.   46

labour market   46, 91–95, 99–101, 125,
    130–135, 140–141, 147–151, 155, 172,
    178–179, 274–276

Laclau, E. & Mouffe, C.   266
LaGraffe, D.   189, 190, 191n
Lannen, D.   317
Laskos, C. & Tsakalotos, E.   258, 262, 264
Latimer, J. & Skeggs, B.   157, 164
Law, J.   108
Lawrence, B. & Dua, E.   320
Lawson, G.   200
Leander, K.M, Phillips, C. & Headrick
    Taylor, K.   96
Leccardi, C.   92
Leftwich, A.   75, 209
Leon, C. de, Desai, M. & Tugal, C.   283
Lesko, N.   289
Levitas, R.   165
Lewin, K.   142
Lipman, P.   196
Lipset, S. M.   282
Loader, B. & Mercea, D.   210
Lowy Institute   247
Lubienski, C.   195
Lubienski, C, Lee, J. & Gordon, L.   195
Luke, P.   30
Lutz, C.   32
Lyon, D. & Crow, G.   155

Madar. C.   34
Madkhul, D.   227
Mahler, V. A., Jesuit, D. K. & Paradowski, P.
    R.   210
Mannheim, K.   273
Manning, N.   77, 212
Manning, N. & Holmes.   210, 211, 212
Manson, J.   126
Manson, P.   5
Maragkidou, M.   209, 218, 220
Marginalisation   61, 66, 150, 152, 227, 233
Martin, A.   77, 242, 255
Maslin, N.S.   313
Matthews, J.   94
May, V.   11
Maynes, M, Pierce, J. & Laslett, B.   158
McCarthy, B, Williams, M. & Hagan, J.   135
McCue, H.   227
McDonald, K.   229
McDonald, P., Bailey, J., Price, R. & Pini,
    R.   134

McGoey, L. 210, 222
McGrath, P. 188
McKenna, B. 33
McKibben, B. 318
McLachlan, R, Gilfillan, G. & Gordon, J. 140
McLeod, J. 94, 314
McLeod, J. & Thomson, R. 92
McWilliams, J. A., & Bonet, S. W. 197
Mellor, N. 278
Memos, C. 261
Memmott, P. & Horsman, R. 142
Meyer, J.W. & Scott, W.R. 209
Mietzner, M. & Aspinall, E. 241
Mignolo, W. 309
Milberry, K. 192
Miles, S. 131
Miller, P. & Rose, N. 94, 127
Mische, A. 158, 178
Mission Australia 140
Mitchell, K. 99
Mitropoulos, A. 197, 198, 320
Mitropolous, A. & Kiem, M. 320
Mizen, P. 210, 213
Mobility 48, 93, 123, 156, 160–162, 165
Moore, P. 198
moral economies 176, 179
Morozov, E. 47
Morton, A. 316
Moslem Brotherhood 282, 285
Mouffe, C. 85, 209, 212, 221
Mukherjee, E. 292
Muldoon, B. 315
Muldoon, J. 314
Muna W.K, Stanton, A. & Mwau, D. M. 283
Murphy, E.C. 273

Nasir, K.M. 230, 232
Nelson, J. 33
Neilson, B. & Rossiter, N. 186, 197, 198
neo-Liberalism 52, 61, 65, 70, 93, 169, 172n, 175, 177–180, 194, 256–257, 263, 266, 290, 305, 311
    health and wellbeing 30, 64, 109, 143, 148, 279, 290–291, 317
    responsibilisation 61, 65, 70
    subjectivity 63, 170
new commodity forms 97, 101
Newman, J. 134

new media 4, 5, 37, 158, 209–210, 233, 281–282
Nichol, G. R. 38, 39
Noueihed, L.& Warren, A. 281
Nussbaum, M. 53

Occupy (movement) 61, 64, 76, 126, 186, 192, 197–200, 211, 281, 307–309, 312–316, 320–321
Occupytogether.org. 6
OECD 27, 49, 50, 109, 189n, 192–196, 198, 262
Ojala, M. 126
Oliver, A. 174
Olson, K. 84, 210
Olsson, U, Petersson, K. & Krejsler, J. 164
O'Neill, B. 125
Ordinariness 156–157, 163–164
Orwell, G. 27, 33
Osman, T. 282
O'Toole, T. & Gale, R. 212, 227, 228
Ovenden, K. 257, 260, 265

Pain, S., Panelli, R., Kindon, S. & Little, J. 124
Pakulski, J. 231
Palmer, D. 151, 152
Panagiotis, S. 220
Paradies, Y., Chandrakumar, L., Klocker, N., Frere, M., Webster, K., & Burrell, M. 176
Park, H., Twenge, J. M., & Greenfield, P. M. 290
participatory practice 55–57, 229–231, 234, 305
    and action research 142, 291, 305
Partnership for 21st Century Skills 176
Patel Stevens, L., Hunter, L., Pendergast, D., Carrington, V., Nahr, N., Kapitzke, C. & Mitchell, J. 187, 188
Patton, C. 232, 233
Paulsen, N. & McDonald, A. 141
Pavlidis, A. 176
Pearson, N. 141
peer to peer technology 53–56
Perkins, K. 284
Peston, R. 33
Petropoulou, C. 261
Peucker, M. 234, 235
Pickard, A. 124

INDEX

Pickard, S. & Bessant, J. 210
Picower, B. 194
Picower, B. & Mayorga, E. 305
Pike, J. & Kelly, P. 107
Piketty, T. 196
Pitty, R. 256, 266
Pledger, D. 319
Politics
   and altruism 152, 214, 215
   and disillusionment 209, 216, 217, 220, 261
   moral emotions (ethics) 211–214, 217, 219, 221, 222
   and *Pancasila* 246–248
   and power and corruption 33, 144, 246, 263, 283
Political engagement (and disengagement) 32, 77, 124–127, 210–214, 217–219, 221–222, 226–230, 233–237, 241–242, 251–255, 258
politics of everyday life 28, 65, 166, 229, 237
polling for justice (PFJ) 290–291
Pollock, J. 6
popular culture 94, 231–233
Population Council 273, 277, 278, 283
Porta, D. & Mattoni, A. 282
Postman, N. 188
Precarity 7, 30, 61–65, 123–128, 131, 134, 170–171, 176–177, 186, 194, 197–198
Premier of Victoria 317
Prentoulis, M. & Thomassen, L. 260, 263, 264, 266
Priest, N., Ferdinand, A., Perry, R., Paradies, Y., & Kelaher, M. 176
Priestley, M. 313
Print, M., Saha, L. & Edwards, K. 210
Psimitis, M. 259
public sphere 35–38, 40, 55, 74, 78–79, 81–85, 100, 163, 179, 194, 210, 221, 231–235
Pykett, J. 209

Quit Coal 316

Racism (and anti-) 129, 175–178, 180, 215, 258, 289, 296, 304, 318, 320–322
Raco, M. 123, 125
radical imagination 36–38, 40
Rambla, X, Valiente, O. & Frias, C. 193

Rancière, J. 221
Rasmussen, M. L. 199
Ratto, M. & Boler, M. 232
Ravitch, D. 196
Razer, H. 319
Reformasi 241, 248
Refugees 107, 123, 131, 180, 216, 220, 265, 310
   and off-shore detention 307, 321
Reid, A. & McCallum, F. 135
Representation 197, 226, 231–234
   in Indonesia 248
   multicultural politics of 226, 234
resilience 35, 61–63, 69, 85, 117, 144, 176, 179
retirement 159–162, 165–166
RISE (REFUGEE SURVIVORS AND EX-DETAINEES) 319, 320
Rizvi, F. 95, 96
Rizzo, H, Abdel-Latif, A-H. & El-Moghazy, A. 280
Roberts, K. 281
Roberts, S. 173, 162
Roberts, Y. 176
Roker, D. 228, 235
Roche, S. 189
Roda, A. 194
Roose, J. 127, 232
Rosa, H. 92, 162
Rosaldo, R. 230
Rose, N. 107, 115, 178
Rose, N. & Miller, P. 108, 127
Rosen, R. J. 5
Roudi, F. 275
Rowe, E. 195, 198
Ruffin, H. 312
Rygiel, K. 127

Saha, L, Print, M. & Edwards, K. 174
Sakbani, M. 199
Sandri, R. 142, 152
Sandywell, B. 75
Sauter, M. 210
Sayer, A. 178
SBS 175
Schell, O. 28
Schmitt, C. 83, 84
Scott, J., Robinson, A., Rosenthal, R., Savage, T., Rabbit, J., Grossman, M., Kellman, B. & Sellar, S. 135

Sennett, R.   39
Serres, M.   45
Shahine, S.H.   281, 282
Shiller, J.T.   126
Shukaitis, S. & Graeber, D.   309
Sika, N.   280
Singer, P.   212
Singerman, D.   273, 282
Sitrin, M.   199, 200
Sitrin, M. & Azzellini, D.   259, 260
Skalli, L.H.   282
Skocpol, T.   72, 210
Skujins, P. & Lim, P.   172, 179
Smith, N., Lister, R., Middleton, S. & Cox, L.   127, 228
Smolan, S.   69
Smyth, J.   197
social contract   35, 272n
social enterprise   141, 142, 177
social justice   40, 62–67, 126, 141
social media   60–61, 98, 134, 158, 191–193, 199–200, 212, 229, 233–235, 241–244, 281–282, 290, 312, 314
social movements (and see also *Arab Spring, Black Lives Matter, Occupy, Syriza and WikiPDR*)
    and general assemblies   200, 260, 315
    climate   112, 307, 308, 315–318, 320–322
Söderberg, J.   97
Soler-i-Marti, R.   212
Song, J.   320
Sotiris, P.   261, 262, 313
Spanish *Indignados*   99, 200, 211, 281, 312–315
Spourdalakis, A.   257, 264
Spourdalakis, M.   258, 259
Staeheli, L. & Nagel, C.   282
Standing, G.   62, 63
Stavrakakis, Y. & Katsambekis, G.   258, 259
Stengel, R.   5, 60
Stoudt, B., Fine, M. & Fox, M.   291
Stoudt, B., Fox, M. & Fine, M.   290, 292
Stoudt, B.G., M.E. Torre, P. Bartley, F. Bracy, H. Caldwell, A. Downs, C. Greene, J. Haldipur, P. Hassan, E. Manoff, N. Sheppard & J. Yates   292, 305, 306
Stromquist, N. & Sanyal, A.   193
Suarez-Villa, L.   186, 197

Sukarieh, M, & Tannock, S.   95, 99, 100
Sundararajan, A.   56, 57n
Susser, A.   187n, 198, 199
Susskind, R. & Susskind, D.   46, 47
Sutter, J.   73, 82
Swan, J.   319
Syriza   18, 20, 209, 256–267
    and limits of reformism   264
    and the eurozone   256, 264–266
    and fragmentation   257

Tabar, P, Noble, G. & Poynting, S.   228
Taylor, A.   193
Taylor, C.   1, 8–10, 213
Technocapitalism   196, 197
Tekin, B. & Tekin, R.   259, 266
Temporality   92, 94, 110
The Internationalist   193
Tholen J.   274–277
Thomson, R, & Holland J.   91
Threadgold, S.   18, 95, 100, 164, 165
Time Magazine   1
Tormey, S.   127, 260
Törnquist, O.   241
Transitional labour market programs (TLMPS)   2, 16, 17, 140–151
Triventi, M.   162
Troika   256, 259, 264, 269, 270
Tronti, M.   309
Trump, D.   60, 188, 290, 313
Tsakatika M. & Elefteriou, C.   258
Tsekeris, C.   80, 83
Tsipras, A.   258, 267
Tugal, C.   283
Turkle, S.   47
Turley, J   31
Turner, B.S.   231
Twenge, J.   215

Unger, R.   45, 47, 53, 54, 56, 85
UNICEF (Conventions on the Right of the Child)   188
Universities Australia   172
Uprichard, E.   92
Urdal, H.   189, 190n, 191n
U.S. Government   190
Üstündağ, N.   312

INDEX

van de Sande, M. 200
Vandewalle, D. 282
Vassadis, A., Karimshah, A., Harris, A. & Youssef, Y. 229n
Verger, A, Lubienski, C. & Steiner-Khamsi, G. 195, 196
Vgontzas, N. 264
Vinken, H. 228
Vinson, T. 140
violence 29, 31, 33, 114, 116, 131, 178, 189, 241
  and neo-Liberalism 27, 32, 35, 105, 110
  and the punishing state 29, 32–34
  new forms of 99
  police 8, 21, 32–34, 66, 127, 174, 193, 261, 279, 280, 285, 291, 292, 304, 315
  symbolic 29, 37, 165
Vromen, A. 210, 236
Vromen, A. & Collin, P. 77, 228
Vromen, & Xenos, M. 77
Vuchnich, A & Chai, C. 30

WACA (Whistle-Blowers and Citizens Alliance) 318
Walkerdine, V. 91
Wallerstein, I. 308
Walsh, L. 62, 169, 171, 176
Walsh, L. & Black, R. 123, 177
Wark, M. 14, 90, 91, 97–101
Watkins, S. 259
Wellington, D. J. 4
Wells, A, Slayton, J. & Scott, J. 194
Wenman, M. 210
Westling, M. 78
Whitty, G. & Power, S. 195
Whitty, G. & Power, S. & Halpin 194
Wierenga, A. & Ratnam, S. 135

Wiggins, J. 307, 318, 320
WikiDPR 18, 20, 241–245, 251–255
Williams, Z. 29
Williamson, H. 127, 134
Windle, J. 195
Wolfe, P. 317
Wood, B.E & Black, R. 190, 191
Woodman, D. 62, 92, 157, 163, 173
Woodman. D. & Threadgold, S. 95, 100
Woodman, D, & Wyn, J. 91
Wright Mills, C. 27n
Wrigley, T, Lingard, B & Thomson, P. 125, 129
Wulf, V., Misaki, K., Atam, M., Randall, D. & Rhode, M. 5
Wyn, J. 99
Wyn, J & Cuervo, H. 173
Wyn, J. & Woodman, D. 62

Xborder 319, 320
Xenos, M., Vromen, A. & Loader, B. 77

Yassin-Kassab, R. & Al-Shami, L. 312
Yeung, P, Passmore, A. & Packer, T. 229
Yifu Lin, J. 190n, 191n
Yin, R.K. 128
Yoon, E. 195
Youth unemployment 1, 15, 30, 100, 155, 189, 192, 198, 258, 262, 266, 275, 277
Yuval-Davis, N. 11

Zakaria, F. 189–191, 197, 199
Zhao, Y. 176
Zipin, L., Sellar, S., Brennan, M. & Gale, T. 131, 134, 135
Žižek, S. 1, 61, 70, 85

Printed in the United States
By Bookmasters